A SACRAMENTAL UNIVERSE

A SACRAMENTAL UNIVERSE

Being
A Study in the Metaphysics of Experience

VANUXEM LECTURES

BY

ARCHIBALD ALLAN BOWMAN
Sometime Professor of Moral Philosophy in the University of Glasgow

Edited by J. W. SCOTT
Professor of Logic and Philosophy, University College, Cardiff, Wales

The King's Library

1939
PRINCETON: PRINCETON UNIVERSITY PRESS
LONDON: HUMPHREY MILFORD, OXFORD UNIVERSITY PRESS

PRINTED AT PRINCETON UNIVERSITY PRESS
PRINCETON, NEW JERSEY, U.S.A.

PREFACE

THE *Vanuxem Lectureship at Princeton University was founded by Louis Clark Vanuxem of the Class of 1879 for the annual delivery before the University of four to six lectures on matters of current interest, including but not confined to topics of a scientific character; and the late Professor Bowman of the University of Glasgow gave, in 1934, the philosophical course which forms the basis of the ensuing book.*

Of the Parts into which the book falls, only Part I—an elaborate redaction of the first three lectures—had been typewritten, ready for the press, at the time of the author's sudden and unexpected death, on the 12th of June 1936.

The duty of an editor in such circumstances is always a responsible one; but for various reasons it proved less onerous in the present instance than it might easily have been. The following are the salient facts:

The lecturer spoke from notes. The book of notes which he had before him was available; and from this it soon became clear what he had intended to give to his audience in his first three lectures—nothing less, namely, than a condensation of the whole metaphysical thesis which he has argued out in full in the eight chapters comprising Part I of the present volume.

Since the author had found it necessary, in preparing his spoken work for publication, to develop his first three lectures to this extent, it was reasonable to suppose that he would also have expanded the remaining three. The opportunity to do this was denied him; and the fact constituted a loss which no editor, however well equipped, could set himself to repair. At first sight, the only feasible plan seemed to be to discard the platform notes altogether, and let our Part I, embodying the first three lectures in expanded form, be the whole book. This, however, implied discarding half the Vanuxem course, and did not seem possible. It would have been to present as a fragment, although a highly impressive fragment, a series of addresses which was, in fact, very much more. It would not have been fair to either publisher, public or Foundation. After considerable discussion and trial of other ways of treating the material, three considerations served to precipitate what I think was the right decision.

Firstly, although the six lectures had not been simply read off by the speaker from a manuscript, it occurred to me that most of them were nonetheless recoverable—all, in fact, except number one—in large part. They existed, not exactly as they were spoken, but as they were composed; that is to say, in scattered notes in the platform book and elsewhere. The method which had been followed in their composition was clear. The author had a large and accumulating mass of manuscript material which it was his habit, in a busy life, to keep in excellent order; and down the margins of some of this, he had red-inked long passages for inclusion in these discourses. All which he had thus marked off, when inserted into its place among the connective material of his platform book, fitted perfectly. I therefore took the responsibility of so inserting it, and printing the result in its entirety, with a minimum of editing, in the middle of this volume, as Part II. Part II consists, therefore, of the notes for the spoken lectures, so far as they exist in writing.

This scheme commended itself the more because, in the second place, these spoken lectures, being allowed to appear in all their "unedited" frankness and freedom, as Part II of this volume, do seem to me to have a real rôle to play. They provide the serious student with a welcome and almost indispensable recapitulation of the difficult first eight chapters comprising Part I. A third consideration favouring their inclusion lay, if one may so put it, in the circumstances of their birth. Composed as they were under high pressure, and with the needs of an audience in prospect, they not only contrive to impart a certain momentum to the somewhat more studied and careful metaphysical argument of Part I; but also they carry the line of thought forward to a finish with a rush and a crescendo which some readers at any rate would not willingly have seen sacrificed.

Part III is supplementary, but it is no "appendix." It consists of materials continuous with those marked for inclusion in the lecture course, and amplificatory of them. It comes—as does a great deal of what was spoken from the platform—from the courses habitually given to the author's large University classes at Glasgow, and it again is a sketch very roughly blocked out and very literally set down as in the author's MS. It discusses human nature and the development of the moral life; that is to say, the process by which man enters into and enjoys the "sacrament" of the universe.

The responsibility incurred by such a policy of literalism in treating the reliquiae of this particular philosopher arises, of course, simply from the fact that he had not finished his work. He had not the opportunity, for example, so to expand the last three lectures as to show in any detail the connection he saw between those theological and even Christological positions to which he hastened in his concluding lecture (Chapter XIII, below) and the elaborate metaphysic which had gone before. Perhaps there may be those to whom it is not clear that there is any connection between the two things. And no doubt for such the work would have been better left as a torso. My only apology for not having left it so is that I do not share the view. This is not the place to say why; but the fact has to be recorded. It is the only excuse for a further feature of the volume, which might otherwise savour of presumption. I refer to the few footnotes with which I have attempted to companion the student on his way through the pages. The point of those, let it be said once for all, is chiefly to try to keep the lineaments of the system in sight lest they scatter, while new details are being drawn in.

I think "system" and "lineaments" are the right terms to use here. I think I am right in believing that the author's conscious criterion, in all his ethical and metaphysical speculation, was what he calls, in these pages, "methodological effectiveness"; not mere linear argument but system; considerations of weight; the finding of a point of view, to be vindicated in the last resort by the degree of systematic cogency which it enabled him to see in the various departments of human experience. System is of the essence of his story. And indications too numerous to detail, and perhaps too subtle to formulate, have convinced me of his cherished intention to make these Vanuxem Lectures in their published form a demonstration, as full and definitive as was possible in short compass, of the conditions for the discovery of such system; of which conditions, the chief is the recognition of the spiritual as a distinctive realm of reality. And although the book cannot, in the nature of things, ever be now the finished and perfectly jointed work which he would himself have turned out, I trust I may not have wholly failed in my main endeavour; which was to make it something that should be in every essential sense, and in the first place, his own book; of which it could be said that he wrote it all; and that it sets out what he wrote, in approximately the sequence in which he intended to make it public.

It should be noted that the general title is that originally chosen by the author; the chapter headings also being his, almost all; and the sub-

*headings, the analytical table of contents and the paragraph numbering
almost all mine. I would add further that it might be of great assistance
to the reader to supplement the study of this argument by some
acquaintance with another book,* Studies in the Philosophy of Religion, *which the author committed to type about a decade earlier than
these lectures, but never printed; and which has been recently published by the Macmillan Company under the editorship of Professor
Kemp Smith.*

*Of many debts incurred in connection with this discharge of a last
duty to a friend, the heaviest is naturally to Mrs. Bowman, for having
given me the opportunity. I have also to offer my best thanks to three
individuals for their various cooperation, assistance and advice; J. A.
Irving, Assistant Professor at Princeton, and two others who were
of the author's inner circle, Dean C. W. Hendel of McGill University,
Montreal, and Professor N. Kemp Smith mentioned above. I am also
deeply indebted at special points to Mr. L. J. D. Richardson and
others of my colleagues of University College, Cardiff. For the rest, it
may perhaps serve a purpose, as indicating something of the relations
between the lecturer and Princeton, and of what he meant to those he
was addressing, if I insert here a few unassuming sentences from a
report of the lectures, by the Mr. Irving just named. He is writing in
the* Princeton Alumni Weekly, *immediately after they were over.*

*"The coming of Dr. Archibald A. Bowman, Professor of Moral
Philosophy in the University of Glasgow, to Princeton, to give the
Vanuxem Lectures was hailed by the undergraduates as the most significant event of the academic year. Dr. Bowman is no stranger to
Princeton. Called here in 1912, he was Professor of Logic in the University until 1926 when he received his appointment to Glasgow. From
1922 to 1926 he was chairman of the Department of Philosophy. His
departure for Scotland in 1926 was deeply and widely regretted, for his
influence had extended far beyond the circle of professional philosophers. His profound thought on philosophical, religious and social
questions had stirred the entire Princeton community; when the present
writer came to the University in the autumn of 1927, Dr. Bowman's
influence was pervasive in every direction."*

*Then, after some further characterization, follows Mr. Irving's
report; my impression of the merits of which I should like to take
occasion to record. The student is hardly likely to find any more*

*adequate rapid summary of the salient points of the lecturer's teaching
than is there contained. The date of the issue is April 6, 1934.*

*The lectures, delivered to very large audiences, seem to have made an
unusually deep impression. And it is, I think, proper, as being a
matter of special interest to many of his hearers and potential American readers who knew the man referred to, that I should close by
reproducing, from the same report, an incident which graced the
opening address. On rising to speak, Dr. Bowman said:*

*"The thought that is uppermost in my mind at this moment is the
thought that when I last spoke from this platform it was to say 'Good-
bye' to Princeton; and the last word was uttered, not by me, but by one
whom I had fondly hoped to greet today. Of President Hibben I cannot
trust myself to speak. He was my friend. It was he who brought me
here; and it is to him that I owe the ten happiest years of my life. For
more than twice that period he presided over the destinies of this great
University with wisdom, courage and devotion. His administration
covered the dark days of the war and the mad race of the years that
followed. But throughout the bewildering oscillations of that period he
remained calm and steadfast at his post, resting his cause on a faith
that never faltered or gave way. For such a life we are moved to profoundest gratitude; and if you will not consider it presumptuous on
my part, I should like to think of these Vanuxem Lectures as in some
sense a belated and imperfect offering to the memory of a friend and
leader, and so to place my tribute of love and reverence upon the spot
where now he rests."*

J. W. SCOTT

University College of
South Wales & Monmouthshire,
Cardiff, Wales

CONTENTS

ANALYSIS

INTRODUCTION

1. The problem. What must the universe be, considering that it has produced man?
2. he being spirit; and spirit, in turn, a distinctive mode of being?
3. Spirit (or personality) is something which we may hope to find sufficiently knowable to justify the attempt to read the *general* nature of things in the light of it.
4. We shall make assumptions in this inquiry—e.g., that time and that consciousness exists.
5. The notions we shall employ, namely, function and system.
6. We shall apply the latter terms to events which are subjective, in the sense that they can constitute personality. Personality will be a system of subjective events functionally related. The world of perceptual experience with its values (the existence of which makes the universe sacramental) will then be a function of the subjective mode of being *in conjunction with* the physical mode.
7. Summary of conclusions to be reached.
8. Use to be made of linguistic material in reaching these conclusions.
9. Their relation to theism.
10. Their relation to contemporary philosophy.
11. There must be a way of explaining the world which will not reduce it to nonentity. There must be some equivalent of the traditional "substantive thing." It is to be found in systems, physical and subjective.   pp. 1-13

PART I

METAPHYSICAL PROLEGOMENA

CHAPTER I
Functions and Systems

1. The notion of function. The linguistic force of the term. Its suggestion of a self-enjoying activity.
2. The physiological application of the term finds a certain analogy in the mathematical.
3. In the last resort, in both usages, terms are found composing a system; and each term is a function of that system. The principle of Reduplication.
4. The resulting concept of system. System is such that the terms within it may only be functions of one another provided each is also a function of the whole system. If $y = F(x)$, it is because, by the principle of Reduplication, $y = F(xy)$.
5. A consequence of the proposal to use the concept of system existentially (cf. Introduction, 11) is that the functional relation, besides subsisting between classes, may hold between the individual events composing the classes.
6. Another consequence. Our systems, being of events, will be in time.
7. We may hope that the discovery of such time-conditioned systems will be found to explain the temporal; and preclude the necessity for other, logically inadmissible, explanations.
8. It sometimes happens that certain terms are found merely to be conjoined while another term is a function of their conjunction. (cf. Introduction, 6.) Even here the double formula required for a complete statement of the functional determination of the terms (paragraphs 3 and 4, above) can be supplied.
9. Defence of the *double* formula of paragraphs 3 and 4 above.

CHAPTER II

*Physical and Spiritual in Modern Philosophy, with
a Special Examination of Professor Santayana's System*

6. (b) They remove all basis for belief in a soul or spiritual substance. (cf. Introduction, 11, and Chap. 1, 10.) No perception can *resemble* a substance.

7. Santayana restores substance, but not as it has been understood in the philosophical tradition. His substance is a mere feeling of "something here, something there." And it is different from the essences given in intuition.

8. Our interest here is in noting the aggravated reemergence, in Santayana's hands, of a duality which has not been confronted and acknowledged at the proper place.

9. Santayana's essences. They are intuited, and carry their own light with them; are eternally what they are; are outside the stream of change, and so do not exist; but they have being.

10. They would cover both Hume's perceptions and, partly, the Platonic forms. While sharing some of the characteristics of the latter, they are precluded by their timelessness and non-existence from all efficiency in the realm of the existent and temporal.

11. But this means that the character in the flux which was to be its meaning, is never allowed to be there. It is always in the timeless realm of essences.

12. We must find another interpretation of those characters which give determinateness to the flux and yet appear not to be themselves in flux.

13. We must labour at the question of *identifying events*. The identity of an event we shall find to be determined by the system of which it is a function, not by the incursion of a timeless essence.

14. The system which determines the identity of such events as colours and sounds cannot be *merely* physical but will include both vibrations and a percipient, which latter must be taken seriously as an independent variable. Only by recognizing this *duality* of psychical and physical can the impasse of *dualism* be avoided.

15. But is it possible to treat mind as an independent determinant of the sensory characteristics of nature? The question of the nature of mind comes in.

16. How Santayana sinks mind in nature. His psyche, soul and spirit.

17. The psyche. It is the life-mechanism in the body.

18. Consciousness or spirit. What is that?

19. Again a pseudo-monism. The psyche is the bodily life and the spirit a higher level of the same.

20. But the duality reemerges in intractable form. That spirit which was to have been sunk in nature will only partly sink. The other part becomes opposed to nature, as something that nature can only violate.

21. We are left with, on the one hand, a self-dirempted subject of experience; on the other, a nature and spirit which are neither nature nor spirit.

22. The widespread disinclination among contemporary philosophers to think that spirit may be something in itself.

23. Whitehead as an example of this tendency. Beginning with a natural world closed against mind, he ends with a reality in which subjective and physical have lost all distinctness.

Appendix A. The contextless character of Santayana's essences.

Appendix B. There must be, yet cannot be, a "realm" of essence.   pp. 51-84

CHAPTER III

Physical and Spiritual in Modern Philosophy, with a Special Examination of Professor Whitehead's System

1. Further consideration of the contemporary tendency to sink mind in nature. Whitehead's general problem: to overcome the rift between the world of ordinary knowledge and the world of science.

2. He asks why the dualism, the bifurcation of the two.

3. But Santayana is committed to a dualism without bifurcation. Is it not the same with Whitehead?

4. Whitehead's doctrine that nature, or what we perceive, is independent of mind. Admittedly, the sensum, "this green," is an object (and not a state) of mind. But has it the same independence of mind, as e.g., "this green leaf"?

5. For Whitehead, at any rate, the sensum is taken over into the flux of natural events. The physical leaf and the green *of* the leaf are not to bifurcate. What then is the place of the distinction between them?

6. In the first place, as Whitehead sees, time must be of the essence of the nature we perceive by the senses. An ordinary so-called object (e.g., Cleopatra's needle) is really a complex event.

7. But we could not recognize pure events, according to Whitehead. Since we do recognize, there must be objects in the sense of "factors which do not pass."

8. Whitehead's objects are confined to such as are "situated in events." They are not exactly coincident with Santayana's essences. Their kinds:

9. (a) Sense objects, which are the various sensa ("this *shade* of blue" which may be perceived here or there, now or at another time, according to the particular event in which it is situated).

10. (b) The perceptual object, a complex of sensa "occurring" in a series of "situations" and judged to be an object. This, when the judgment is not delusive, is a physical object.

11. (c) Scientific objects—atoms, electrons, etc. These seem to mean the physical objects which condition the appearing of any sensory or perceptual object, if the requisite "percipient event" be forthcoming. This introduces a cardinal issue.

12. Does the physical, as construed by Whitehead, explain the perceptual; or is there a rebifurcation?

13. That the physical objects which are to furnish the explanation are hypothetical is no presumption against them.

14. But what is a physical object? It is a certain group of sense objects appearing repeatedly, the whole series of appearances being viewed as a group and judged to be an object. This judgment, placing the group in nature, makes us inquire after the "active conditioning events" presupposed in its (the object's) appearing;

15. which means asking how these events make possible a *perceptual* which is *physical*.

16. It is of course logically inadmissible that such "active conditioning events" should be enabled to explain an object, merely in virtue of something in them that has been *defined* as giving them that power.

17. How, exactly, then, does their relation to "scientific objects" enable events actively to condition the physical objects of our perception? Apparently in the sense that events "occupied" by such scientific objects (electrons) are the "all," of which any given perceptual object is "some"—a contention which seems demonstrably inadmissible.

18. For a bifurcation which was only a challenge to further thought, Whitehead has substituted one which is irresolvable.

19. The real desideratum is to recognize the initial duality of nature and mind, whereupon we may find events which *are* objects, and objects which are temporal.

20. How can sense objects be eternal? Only if we can, e.g., take a content "red" apart from the instances and make an "object" of the one and "events" of the other. Whitehead sins against himself here.

21. And does a sense object as given ever have the *sameness* which Whitehead's theory must attribute to it? He must *mean* to attribute to it sameness in difference.

22. But apparently he unconsciously postulates an identity *without* difference. Where his thinking goes wrong.

23. Are scientific objects eternal and the negation of events? Molecules can hardly be; nor yet electrons.

24. The reorientation we propose. We think it better to speak simply of physical events than of scientific objects, and regard them as becoming "objects" when we attend to them. (cf. Chap. VI, 10-11.) The sensa—and similarly the percepta—will then be primarily functions of the subjective and the physical in conjunction. (cf. Chap. I, 8.)

25. Another difficulty. How can that which by definition does not pass, be the character of that whose nature it is to pass? Whitehead's "ingression" does not bridge this gap.

26. If nature is closed to mind, why percipient events? What *are* those?

27. They have to be physiological processes and, as such, part of the events of nature; yet the corresponding object is apparently a unity of consciousness!

28. This latter it must be if it is to serve Whitehead's purpose. Whereupon an entirely different conception of sense-objects becomes unavoidable. They are no longer *situated* in events. They are objects of consciousness, themselves persisting in time.

29. Similarly if the "creative advance" of nature is in evidence in the percipient event this must be a psychical process, not a physiological.

30. And the psychical process must, further, include consciousness.

31. The remarkable result of the contemporary tendency to reduce the whole of reality to nature is to throw mind back into nature, in quasi-animistic fashion. It suggests something definitely anti-scientific in a theory which has sacrificed everything to science.

Appendix A. The existence of objects in a definitely physical mode.

Appendix B. Ingression. pp. 85-133

CHAPTER IV
Mind and Space

1. In the modern tendency to obscure the distinction between the natural and the spiritual, much has been made of a supposed spatial character in conscious processes. Is mind something spatial? The question is important.

2. Locke's implied "yes" to this question.

3. Alexander's "yes."

4. (A) The epistemological argument for this position.

5. Holt: unless the mind's ideas were spatial they could not mediate knowledge of the spatial.

6. But what is an idea? If the object be mind-indifferent, the idea of it is clearly a subjective activity or state.

7. But the object may be subjectively conditioned, e.g., a mental image (cf. Chap. VI, 16, 17.) when the object itself may be the "idea" intended.

8. There is no need for the idea of space to be spatial, in the first of these cases;

9. or in the second; for even here there is a constructing, outside of imaged space.

10. And a mental image symbolizing an object in outer space (a) need not itself be spatial at all, and (b) must, if spatial, have a spatiality distinct from that of the object it symbolizes.

11. But what if we altogether deny the conditioning subjective activity of paragraph 6 above, and say with Holt that there are only neutral entities, each capable of entering into various contexts?

12. How, in that case, would my knowledge of a distant town be interpreted?

13. The answer given: As part of the manifold called the town, having become part of a conscious manifold. In virtue of such partial identity my knowledge-mass will "represent" the town.

14. My consciousness of an object, on this view, is a selection from it; as a map is a selection from the geographical features mapped.

15. But apart from consciousness, does a map *represent*?

16. Resemblance in the sense of partial identity is obviously not yet representation.

17. There must be logical identity. What is identical is an abstract logical scheme.

18. But this unity must appear in a manifold.

19. And the "primary representation" which this implies involves an act of positing which cannot be a function either of the spatial systems or of the human nervous system.

20. We must always have these difficulties till we can look on experience as something prior to objects *qua* objects.

21. To mediate between represented object and representative object we need—not a further set of objects but—a subjective being.

22. Mind, then, is not epistemologically shown to be in space. Then the situation becomes clear.

23. (B) Alexander's psychological argument: that mind is conscious of being itself in space, in its "enjoyments" of space.

24. Here it may be admitted that there is in some sense "enjoyment" of space—i.e. a non-contemplative way of being aware of space. It is rooted in coenaesthesis or body feeling.

25. We first know our bodies via feeling from within.

26. The body feelings are "common" in their nature; and they are primarily (if nebulously) cognitive, i.e. they are a consciousness "of" something, though they are very rudimentary in type.

27. In what are these "common" feelings distinct from the five special senses?

28. They cannot be distinguished either as specially subjective or as internally stimulated.

29. Their first distinction is their having no reference outside the organism.

30. But they do refer to the organism, however obscurely. Whether they refer to it as an object, exactly, is a further question.

31. To see, however, whether, in its body feelings the mind is aware of being in space, we must ask what place these feelings occupy in the subjective system.

32. They would seem to be a consciousness "of" the body; but not as seeing is, of colour; or as hearing is, of sound; or as touching is, of a surface.

33. They seem, that is, to be (a) of the body as a spatial system isolated from every frame of reference other than itself. It is possible to have such experience. Other instances e.g. the space in mirrors and pictures.

34. None of the "objects" of the body feelings are localized at points in *public* space. (cf. 40 below.)

35. (The reason why the detachment of the body can be overcome is that, sacrificing the coenaesthetic consciousness of the body, we can have the other kind of consciousness of it, characteristic of seeing or of touching.)

36. And the "objects" to which coenaesthetic consciousness has "reference" are not in any literal sense objects. The reference is different. It is a direct relation.

37. And but for our habit of confusing our coenaesthetic sensations with the places in the organism *to which they refer*, we would not imagine the sensations themselves to be an experience of spatiality in the mental processes.

38. Thus (b) the space term in our coenaesthetic consciousness of space is related directly to the consciousness; and (c) the space of coenaesthetic experience must always be private.

39. To construe the immediate reference which our coenaesthetic experience has to loci and areas in the organism, as an experience of the spatiality of mental processes, is to misconstrue it. What is mistakenly felt as the spatiality of the mind is really only the enjoyed spatiality of the body.

40. The system of points which constitute the correlatives of body feeling can never be identical with the interpunctual system of coordinates in objective space. The difficulty of "referred pain," etc., only arises from our forgetting this.

Appendix A. The terms for body feeling.

Appendix B. The sensations involved in general sensibility.   pp. 134-175

CHAPTER V

The Modality of Spirit: Subjects and
Systems of Experience

1. Our task: to see how far the hypothesis that nature and spirit are original modalities in real being is methodologically effective within the continuity of a certain "tradition of understanding."

2. Examples of methodological effectiveness within such a tradition.

3. We begin by finding two original and antithetical modes of being, physical and spiritual.

4. We find further that they may occur together, either in bare conjunction or in functional relation. (cf. Introduction, 6, and Chap. 1, 8; also Chap. 1, 14-19.)

5. In the latter case we have the embodied spirit, a heterogeneous, a psycho-physical mode of being.

6. In the former, the "derivative" mode, the world of sensory properties, values, etc. (cf. Chap. 1, 17.)

7. The method to be adopted in exploring the modes of being will be "empirico-critical"; and the experience it will criticize will be developed experience.

8. First, the spiritual. The way in which this mode of being has revealed itself to man's developed experience is partly recorded in his language.

9. Some differences between the synonyms for the spiritual. I *have* a "mind" but *am* a "person." Apparently, what I *am* is the whole of me. What I *have* is some part.

10. Again, I am not "person" but "*a* person"; whereas I am *both* "mind," "soul" *and* "a mind," "a soul."

11. But only in the term "spirit" are abstract and concrete perfectly thus poised.

12. Because "spirit" can be abstract, "spiritual" is free to attach itself to the spiritually conditioned. That may be spiritually or subjectively conditioned, which is entirely *objective* to the spirit or subject.

13. We shall not use the terms mental or spiritual for the mentally or spiritually conditioned.

14. What then is spirit; and what does it mean to be a spirit? Spirit is experience, and a spirit is an individual who experiences.

15. In what sense can there be an *individual who* experiences?

16. There is a parallel problem, in the sphere of life, where we may ask how there can be an individual which is alive. In this case the problem is easier because the individual appears in space.

17. Really, however, the biological individual is a functional integration of events in a spatio-temporal system.

18. And the experiencing individual is also a functional system; only, he is not *spatio-temporal*. He is the system of his experiences, which are events.

19. But (1) can a system of experiences be the conscious *subject* of them?

20. And in any case (2) can systems at once be in time and be definable?

21. As to (2) we shall see later that the time in which spirit exists compels us to postulate it as systematic.

22. As to (1) if the system be *of experiences* then it *is* the subject of them. The system not only precedes its constituents but sustains them as its activities.

23. For an activity itself does not act. (To think that it can is a confusion conspicuous in the writing of William James.)

24. And neither can it be "of" something detached from it.

25. If, however, we can take the activities as *mutually* correlated (and not merely as correlated each separately to something detached from them all) we get the subject the case requires.

26. The subject being thus a subjective system or system of experience, the question, What is experience? arises. Our answer. It is that which includes the possibility of being conscious.

27. We take consciousness to be indefinable.

28. Holt's opposite view. He can place consciousness within being.

29. It is for him a special aggregate of neutral objects. Awareness *is* these objects.

30. But such a neutrum cannot be *fundamental* in the sense that the different forms found *in* it are forms taken *by* it. And if it were, it would not be simple.

31. Being must be defined by reference to its modes, and consciousness cannot be defined by reference to being.

32. What reference to consciousness does experience require? For experience can be unconscious.

33. But while conscious and unconscious mental states are opposites, *both* are opposed to the non-mental as to another mode of being. (cf. diagram, Appendix D.)

34. We experience both the former two; and as modally homogeneous.

35. There is no insuperable paradox in this. An unconscious *phase* may be the subjective content of a *conscious experience*, and the latter may owe its identity to that fact.

36. The principle behind our recognition of a subjective unconscious: if a consciousness of *what it means* to be unconscious, being unconscious is an experience.

37. Actual instances of experiencing unconsciousness: trying to recall, warding off threatened unconsciousness, courting unconsciousness.

38. The experience of being unconscious in varying degrees.

39. The grade of unconsciousness is always a function (cf. Chap. 1) of subjective or psycho-physical conditions.

40. Having seen the spiritual mode of being as a system of that which includes the possibility of being conscious, we must next inquire into its relation to selfhood, and to the subject-object distinction.

Appendix A. The word "person."
Appendix B. Berkeley and contemporary philosophy.
Appendix C. The New Testament use of the word "spirit."
Appendix D. Conscious and unconscious—a diagrammatic representation.

Chapter VI

Subject-Object and Self

1. The subjective. It is a mode of being; and it is constituted of experience as distinct from all that is non-subjective, i.e. either physical or "derivative" in its mode of being. (cf. the first paragraph of Chap. v, 7.)

2. This experience occurs in systems. These constitute subjects. The definitory force of the concept of consciousness, in the experience in which a subject consists. Such experience includes the possibility of being conscious. (cf. Chap. v, 32-39, also Appendix D.)

3. The subjective systems are persons; but they are human persons only when incorporated in human bodies.

4. Man is thus a personality with a body; but personality does not require a body.

5. Are animals too persons? Their momentary experiences do not appear to individuate themselves within a comprehensive experience, in the manner requisite for responsibility; which seems decisive against the view.

6. But animals have consciousness, and thus must be taken as examples of the subjective mode of being.

7. To understand the relations of subjective and physical, both must be articulated; the physical by the help of science (cf. Chap. VIII), and the subjective by an exploration of the distinction between conscious and self-conscious. (cf. Chap. VII.)

8. And first we must be clear (A) on the subject-object distinction, and (B) on the concept of self.

9. (A) the term subjective. It connotes a mode of being.

10. To be objective, on the other hand, is only to be related to that mode of being in a certain way. (cf. Chap. III, 24.) The way can only be described by saying that it is what gives meaning to "of" in the phrase "conscious of."

11. Thus every entity is objective in so far as there is consciousness of it.

12. But its objectivity may be (1) purely accidental to, or (2) necessary to the mode of existence of, an entity.

13. Independent of their objectivity to consciousness are (a) the subjective itself. (Mental states or persons may become objects of attention, but they always *exist* subjectively.)

14. And (b) the physical.

15. (2) Their objectivity to consciousness is, on the other hand, *essential* to (a) mental processes which are altered (though their modality is not changed) by becoming objects of consciousness (cf. Chap. VII, 24, 25); and (b) entities which, though having a non-mental mode of being, do owe it to their objectivity.

16. (b) may be in various degrees coercive of mind though they are mind-conditioned. Examples of (b) are, mathematical and other truths, ideal objects, objects of perceptual experience, mental creations the last being relatively highly uncoercive.

17. We are not yet in a position to place "things" or living bodies.

18. Physical and spiritual together make up that part of the objective which is unaffected ontologically by its objectivity.

19. Yet the spiritual is farther removed from being *only* objective than the physical is.

20. (B) The self. If human subjectivity is self-conscious subjectivity, the presupposition is that in this case the subject is a self. What is a self? Linguistically, as the term becomes a noun, it comes to *mean* that *inward sameness in an individual* which at first it helped the pronoun to express.

21. Its significance varies all the way from a momentary focus of attention till it comes to rest indicating a system.

22. But what kind of a system merits the name of self? At least an existing one. (cf. Introduction, II, and Chap. I, 4ff.)

23. Is a physical system, then, necessarily a self? Apparently not.

24. Is a subjective system a self? Is a system in a derived mode? Is a living body? or a "thing"?

25. Man senses a self in a system, only if the system (1) exists as an individual, (2) is not a mere function of anything else, and (3) is capable, besides being a unity of mutually determining contents, of surviving vicissitudes. What "vicissitudes" are.

26. What *except* a subjective system fulfils these requirements? Not a system in a derived mode (cf. Chap. V, 3-6) and not a living body, if it is only physical—unless the physical itself can have selfhood.

27. And "things" are disqualified because the organizing principle of the thing would not seem to be anything internal to it. Things (up to a point) are selections by *us*.

28. The limiting case of the crystal. Not a living body, yet not a thing outlined by our interests.

29. If the crystal be what a *mathematical account* expresses it as being, then it is not a system which survives vicissitudes.

30. If the crystal be that which *physico-chemically* it is, it has features suggestive of selfhood; it is built up from a unit cell.

31. But its changes are not something which happens *to* the structure; i.e. something destructive which it survives and turns to account.

32. It is not a self.

33. Living bodies apart, selfhood would seem to be confined to (and exemplified in all of) such homogeneous systems of being as include conscious states; and further, it is consciousness which confers the selfhood.

34. *What* consciousness? The answer is *self*-consciousness; and we shall see that there is no consciousness without self-consciousness.

Appendix A. The realm of nature.

Appendix B. Philosophy and the interpretation of animal life.

Appendix C. Timeless truths and existence. They have existence only as objects of consciousness; not as that *to* which the said objects *refer*.   pp. 216-254

CHAPTER VII

Consciousness and Self-Consciousness

1. We only find selfhood unmistakably in subjective systems. Here, external relations are experiences; and so vicissitudes become the very material sustaining the continuity of an inner life. The principle of such superiority to vicissitude is self-consciousness.

2. Consciousness of self is necessarily involved in being conscious of anything. We cannot be conscious of an object only.

3. A conscious state within a subjective system must be a consciousness of the system.

4. Awareness of an object is so far a consciousness of what it means to be a subject.

5. What is this latter consciousness of self? Not anything introspective. It is something prior to the introspective type of self-consciousness and making it possible.

6. There are thus two ways of being self-conscious, a primary and a secondary.

7. The primary is largely independent of variations in the object. It may even be intensely present in the absence of a definitely assignable object.

8. A self's past states and its future states, are not its memories and anticipations merely, but internal differentiations of its present being. For a self appropriates *to itself* the things that happen to it.

9. Self-consciousness implies something more than that power of remembering isolated past states, on which Mill grounded his defence of introspection against Comte.

10. Such introspection reveals only artificially isolated states, not the system which is the self. A subjective system must be subjectively revealed.

11. But there is a genuine secondary self-consciousness of which introspection in this ordinary sense is a weakened form. It is, firstly, an observing of the process, say, of observing a physical object.

12. Part of the object inspected, that is, is something the primary nature of which is *to be a subjective state*; and so, something not known *only* (or even primarily) in this relation of objectivity.

13. This gives the observed act a place along with the act of observing it—not as the latter's object, but—within the unity of a subjective system.

14. But there is a still less artificial secondary self-consciousness which introspects— not brief states but—tracts of subjective time of appreciable compass.

15. We may call it reflection. It is subject apparently to a disability in being dependent on memory.

16. But this is really a deeper difficulty; namely, the possibility of *anything* subjective (i.e. that has been lived) being *remembered*. How can our own past experience ever be mediated to us in a merely presented *idea*?

17. Apparently, the genuinely indubitable ego cannot be found if it be a time-conditioned ego. For what is remembered from the past is always dubitable.

18. The fallacy in this. The assumption is being made that the past cannot at all be present and that it is purely objective. Actually, it cannot be wholly outside the present of experience which is subjective.

19. There is admittedly consciousness of past self in idea, or as object. Is this in any instance demonstrably more, namely present *experience* of past self?

20. An illustration of how a self may be *actually in* the past state it is objectifying. Here are primary and secondary self-consciousness in one;

21. an earlier subjective state being objectified without ceasing to be subjectively present.

22. This objectification of a past self is not its ideal reproduction but its real presence. The objectified past self and the present self are functionally related.

23. Can the same functional relation appear between acts of primary and secondary self-consciousness if they are more widely apart in time?

24. Yes, if for any reason the later state of mind cannot possibly be a mere contemplation of its peculiar object (the earlier state) which leaves the latter unaffected.

25. And there seem to be such cases.

26. Similarly the future subject may be *in* present experience and not a mere object *to* it.

27. Consciousness of the past and future self, then, is a function of consciousness of the present self. In existence and in meaning the two are one system.

28. Degrees of selfhood. Man and animal.

29. The animal has (primary) self-consciousness.

30. But it is with the enlarging union of primary and secondary self-consciousness that increment of being occurs. Summary of the chapter in three propositions.

Appendix. Primary self-consciousness as recorded in French linguistic expression.

CHAPTER VIII
The Physical World

1. After the spiritual, the physical. The paradox in recent physics: it seems to leave us with a highly un-physical world. Reasons for this.

2. We are to try to construe the most general nature of the physical in a way that will not run counter to the positive findings of science.

3. And first, a physical must *exist*.

4. It must exist as that non-subjective object, modally indifferent to its objectivity, which experience is "of" when it is not "of" itself or the subjectively conditioned,

5. and (A) it is *qua spatial* that it exists in independence of its objectivity. What "spatial" is that?

6. Is, e.g., *perceptual* space thus physical? How does the latter compare with the more obviously mind-dependent spatial orders? It is plainly less mind-dependent than they.

7. (a) It underlies most of them.

8. (b) It is removed from them in varying degree. Mirror space is the nearest to it.

9. Yet it and (even) mirror space, are not one space.

10. Those two, however, though heterogeneous, are functionally related in a system.

11. Our question concerns the ontological status of such differing systems of space. (a) Mirror space. It is not physical. Its objects are not amenable to physical treatment. Mirror space has a mind-derived mode of being.

12. (b) Perceptual space. Amid much that is mind-dependent—since the "things" in it are largely mind-conditioned, and even the element of extension too—

13. there is an aspect of perceptual space, namely the measurable in it, which is entirely independent of its objectivity-to-consciousness, and *is* physical.

14. (c) That in the heterogeneous system—the system composed of a piece of "real" space and its mirror reflection—which expresses the laws of optics is physical, and independent.

15. (B) The physical is also *that temporal* which exists in independence of its objectivity. What "temporal" is that? Clearly it will be the *spatially* temporal. How are these two correlated in the physical mode of being?

16. It is necessary to take a cue here from the history of science. There is a physically temporal which science has been gradually learning to acknowledge.

17. In reading *structure* as *process*, recent physics is only now mastering a principle vaguely divined from the beginning of science, namely the part played by time in constituting the physical.

18. (a) We find the earliest Milesian scientists, seeking being, already forced to include becoming in it. They are preoccupied with the *temporal* aspect of their "physical."

19. The first successor of Thales finds he needs, as primordial being, something which will allow him to bring in *change*.

20. His opposites become opposites by changing—separating.

21. A still more pronounced stress on becoming or process is found in Anaximenes.

22. With Heraclitus, who can find becoming thinkable only if there is no being, science leaps to a position greatly in advance of anything for which it is as yet ready.

23. Like all his compeers (and unlike M. Bergson) Heraclitus seeks the thinkable.

24. But science was not yet prepared to deal with a temporal continuum, except by translating it into the form of successive configurations of matter in space.

25. Greek opposition-thinking is in the presence of a problem of the temporal, which science cannot confront until the whole spatio-mechanical phase of its development has been gone through.

26. The initiation of the latter development. Parmenides' logic. He finds it unthinkable that non-being should be.

27. But the atomists (not confining their attention to *logical* non-being) find empty space perfectly thinkable. They postulate atoms changing their places in it, and so launch the spatio-mechanical development of science.

28. Science can now utilize change. It can take change to be change of place—motion—and become fruitful. It need not ask about the origin, but can interest itself in the characteristics, of motion.

29. (b) The modern era in science. Precisely the facts most redolent of the nature of the physically real, have been found *not* to be reducible to bodies moving in space. The temporal factor in the mechanistic scheme gradually upsets the scheme.

30. The limits of the body-in-motion cue to the problem of rest. Rest can be a kind of motion. In "force" is found something of which both are manifestations.

31. But there remains the duality of body and force (matter and energy). The nineteenth century still accepts this duality.

32. But those two are gradually found not to yield a tenable theory of the atom, in which time begins to take its place as a constitutive factor. Events begin to enter the constitution of things, instead of merely happening to them.

33. Matter today is replaced by a universal energy, which takes on the aspect of body under conditions of ordinary human experience.

34. The episodes of the advance. (i) Kelvin's vortex rings. The atoms constituted of a rotatory motion.

35. But motion, since it presupposes matter, cannot constitute it; as Kelvin virtually makes it do; thereby practically discarding the older conception of matter.

36. Here matter is being reduced to a concentration of energy; and motion may thus be taken as a manifestation of it.

37. The story of this. (ii) Relativity. Here, the motion of bodies is brought into their magnitude; and so into their quantitative (i.e. their physical) identity.

38. (iii) Theory of the atom. First, mass (the quantitative-physical) is seen to be energy.

39. Then the time factor in energy contributes to the *existence* of energy.

CHAPTER XV

The Development of Man's Spiritual Being, Cognitive and Conative

CHAPTER XVI

The Development of Man's Spiritual Being, Affective and Conative

1. (C) The affective life. Complex versus simple emotions.
2. The synthesis of emotions into sentiments. Characteristics of the sentiments.
3. (a) Permanence. (b) Same emotions ingredient in different sentiments.
4. (c) Sentiments prior to the emotions.
5. A difficulty in the relation of the sentiments to the emotions. How, being *after* the emotions, may they also be *before* them? It is the nature of spirit to admit of this.
6. Correlation of the cognitive and the emotional aspects of experience.
7. The moral life in its emotional aspect. The master feeling—affective correlate of a policy. Its consequences.
8. The nature of the master feeling as affective correlate of the good man's policy. The moral sentiment. Reverence or the subjective realization of sanctity.
9. Analysis of reverence.
10. The kind of "fear" involved in it.
11. Why fear at all?
12. The kind of wonder involved.
13. The kind of negative self-feeling involved.
14. How reverence works. (a) In a man's relations to the natural world. The spiritual as the end of the natural.
15. (b) In his relations with other persons. Its transformation of the instincts.
16. (c) In his relations with himself. Self-respect.
17. The emotions and the ethical imperative. May there be a duty to feel? Further considerations on the conative life.
18. How the will must operate to induce a new emotional disposition.
19. The evolution of a will.
20. How the conative impulses come to be organized into volitional systems.
21. How the conative life develops. Its parallelism to cognitive development.
22. The point in which the parallelism fails.
23. Relation of the volitions to the will in the evolution of the conative life. How the proleptic principle works in this instance.
24. Will and freedom.   PP. 393-411

INTRODUCTION

The Problem: to Read the Nature of the Universe in the Light of the Fact That "Spirit" Exists

1. The age in which we live is notable for two things, man's progressive triumph over nature in the sphere of theoretical and applied science, and his tragic inability to order his own life. Every year adds appreciably to our knowledge of the physical world: every year brings home to us the baffling inscrutability of human nature as revealed in our disordered civilization. We have learned to deal with objects and events unimaginably remote in space and time, with magnitudes so great and so small that the very units in which we compute them are beyond the range of our perceptual experience. The geologist can reconstruct for us the scenery of the Jurassic age, and the astronomer can predict with mathematical exactitude and perfect confidence the configuration of the heavenly bodies for centuries to come. In the face of all this intellectual penetration man remains a mystery to himself. There is no consensus of opinion as to what he is, or how he came to be, or what is ultimately in store for him; and it is significant of the obscurity in which the problem is involved that if we were asked to designate the principle of being that gives us our identity as conscious subjects, we should be unable to agree upon its name. We speak of mind, of soul, of personality, of spirit; but there is about each of these terms a vagueness which, as often as we have recourse to any one of them, lays us open to the charge of obscurantism.

This astonishing contrast between man's failure in one sphere and his achievement in another reveals itself mainly in two ways.

(a) A scientific knowledge of the world is characterized by a certain explicitness, exactitude and communicability. The propositions in which it expresses itself, the terms of which it makes use, are definite and unambiguous. An extreme instance is that of pure mathematics, the science of rational implication. Of course the mathematician enjoys the privilege of defining his terms in advance. When he speaks of a point, a straight line, a parabola, the series ℵ, he tells us how these concepts are to be understood. With the physicist, the chemist and the biologist the procedure is necessarily different, and different in varying degrees; but the upshot is much the same—a definite body of doctrine, profusely documented from the growingly decipherable records of nature, and worked out in reasonings to conclusions which may be right or may be wrong, but are certainly intelligible. If it is not given to the natural sciences to define their data at the outset, they can at least describe the latter and show them to us; and they can do so with the assurance that the objects and processes to which they wish to draw attention are generally such as can be identified, directly or by analogy, from the description. Not only so, but the problematic factors to which at times they have recourse—atoms, for example, and electrons, which, unlike cells and chromosomes, cannot be detected by any direct process of microscopic observation—have about them something of the same definiteness which accrues to the objects of mathematical definition. They are the postulated equivalents, in the physical world, of conceptual constructs which we work up for ourselves upon circumstantial evidence. Hence we know exactly what is in them. Of course it is open to anyone to dispute the evidence and to criticize the construct: it is reasonable to raise the question whether atoms and electrons, positrons and neutrons exist. The point is that there need be no uncertainty as to what, at any moment in the history of these concepts, *is meant* by an atom or an electron, a neutron or a positron.

When we pass from our knowledge of the outer world to the knowledge of ourselves, everything is altered. Man's being is obscured for the understanding, perhaps by the very closeness and intimacy of the theme. Our predicament resembles that of the people referred to by Socrates in Plato's *Republic*, who "go about searching for what they have in their hands."[1] The paradox is well illustrated by the fact that (as the whole history of science goes to prove) it is easier to understand the outer world of space, conceived as a system of external relations, than it is to understand the world of time, which, in one of its phases, we actually experience as the sequence of our own inner states. As Sir Arthur Eddington has expressed it: "We know nothing about the intrinsic nature of space, and so it is quite easy to conceive it satisfactorily. We have intimate acquaintance with the nature of time and so it baffles our comprehension."[2]

[1] *Rep.*, IV, 432 d-e.
[2] *The Nature of the Physical World*, Chap. III, pp. 51-2.

(b) Not only is our knowledge of ourselves, when compared with a scientific knowledge of the world, deficient in clarity and exactitude, but it is characterized by a notable want of continuity and progressiveness. There is no authentic tradition of development behind it, no steadily accumulating and generally accepted fund of insights to its credit, no unmistakable dialectic in its movement. Rather is the life of man the sphere of an unending and many-sided polemic. Except in superficial ways it would be hard to show that the modern mind has a firmer grasp of the essential truths of human nature than the mind of classical antiquity. The measure of our shortcoming is the calamitous condition of the world of men today.

Now man's failure to understand himself is a predicament with which we cannot hope to deal effectively so long as we isolate the problem of human life from all other problems. That man does not know his own nature is in the last analysis a truth which compels us to admit that he does not know the nature of the world to which he belongs. This is no reflection upon science as such: science stands in the strength of its own achievements. What is really wanting is the ability to interpret the truths of science in the light of truths more comprehensive than themselves. Physics and chemistry have taught us what the world is like when the presence of conscious subjects is ignored: they cannot tell us how it is to be conceived when the purely physical takes its place in the larger system of being which includes the spiritual as well.

These remarks will serve to prepare the way for a statement of my problem—a statement which, at this stage, must necessarily be both tentative and vague. Paradoxical as the assertion will appear, the exact nature of the inquiry will become manifest only when a certain amount of progress has been made towards its completion. Some inkling of the answer is required to enable us to understand the question we are propounding. For the moment the following will have to suffice.

I suggest that it is in some sense possible to view man's life in the widest of all contexts, that of "the total scheme of things."

The latter of course exists for our consciousness as an ideal concept. But the concept may be more or less articulated. My purpose is to contribute certain elements of meaning to it. One of these follows of its own accord from the statement that has just been made about man's position in a larger world. If human beings exist (a proposition which I am not going to question), they must constitute an appreciable portion of all that is, and we can have no adequate notion of reality as a whole until we have considered it from the standpoint of this fact. We shall have, therefore, to inquire into the significance of the truth that being sometimes takes the human form.

2. But what is meant by the *human* form? It is one thing to think of man as an animal organism, and quite another to think of him as a person. Perhaps we shall find reason to think of him as both.

Each of these possibilities is pregnant with suggestions for the interpretation of the real. If, for example, human beings are persons, then persons exist, and existence includes the possibility of being personal. If personality and animal organization come together in living men and women, this circumstance is a further revelation of the possibilities of being. That is to say, beings will exist that are both persons and animals.

I wish to make it plain that for the purposes of this inquiry our interest in men and women and in the predicaments of their existence must be placed on a definitely philosophical basis. This means that the aspects of the subject with which we are primarily concerned are those which represent the highest degree of generality. From this point of view personality is more significant than humanity. Or, to put the matter otherwise, the proposition: "Persons exist," or "Being takes the personal form" is, metaphysically speaking, more important than the proposition: "Human beings are persons" or "Personality takes the form of men and women." My ultimate object will have to be expressed in some such words as these: "To obtain a general impression of the world as a whole in a perspective determined by the recognition of personality—or, as I prefer to say, *spirit*—as a distinctive mode of being." Of course I shall have to make good my right to the preliminary act of recognition upon which the problem turns.

Spirit Sufficiently Knowable for our Purposes

3. At first sight there will appear to be something perverse in this procedure. Personality is most familiar to us in the human form; and there are many who would question whether it is known in any other. Now I have been dwelling upon our ignorance of man's nature as contrasted with our knowledge of the world

around us. I therefore seem to be proposing to throw light upon the relatively known from a source in the relatively unknown.

The objection may be dealt with in two phases.

(a) There is the difficulty of seeing how a knowledge of personality, in whatever form, can possibly contribute to our knowledge of the world. The difficulty would be insuperable if by a "knowledge of the world" were necessarily meant a scientific understanding of natural phenomena. The condition upon which this is attainable—the condition upon which our knowledge of the world acquires the character of science—is the elimination of the conscious subject, and of all that is specifically due to his presence as a percipient organism, from the field of the data. My suggestion is not that our acquaintance with spiritual beings can in any way be utilized by the sciences, but that when the sciences have done their utmost, when, ideally speaking, they have reached the limit of comprehensiveness and exactitude, there remain essential aspects of the truth about the world that lie, and must necessarily lie, for ever beyond their ken. It is with these aspects that I wish to deal; and my contention is that they come into view and assert themselves as actual objects of our common experience, and as potential objects of intellectual curiosity, only when the phenomena of nature appear in a single context or perspective with the activities of spiritual beings. The problem that lies before us, therefore, rests upon the assumption that there is a way of knowing the world that is not the scientific way.

(b) The second difficulty arises from man's acknowledged ignorance of personality or spirit. What is the use, it will be asked, of placing our knowledge of the world in a single perspective with the spiritual mode of being, if we have next to no authentic information as to the precise nature of the latter? Well, here again the point of the objection may be turned by a further observation upon the limits of scientific knowledge. It is true that we have no science of spirit, as we have a science of the physical. But if it is permissible to assume that there may be a non-scientific, as well as a scientific, knowledge of the world, may it not with equal reason be assumed that even in the absence of a corresponding science, it may be possible for us to achieve a very genuine insight into the nature of personality? As a matter of fact all that I have said about man's ignorance of man amounts only to a recognition of the fact that scientific knowledge is not here available. In other words, for reasons that are perhaps fundamental, it has not been found possible, in dealing with the personal mode of being, to establish a body of interrelated, abstract propositions, capable of commanding the general assent of those who understand them, and of furnishing the nucleus or starting-point for an indefinitely extensible body of similar propositions. But this is not to say that among the numberless thoughts which men have entertained about themselves—whether the thinkers were poets and prophets or ordinary, unpretentious individuals, and whether or not the thoughts were set forth in coherent fashion, as a creed or as an aesthetic representation of human nature—there may not be some which embody a profound insight into the nature and meaning of spiritual existence.' In view of this possibility we shall have to qualify what was said about man's ignorance of man by adding that the fact referred to was merely the absence of anything corresponding to the universal currency and progressive fertility of scientific truth.

Of course this in itself is a sufficiently serious disability, and one which would seem to preclude the very application we wish to make of the concept of personality. Since men are not agreed about their own nature, what hope is there that any presentation of the latter upon which we may venture will enable us to see the nature of the world as a whole more clearly and more adequately?

To this question I can only reply that the application must itself be made to justify the presentation of the concept. I claim no special insight into the nature of personality. In the absence of such insight I place my reliance upon a method or special way of dealing with the subject. The purpose of the latter is to render the concept of personality available for metaphysical investigation, (a) by making clear the assumptions which seem to me absolutely indispensable if the concept is to be recognized at all, and (b) by the use of certain notions, already familiar in other spheres of knowledge, and specially designed to render the concept luminous and persuasive, while restricting the assumptions to a bare minimum.

Assumptions to Be Made and Notions to Be Employed in the Inquiry

4. (a) Assumptions of course there must be, as in the sciences themselves. There can be no objection to this so long as everything is made explicit. I shall assume, for example, that there is such a thing as being conscious. To those who doubt or actually deny this

possibility the ensuing argument will be of no value. I shall further assume that consciousness occurs in a variety of forms—that it has its characteristic modes, its episodes, its incidents, and that these can be identified and indicated, perhaps not so easily, but in the end with as high a degree of certainty, as in the case of sensory objects. Of course I shall have to assume time. This I take to be the universal form of existence, and without it everything would fall to the ground. But granted time, and granted events which are also states of consciousness, identifiable in all their subjective particularity, I have virtually everything necessary to render the application of my special notions metaphysically fruitful. By means of these I hope to obtain a conception of the spiritual mode of being sufficiently exact to justify the attempt to relate the latter to the concept of the physical as developed by scientific investigation.

5. (b) The special notions to which I have referred, and by means of which I hope to restrict the element of sheer assumption, are most easily recognized by the part they play in the science of mathematics. This science is doubtless best defined, without reference to anything beyond its own characteristic processes, as the science of rational implication.[3] But there is a sense in which it may also be characterized as the final generalization of scientific knowledge. By this I mean that it gives a purely abstract and completely universal expression to truths which the various sciences of nature discover for themselves in the world of actually existing objects and events, and by methods which are in part at least empirical. In the last analysis every scientific problem is a problem in identity. The purpose in each case is to render things clear by telling us *what they are*. In practice this frequently means explaining *how they come to be*. A motion in space, for example, is defined as the product of antecedent forces, a geological formation, a plant or an animal species as the ultimate term in an evolutionary process. But the abstract type of all such explanations, whatever the mode of being or the nature of the phenomenon to which they have

---

[3] The difference between mathematics and logic seems to me to be this, that whereas mathematics seeks to discover the implications of propositions or propositional functions, logic studies *the fact of implication* itself from a point of view which I should describe as *critical*. The modern tendency to assimilate logic to mathematics is really detrimental to the former. Its effect is to render logic dogmatic and therefore unphilosophical. Thus the altogether praiseworthy attempt to escape from *one* dogmatism—that inherent in the uncritical acceptance of the Aristotelian tradition—has given rise to *another*—the dogmatism inseparable from the cult of a specialized science.

reference, is the mathematical equation. Here we seek to fix the identity of the expression on the left-hand side by means of the expression on the right. When the latter is an independent variable, the relation between the two is functional, and the dependent expression is called a *function* of the independent. Furthermore, quantities that are functionally related are said to constitute a system.

In mathematics all of this is purely theoretical, and has nothing to do with actually existing entities, whether physical or spiritual. My proposal, which might be described as an experiment in the methodology of metaphysics, is to invert the procedure whereby mathematics eliminates the actual, and to apply the notions of function and system, with whatever modifications may be found necessary, to the concrete actualities of human experience. In this way the concepts themselves will gain a certain concreteness. From another point of view they will have to be thought of as increasing in generality. For whereas in mathematics the identities with which we have to deal are definitely quantitative in character, my suggestion is that the conception of functional relationship be extended to every instance in which the identity of a term, irrespective of its nature, is seen to be dependent upon that of another. This is obviously to generalize the conception of a functional relation as understood by mathematics.

That such relations are to be found between actually existing entities in the natural world may be taken as a *prima facie* probability, supported by a vast weight of scientific evidence. But if so, it follows that systems exist in nature. Whether the world in its entirety is a system may be open to question. The unreflective assumption of a single Universe is certainly subject to theoretical objections; but it may well be that on a reflective view there are strong reasons for adopting the notion at least as a working hypothesis or (in Kant's phrase) a "regulative idea."

6. Now the suggestion which I wish to develop is that the concepts of function and system be applied to the events and modes of being which we designate "subjective," and which include the possibility of being conscious. Thus a functionally organized manifold of subjective events will constitute a subjective system. For purposes of theory this may be taken as the definitory formula of personality. Throughout my argument, then, the expressions "a

person," "a spirit" must be understood to connote a system of subjective events.

Finally, I shall have to deal with certain possibilities of experience and of existence which seem to me to have their origin in the compresence, in the total scheme of things, of subjective and physical systems. In particular I hope to show that the world of perceptual experience, with all the values characteristic of the latter, may with advantage be represented as functionally dependent upon the conjunction of physical and subjective systems. This is the condition upon which the world acquires the character that I have called "sacramental." We shall have to ask how this character is possible. My answer to the question is that sacramentality arises through a prior union of the physical and the subjective in a mode of being which reveals itself from different points of view either as the embodied spirit or as the living body.*

Conclusions to Be Reached

7. To anticipate conclusions, my contention is reducible, in the main, to the following four points. (1) There are grounds for conceiving the physical world as a self-contained and indefeasibly non-subjective system of functionally related particulars—many of the latter themselves physical systems. (2) There are grounds for believing in the existence of subjective systems, otherwise known as spiritual beings or persons, and for thinking of these as irreducibly non-physical in character. (3) Any attempt to qualify the duality

[*One way of elucidating the author's position here would be to relate it to Fechner's well known antithesis between the day view and the night view of the world.

The sacramental universe is the universe in the full light of day; the night view being what we obtain when we take the physical barely by itself. Both that which clothes the physical—the panoply of light and colour in which it is wrapped—and, on the other hand, the existence of living beings on the earth, presuppose a union of subjective and physical, their conjunctive union in the former case and their organic union in the latter.

Now the organic union in some sense underlies the conjunctive. Hence the point of the word "prior" above.

The emergence of the perceptual or day world (the metamorphosis of bare physical being into what the author calls nature, together with the further emergence upon nature itself of the world of values) occurs, in a way which is ultimately mysterious to us, merely upon occasion of the conjunction of spirit and matter in the subject-object relationship. But before it can happen—before spirit can enter into this all-creative subject-object relationship with matter—there has to be a prior organic union of the two modes of being, in or as that heterogeneous system which we call the embodied spirit; not the imperfect embodiment of spirit which we find in all the phenomena of life, but the fuller embodiment which we find in humanity.—Ed.]

of the spiritual and the physical, any monistic prejudice which tends to obscure the absoluteness of the cleavage between these two ultimate modes of being, is fatal to an understanding of either, and is indeed apt to issue, not in a genuine monism, but in a dualism more invidious than that which it is designed to obviate. And (4), while nothing can detract from the ontological distinctiveness of the dual opposites, the spiritual and the physical enter into relations of a highly determinate character, from which arise certain new possibilities of being, (a) the forms of life and (b) the various types of value. Among the latter are the sensory and perceptual qualities of things, and the characters which we denote by the names *charm* or *agreeableness, utility, beauty, wistfulness, glamour, sublimity, sanctity.** I recognize a realm of being, an order or domain to which each of these belongs. One such domain is that which we ordinarily call the natural world. Nature on this view is the objective world of our perceptual experience, and the explanation of it is to be found in a functional dependence upon the relationship between the physical and the spiritual modes of being. Thus nature reflects the life of spirit in meanings that spirit imparts to the inanimate and non-spiritual. A universe in which such possibilities exist is a sacramental universe. That is to say, not only do its impersonal forms and processes propagate themselves in endless characteristic rhythms and purposeless recurrences: in relation to the consciousness of spiritual agents they contract meanings which minister to the power that calls them into being. And thus the spirit, having sanctified them to its use, renews the power from which all sanctity proceeds through their appropriation.

8. In working out the detail I shall avail myself of light from every accessible source. Linguistic considerations will count for what they are worth. A certain sensitiveness to the latter may possibly expose me to the charge, so prevalent today, of a *verbal* philosophy. To this I can only reply that while there are numberless inducements to confused thinking in the uncritical use of a symbolism which has grown up without regard to scientific exactitude, nonetheless language is the product of man's ar-

[*The outline of these (in Chap. xiv below) is doubtless one of the parts of his work which the author hoped to elaborate in much greater detail.—Ed.]

ticulated consciousness both of himself and of the world, and for this reason it cannot be ignored as a repository of truth.

Their Relation to Theism and to Contemporary Philosophy

9. This is a book about the world rather than a book about God. Yet it is my opinion that the view set forth cannot be fully substantiated on any but a definitely theistic basis; and while I have decided that the theistic argument is beyond the scope of the present investigation, which is accordingly limited and incomplete, I hope to indicate in a general way how the conception of a divine being relates itself in theory to the set of ideas with which I propose to work. My argument must be regarded as tentative and provisional, an experiment in method and an assemblage of considerations bearing upon an inquiry more comprehensive and fundamental than I care at present to attempt.*

10. I am painfully aware that the trend of my thoughts runs directly counter to the philosophical movement of the age. That movement is of the greatest value as a corrective to the presumptuousness of metaphysical system-building; but in its final issue it leads to a position that is nothing short of nihilism. The thesis of Gorgias that *nothing is* would seem to be the logical conclusion of the most advanced thinking in the sphere both of science and of philosophy.

This has become growingly clear of late in the sphere of science. From the time when the late Lord Kelvin broke new ground with his long exploded theory of the vortex atom the tendency has been to treat *the laws of physics* (in this instance the laws of motion) as an actual substitute for the physically real, to displace the independently existing world of nature by an intellectual construction which physicists themselves have not hesitated to describe as "subjective." That tendency (as I shall have occasion to point out in the appropriate place) was long ago exposed by Clerk Maxwell in a discussion of the vortex theory; but the movement has continued, latterly with greatly enhanced momentum.

In philosophy the same perversion of the truth has emerged through the framework of that realism which at first sight appears most adverse to it; and the whole development finds a fitting

[*For the author's treatment of certain aspects of this more comprehensive inquiry cf. *Studies in the Philosophy of Religion*, edited by Professor N. Kemp Smith, The Macmillan Co., 1938.—Ed.]

climax in the logical positivism which has so captivated the younger generation of thinkers. Philosophy must be rendered scientific by an application of the same device which has enabled physics in the recent past to make its most signal advances—"the elimination of the substantive thing." And what is the result? In the opening proposition of his *Tractatus Logico-Philosophicus* Mr. Ludwig Wittgenstein has defined the world as "everything that is the case" (alles, was der Fall ist). Now "everything that is the case" is a possible concept; it is quite thinkable, but surely it cannot be taken as a definition of "the world." Strictly speaking "the case" is the timeless content of a judgment or of a noun clause. It is the non-existent abstractum of truth, detached by thought from its original context of space, time and circumstance, and presented to us in a form that has no other significance than that of a logical symbol. Events and objects cannot be the case, although it may be the case that such events and objects either have been or now are. If therefore the world could really be identified with all that is the case, it would lose the character of a time-conditioned manifold, which is its claim to existence.

11. From such a conclusion I cannot but recoil. And yet it may be that the conclusion follows of necessity from the premises. If so, the premises must be revised. By that I mean that in the search for conditions under which the explanation of the world may be undertaken without reducing it to nonentity, we shall have to supplement the principles which serve the practical needs of science by the recognition of principles derived from a different source. It is not my suggestion that we should reinstate "the substantive thing" with its mysterious equipment of imputed qualities. Rather we must seek an equivalent of the substantive— something more in keeping with the modern outlook, yet capable of sustaining the once familiar and for ever indispensable rôle of furnishing a subject of reference for the deliverances of experience.

The substitute which I propose is best expressed by the word "system." Only, the concept of system must be brought into relation with the conditions of existence. The principle which I intend to assume is that whenever anything comes to be, a system is *eo ipso* presupposed. The latter is the ontological *prius* of the former. Functional dependence upon a system—or, to express the same thought from the opposite point of view, the ontological priority of systems to their constituents—is what I take to be the principle of being in whatever form; and the extension of the principle to the sum-total of things is in my view the condition required for the concept of a world. What I wish to show in particular is that the world we know, the world of our actual experience, is unthinkable except in so far as we recognize the existence of systems having the character of subjectivity.

PART I

METAPHYSICAL PROLEGOMENA

PART I

METAPHYSICAL PROLEGOMENA

CHAPTER I

FUNCTIONS AND SYSTEMS

The Notion of Function Linguistically Considered

1. The word "function" has two meanings that specially concern our inquiry. It connotes an activity, and it connotes a mathematical relation. These meanings, at first sight only remotely if at all connected, can, I think, be shown to emerge from a common background of thought.

Etymologically speaking, "function" is derived from the past participle of one of those anomalous Latin verbs which we call "deponents." Deponent verbs represent an intermediate class between active and passive. Passive in form, they commonly express an activity of the subject, but an activity that terminates in itself rather than in some definitely traceable effect in the world beyond. If an *object* is implied, its relation to the subject is oblique—that is to say, the kind of relation that would ordinarily be expressed by a preposition; and it is for this reason that the object of a deponent verb is commonly, though not invariably, in the genitive or the ablative case.[1] The underlying idea would seem to be that of a self-contained or self-reflecting activity, directly expressive of some inherent potency in the subject, and indirectly of some relation to an object.[2]

Of this the verb "fungor" is a perfect example. But what is specially significant is the fact that the verb not only illustrates, it actually *means*, what has just been said about deponents. Indeed it might be taken as giving generalized expression to any activity or experience of self-realization[3] within a well defined relationship

[*Chapter heading the author's, sub-headings mine. So throughout, except where otherwise indicated.—Ed.]

[1] Ablative: fruor, utor, abutor, potior, vescor, pascor, fungor, laetor (abl. or prep.). Genitive: potior, reminiscor, recordor (the latter usually with acc.), obliviscor.

[2] *vid.* Appendix A to this chapter, p. 48.

[3] The basic connotation is that of *enjoyment*. Brugmann gives the Sanscrit equivalent in factitive form: *bhuñj-a-ti*, "makes to eat or enjoy." *A Comparative Grammar of the Indo-Germanic Languages*, §628. (English tr. by Conway & Rouse, Vol. IV, p. 164.)

or set of conditions; and this meaning has been perpetuated in its English derivative.

The Notion of Function in Its Physiological and in Its Mathematical Context

2. A function then is an activity. But it is more than that. It is the activity proper to a structure organized for the performance of it, and for the performance of any other activities either inseparably connected with it or at least in some way uniquely characteristic of the structure. Thus we think of the function peculiar to a mechanism, an organ or organism, a society, a profession or associative group of human beings.[4] Until we know the nature of the structure we cannot have a really well defined idea of the function. We realize what *breathing* is when anatomy, chemistry, and physiology, by furnishing the necessary particulars, have taught us to regard it as the peculiar function of the respiratory system.[5] In this way what to begin with was a vague notion, calling for a more precise identification, acquires something of the exactitude characteristic of a mathematical expression for which a "value" has been found. And so of the other bodily processes. Ordinary unscientific experience has rendered us familiar with the impulsive movements which the body executes without the aid of definite volition. But the nature of the processes involved remains obscure until we have learned to *identify* the movements as instances of reflex action—the characteristic function of a structure designed for just such operations.

Thus the method we employ when we interpret a vaguely apprehended physiological activity as the function of a well defined anatomical structure has a close analogy to that of the mathematician who assigns a "value" to a dependent variable by representing it as the *function* of an independent. This brings us to the second meaning of the word.

[4] It is true that many structures (human bodies, for example) have more than one characteristic activity. But where this is so it will be found that the structure in question includes a variety of subordinate structures, to each of which one or other of the different functions is assigned.

[5] This of course is only one side of the truth. There is a sense in which breathing is not a physiological function but an *experience* or subjective activity. In this case it belongs to a different system—the system of some subject-self. The authors of the Upanishads were alive to this truth when they included such activities as breathing and digesting along with the more obviously mental processes of thinking, willing and feeling under the single rubric of the *devatâs* or vital powers.

In mathematics one expression is said to be a function of another if the value (that is, the *quantitative identity*) of the former is determined by, and varies with, the value or quantitative identity of the latter.

The term itself was introduced into the language of mathematics by Leibniz, whose original definition is to be found in the *Acta Eruditorum* of July 1694. Leibniz explains that what he has in mind is a portion of a straight line cut off by two other lines determined by a fixed point and a point upon a given curve.[6] The fixation of value, of identity, is the essential feature. Four years later, we gather from his voluminous correspondence with John Bernoulli, he has extended the conception to the solution of isoperimetrical problems.[7] Here his contention seems to be that better results are obtained by arguing from content or capacity to perimeter than by arguing (as was then customary) from perimeter to content.[8] Once more the question is one of the fixation of values by a definite operation of the mathematical laws involved. An equality of volumes is first established in accordance

[6] "*Functionem* voco portionem rectae, quae ductis ope sola puncti fixi et puncti curvae cum curvedine sua dati rectis, abscinditur. Tales sunt: Abscissa . . . ordinata . . . tangens." G. G. L., "Nova Calculi Differentialis Applicatio et Usus, ad multiplicem linearum constructionem, ex data tangentium conditione," *A. E.*, 1694, p. 316. Jakob Bernoulli uses the word in a similar sense. F. Cajori, *A History of Mathematics*, 2nd ed., 1919, p. 211. cf. Cantor, *Geschichte der Mathematik*, Leipzig, 1898, Vol. III, p. 438.

[7] *vid.* the letters numbered LXXVI, LXXIX and LXXX, *Leibnizens mathematische Schriften*, Gerhardt, Vol. XXXII, Halle, 1856. Also the collection, *Got. Gul. Leibnitii et Johan. Bernoullii Commercium Philosophicum et Mathematicum, ab Anno 1694 ad Annum 1716*, Lausanne and Geneva, 1745, 2 vols. Ep. LXXV and LXXVI correspond to Nos. LXXIX and LXXX in Gerhardt's collection.

[8] Leibniz to Bernoulli: "Placet etiam, quod appellatione Functionum uteris more meo. Loco Isoperimetrarum liceret generalius adhibere figuras Isodynamas, secundum unam fungendi rationem, et ex iis reperire vel eligere eam, quae Maximum aut Minimum praestet alia fungendi ratione, v. qr. in simplicissimo eam, quae ex aeque capacibus est brevissimi ambitus, quae est Circulus, decussata, ut sic dicam, quaestione cum inquisitione capacissimae ex Isoperimetris. . . ." (July 29, 1698.)

Bernoulli to Leibniz: "Elegans est conversio Tua quaestionis Isoperimetrarum in Isodynamarum, ubi scilicet ex omnibus figuris Isodynamis seu ejusdem capacitatis quaeritur illa, quae certa fungendi ratione producat aliam figuram brevissimi ambitus inter omnes illas quae eadem functione ab aliis Isodynamis produci possent." (August 16/26, 1698.) Gerhardt, Nos. LXXIX and LXXX. That the unusual expression "Isodynamae" (figurae) refers to area or content (capacitas) is apparent from the words of Bernoulli, and it is borne out by incidental utterances of Leibniz. "*Nomen* est terminus rem significans pro arbitrio assumtus. Ita circulus est hujusmodi figurae nomen, at figuram esse, uniformem esse, capacissimum esse isoperimetrorum sunt attributa." L. Couturat, *Opuscules et fragments inédits de Leibniz*, Paris, 1903, p. 241. "Circulus isoperimetrorum maximus est Ens necessarium." *ibid.*, p. 272.

with one way of working ("secundum unam fungendi rationem"). Then from among the volumes thus equated it is possible to discover or to select that which, by another way of working ("alia fungendi ratione," "eadem functione"), is found to have the longest or the shortest perimeter. From the expressions used it appears that the word "functio" is the equivalent of "ratio fungendi," a working out of principles to their conclusion, hence the conclusion itself, the end-term of a mathematical *process*. This is in complete accord with the original deponential sense of the word (a crossing of active and passive), and with the English idiom. A function is a *doing* construed as *done*, a *working* viewed as an effect *wrought*, as when we speak of the *working* of a tariff system, or refer to a providential issue as "the Lord's *doing*."[9]

It remained only to give the concept an abstract turn by removing the distinction of active and passive altogether. What is left is the relation of *determined* to *determinant*. The concept has attained not only a high degree of abstractness, but a high degree of generality.[10] Already in Leibniz' theory it is not with actual discrete quantities and the relation between them that we have to do, but with the general laws to which all quantities are subject in so far as they are mutually interdependent and vary together.[11] Reciprocity is the essence of functional relationship. Indeed it is all a matter of the point of view and the special angle of inquiry, which of the two variables we consider the independent and which the dependent. If, for example, our problem is to determine the *distance traversed*, we do so by representing it as a function of the time during which the motion is uniformly maintained: $d = F(t)$. If the subject of inquiry is the *time* it takes the moving body to reach a fixed point, the answer is given as a function of the distance: $t = F(d)$. The functional relation may thus be looked at from either end; and between them the variables, independent and dependent, may be regarded as constituting a *system* of mutual determinants expressible in the formula xy.[12]

---

[9] For further examples of an active form with a passive meaning cf. the expressions "a baking," "a boiling," "a washing," "a catch."

[10] The arithmetization of the doctrine by Weierstrass represents a further step in the logic of this universalizing process.

[11] E. Cassirer, *G. W. Leibniz Hauptschriften*, Einleitung, Vol. I, p. 10.

[12] *op. cit.*, Vol. I, p. 184, Streitschriften zwischen Leibniz und Clarke, with editor's note.

Function and Existing *System*

3. It will be seen, then, that both meanings of the word "function" imply the concept of a system. The concept, however, to begin with, appears to come in somewhat differently in the two cases. When we say, in the mathematical sense, that *y* is a function of *x*, we do not mean that *x* is a system and *y* its function, but that between them the two variables *constitute* a system of changing values held together by a relation that remains constant. When, on the contrary, we speak of breathing (*y*) as a function of the respiratory system (*x*), it is obviously to the *system* (of respiration) that we are referring the function. The two cases, therefore, differ in this, that whereas in the latter the terms divide as function and system respectively, in the former they combine with one another, and with the characteristic relation between them, to constitute the unity of a system within which the variables differentiate themselves as independent and dependent.

A moment's reflection, however, will show that beneath this divergence in usage there is a common substratum of meaning. Thus (a) if the proposition "*y* is a function of *x*" means that all the possible values of the first term are determined by all the possible values of the second, it is upon *this fact* rather than upon the values of *x* as such that *y* depends. In the end, therefore, the true determinant is the systematic character of the relationship that unites the two terms; and so the formula $y = F(x)$ is seen to be a superficial rendering of the formula $y = F(xy)$. The second of these propositions stands to the first as a principle to its application or as a presupposition to the assertion which it conditions. The principle involved might be called the Principle of Reduplication. (b) A similar construction must be placed upon the other case. Except from a narrowly anatomical point of view we do not really separate breathing as a function from the system that sustains it. The truth is rather that the various organs and parts which combine to constitute the system acquire the character of a single anatomical structure only in relation to the function which they render possible. In the characteristic activity there is something of definitory force, something that serves to concentrate our impressions at the relevant points, and enables us to view just this plurality as one. Anatomical description is here guided by considerations derived from physiology and the chemistry of the living body. It is specifically in relation to vital process that the various parts and organs involved define themselves as a respiratory system. In so far, then, as we describe breathing as a function of that system, we *ipso facto* postulate a more complex structure definable as "the respiratory-system-in-action." It is of this rather than of any mere anatomical organization that breathing is the characteristic function.

4. These considerations are of decisive import in determining the concept of system as I intend to apply it to our metaphysical problem. That is to say, the formula $y = F(x)$ must be interpreted as founded upon the formula $y = F(xy)$. The expression xy denotes a system, and the special truths which the basic formula is intended to convey are (a) that every term which is a function of the system must have a place within the system, and (b) that every term within the system is a function of the latter.[13] The systems with which I shall have occasion to deal will be such that within their unity one term may be rightly described as a function of another, but only in a sense which presupposes that every term is a function of the system as such.

5. It should be remembered that the symbols x and y stand for variables. Each of them represents a range of values, and the system which between them they constitute is a system of concomitant variations. From the mathematical and abstractly logical point of view this is as far as we have a right to go; but if the conception of functional relations is to be made available for the interpretation of actual fact, there must be some way of relating the concept to the particulars of experience. I do not mean that instances of functional relationship must occur, but that when such instances are brought to light, it ought to be possible to attribute the relation in question not only to the variables, but to the individual "values" or specific occasions which exemplify the latter.

A case in point is the relation of any cause to its effect, when viewed in the light of the causal law involved. This law declares that every time a y (that is, any member of a y set or class of y's) occurs, we must assume an x (that is, a member of an x-set or class of x's) as its cause. Here the relation is obviously between sets or classes, and the reference is not to any individual x and y,

[13] The second of these propositions is subject to a certain qualification in the case of complex and incompletely coherent systems. This will be brought out presently.

but to the *series of individuals* which constitutes each of these expressions a variable. My contention (which is diametrically opposed to that of logical positivism, but is quite compatible with logical principle) is as follows:

If x and y are variables, and x^1, x^2, x^3, x^4 . . . and y^1, y^2, y^3, y^4 . . . are the specific values or individual instances of x and y respectively, then in so far as y is a function of x, y^1 has a right to be considered a *function* of x^1, y^2 of x^2, y^3 of x^3, etc. In other words, if there is any point in assuming that the concept of a functional relation between variables is exemplified in the world of experience (which the positivists themselves assume), it can only be on the ground that the relation which obtains when the terms are variables is formally identical with that which obtains when the terms are individual events or existents. It may be true in all cases (as it certainly is in most)[14] that a "determinate causal situation" presupposes a general causal law as just defined; but there could be no such thing as a causal law apart from the determinate situations in which it is exemplified. The difference involved is merely that between a principle of interpretation and the empirical confirmation of the principle. In the one case the principle is *posited*, in the other it is *recognized*; and the significance of both operations depends upon the identity of what is recognized with what is posited. That identity is definable as the relation of a *determinant* to a *determined*. In view of this the difference between functional and causal dependence is reducible to the difference between the thinkable and the actual. Where the actual and the thinkable coincide, the difference disappears.[15]

[14] My reason for this guarded expression is that I am not prepared without further thought to rule out the possibility of an absolutely unique causal occasion. Perhaps there is some way in which the latter contingency might be brought within the scope of the general rule. As there is a *null* class, might there not be a class of one? Failing this, it is still conceivable that the ordinary conception and the unique occasion might be brought together under a more comprehensive conception of what causality really implies.

[15] In practice, however, it *makes a difference* whether we begin with the thinkable or with the actual. It is my assumption that the actual is always thinkable, and that when the former is given, the latter may be taken for granted. On the other hand, it cannot be assumed that the thinkable is always exemplified in the world of actual happenings. If, therefore, we begin with the pure concept, the actual may have to be brought in as a postulate of being. From this point of view functional dependence may still be distinguished from causality on the ground that the latter is what the former becomes when the postulate of being is added to the concept. But between the two cases there is no difference *of form*. In both the notion is that of a *determinant* in relation to a *determined*.

This reinterpretation of functional relationship has its effect upon the corresponding notion of system. The latter acquires a concreteness commensurate with the former. That is to say, the system in question need no longer be a system of concomitant variations. It may (and indeed throughout my argument *will normally*) be the specific unity (historical and unique) of two or more events which, in accordance with the revised conception, are found to stand in functional relation to one another. Thus the expression *xy* which occurs in the formula $y = F(xy)$ will normally denote a system of events of which *x* and *y* are the functionally related constituents.[16]

Advantages of Taking System Existentially

6. What I have said about the identity of the functional relationship with that implied in any specific causal occasion has brought out a further point, which, however, I wish to make independently. In mathematics and logic the conception of variability has of course nothing to do with the empirical fact of change in time—although for certain purposes it may be taken as an abstractum of that fact. The variables with which we are here concerned are, however, not mathematical abstractions, but actualities of experience. This will have its effect on the concept of system which I am trying to formulate. The expressions for which a value is sought by referring them as functions to some system will be time-conditioned processes or phases in a time-conditioned process. In other words, they will be, at least in one aspect, sequences of concatenated events. Hence the systems which enclose them will likewise be characterized by progression in time. This is in entire agreement with conclusions already reached as to the biological interpretation of the concepts with which we have been dealing. In the case of breathing, for example, although we commonly describe the process as a function of the structure, the statement, as I have insisted, is of little value so long as the structure is considered apart from the process. But the addition of the process to the structure implies that the system with which we have to do is the ordered series of events in which the apparatus of respiration is involved. The significance of these observations will, I hope, be

---

[16] The background against which my view is developed is furnished by the account of functions to be found in any logical treatise written from the modern point of view. *vid.*, e.g., Miss Stebbing's *A Modern Introduction to Logic*, 2nd ed., pp. 128 *sq.*, 352 *sq.*, 380; Professor C. A. Mace, *The Principles of Logic*, pp. 70 *sq.* and Chap. xvi.

more apparent when we come to deal with the nature of life in general and with experience in its temporal aspect, but more especially when the question is raised whether consciousness can be considered a function of the brain and spirit a phenomenon of bodily structure as such.

7. It is my hope, also, that the recognition of time as integral to the constitution of all actually existing systems will be of some use as indicating a possible way of escape from an impasse which is as old as Plato, and into which (in a greatly aggravated form) modern philosophy has been led by some of its ablest exponents. I am thinking principally of the systems of Professor Whitehead and Professor Santayana, in which nature figures as a process in time, all of whose distinguishable characters are timeless essences or eternal objects. Of course essences are reputable entities. In a sense they are quite exceptionally manageable. They are so because of the mental operation by which we insulate them from all perplexing contexts and so get them by themselves. The trouble is that when they have been thus tamed to our use, there seems to be nothing we can do with them. It is true that the Platonic ideas, which are among the essences, have been utilized by their inventor as causal principles or principles of explanation. But there is one thing which they cannot possibly explain, and that is how there comes to be such a thing as a time-conditioned manifold or natural world. Moreover, as *characters of the flux* they completely lose their abstract intelligibility. Indeed we may go further and say that if there is anything about them that is altogether clear, it is that they cannot be regarded *as characters of the flux*. In the end we are confronted by a series of paradoxes so extreme that, when the logic of the position is unfolded, it is seen that the natural world and the realm of essences (as nearly happened in Plato's theory) have both alike virtually disappeared in sheer non-entity. As Professor Santayana puts it, the flux has existence, but no being, whereas the essences have being, but no existence. From these perplexities I think we may be delivered by a method of thought in which the distinction of essence and existence fades away in the concept of time-conditioned systems,[17] and in which explanation means not

[17] The same would have to be said of the distinction of Sein and Dasein in the philosophies of Fichte and Hegel.

the identification of an essence, but the discovery, upon evidence which is bound to be in the end chiefly empirical, of functional relations in the manifold of experience.

Degrees of Coherence in Systems

8. As regards internal organization, everything in a system need not be a function of everything else. If the structure is at all complicated, it is likely to contain terms which are not functionally related to one another. Moreover it is necessary to recognize varying degrees of integration. Some systems are more closely organized than others. Where two or more terms do not stand in functional relation, their connection may be no more than conjunctive or additive. All that is implied in this is compresence of some sort, for example, in space or in time. A manifold of terms, between which the relation is purely conjunctive, does not constitute a system; and no term can be considered as belonging to a system if its sole relation to everything within the latter is conjunctive. If a plurality of terms is to constitute a system, therefore, what is really implied (and this is a minimal requirement) is that every member should be a function of *some other member*.[18]

Although in itself of no definitory force, the conjunctive relation may nevertheless under certain circumstances contribute to the sum-total of the conditions under which a manifold acquires the significance of systematic organization. For example, the elements a, b, and c may constitute a conjunctive plurality and nothing more. Hence in their relation to one another there is no suggestion of a system. But if there is a term x which can be seen to be a function of these elements taken *in conjunction*, that is, of the relation of mere compresence which subsists between them, then we are confronted with the proposition $x = F(a + b + c)$ and with the system $\{x(a + b + c)\}$. The basic formula would of course be $x = F\{x(a + b + c)\}$.[19]

[18] On this aspect of the subject *vid.* L. S. Stebbing, *A Modern Introduction to Logic*, p. 198.

[19] When this contingency arises, there may be grounds for suspecting that behind the conjunctive relation of a, b and c there lies hidden a relation much more fundamental. But it is not necessary to assume that this must be the case. Instances occur in which a certain possibility of human experience may be clearly perceived to depend upon a conjunction of conditions that is in itself quite unintelligible. Beauty in nature, for example, implies the compresence of a percipient organism and certain physical conditions in the outer world. How these two come together we do not know. So far as our human insight is concerned, their compresence is purely conjunctive. But of the conjunction beauty is a function. [cf. similar footnote, p. 32.—Ed.]

I must here notice a difficulty with regard to the relation of what I have called the *basic* to the primary or subsidiary formula. For purposes of philosophical inquiry, where presuppositions must be made explicit, the proposition $y = F(x)$ must be read in the light of the proposition (which in relation to the other has the force of a principle): $y = F(xy)$. But how is this principle to be expressed in the case of complex and loosely integrated or incompletely coherent systems? If, for example, y is a function of $(a + b)$, and p and q are functions of a and b respectively, there is obviously a systematic connection between the elements $a, b, (a + b), y, p$ and q; but the connection is incompletely coherent. The relation between a and b is merely conjunctive. Can it be maintained that the propositions $p = F(a)$ and $y = F(a + b)$ necessarily imply the propositions $p = F\{ab(a + b)ypq\}$ and $y = F\{ab(a + b)ypq\}$* respectively? Obviously not. There are elements within the system which have nothing to do with the conditions by which p and y are determined. Suppose, for example, that a stands for a state of consciousness in some percipient organism, b for a state of the physical world, and y for an object of perceptual experience (a *percept*) determined by the conjunction of a and b. In this case p might conceivably represent a subsequent state of consciousness in the same organism, determined by a, and q a physical event in the outer world, related to b as effect to cause. If the downward-pointing arrow is taken to symbolize functional dependence, the total system might be represented thus:

From this it is clear that the percept y is in no way dependent upon either p or q, and that p, which follows by some psychical necessity from a, is not necessarily affected by any physical event resulting from the causal efficacy of b. In brief, we can detect no functional connection between p, y, and q, and none between $(a + b)$ on the one hand and either p or q on the other. Nonetheless within this loosely integrated system there are subordinate systems which are

[*It may be well to point out that in his use of algebraic symbols the author pays little attention to ordinary mathematical conventions. Thus while his + means *plus*, his *ab*, etc., have nothing to do with multiplication.—Ed.]

coherent, and these supply the principles required for a complete statement of the functional determination of p and y. Thus: $p = F(pa)$ and $y = Fy(a + b)$.

9. As an example of a thoroughly coherent system we may take the following. Let a and b represent past and future time. It will be agreed that the relation here is not merely conjunctive, but that the terms stand in definitory relation to one another. To know that the one is identifiable as either past or future is to know that the other is identifiable as either future or past. Suppose now that y = present time. This is determined by a relation to both past and future. But, since a and b are functionally and not conjunctively related, the primary formula would have to be, not $y = F(a + b)$, but $y = F(ab)$. Present time is a function of that which precedes it in a highly determinate relation to that which follows it. In other words, given a and b in the relation which is definitory of these terms as past and future, we know where y must of necessity come in: given y, we understand the rôle it plays in the determination of a and b. The mutual implication of the terms in question is complete. In this way the order which is of the essence of time has definitory significance for all of time's articulations. Hence we may say that a, y and b each $= F(ayb)$.

The value of such propositions is that they give expression to the principle in the light of which, as I have said, the primary formula must be construed. But it is no less true that the basic formula, if taken by itself, obscures the differences between the various terms which it serves to define. If the expression $F(ayb)$ is the definitory formula alike of a, y and b, we have no means of distinguishing between these three terms. To obviate this inconvenience we must have recourse to the primary formulae: $y = F(ab)$, $a = F(yb)$ and $b = F(ay)$. Thus, having interpreted the primary in terms of the basic formula, we must invert the process, and articulate the latter in terms of the former.

Problems Inseparable from the Proposal to Take System Existentially

10. Among the problems which call for special attention is that of relating the concepts of function and system to the postulate of being in each of its fundamental modes. We shall have to ask how far and in what ways the conditions implied in the functional relation are realized in the world of actually existing objects and events. For of course functions and systems do not in themselves

imply existence. The terms between which the characteristic relation obtains, and which therefore become the constituents of some systematic organization, may be anything whatever. They may be parts of a physical structure, objects of sensory experience[20] or of pure thought, meanings, qualities, events in the natural world or in human minds: they may exist or they may not: they may exist in one way and not in another. The only thing that matters is that they should have an identity, actual or ideal, which is determined by a relation in which they stand to other identities. When this condition is realized, we are bound in some sense to think them together—in other words, to postulate a system.

11. Now if this is so, if the concept of system does not imply being, whereas being may well assume the systematic form, it follows that where the question is one of actual existence, we are altogether dependent upon evidence derived from another source. That source can only be experience. Experience alone can inform us whether anything exists, and to what particular mode of being it is to be assigned. In relation to the purely theoretical concept of system, therefore, being can be introduced only as an independent postulate. But granted the postulate, and granted the concept of system, the concept may acquire ontological significance through its relation to the postulate. Questions like these arise. To what extent are the phenomena of the physical world organized in systematic structures? Is there any evidence for the view that what we call "Nature" is itself a comprehensive system of being? And if so, does the evidence suggest that the system is completely or incompletely coherent? How far is it possible to extend the concept of system to the spiritual mode of being? Do subjective events cohere in organized wholes, of which the principle is the relation of *determined* to *determinant*? Is anything to be gained *for theory*

[20] In the philosophies of Mach and Avenarius the application of the concept of functions is limited to the elements of sensory experience, and the existence of a system must not be taken to imply more than the existence of these elements in functional relation. The connection of systems and functions is set forth with great explicitness by Avenarius. "Let V_1 and V_2 be two of the variables assumed in our general empirico-critical scheme; and suppose that these are mutually dependent—exactly how it does not matter except that every time a change occurs in V_1 a change occurs in V_2. Thus we designate V_1 in relation to V_2 a 'determinant' (Änderungsbedingung); whereas the changes which occur in the second variable V_2 in relation to V_1 we designate 'determined' or 'dependent' (bedingte oder abhängige)—in brief, as determined by or dependent upon V_1. Finally, when we think the two variables together, the resulting concept is that of a *System*." *Kritik der reinen Erfahrung*, Teil I, I, pp. 25-6.

by substituting the notion of a subjective *system* or *system of experiences* for that of a *subject* in the treatment of the self or ego?

12. Behind these problems there are others of a general metaphysical character having to do with the relation between *systems* of being, considered in conjunction with the diverse *modes* of being. For example, a well defined series of events in the physical world is knit together by the bond of causal connection. This is an obvious instance of the functional relation of determinant and determined. Hence the events involved constitute the kind of system we call causal. That many such systems exist can hardly be doubted. But the question remains whether the existence of causal systems implies the existence of a universal causal law, as the existence of causally related events implies the existence of causal systems. The problem is one in which evidence and interpretation must go hand in hand. But whatever the solution, the unmistakable prevalence of systematic organization in the actually existing outer world is in itself a fact of significance. It proves at least that nature (metaphorically speaking) does not abhor system—that nature in fact is prone to system—and it suggests that system may be the universal *form* of being in the physical mode. But it is hardly possible to entertain such a suggestion without extending the question to being in general and asking whether anything can exist except in some organized structure and in functional relation to other things. If the answer, however tentative, should turn out to be in the affirmative, the conclusion forced upon the mind would be that while the concept of system does not imply being, it is quite possible that being implies system.

13. The restriction of the concepts of system and function to the sphere of the actual by the introduction of the postulate of existence suggests a further problem. So far determination has been taken to mean the fixation of identity; but in the real world (so at least it would seem) the identity of things is not revealed to us through their relations to other things, but is given directly with their existence, as this reveals itself to our experience. Since Hume made this clear in the case of causal connection it has been generally realized that where we are dealing with empirically apprehensible phenomena there is no analogue to the way in which the expression on the left-hand side of an equation is determined by the expression on the right, or the conclusion of a syllogism by the conjunction of the premises. Such being the case, it looks as if

the concept of functional determination, when applied to the *de facto* contents of the real world, must have reference, not to the *identity*, but to the *existence* of the terms affected.

This interpretation is hardly warranted. It is true that in the world of experience determination does not mean the correlation of identities *by implication*. Nonetheless it means the correlation of *identities*. In the case of the causal relation, for example, the point is not merely that *y comes into existence* under conditions which can be stated, but that what comes into existence under these conditions *is y*. Indeed the very essence of causal explanation is to be found in the assumption that if the sum-total of the determining conditions could be known, we should know exactly what to expect by way of result. As in other contexts, the "what" must not be divorced from the "that" nor the "that" from the "what."

Homogeneous and Heterogeneous Systems

14. Among the complications that arise when we try to relate the concept of system to the postulate of being is one that has to do with the "modes" of the latter. I have not hesitated to make use of this expression (without explanation), and to cite the physical and the spiritual as illustrations of what I mean by it. That the illustrations will be accepted in the sense which I intend is something which I have no right to assume. Indeed it will be a main part of my effort in succeeding chapters to make good my right to regard the physical and the spiritual as separate modalities. Meanwhile let me explain what I mean by "modality" or "mode." The idea is that of a certain ontological exclusiveness which I take to be absolute. Thus, if it is correct to describe the spiritual and the physical as two modes of being, it follows that nothing which can be rightly described as physical can be rightly described as spiritual, and vice versa.

We must now consider the concept of system in relation to the modes. Where functional relations occur between terms having the same modality, it is necessary to assume a system having the modality of the terms. Thus if there are subjective states which are functions of other subjective states, there is such a thing as a subjective system. The word "subjective" here refers to the modality of being, the word "system" to the principle of organization, and the expression as a whole may be taken to denote a complex structure characterized by the ontological exclusiveness which (upon this hypothesis) the word "subjective" implies. Upon the same hypothesis an exactly similar statement could be made with regard to any system characterized as "physical." Thus systems partake of the modality or ontological exclusiveness characteristic of their contents.

From these considerations it follows that (under the conditions assumed) no term can enter directly into a system which differs from it in its mode of being. There is no place for a state of consciousness in a physical structure, and no place for a physical event in a system of subjective processes. This truth may be generalized in the provisional maxim that where a system and its constituent terms are modally homogeneous, no one of the latter can be transferred from the system to which it belongs to a system which differs in modality from the former.

I have described the maxim as *provisional*. The reason for this is that in view of certain possibilities which have yet to be considered, the maxim fails to express the whole truth as to the relation of terms and systems from the standpoint of modality. In the case which has been dealt with, the modal homogeneity of a system with itself and with its constituent terms is conditioned by the homogeneity of the latter. Thus if *a* and *b* are modally identical, the system (*ab*) is modally identical with each. But the question remains open whether terms which differ in modality may not stand in functional relation to one another, and so unite in a single system. The possibility can hardly be doubted. Cerebral changes, which are physical events, have a determining effect upon states of consciousness, which are spiritual events. The latter are functions of the former. Conversely, bodily movements are functions of the volitional activities which call them into being.[21] The connection is as unmistakably functional as is the causal nexus between modally homogeneous events in the outer world. But if so, we are bound to recognize the existence of systems in which the *determinant* is in one mode and the *determined* in another—systems, therefore, which are not modally homogeneous either *in themselves* or *with their terms*.

[21] In the end it might be necessary to modify or to amplify these statements. The acting cerebrum and the moving body are not merely physical structures: they are living organisms, and as yet we have no clear conception of life. The illustration may, however, stand. In certain of its aspects at least the living body is also a physical structure, and movement in space a highly characteristic physical phenomenon.

The existence of modally heterogeneous, like that of modally homogeneous, systems is subject to special conditions. In the first place they are never found except where the terms which enter into them are at the same time functions of systems modally identical with themselves. To put the situation symbolically, if p and q are the functionally related but modally divergent terms in question, and x and y are their respective modalities, then the condition upon which alone p and q can come together into the modally heterogeneous system (pq) is that there already exist an x-system, M, of which p is a function, and a y-system, B, of which q is a function. In terms of our previous tentative illustration, the volition presupposes a subjective system or *mind*, and the physical movement a corporeal system or living body. Of these p and q are the respective functions, and as such they are modally homogeneous with the systems M and B to which they belong. All of this is presupposed in the possibility of their entering into functional relation with one another in the modally heterogeneous system (pq).

15. In the second place, the modal character of p and q is entirely unaffected by the mutual relation into which these terms are assumed to have entered. That character is fixed in them for all time as x and y by their respective membership in the systems M and B. In the system pq the individual terms retain what I shall call their native modality. A volition is indefeasibly subjective even if it is cerebrally conditioned and issues in a movement of the body; and there is not a trace of subjectivity in the cerebral process which initiates the volitional activity, or in the bodily movements by which the latter is followed.[22]

Why the Heterogeneous System Is of the Higher Ontological Rank

16. It is not difficult to see that these considerations have a bearing on the ontological character of heterogeneous systems. The latter differ from homogeneous systems not only as one homogeneous system differs from another, or as modality differs from

___

[22] Where the heterogeneity is that of the physical and the subjective, the modality of the system will be best described as "psycho-physical." Obviously this expression does not imply that what is psychical is also physical, but that the system so characterized comprises both modalities. A psycho-physical *system* must of course be distinguished from a psycho-physical *conjunction*. The case with which I have been dealing is quite different from that already noted, in which a factor y (e.g., beauty or the sensory properties) is seen to be a function of the physical and the psychical in conjunctive relation.

modality in general. Rather the distinction is ordinal. It is so, however, in a sense that varies with the point of view. In the case of finite beings like ourselves a certain metaphysical priority must be assigned to the homogeneous in relation to the heterogeneous. We understand the way in which a volition *exists* (the kind of *being* which must be attributed to it) much better when we think of it as an activity of some mind than when we think of it as a principle of bodily change. Its causal efficacy, which is something of a mystery, throws little light upon its ontological status. In the same way we grasp the nature of a bodily movement as a possibility of *being* more adequately when we view it in a context of similar movements, or as a function of the living body, than when we relate it to an actuating volition. This is the truth which enables biological science to make its characteristic abstraction and to exclude all considerations of a psychical nature from the treatment of biological phenomena as such. In the order of being, therefore, there is something basic and original in modally homogeneous systems, something derivative, conditional and ontologically superficial in systems which combine mutually exclusive homogeneous modes. All that religious thinkers have had to say about the triviality, the precariousness and the insignificance of man's existence as an embodied spirit, in contrast to the significance and the indestructibility of his being as an immortal soul, may be taken as a commentary on this last observation. All that we have learned about the dependency of our composite natures upon physical and chemical conditions, all that we have felt as conscious animals, when viewing our human lives in the vast perspectives of evolutionary process, goes to reinforce the same evaluation of the heterogeneous from the opposite standpoint.

17. On the other hand, granted the ontological dependence and secondary character of modally heterogeneous systems, it is still possible to conceive the existence of such systems as an enhancement of being—not in the superficial sense that it brings an appreciable increment to the sum-total of what was already there, but in the deeper sense that existence itself may acquire new elements of content, new meanings and values, through the union of diverse modes in functionally organized heterogeneous structures. I have instanced beauty as a function of the compresence of the physical and the spiritual modes of being, and have pointed out that all that is implied here is a conjunctive connection between

these modes. As a matter of fact the statement is incomplete. For before the conjunction of the physical and the spiritual can give rise to the value we call beauty, it is necessary that the two modalities should also come together (in quite a different way) in the functionally organized, heterogeneous system of the percipient organism. The physically real contracts the property of beauty in conjunction with an appreciative consciousness only when the consciousness in question is that of a living animal endowed with organs of sense. The quality of being, in any such composite system as renders the conjunction of heterogeneous modalities capable of generating a value, I shall call *power*. Being in the form of power is itself a value in the being that possesses it: it is an element of content in the absence of which being would not be what it is; and for this reason it makes up in significance what it lacks in ontological independence.

18. It is possible to go further than this. If consciousness is a condition of all the higher possibilities of spiritual self-realization, and if spiritual beings require a living brain in order to achieve the experience of consciousness, it would seem to follow that even in its ontological exclusiveness the spiritual is dependent for what is most of value to it upon the union, in a single system, of cerebral and purely spiritual factors. Finally, there is a point of view from which it is necessary to reverse all that has been said about the ontological inferiority of the heterogeneous to the homogeneous. There may be grounds for supposing that the universe itself is a comprehensive system of all the modalities. In this case the supreme reality will be a heterogeneous system of being.

19. Before proceeding further I must complete and restate the maxim which governs the relationship of terms and systems to the modalities of their existence. The rule may be given under two main headings. (a) No term within a modally homogeneous system may occupy a place within another homogeneous system which differs in modality from the first; and (b), a term in any one mode may enter into functional relation with a term in another, and the two between them may constitute a system, provided (i) that these terms already belong to systems which are modally homogeneous with them, (ii) that in entering into the new system they do not forfeit their native modality, and (iii) that the systems implied in the functional connection of the modally dissimilar terms are char-

acterized by the same heterogeneity as the terms of which they are composed.

The Question What Systems Exist

20. Leaving these more abstract considerations, let us now devote some thought to the question how far the actual world of our experience gives evidence of functional organization. Here again method is all-important. In view of the multiplicity and the inexhaustible complexity of things, induction in any of the ordinary forms is obviously quite inadequate. My plan is rather to make use of what I shall call considerations of weight—forms of evidence which, because of their intrinsic character, appear to warrant a *right to believe*. If, for example, functional relations are found to exist between objects removed from one another by astronomical distances in space, that would count for something in favour of the view that the world is one. If chemical phenomena on a remote heavenly body are functionally correlated with physical phenomena on the surface of the earth, the suggestions of a physico-chemical cosmos or world-system would be hard to ignore. But the weightiest type of argument is that derived from the conditions under which our knowledge advances in scientific exactitude and comprehensiveness. If with every forward movement in this direction there goes a further revelation of the truth that things apparently unconnected or perhaps even opposed in nature are really manifestations of one and the same set of laws, and if the substance of these laws is always the determination of some identity by functional correlation, we have every right to treat the argument (so far as this is ever possible under the conditions of empirical inquiry) as completely conclusive. What follows must perforce be no better than a selection of specimens derived almost at random from the history of scientific knowledge, designed to bring out the general trend of the available evidence.

21. It will be agreed that physical systems exist. We speak, for example, of the solar system, and the term denotes a group of planetary bodies whose movements are so completely interdependent that we can view them as the diversified expression of a single complex process. In order to understand the behaviour of any individual in the group we must consider it in the light of its changing relations to all the others: we must *think* the moving

bodies together, and view the sequent phases of their motions from the standpoint of determinant and determined.[23]

The principle involved is as follows. Each planetary orbit (by which we must here understand not merely the path delineated in space, but the delineation of the path—hence actual orbital movement) has an identity of its own, which is determined by, and in turn determines, the identity of every other orbit. Here then we have a concrete illustration of the abstract concept: here the essence of system is revealed as the mutual determination of variable identities.

Nature abounds in systems so determined. When we look at a spectrum containing what appears to the eye to be one yellow band shading off on each side into darkness, we at once think of the yellow flame of sodium. A blue and a violet band towards the right end of the spectrum announce the presence of indium. In this way the chemical identity of the substances of which the heavenly bodies consist can be determined by the observation of terrestrial phenomena—and, incidentally, phenomena which fall within the province not of chemistry, but of physics. There is no more impressive evidence that nature's processes tend to be functionally ordered, and that therefore they constitute systems of correlated fact, than the union of astronomical and chemical investigation in the science of spectroscopy. So great has been the measure of success achieved that astronomers already believe themselves entitled to the conclusion that none of the known elements is absent from the sun. Thus empirical evidence is accumulating in favour of the proposition, advanced by Descartes on a priori grounds, that the earth and heavens are formed of the same matter.[24] Spectroscopic methods further illustrate what has been said about the reci-

---

[23] Professor Stebbing instances the solar system as an example of "an ordered set of elements" or an "order," "since from the fact that a planet has such and such a position inferences can be drawn." While this assertion is of course accurate, I think it is an understatement of what is meant by thinking of the planets as constituting a system. It is not merely that inferences can be drawn from the fact that a planet occupies a certain position, but that the position which the planet occupies can be deduced as an inference from the position of other planets. And as this applies to every planet in turn and to every possible position, a certain completeness can be attained in the statement. Miss Stebbing adds: "Such inferences are to be distinguished from those that are dependent upon the general laws of planetary motion, e.g., Newtonian law of gravitation." This is also true; but so long as the general laws of planetary motion are excluded, it will be impossible to form an adequate idea of the orderliness of the solar system as a system of *moving* bodies. *vid. A Modern Introduction to Logic*, pp. 228-9, footnote.

[24] *Princs.*, II, xxii.

procity of the functional relation. Generally speaking, the isolation of the elements by chemical analysis has preceded the discovery of their spectra; in which case the spectra appear as functions of the elements. But in one instance the first step was taken by spectroscopic observation. The discovery of helium in the sun (from which the element derives its name) was achieved by spectroscopic investigation as early as 1868, whereas its presence in the terrestrial atmosphere was detected for the first time by Sir William Ramsay as late as 1895.[25] Until the element was actually isolated, it could only be thought of as a function of its spectrum.

Turning for further illustrations to the more highly generalized aspects of the changing world of nature, we immediately think of the numberless conjunctions of events which experience has taught us to regard as causally connected. Every one of these conjunctions is a causal system with a structure of its own. That is to say, the events in question acquire the identity of cause or effect from the relation in which they stand to associated events. The structures are generally, even to our imperfect human knowledge of them, enormously complex.

Considerations in Favour of the View That Nature as a Whole Is Systematic: (a) Leibniz' Advance upon Descartes

22. Whether nature as a whole may be conceived as a single comprehensive causal system, whether we are entitled to postulate an all-embracing law of causation, is a question which has given occasion to one of the most significant controversies in the history of philosophy. The answer turns upon our right to assume that the identity of every event, in relation to the sum-total of physical events, is determined with the same precision which we know to characterize the movements of the planets in the solar system. Such an assumption is of course immeasurably beyond the possibility of detailed empirical verification; and a cautious thinker like Professor C. D. Broad is constrained to rest content with the idea that causal laws exist, while leaving unanswered the question of a single all-embracing Causal Law.[26]

23. It is, however, significant that every great advance in scientific analysis, while teaching us to draw more firmly and distinctly

---

[25] Young's *Astronomy*, revised (1927) by Russell, Dugan and Stewart, Vol. II, p. 504.
[26] *Perception, Physics and Reality*, p. 161. Mr. Broad agrees that it is "advantageous" to assume the general Law of Causality "as a methodological postulate."

the line that divides one group of phenomena from another, has at the same time revealed more and more unmistakably the existence of a common principle running through the most widely severed provinces of reality, and bringing the most diverse phenomena into just such relations as I have described. Even where the appearances were all against the application of a single interpretative concept to the data, the adoption of this procedure on grounds of methodological convenience has fully justified the risk taken, by bringing the facts into new and scientifically illuminating perspectives. The history of the sciences is rich in illustrations. Let us consider one or two typical cases.

24. Descartes, for example, trusting to appearances, and content to take things in the way that seemed most natural, represented motion and rest in the usual way as two opposing states of matter.[27] Leibniz, with greater insight, by an application of the principle of continuity, showed how the two phenomena could be viewed as one, by interpreting rest as a limiting case of motion.[28]

The advantages of the new point of view are more than methodological. There are phenomena which by their very nature defy all attempts to dispose of them neatly in one or other of the Cartesian categories, and which consequently bring these categories into direct conflict. A striking example of this is to be found in a further use which Leibniz makes of the new principle he has just enunciated.

Descartes had maintained that the quantity of motion in the universe is constant.[29] On the basis of this doctrine he proceeds to formulate two rules for moving bodies—rules which, as Leibniz shows, in one specific instance are mutually incompatible. The first applies to bodies of equal size approaching one another at the same rate. By the principle of the conservation of motion, when these bodies meet they must both immediately reverse the direction of their movement, while maintaining their original velocity.[30] The

[27] *Princs.*, II, xliv. "Movement is not contrary to movement, but to repose. . . ." It is true that he thinks of the bodies which sustain these opposite states or modes as themselves in motion (*ibid.*, xxvii); but this hardly improves the situation.

[28] *Animadversiones in partem generalem Principiorum Cartesianorum*, Gerhardt, Vol. IV, p. 376. cf. the letter (d. 1687) addressed to Bayle "sur un principe général utile à l'explication des lois de la nature . . . pour servir de réplique à la réponse du R. P. D. Malebranche," Gerhardt, Vol. III, p. 53. Erdmann, Vol. I, p. 105: ". . . La règle du repos doit être considérée comme un cas particulier de la règle du mouvement."

[29] *Princs.*, II, xxxvi.

[30] *op. cit.*, II, xlvi.

second rule is designed to meet the case of unequal bodies which come together under similar conditions. When the impact occurs, only the smaller is reversed, the larger continuing as before.[31] According to the first law, the later movements of the two bodies are in opposite directions, according to the second, in the same. It will thus be seen that between these laws there is a complete break. Each is separately conceived, to meet what Descartes assumes to be an irresolvable difference in the supposed facts of the case. The one holds only for equal bodies, the other only for unequal; and no allowance is made for any difficulty as to the precise class to which any pair of bodies is to be assigned. They must be either equal or unequal.

Now Leibniz argues that there is a third relevant consideration, the *degree* of inequality, and that the demands of theory are not exhausted until this has been taken into account. Thus it is possible to imagine the inequality between two bodies diminishing continuously until it disappears in complete equality. Clearly the recognition of continuity in the series of differences reduces the Cartesian construction of the facts to unworkability. For Descartes equality is one thing, inequality another; and to each, under the conditions stated, there corresponds a separate law of motion. But what of the case where the difference is infinitesimal? The infinitesimally unequal cannot, strictly speaking, be placed in either class, so long as the classes are regarded as rigidly distinct. As *un*equal, it cannot sustain the character of equality; and since the degree of inequality is less than any assignable quantity, it cannot claim the differentiating mark by which inequality itself is given a definite identity.[32] Hence there is no means of deciding which of the two rules of motion comes into effect. The obvious expedient is to apply them both; but the attempt to do so leads to the difficulty which I have just pointed out. The rules conflict, and cannot be made to apply to the same instance. From this impasse the natural way of escape is that suggested by Leibniz. The one case must be read in the light of the other. As rest was interpreted in terms of motion, equality must be interpreted in terms of inequality. When this is done, it is found that where two laws were

[31] *op. cit.*, II, xlvii.
[32] ". . . La différence qui est dans les suppositions de ces deux cas, sçavoir la différence entre une telle inégalité et entre une égalité parfaite pourra estre moindre qu'aucune donnée. . . ." Letter to Bayle, Gerhardt, III, 53.

unable to cover every possible instance, one law is now sufficient.

The point upon which Leibniz' argument turns is the irrationality of a theory which compels us to assume that as inequality passes by continuous gradations into equality, the first Cartesian law of motion, which up to this point has not varied in its application, is miraculously displaced by the second.[33] In order to avoid this "leap from one extreme to the other," this sudden transformation of "absolute repulsion" into "absolute continuity" of motion it is necessary to rethink the whole problem in such a way that any variation in the initial situation (what is given or presupposed)[34] is at once reflected in the end situation (what results from the former and is the object of inquiry).[35] In brief, Leibniz shows how all the factors in the case can be accounted for by the principle of functional variation.[36] Regarded from this point of view the motions resulting from the impact are seen to be dependent variables for which we seek to find exact values by relating them to the corresponding independents—the motions of the bodies originally given.

The essence of Leibniz' procedure is the fact that he applies the concept of continuity or infinitesimal differences to the principle of concomitant variations, expressible in the formula: "datis ordinatis etiam quaesita sunt ordinata." This principle (which he describes as the "more general" of the two), when read in the light of the former, becomes a universal law of order in nature; and the justification of the assumption lies in the extent of the corrections which it enables us to effect.[37]

(b) Newton's Advance upon Aristotle

25. A further striking illustration of the way in which the world, as our scientific knowledge of it advances, takes on more and more the aspect of a single ordered system, is derived from a comparison of Aristotle's physics with the general outlook in physical science

[33] ". . . Cette différence des événemens de ces deux cas n'est pas raisonnable." *ibid.*, p. 53.

[34] In this case the two moving bodies considered from the standpoint of their relative size. Leibniz uses the expressions "hypotheses duae seu duo data" (*Animadversiones*); "in datis ou dans ce qui est posé"; "ce qui est donné" (Letter).

[35] The motions of the two bodies resulting from their impact—"quaesita sive eventa" (*Animadversiones*); "in quaesitis ou dans ce qui en résulte"; "les suites ou événemens (ou ce qui est demandé)" (Letter).

[36] *vid.* Cassirer and Buchenau, Vol. I, p. 84, footnote.

[37] cf. the "principe de l'ordre général" of the letter to Bayle.

in more recent times. In the doctrine of Aristotle the phenomenon of motion in its various manifestations is governed by a set of completely unrelated laws. There is a law for light bodies and a law for heavy,[38] the former moving, by a principle of nature inherent in them, from the centre outwards, the latter, by an opposite principle, moving inwards towards the centre. Both alike proceed in straight lines.

But rectilinear motion is only one of the forms which experience forces upon our attention. The revolution of the heavenly bodies was a phenomenon which early attracted the scientific interest of the Greeks. For Aristotle circular motion ($\dot{\eta}$ κυκλοφορία)[39] differs specifically from rectilinear ($\dot{\eta}$ εὐθυφορία) (and indeed from all the forms of change) in this, that in it alone the direction is reversed without a break in the continuity of the process. Thus an object moving in a straight line from A to C cannot return to A without a momentary interval of rest at C, whereas if A be the starting-point of a circular movement, the process which begins at A terminates at the same point and yet remains a single movement. In this case motion *to* is at the same time motion *from*. We are dealing, not, as in the previous instance, with two distinct and opposite processes,[40] but with a process which is one and continuous throughout.[41] From this analysis Aristotle concludes that "there cannot be a continuous rectilinear motion that is eternal."[42] The attribute of eternity is therefore peculiar to circular motion.[43]

Thus confining ourselves to the types of movement which have been considered, we find that Aristotle recognizes three distinct and mutually irreducible ways in which bodies may pass from place to place. Of these two are rectilinear, and one is circular. The former are opposed to one another, and the latter is opposed to both. There is thus a double break in the world of moving things. By associating the local distinction of *up* and *down* with the qualitative distinction of light and heavy, and by interpreting the

---

[38] *vid.* Appendix B, p. 49.

[39] *Phys.*, E, IV, 227, b, 19-20.

[40] *op. cit.*, Θ, IX, 265, a, 21.

[41] *op. cit.*, Θ, VIII, 261, b, 27 *sq.*, 264, b, 9, 18. *vid.* also Appendix C, p. 50.

[42] οὐκ ἄρα ἐνδέχεται συνεχῆ κίνησιν εἶναι ἐπὶ τῆς εὐθείας ἀίδιον—reading and rendering of the Oxford tr. by Hardie and Gaye, for Bekker's ἐπὶ ἀίδιον τῆς εὐθείας. *op. cit.*, Θ, VIII, 263, a, 2-3.

[43] τὴν μὲν οὖν κύκλῳ ἐνδέχεται ἀίδιον εἶναι, τῶν δ᾽ ἄλλων οὔτε φορὰν οὔτ᾽ ἄλλην οὐδεμίαν. *op. cit.*, Θ, IX, 265, a, 25.

latter as an ultimate difference or oppositeness in the inherent properties of matter (an oppositeness *in kind*), Aristotle is unable to combine these various concepts in the synthetic category of *weight*; and by treating circular motion as specifically distinct from rectilinear, he effectively segregates the system of celestial phenomena from the terrestrial. The heavenly bodies which by nature move in circles are by definition neither light nor heavy.[44] They have no place in any gravitational system. Their movements are not interpretable in terms of any available concept (for example, mass) which might place them in a single category with the movements of terrestrial bodies.

Thus for Aristotle the universe remains the theatre of uncorrelated principles working without intelligible relation to one another. His failure was largely due to the same cause which we trace, through its effects, in the theory of Descartes—the attempt to understand the changing manifold by treating the phenomenon of motion as a thing in itself. So long as this standpoint is maintained, the various types of movement which we generalize from observation remain phenomenally isolated in the classes to which, on superficial grounds, we are constrained to relegate them. Leibniz took a great step forward when he insisted that the phenomena of motion be interpreted as manifestations of the laws of force. Only so can they reveal the functional relations which permit us to correlate them as a whole. By means of these laws we are able to view the most diverse and seemingly opposed phenomena as the outward expression of uniformly and universally operating principles; and once the proper standpoint has been attained, the synoptic method is indefinitely promoted by the fact that where the laws of motion stand out against one another in unresolved contradiction, the laws of force (or, as we should now say, *energy*), lend themselves to mutual adjustment and combination. Newton's supreme contribution to scientific progress—a contribution rendered possible by the preliminary labours of Tycho Brahe, Galileo and Kepler—lay in the fact that by crossing the Law of Inertia with the Law of Gravitation, he succeeded in producing a synthetic principle to which all movements within the solar system, terrestrial and celestial alike, are subject. In brief, he postulated a single system where Aristotle had postulated several. The point at

[44] *De Coelo*, A, III, 269, b, 29-31.

which the ancients failed was in finding a physics that would harmonize with their astronomy, and an astronomy that would not give the lie to their physics—whereas Newton, in the words of a recent popular but competent exponent of Relativity, "with his dynamics and gravitation, supplied a new physics for the new astronomy."[45] It is an interesting commentary on the methodological soundness of Newton's procedure that Einstein, in reformulating the conception of gravitation in a further synthesis of gravitational and electrical phenomena, carries over into his system the same conception of the relationship of gravity to inertia, which had proved so fruitful in the work of his great predecessor.[46]

26. As these instances show, being in the physical mode has revealed itself to our progressive knowledge of it in ways that emphasize more and more the ordering of its contents in systems of functionally related terms. This statement, however, leaves many problems undecided, and for the sake of clarity and explicitness I should like to indicate precisely (though without dogmatic insistence) what conclusions seem to me to be warranted by what I have called "considerations of weight." These may be summarized as follows:

(a) System is the universal form of the physical. That is to say, wherever entities of an unmistakably physical character occur— events in space, for example—we may be sure that a system of some sort is presupposed, and that the entity in question is a function of that system. More briefly, in the physical world nothing exists, nothing occurs, which is not a function of something.

(b) These statements hold good where the functional relation involved is defined as causality. Not only do causal systems occur in the physical world, but nothing occurs there except in a relation of causal dependence.

(c) In a sense determined by the preceding proposition causal law must therefore be conceived as universal. This, however, it must be noted, is not to say that nature is a single causal *system*. It is theoretically conceivable that there should be a number of independent causal systems organized upon the same principle of functional relationship. These would necessarily take the form of

[45] Rice, *Relativity without Mathematics*, p. 19.
[46] *ibid.*, p. 21.

parallel, yet functionally unconnected, series of causally determined events.

(d) Nevertheless there are considerations of weight against such a hypothesis. In particular it is significant that the assumption of independent systems of events finds its best exemplification in such obsolete world-pictures as the Aristotelian with its complete disjunction of stellar and terrestrial physics, and that the normal result of scientific progress (as in the advance from Aristotle to Newton) is the explosion of such disjunctions by the discovery of what I might here call functionally ordered interserial events.[47] It appears to me, therefore, that there are conclusive grounds for preferring the hypothesis that the world is a single system of causally connected events to the hypothesis that there are many causal systems in the world.

(e) I find no such grounds, in the present state of human knowledge, for concluding that the world-system is completely coherent. While every event must *be* a function, it does not seem necessary that it should *have* a function, or even that there should be a place for it in some conjunctive or other combination upon which physical events are functionally dependent. Relationship of some sort there must of course be—were it only spatial compresence or temporal succession; but I know of no considerations sufficiently weighty to exclude the possibility that trains of functionally ordered events may come to an abrupt end, or that nature should include blind alleys and relatively unorganized areas. Even with this qualification, however, which in the end may prove unnecessary, the functional organization of the outer world remains a fact of the utmost impressiveness; and it becomes growingly clear that even if the postulate of being must be introduced independently, existence in the physical mode is inseparable from system.

[47] It may be said that the illustration has not been accurately stated. What Aristotle assumed was not a number of independent systems organized upon the same principle, but a number of distinct principles at work in different areas and upon different modes of physical being. This I admit, and my contention is thereby strengthened. The new truth destroyed the old world-picture, not by showing that the same causal principles which govern the movements of terrestrial bodies govern the movements of the stars, and that therefore sidereal and earthly events may be regarded as parallel series of causally determined physical phenomena, but rather by showing that celestial and terrestrial events, through their reciprocal relations, belong to one and the same system of causal determination.

Plan of the Ensuing Discussion: to Consider the Modalities of Being, with a View to Finding if There Is System in the Spiritual Realm; and, as a Preliminary, to Examine Those Current Doctrines Which Would Virtually Deny the Distinctive Existence of a Spiritual Realm

27. Now my suggestion is that the concepts of system and function, which have proved so fruitful in the exploration of one mode of being, may be, at least experimentally and tentatively, adopted as a clue to the exploration of others. I have more than hinted at a spiritual modality as ontologically distinct from the physical, and having about it something of the same originality and independence, and at modes which are not thus independent, but are the derivative products—indeed the functions—of various types of relationship between the two original modalities. These suppositions must be substantiated and developed. The succeeding phase of my argument, therefore, will have to do with the postulate and the modalities of being rather than with the concept of system.*

28. Above all, and as a preliminary to any progress whatever along these lines, we must ask what reasons can be given for representing the spiritual as ontologically independent and not a mere predicament of the physical. To some this inquiry will appear no better than a forlorn hope; to others it will appear a work of supererogation. In the eyes of the latter class it is the simplest and most transparent of all certainties that the spiritual mode of being is necessarily known as independent and irreducible by everyone who appreciates the fact of his own personality, and experiences within him the ceaseless interplay of its subjective forces. But the fact remains that among leading thinkers of the present day the distinction of physical and spiritual has become blurred and uncertain—sometimes almost to the point of obliteration. Even where it is in some sense frankly recognized, it is not accorded fundamental ontological significance. Reality, it is assumed, must be taken as altogether one; but, it is said, we may take it at different depths. In this analysis process, organism, life, psyche and spirit come successively into view, but only as theoretically distinguishable dimensions of an ever-identical fund of being. Within the unity of the latter there is a subjectivity in the physical,

[*Compare what the author now speaks of, as the distinction between the spiritual and the physical *modes of being*, with what he spoke of in his earlier work as the distinction between *modes* of experience and *facts* of experience. See *Studies in the Philosophy of Religion*, Vol. II, Chaps. XXI-XXII.—Ed.]

and there is a naturalness in the subjective. Not only so, but even in the strictly objective manifold there must be no diremption, no "bifurcation," as into primary and secondary qualities—a mode of thought which has its origin in the totally erroneous idea that some of nature's properties are self-subsistent and scientifically apprehensible, while others are additions due to mind.

The procedure I propose to adopt is to begin with this modern tendency, and to trace its implications through the writings of some of its most expert representatives. It is my hope that these implications, once they are made clear, will throw light upon the validity of the assumptions in which they have their origin, and that in this way we shall be enabled to decide how far the distinction of physical and spiritual is to be treated as metaphysically serious.

APPENDIX A (*See note 2, page* 17)

THE DEPONENT VERB AS EXPRESSIVE OF THE SUBJECTIVE

A closely analogous construction is that of the reflexive verb (= middle voice in Sanskrit and Greek), or the impersonal with pronominal accusative and oblique construction (genitive or prepositional equivalent). e.g., taedet, pudet, piget, paenitet *me*—with genitive; *sich* erinnern (gen. or *an* with acc.), *sich* schämen (gen. or prep., *über*, *wegen*), sich freuen (prep. or gen.); *se* défier, repentir, soucier, souvenir, moquer, méfier, gausser—with *de*; pentirsi, addarsi (apply oneself to), rammaricarsi (complain, grieve). For a thorough treatment of the whole subject *vid*. F. Diaz, *Grammatik der Romanischen Sprachen*, 3rd ed., Vol. III, pp. 190 *sq*. Such forms represent an early phase in the development of linguistic self-expression. In the Indo-European languages the passive voice is derived from a previous middle; and in relatively recent times we find in Scandinavian a similar development, H. Paul, *Prinzipien der Sprachgeschichte*, 4th ed., p. 281. When we consider the matter with attention, the surprising thing is that the middle voice and the deponent and reflexive forms have not played an even greater part in the evolution of the verb. So many of the activities which we describe by means of a transitive governing an accusative are really confined to the inner experience of the subject and do not necessarily affect the object at all. There is no analogy except that of verbal form between "Peter *seized* the stone" and "Peter *saw* the stone." Certain languages, e.g., German, have made provision for the difference by supplying alternative expressions. The point is well brought out in an article by H. Schuchart on "The Passive Character of the Transitive in the Caucasian Languages," from which I quote the following. "In our tongues the subject of transitive assertion corresponds in most instances to the real subject. But if I say: 'I see a house,' 'I hear a noise,' 'I love the girl,' the transitive significance is not comparable to that of the assertion: 'I strike him.' The truth of the matter is better brought out in the expressions: 'ein Haus fällt mir in die Augen,' 'ein Geräusch trifft mein Ohr,' 'das Mädchen flösst mir Liebe ein.'" *Sitzungsberichte der Wiener Akademie, Phil.-Hist.*, 1896. cf. J. Vendryes, *Le Langage*: *Introduction Linguistique à l'Histoire*, Paris, 1921, p. 123.

APPENDIX B (*See note 38, page* 42)

LIGHT AND HEAVY

These laws rest upon a fundamental opposition running through the whole of nature, and typified by the hot and the cold of Anaximander and Parmenides, and the solid and the void of Democritus. The specific opposition here involved is that of position (θέσις), in respect of which "up" and "down" are irreducible contraries, having all the characteristics of ultimate principles, *Phys.*, A, V, 188, a, 19-28. Position must here be understood in an absolute sense, and not relatively to the observer. This is made clear in a later passage. "Up and down . . . are not merely relative to us. For to us they are not always the same, but they vary with our position and the direction in which we are facing, whence the same thing is frequently both right and left, up and down, before and behind. In nature, on the other hand, each of these positions is sharply distinguished. 'Up' is not what you will, but the place where the movements of fire and of light bodies occur. Likewise 'down' is not what you will, but the locus of the motions of heavy and earthy bodies. Thus the distinction is not one of position only, but also of potency" (ὡς οὐ τῇ θέσει διαφέροντα μόνον ἀλλὰ καὶ τῇ δυνάμει). *ibid.*, Δ, I, 208, b, 14-22. cf. *De Coelo*, B, II, 284-5, where Aristotle, in opposition to the Pythagoreans, propounds the curious theory that we live in the under hemisphere and not in the upper.

APPENDIX C *(See note 41, page 42)*

Rotatory Motion in Aristotle

It is unfortunate that the Oxford translators should have chosen to render the Aristotelian ἡ κύκλῳ (= ἡ κυκλοφορία) "rotatory" motion, as this is a distinct conception in Aristotle (= δίνησις), the motion of a compact body or system of bodies (not necessarily solid) turning as one, and without change of place, upon its axis. The movement of the stars is circular, but not, according to Aristotle, rotatory. *De Coelo*, B, VIII, 290, a, 11-13. The inappropriateness of the translation is specially marked in *Phys.*, Θ, VIII, 264, b, 18-19, where change of place is part of the definition, ἡ μὲν γὰρ κύκλῳ κίνησίς ἐστιν ἀφ' αὐτοῦ εἰς αὐτό. Contrast the passage referred to from *De Coelo*: δινούμενα μὲν γὰρ ἔμενεν ἂν ἐν ταὐτῷ καὶ οὐ μετέβαλλε τὸν τόπον. (The allusion is to the motion of the stars.)

Physical and Spiritual in Modern Philosophy—with a Special Examination of Professor Santayana's System

The Monisms of the Present in Their Distinction from the Idealistic Monisms of the Past

1. In the philosophical writing of recent times (as I have indicated at the close of the last chapter) there has been a marked tendency to minimize and to obscure the distinction between what I have represented (provisionally) as two fundamental modes of being. This is, of course, in a sense, in keeping with the metaphysical tradition, in which the abhorrence of an ultimate dualism and the desire for a monistic construction of reality have played a preponderating rôle. But the tendency to which I have referred and of which Alexander, Whitehead and Santayana are outstanding representatives, is marked by certain features which differentiate it sharply from the monistic movement of the past.

The great constructive systems of Continental thought from Descartes on, have on the whole been marked by a profound consciousness of the duality of nature and spirit, subject and object, self and not-self; and in so far as they have achieved an eventual monism, they have done so in ways which imply no abatement, but rather a heightened appreciation of this distinction. Indeed their dualistic assumptions have been made to contribute to their monistic conclusions.*

The Divine Substance of Descartes presupposes the duality of thought and extension which it serves to mediate. Spinoza's two known attributes of God are among the necessities of the Divine nature, and since each of them expresses that nature in its complete extent,[1] and expresses it differently,[2] they are for ever irreducible to one another.

It is true that in his principle of continuity and in his Monadology Leibniz attained a point of view from which the antithesis of soul and body loses much of its force; but a consciousness of that

[* The author had similar aims as is shown by Chap. XIII below.—Ed.]

[1] *Eth.* I, x, Schol.

[2] ". . . Substantia cogitans et substantia extensa una eademque est substantia, quae iam sub hoc, iam sub illo attributo comprehenditur." *Eth.*, II, vii, Schol.

antithesis and of the inadequacy of current attempts (Occasional-
ism, for example) to overcome its more disturbing consequences is
closely interwoven with the motives that led him to formulate the
doctrine of monads in the form in which we know it.[3] It is in relation to the problem of body and mind that the first suggestions of
the conception of a preestablished harmony appear;[4] and although
the significance of the body-mind problem fades away as a dualistic becomes a pluralistic universe,[5] nonetheless the distinction of
spirit and matter breaks out afresh as that between two distinct
levels of dignity in the hierarchy of monads;[6] and in a world where
all being takes the monadic form there is still a place of unique
distinction for what Leibniz calls the dominant entelechy or soul.[7]

Kant's Critical Philosophy turns upon the cleavage between a
natural world of causally determined appearances and a world of
ideal possibilities, of which the active principle is the free will of a
moral agent. The German Idealistic movement begins with a profound sense of the same cleavage. For Fichte it was Kant's supreme achievement to have unbound spirit from the shackles of
circumstance, and from all forms of determinism, whether physical
or religious. In letters to Achelis, to Weisshuhn, to Johanna Rahn,
he celebrates, with characteristic enthusiasm, his consciousness of
inward emancipation, secured to him for the first time by arguments which he conceived to be conclusive.[8]

Fichte's system is weighted heavily in favour of the Ego, which
posits both itself and the Non-Ego. Of this his successor Schelling

[3] *Système Nouveau de la Nature et de la Communication des Substances, aussi bien que de l'Union qu'il y a entre l'Âme et le Corps*, 1695, 12 *sq.*

[4] "C'est qu'il faut donc dire que Dieu a créé d'abord l'âme, ou toute autre unité réelle, en sorte que tout lui naisse de son propre fonds, par une parfaite spontanéité a l'égard d'elle-même, et pourtant avec une parfaite conformité aux choses de dehors." *op. cit.*, §14. The expression "harmonie préétablie" occurs for the first time in the "Éclaircissement du Nouveau Système," written in reply to certain observations by Simon Foucher and published in the *Journal des Savants*, 2nd and 9th April, 1696. *vid.* Latta, *Leibniz*, p. 326, note.

[5] "Body, for Leibniz, is nothing but a collection of Monads (or phenomena of Mo-nads), and consequently the question of the connexion between soul and body is only a confused and imperfect form of the question as to the relation between any one Monad and another." Latta, *op. cit.*, p. 46.

[6] "Je jugeois pourtant qu'il n'y faloit point mêler indifféremment les E s p r i t s ni l'Âme raisonnable, qui sont d'un ordre supérieur, et ont incomparablement plus de perfection que ces formes enfoncées dans la matière" &c. *Système Nouveau*, §5.

[7] *Monadology*, 70.

[8] Selections from these letters will be found in the brief but excellent English *Memoir* by William Smith, 1848.

took a seriously critical view. Indeed, to Schelling it seemed that the natural world as defined by Fichte in terms of a limit or obstruction (Schranke) of the divine life,[9] and hence as something stiff and dead, was a sheer negation of being.[10] To avoid this conclusion nature must be invested with something of the character of spirit. The life which is one with being, and which Fichte assigns without qualification[11] to God or the Absolute alone, must be shown to be implicit in nature also. It is therefore necessary to abandon the view which would reduce the physical to a negation. Body and soul must be thought together. Neither has an independent existence. There is no such thing as pure body or pure soul.[12] The difference between the two is that between *an affirming or a knowing* and *a known or affirmed*.[13] The result is a pan-psychic philosophy of nature and a naturalistic philosophy of spirit. But the two moments in the act of identification are clearly articulated. To find spirit in nature demands a certain attitude to the truth: to find nature in spirit demands another. It remained for Hegel to place the relationship on a specifically dialectical basis.[14]

Now throughout this vast movement of thought, however monistic the conclusion reached, the duality of nature and spirit was ever present *as a problem* and an actuating motive. What is characteristic of the present-day movement is the relative absence of the motive which springs from a profound consciousness of this duality. It is symptomatic of the current tendency that the Continental thinkers whose influence of late has been most noticeable are on the whole those who have felt least deeply the opposition of the two modes of being. Thus Leibniz and Spinoza have grown in influence, and Kant is perhaps less of an inspiration than he has been at any time since the appearance of the *Critique of Pure Reason*. Epistemology has fallen back appreciably before a revived interest in metaphysics on the one hand, and (more recently) the sudden development of logical positivism on the other. It is with the former rather than the latter that I wish to deal. I am thinking

[9] *Ueber das Wesen des Gelehrten, Vorles. II.* Werke, ed. by J. H. Fichte, Vol. VI, p. 363.
[10] "Ein vollkommenes Non-ens." *Darlegung des wahren Verhältnisses der Naturphilosophie zu der verbesserten Fichteschen Lehre,* 1806. Schelling's Werke, 1860, Vol. VII, p. 10.
[11] ". . . Es giebt kein anderes Seyn, als das Leben." *op. cit.,* p. 361.
[12] *System der gesammten Philosophie,* Werke, Vol. VI, p. 217.
[13] *ibid.,* p. 217.
[14] *vid. Phänomenologie des Geistes,* Einleitung. Werke, 1841, Vol. II, p. 67.

of such impressive constructive efforts as Alexander's *Space, Time and Deity* and Whitehead's *Process and Reality*.

2. In view of what has just been said it might seem a little strange that there have been so few signs of an effective return to the great Idealistic systems of Schelling and Hegel. The explanation is perhaps to be found in the obsolete science of these systems. There is certainly something in Schelling (and more particularly in his conception of organism as a cosmic principle) that suggests the developed theories of Whitehead;[15] but the chemistry and physics of the *Naturphilosophie* are not the chemistry and physics of the twentieth century, and there is no inspiration in them for a philosophy that is definitely rooted in the science of the day. It is different with Leibniz, whose work, unlike that of Schelling, belongs to the authentic scientific tradition, and has therefore, on this side of it, a permanent interest and value to which the *Naturphilosophie* can hardly lay claim.

The Influence of Locke and Hume upon Contemporary Thinkers

3. As regards the remaining influences, and more particularly those derived from the empirical movement in British philosophy, there is significance in the position which Locke and Hume have come to occupy in the minds of contemporary thinkers. Although the problem of these two philosophers is essentially the problem of *the knowable*,[16] their handling of the subject obscures the issue in its most critical aspects—especially those which derive their point from the duality of consciousness and its object. In neither Locke nor Hume do we find a genuine epistemology.

It is true that the background of Locke's thinking is a naïve dualistic realism; but the implications of this position are never

---

[15] *vid. Von der Weltseele, eine Hypothese über der höheren Physik zur Erklärung des allgemeinen Organismus*, 1798. Werke, Vol. II.

[16] I do not say *the problem of knowledge*. The difference between Locke and Kant might be expressed as that between asking: "What can I know?" and: "Granted knowledge, what are the conditions that render it possible?" This explains the distinction between a genuine criticism and Locke's "historical plain method"—the method of an inventory or investigation applied to ideas, very much as Bacon had applied the methods of natural history to the phenomena of the physical world, cf. the phrase: "the collecting and perfecting of a Natural and Experimental History" in the Dedication to *The Great Instauration*. The point of view is maintained throughout the *Novum Organum* and *The Advancement of Learning*. e.g., ". . . we must first of all have a muster or presentation before the understanding of all known instances . . . and such collection must be made in the manner of a history. . . ." *Nov. Org.*, II, xi.

fully grasped, and it is not permitted to reveal itself completely in the precise form which the inquiry assumes. The distinction of mind and body, moreover, loses much of its force through the unfortunate circumstance that Locke refers all mental and all non-mental facts to a spiritual and a corporeal substance respectively, neither of which is really known or even knowable. Such being the case, it is impossible to make profitable use of the distinction; and in the end there seems to be no conclusive reason why we should refuse to attribute the power of thought to body (duly modified for the purpose by the Creator),[17] or why the soul and the body should be distinguished as immaterial and material.[18]

Hume was merely pushing the argument to its logical conclusion when he disposed of substance altogether, whether in the material or the immaterial form, and so reduced the question of the immateriality of the soul to meaninglessness.[19] What remains is a manifold of superficially concatenated particulars from which the distinction of subjective and objective has disappeared. This manifold can only be accepted: it cannot be explained. The "impressions" and "ideas" of which it consists, and which differ only in the order of experience and in their relative vividness, are not, *so far as we know*, the manifestations of a reality more fundamental than themselves. On the contrary they are the surds which we strike when we have probed reality to the limit—the dregs of a world that is nothing but dregs. It is a fact of the greatest significance that in the philosophies of the last thirty years which resemble that of Hume in obscuring the distinction of physical and spiritual there reappears a class of entities closely akin to these homeless apparitions which emanate from nowhere, and mean nothing but themselves.

4. The "essences" of Professor Santayana, for example, like the "perceptions" of Hume, are the grounds that remain at the bottom when the cup of scepticism has been drained dry. "The approach to essence," we are told, "is through scepticism";[20] and the

---

[17] "We have the ideas of matter and thinking, but possibly shall never be able to know, whether any mere material being thinks, or no; it being impossible for us, by the contemplation of our own ideas, without revelation, to discover, whether omnipotency has not given to some systems of matter fitly disposed a power to perceive and think." *Essay*, IV, Chap. III, §6.

[18] Reply to Stillingfleet in note to the chapter cited.

[19] *Treatise*, IV, sect. v, Green and Grose, Vol. I, p. 518.

[20] *The Realm of Essence* (to which in future I shall refer as *R.E.*), p. 1.

writer explains that "that which appears when all gratuitous implications of a world beyond or of a self . . . are discarded, will be an essence.[21] A similar entity is that to which Professor Whitehead has given the name of "eternal object." Under whatever designation, the conception is one that involves the whole problem of the duality with which we are dealing; and it is reasonable to look for light to these two writers, from the standpoint of what is common to them, and from that of any points in which they may be found to differ from Hume.[22]

Hume's Excision of Substance, and Santayana's Manner of Restoring It. Animal Faith

5. To begin with what has already been stated, so far as the distinction of subjective and objective is concerned the "perceptions" of Hume are neutral. It follows that there is a class of relations into which, strictly speaking, they cannot enter—the relations that connect and contrast an object of consciousness with a consciousness of the object.[23] In this the "perceptions" differ from the "ideas" of Locke, to which in other respects they correspond. The latter, despite the precariousness of the distinction between mind and body, and (what is no less important) a constant tendency to confuse *states* with *objects* of consciousness, are definitely conditioned by the relations in which they stand on the one hand to the mind whose objects, by definition, they are, and on the other to the material which they *represent* to the mind. Hume's "perceptions" are not thus definable in terms of any relationship to a percipient consciousness. Rather the consciousness of them is part of what they are and mean. That is to say, each "perception" carries its own specific consciousness with it, and there is no awareness except in the form of a particular "impression" or "idea." Thus whereas for Locke it was natural to define perceptions or "ideas" as *objects*, for Hume it is *necessary* to define objects as per-

---

[21] *op. cit.*, p. 2.

[22] My initial warrant for classing them together will be found in Santayana's recognition of Whitehead's "eternal objects" as the equivalent of his "essences" (*vid.* Postscript to *R.E.*, p. 169 *sq.*), and in Whitehead's repeated tribute to Santayana in *Process and Reality*.

[23] Hume, it is true, habitually refers to the *objects* of our perceptual experience, but the expression is purely conventional. To be exact, the "objects" and the "perceptions" are one. ". . . To form the idea of an object, and to form an idea simply, is the same thing; the reference of the idea to an object being an extraneous denomination, of which in itself it bears no mark or character." *Treatise*, I, sect. vii, G. & G., Vol. I, p. 327.

ceptions. ". . . Let us remember," he says, "that as every idea is derived from a preceding perception, 'tis impossible our idea of a perception, or that of an object or external existence can ever represent what are specifically different from each other. Whatever difference we may suppose betwixt them, 'tis still incomprehensible to us; and we are obliged either to conceive an external object merely as a relation without a relative, or to make it the very same with a perception or impression."[24]

6. With this change of viewpoint there is bound up another which has to do with the conception of representation itself. For Locke representation does not mean resemblance. This is precisely what it means for Hume. ". . . How," he asks, "can an impression represent a substance, otherwise than by resembling it?"[25] The conclusion of course is that as there is no similarity of nature between a substance and an impression, the latter cannot represent the former. Hence, having no *impression* of substance, we have no guarantee of the *idea*. In this way Hume disposes of the belief, already shaken by Locke, that the soul can be regarded as an immaterial substance; and with this there goes the belief in the very existence of a soul.

7. Now Santayana restores the conception of substance, but in a form and upon grounds profoundly different from those of the Scholastic or Cartesian notion. The latter is the product of thought —an intellectual construction backed by reasons. Not so Mr. Santayana's conception. Indeed the argument employed, although it leads its author to an opposite conclusion, brings him much nearer to Hume's position than to that which is usually associated with a belief in substance. To be exact, reasons and arguments have nothing to do with the matter.[26] The determining factor is the compulsion of that animal faith to which we are all subject by nature. We are here in the region of brute fact, where every denial rebounds upon our heads with the force of an affirmation.[27] In short, a belief in substance is the essence of belief in the existence of anything; and substance, as conceived by Mr. Santayana, might

---

[24] *Treatise*, IV, sect. v, G. & G., Vol. I, p. 524. cf. pp. 499, 502, 504.
[25] *ibid.*, p. 517.
[26] "It is not to external pressure, through evidence or argument, that faith in substance is due." *Scepticism and Animal Faith* (hereafter *S.A.*), p. 185.
[27] "Belief in substance is . . . so fundamental that no evidence can be adduced for it which does not presuppose it." *S.A.*, p. 185.

be defined as the independently existing correlate[28] of the believing
attitude.[29] It makes no difference how existence is interpreted in
theory. The belief in question survives even the doctrine known as
phenomenalism, which would reduce all things to appearances.[30]
This is one of the points in which Santayana's position differs from
that of Hume. For Hume phenomenalism implies the negation, for
Santayana the affirmation, of substance.[31]

It is obvious that a conception so defined is vague, and that its
content is bound to be highly variable. Behind it there is merely a
feeling of *something here, something there*. Its guarantee is a certain
"animal watchfulness"[32] promoted by nature to guard the vital
interests of the organism. From the standpoint of knowledge and
the critic of knowledge "belief in substance . . . is the most irrational, animal and primitive of beliefs: it is the voice of hunger";[33]
and the first revelation of it is in the appetitions and aversions of
the animal ego.[34] What that ego discovers of *self* or of *other* assumes,
in the first instance, the form of materiality;[35] and the belief in
substance so generated is confirmed by the findings of a more developed experience. ". . . The substance in which I am proposing

---

[28] *S.A.*, pp. 202-3.

[29] "All knowledge, being faith in an object posited and partially described, is belief in
substance . . . it is belief in a thing or event subsisting in its own plane, and waiting
for the light of knowledge to explore it eventually, and perhaps name or define it." "It
is impossible to eliminate belief in substance so long as belief in existence is retained."
S.A., p. 182.

[30] ". . . From the point of view of knowledge, every event, even if wholly psychological or phenomenal, is a substance." *S.A.*, p. 182. "Substance is not more real
than appearance, . . . but only differently real. . . . When substance is asserted,
appearance is not denied; its actuality is not diminished, but a significance is added to it
which, as a bare datum, it could not have." *ibid.*, p. 210. "In recognizing any appearance
as a witness to substance and in admitting (or even in rejecting) the validity of such
testimony, I have already made a substance of the appearance; and if I admit other
phenomena as well, I have placed that substance in a world of substances having a
substantial unity." *ibid.*, p. 185.

[31] "In so far as the instinctive claims and transcendent scope of knowledge are concerned, phenomenalism fully retains the belief in substance." *S.A.*, p. 183.

[32] *S.A.*, p. 190.

[33] *S.A.*, pp. 190-1.

[34] ". . . I must insist here that trust in knowledge, and belief in anything to know,
are merely instinctive and, in a manner, pathological." *S.A.*, p. 186.

[35] "In the genesis of human knowledge . . . the substance first posited is doubtless
matter, some alluring or threatening or tormenting thing. . . . As a matter of fact, the
active ego is an animal living in a material world; both the ego and the non-ego exist
substantially before acquiring this relation of positing and being posited." *S.A.*, pp.
183-4. (The reference is to Fichte's theory.)

to believe is not metaphysical but physical substance.[36] It is the varied stuff of the world which I meet in action—the wood of this tree I am felling, the wind that is stirring its branches, the flesh and bones of the man who is jumping out of the way. Belief in substance is not imported into animal perception by language or by philosophy, but is the soul of animal perception from the beginning, and the perpetual deliverance of animal experience."[37] Of course our first crude apprehension of substance must be rectified and refined by more adequate descriptive identification of its forms. But this process leads merely to an exacter knowledge of its constituents, and these, as they disclose themselves to our inquiry, stand revealed as neither more nor less than substances.[38]

To sum up, substances are "objects of belief posited in action,"[39] and as such they are to be sharply distinguished from essences, which are "images given in intuition." The contrast is between what Santayana calls the "two phases or movements" of transcendentalism[40]—"the sceptical one retreating to the immediate, and the assertive one, by which objects of belief are defined and marshalled, of such a character and in such an order as intelligent action demands."[41] We must now attempt to view the doctrine of essence in the light of the doctrine of substance, and more particularly of the fact that Santayana recognizes substance only in the physical or material form.

8. But before proceeding to this I ought to add one further word of explanation to what has already been said as to my reason for so prolonged an excursus into contemporary philosophy. As I have already pointed out, Professor Santayana and Professor Whitehead are outstanding representatives of the current tendency to pass over the duality of body and mind as if the distinction were wanting in depth and reality. From the standpoint of the psychophysical problem this tendency must be characterized as monistic; but I hope to show that the elimination of dualism in one form only

[36] cf. R.E., p. 51. Also The Realm of Matter (R.M.), pp. 17 sq.

[37] S.A., p. 201.

[38] S.A., pp. 201-2.

[39] S.A., p. 202. The object must be conceived as independently existing or "external to the thought which posits it," (S.A., pp. 202-3. R.M., p. 10), a fact which the word "object" tends to obscure.

[40] By transcendentalism or "transcendental reflection" we are to understand "reversion, in the presence of any object or affirmation, to the immediate experience which discloses that object or prompts that affirmation." R.M., p. 8.

[41] R.M., p. 8.

serves to aggravate it in another—and that other a form which is fatal alike to the interests of spiritual life and to the scientific interpretation of nature. Behind this whole movement of thought is a reluctance to take spirit seriously, and a manifest determination to exalt the natural to a position of complete preeminence. The result is that the natural, thus left to itself, assumes the aspect of a conjunction of incompatibles. This conclusion is not peculiar to the two writers with whom I propose to deal. It is implicit in all systems—idealistic as well as naturalistic—which fail to recognize the ontological claims of the spiritual mode of being. But Santayana and Whitehead between them offer a particularly striking illustration of the effects I am trying to trace; and for this reason I shall develop my argument with special reference to their views.

Santayana's "Essences," vis à vis the Forms of Plato and the Perceptions of Hume

9. Santayana's concept of essence, then, as has been explained, is the product of a sceptical movement which refuses to stop until it has removed all interpretative accretions from the bare deliverances of experience. When this point has been reached, what remains is essence. A survey of the examples which the writer incidentally lets drop reveals the immensely varied character of the "realm" to which they belong. They are infinite in number.[42] Indeed it becomes clear that everything is an essence in so far as it does not involve a believing attitude, is indifferent to its contexts, and independent of the affirmations and negations with which from time to time it may be interwoven.[43] Thus essences are altogether unaffected by the conjunctions in which they occur, the flux of nature which "sustains" them, the existences which they qualify.[44] They are absolutely "pure" in the sense that "intuition permeates them and rests in them without the intervention of any ulterior intent or cross-lights, as we might speak of pure mathematics or pure pleasure."[45] Essence, so to say, carries its own light with it, and, while unilluminated from any other source, serves to illuminate everything else. Its "being" is entirely exhausted by its definition—meaning thereby not a verbal statement, but what is

[42] *R.E.*, pp. 20-1.
[43] *vid.* Appendix A, p. 81.
[44] *R.E.*, pp. 39-40.
[45] *R.E.*, p. 49.

specific in the essence as such, what distinguishes one essence from another.[46] Eternal self-identity is the principle involved;[47] and from this we can see the part played by essences in the economy of an ever-changing world of existence. "Essences, by being eternally what they are, enable existence to pass from one phase to another, and enable the mind to note and describe the change."[48] Since existence is flux,[49] and therefore in accordance with the Platonic conception, non-being,[50] it follows that essences do not *exist*.[51] Yet they have "being" in an eminent degree,[52] and may be objects of exact science.[53]

10. The being thus assigned them is obviously the being (οὐσία) of the Platonic ideas, the being of all ideal entities, standards, authenticities, invariables beyond the stream of time. The essences *are*: they are in their own right. Hence they cannot properly be conceived as abstractions[54] or as "unrealizable generalities."[55] There is no community of nature between a general term as such and an essence. Yet the latter is *universal*. It is so because it is completely independent of position in the flux, and is therefore definable by reference to its intrinsic character, and not to its extraneous relations. In this realm repetition is of no avail to sort out the common, which is the essential, from the occasion, which is the adventitious, and so to concentrate the relevant points into the unity of the definition. But a universality which owes nothing to repetition and generalization, and everything to the self-com-

---

[46] *R.E.*, p. 18.
[47] *R.E.*, pp. 5, 18.
[48] *R.E.*, p. 5.
[49] *R.E.*, p. 22.
[50] *R.E.*, p. 48.
[51] *R.E.*, p. 21.
[52] *R.E.*, Chap. iv.
[53] *R.E.*, p. 5. Being and existence for Santayana, so far from being "almost interchangeable terms," are "exact opposites." *ibid*, p. 48.
[54] *R.E.*, pp. 16, 31 *sq.*
[55] *R.E.*, p. 40. Santayana's statement calls for a little amplification. Thus while the definitory notion is not that of *something abstracted*, but of *something intuited*, abstractions and generalizations, since they are intuitable, must have a place among the essences. Again, a very large number of essences can only be arrived at by an active process of abstraction, whereby they are forcibly removed from the contexts of experience in which they most naturally occur and the judgments which habitually sustain them. When the retreat to immediacy assumes the aspect of a deliberate manœuvre, when its products are excisions, siftings, strainings of the flux, scepticism and abstraction are hardly distinguishable. To get at the grounds in the bottom of the cup, the cup must be drained dry.

pleteness and self-illumination of the entity in question, is the same thing as perfect individuality. "Every essence is universal not because there are repeated manifestations of it (for there need be no manifestations at all) but because it is individuated internally by its character, not externally by its position in the flux of nature: and no essence is general for the same reason."[56] Again the obvious parallel is the Platonic idea; and the resemblance is further reinforced by the relation in which the ideas on the one hand and the essences on the other stand to the particulars of experience or the phases of the flux. This is well expressed for both in the passage from which quotation has just been made, where Santayana explains that essence "may define things numerically distinct," but is not itself among the things which it so defines. It remains to add (and here the analogy with the Platonic ideas breaks down completely) that in relation to the flux of nature the essences are powerless and inert.

This much of description and illustration will suffice. We must proceed to draw out the implications of the concept in relation to the duality (or otherwise) of spirit and nature. But before we do so it will be well to reorient ourselves towards the notion of essence by viewing it from the standpoint of the two great thinkers with whom Santayana seems to have the closest affinity. The conjunction of Hume and Plato might at first sight appear somewhat startling. As a matter of fact it is quite natural. Where they are dealing with the same subject, the flux of human experience and of natural events, Plato and Hume are very close to one another; and in the *Theaetetus* the former accepts a position to which the latter would have largely subscribed. The flux of Heraclitus and the *homo mensura* of Protagoras are the objective and subjective expressions of a view of things of which the essence is relativity, and the ultimate implication the scepticism of Aenesidemus. The same view represents the negative side of Platonism; and the negative side of Platonism anticipates the positive teaching of Hume. What is remarkable, therefore, is not so much the way in which Hume's theory of perceptions and Plato's doctrine of forms are alike made to contribute to Santayana's concept of essence, but the fact that forms and perceptions are classed together under this concept. The various relations involved can be exhibited as follows:

[56] *R.E.*, p. 36.

(a) The "essences" include the "perceptions," although Hume's habitual demand that the impressions upon which ideas are founded should be *produced* in evidence would exclude a very large class of essences.

(b) The existence which Santayana denies to the essences is expressly attributed by Hume to the "perceptions." Indeed existence, like awareness, is given with the latter and in no other way.[57] In general the distinction which Santayana draws between existence and being is one which has no meaning for Hume.[58] For him the difference at the most is merely that between an impression and an idea.[59]

(c) The general characteristics which Santayana assigns to the essences, universality, eternity, individuality, being and the power to give significance to the existent in the flux of nature (the world of becoming) are all in accord with the definitory concept of the Platonic forms. The latter, moreover, would all be included in the class of essences. But this class contains a vast array of instances which the Platonic conception definitely excludes.[60] For Plato the sensory properties belong to the world of becoming, and to him it would have seemed the height of paradox to attribute eternity and universality to what he conceived as the very type of the transient, conditioned and relative. Along with this there goes a difference as to the nature of the knowledge involved.

(d) The Platonic forms are *thinkables*, the ontological equivalents of their own λόγοι or definitory concepts. In this context the word "thinkable" must be interpreted as opposed to the merely intuitable. Not so in the case of Santayana's doctrine. "Essences are definite and thinkable: existence is indefinite and only endured. That is the Platonic experience which I cannot help repeating and confirming at every turn; only that by 'thinkable' we must not

[57] *Treatise*, II, sect. vi, G. & G., Vol. I, pp. 370-1. Our impressions "may be considered as separately existent, and may exist separately, and have no need of any thing else to support their existence." *op. cit.*, sect. v, p. 518.

[58] "There is no impression nor idea of any kind, of which we have any consciousness or memory, that is not conceived as existent; and 'tis evident, that from this consciousness the most perfect idea and assurance of *being* is deriv'd." *op. cit.*, II, sect. vi, G. & G., Vol. I, p. 370.

[59] Contrast Locke: ". . . Our ideas are not always proofs of the existence of things." *Essay*, II, Chap. XVII, §4.

[60] *S.A.*, p. 225.

understand definable in words, but open to intuition in the terms of any sense or of any logic."[61]

(e) Although the ideas and the essences alike may be described as determining the many in the flux of nature, they are conceived to do so in very different ways. Santayana accuses Plato of turning the doctrine partly into a false physics, partly into a theology. As for the essences themselves, in the Platonic theory of ideas they appear in a false character as "natural magnets, as a background of metaphysical powers, more selective than nature itself, and con-stituting a world of substances behind the flux of appearances. Physics and theology," the writer adds, "may appeal to such patron substances if they think fit; but in the theory of essence they have no place whatever. Essences . . . cannot be a material source of anything."[62]

In this way Santayana disposes of the causal function which Plato assigns to the ideas in the natural world. Nothing in that world owes its existence to the essences: nothing comes to be be-cause the essences are brought to bear upon the plastic stuff of nature. Whatever be the process whereby the forms of "pure" being "enable existence to pass from one phase to another," of this we can be well assured—there is here no dynamism, no influence at work, no passage of effective energy from the realm of being or essence to that of nature or existence. When the physical world acquires qualities and meanings which we recognize as essences, the fact must not be construed as an *event*. Events belong to the ever-streaming flux: the essences are changeless and eternal. We cannot therefore think of them as passing into and out of the stream: it is the stream that passes from one essence to another, and it does so under a compulsion that is entirely its own.

In thus modifying the Platonic theory, Santayana deprives the ideas of that character of metaphysical priority, effectiveness and privilege which we usually express by the word "principle." The conception of the ideas as principles has been maintained, he thinks, by an unscientific fusion of the physical and ethical points of view in a cosmology that was largely fanciful. Such is the error of idealism as understood by Santayana, and from this error the doctrine of essences is free. ". . . Although essences have the texture and ontological status of Platonic ideas, they can lay claim

[61] *R.E.*, pp. 39-40. cf. *S.A.*, p. 225.
[62] *R.E.*, pp. 30-1.

to none of the cosmological, metaphysical, or moral prerogatives attributed to ideas";[63] and if idealism, as we are told, is "a moral interest dictating a physical system," if "those who have been idealists by temperament have been . . . inclined to substitute essence for matter in their theory of the universe," if they have been guilty of "fusing their physics with their visions," then we can only conclude that Santayana is altogether right in repudiating idealism and in driving still further the wedge that separates the realm of matter from the realm of essence.

Failure of Timeless Essences to Interpret Existence. Events Must Be Functions of the Temporal Systems to Which They Belong

11. But having secured the realm of matter (which is the flux of natural existence) against the intrusions of timeless being by the simple process of segregating each from each in thought, we find that we have by no means disposed of all our difficulties. For after all it is mostly in the flux of nature that essences reveal their timeless presence.[64] As an interpretation of existence Santayana's philosophy is a highly representative form of naturalism: as an interpretation of life it is a naturalism of the animal ego. In the world around us and in living things existence reveals itself as a forward-plunging, onward-streaming force, rising in man to "animation,"[65] and making for ends to which the body holds the key. But this philosophy has a second side to it. It undertakes to explain that character in the existent whereby we distinguish one episode in the flux of nature from another. The character in question, which supplies the element of necessary description or *meaning*, is always an intuitable identity, and can never be anything more. It is not itself an episode in the flux, of which it enables us to obtain an articulated apprehension. Rather it belongs to a "realm" of essences—a phantasmagoria of apparitions—a manifold of universals unanchored to the actual and uncircumscribed by circumstance, adding nothing to existence, yet touching the successive phases of the latter with a characteristic coloration. By no possibility can this interpretation of existence and this philosophy of meanings be brought into intelligible relation. The mere attempt to harmonize the two points of view reveals the implicit

[63] *S.A.*, pp. 77-8.
[64] *vid.* Appendix B, p. 82.
[65] Defined as "material life quickened into intuitions." *S.A.*, Chap. XXXIII, pp. 242-3.

contradictoriness of the situation. The *being* of the essences and the *existence* of a natural world are opposites, and cannot be lodged together either in the realm of essence or in that of matter. At the same time they cannot be separated. What is there, for example, to intuit in sound, colour or beauty except as these essences unveil themselves in the actual world around us? And how do nature's laws (which are essences) obtain their meaning (which is what *essence* signifies) except in the time-conditioned flux of natural events? Is goodness intuitable in any other realm than that of action, circumstance and animal endeavour? Wherever we turn, and however we view the subject, we are confronted by alternative impossibilities. The worlds of essence and fact can neither be segregated nor united.

12. Our problem is to convert these alternative impossibilities into conjunctive truths and complementary necessities—in other words, to show that the processes of which nature consists and the essences required for the description of these processes[66] must be at the same time distinguishable and inseparable. The *necessity* will, I think, readily be granted: our difficulty has to do with the *possibility*. The question is therefore one of finding a formula which will do justice at once to the constitution of the natural world as a time-conditioned manifold of matter and to those characters which, like the sensory properties on the one hand and the laws of physics on the other, give determinateness to the flux, but are not themselves, to all appearances, definable as events. In brief, we are in search of a consistent methodology—a methodology which will enable us to avoid the absurdity of representing the essences, in relation to the world-process, as the non-existent,[67] and yet depicting the world-process as articulating itself in phases of which the essences are the description.

13. Now the procedure I wish to suggest is one that involves a radical change of viewpoint. If nature is an ordered sequence of events, the relevant question has to do with the fixation of identities. How is each successive phase determined? Under what conditions does it come to have the precise character, quantitative or qualitative, which, by methods of empirical observation, we perceive it to possess? It will be seen that when the question is so put, essence and existence are assumed to be inseparably united

[66] It is with these alone that we are concerned.
[67] " 'The non-existent' is . . . not a bad name for the realm of essence." *R.E.*, p. 54.

under the postulate of being. The former is nothing but the *identity* of the latter, the latter nothing but the *realization* of that identity.

As for the answer to the question, this obviously involves the conception of functional relationship. The identity of any event can be represented as a function of the conditions by which it is determined. Sometimes these conditions must be sought among the laws of physics,[68] but not in the aspect of abstract universality. The movement of a body in space, for example, is the product of specific forces brought to bear upon the latter in measurable quantities and in definite directions. These forces, together with the movement which they condition, constitute a system; and of this system, which is physically existent, the event in question is a function. Thus each distinguishable phase in the process of nature has an identity which is determined by its character as a product of its own antecedents and as a function of the system to which they and it alike belong, rather than by the miraculous incursion of timeless essences from a realm of the non-existent.

Objects of Sense May Belong to Temporal Systems, if There Is an Independent Psychical Factor

14. There are, however, events and aspects of events in the natural world, which call for a different explanation—though one which still involves the conceptions of system and function. Many processes of nature articulate themselves not only in the way I have indicated—that is, as functions of purely physical conditions —but also through differentiations of a sensory character. But in Santayana's theory sensory representations belong to the realm of essence. It is not difficult to divine the reasons which led to this view. The colour red or the note G sounded on a bugle has an intuitable identity which seems entirely different from that of an event in time, and as a matter of fact *is* different from that of events in their purely physical character. Moreover the data of sense do not differ from one another only, or most characteristically, as event differs from event in some well defined sequence, or as one phase in an event differs from another. The most obvious distinction between red and blue, or between a colour and a sound, is not that which has to do with the times at which these sensa are

---

[68] Santayana specifically cites the laws of motion as examples of essence.

experienced. In so far then as characters of this sort contribute to the articulation of nature's successive episodes they might appear to do so not in the sense that they are themselves articulated episodes in the total process, but in the very different sense that the stream of natural events is constantly traversed by these vivid identities from a profoundly different realm—a realm where being excludes existence.

The untenability of this view has been sufficiently exposed. Our business is to find a substitute for it. Again the question is one of identity. We naturally ask whether there is anything of which the sensory data, as these reveal themselves in all the circumstance of time and place, can be represented as functions. Enough is known of the physical conditions which underlie the production of sound and colour (to take the most obvious examples) to suggest that in these we have a relevant factor in the case. Vibrations in the physical world are undoubtedly among the conditions by which sound and colour are determined. They can hardly, however, be considered the only conditions. For the entities which relate themselves to physical vibrations as functions to their determinants do not, in the absence of certain other factors, assume the form of sound and colour. These additional factors may be summarized as the presence of a conscious receptor or percipient organism, reacting to the vibrations in the manner of a resonator.[69] The recognition of a percipient enables us to represent the objects of sense, which clearly have their locus in the natural world, not as intruders from an alien realm, but as functions of a relation between certain physical and certain psychical or psycho-physical events, and hence as themselves natural occupants of the time-stream, coming into being and passing away with the conjunction of events which promotes their existence.

There is one condition, however, upon which all this is contingent. The psychical factor must be taken seriously.[70] What exactly this means is a question to which from first to last we shall have to devote a great deal of attention. For the present it will be enough to say that by taking the psychical seriously I here under-

[69] This conception, which of course, in the present context, must be taken, at least in part, as figurative, I owe to a suggestive paper by Professor Hallett.

[70] So far as my argument is concerned, it makes no difference whether we consider the psychical by itself, as in some sense the opposite of the physical, or take it as a component of those compounds which we call the psycho-physical and the percipient organism.

stand treating it as an independent variable, and as sustaining this character, under the postulate of being, in the conjunctive relationship in which it stands to the physical. Of course this will involve what for Santayana is nothing less than a reversion to "the most primitive of dualisms,"[71] the dualism of body and spirit; but apart altogether from the fact that the recognition of a *duality* in the modes of being does not necessarily imply a *dualism*, it may be pointed out that the course proposed, even if it does involve the offence in question, is designed to obviate the same offence in a form that ought to be even more objectionable to a thinker of markedly naturalistic tendencies. After all it is no outrage upon reason to maintain that within the total system of *reality* there may be more than one way of *being*; but if it is assumed that there *is* only one way, and that *the way of nature*, it must be exceedingly disconcerting to find that in the explanation of it we are compelled to have recourse to two fundamental principles, which are not merely distinct, but are definitely at variance with one another. The introduction of mind as an independent variable is a methodological expedient which enables us, in the interpretation of the natural world of our perceptual experience, to escape from the dualism of process and essence, and to show how the meanings which, in Santayana's theory, nature at once annexes as sensory qualifications and rejects as essences, can find a locus in the physical without violating the metaphysical character of the latter.

Santayana Leaves no Room for an Independent Psychical Factor

15. It may be, however, that in thus venturing to posit mind as an independent, we are taking liberties with the psychical as revealed to us in experience. And certainly we have no right to prejudice the treatment of the latter for reasons quite extrinsic to the problem of spirit as such. Before proceeding further, therefore, we must ask whether in the intrinsic nature of spirit, mind or soul there are cogent grounds for rejecting the proposal to treat the psychical, in relation to the sensory, as an independent determinant in relation to a dependent function. Once more the ground can best be cleared, and the way prepared for an answer, by a careful consideration of the opposite view. In this the spiritual is

[71] *R.M.*, p. 136.

represented sometimes as immersed in matter, sometimes as an unsubstantial epiphenomenon, but in either case as in a state of functional (which is also a state of ontological) dependence.

16. As before, Professor Santayana furnishes invaluable guidance. There is no failure on his part to employ the phraseology of the spiritual life; nor does he refuse to recognize its characteristic manifestations. The negations of his system have all to do with the question of ontological status. Psyche or self, soul and spirit appear and reappear in his fascinating pages, but never in the character of independent substance. Their status is that of adjectival or adverbial qualifications or predicaments—dependents upon a reality which to the end remains obdurately physical. Thus the psyche goes over unreservedly to the side of body, while spirit, which Santayana distinguishes from the psyche, maintains an ambiguous position as a last emanation of bodily life—a kind of luminosity, revealed as an activity of discernment generated in the flesh,[72] yet in a way passing beyond the confines of the purely physiological by opposing the power of impartial discernment to the bias of vital adjustment.[73] As for soul, its fate is to be parcelled out between the spirit and the psyche,[74] and in the end to be dismissed as a poetical equivocation.[75]

17. A more detailed statement is, however, called for. I shall attempt to give it as far as possible in the author's own words.[76]

The psyche is variously defined as "the inherited mechanism of life and of the body,"[77] as "the hereditary organization and movement of life in an animal,"[78] "the principle of bodily life"[79]—which, we are told, is yet "the fountain of my thoughts, that is, the self who thinks them"[80]—as the "central part" of organism,

---

[72] S.A., p. 279.

[73] op. cit., p. 214.

[74] op. cit., pp. 216 sq. The soul is included among "false substances," ibid., pp. 218 sq.

[75] R.M., p. 139.

[76] In the two earlier works from which I have chiefly quoted the allusions to the psyche are scattered and incidental. A special chapter is devoted to the subject in The Realm of Matter.

[77] S.A., p. 218.

[78] R.E., p. 9.

[79] S.A., p. 280.

[80] S.A., p. 245. cf. the words: "Now that part of nature which is the organ of mind, the psyche, is a relatively closed system of movements, and hereditary; the living seed, as it matures, puts forth predeterminate organs and imposes specific actions and feelings on the young creature: he must eat, fall in love, build a nest, resent interference or injury. But this predetermination is not exact, only generic," etc. R.E., p. 97.

"the substance of the ego,"[81] which "leaps to meet its opportunities," "develops new organs to serve its old necessities," "kindles itself to intuition of essences,"[82] and sustains "the whole life of imagination and knowledge"—that life which "comes from within, from the restlessness, eagerness, curiosity, and terror of the animal bent on hunting, feeding, and breeding."[83]

From these statements it is clear that what the writer has in mind is the animation of the body displaying itself in characteristic modes or "tropes"; that is to say, in biologically inherited or otherwise acquired dispositions to reaction, or life-habits. And this in effect is how Santayana in his later treatment of the subject actually defines the psyche.[84]

18. The question arises: Where does consciousness, mind, intelligence come in? The answer is that so far as the psyche is concerned, it does not seem to come in at all. And yet it can hardly be denied. Nor does Santayana attempt to deny it. On the contrary, under the rubric of *spirit* he has a great deal to say about it. Indeed he expressly asserts that "the existence of spirit really demands an explanation." "Spirit, since it *can* ask how it came to exist, has a right to put the question and to look for an answer."[85] The point is that the spiritual mode of existence, of which conscious intelligence is the characteristic mark, is not *self-explanatory*. It must look elsewhere for an intelligible account of itself. But where can it look if not to the realm of matter? The underlying assumption is that in the existence of a physical world and of animal bodies we have a fact so obvious and so fundamental as to render the very idea of explaining it an impertinence; whereas the existence of consciousness is an utter enigma, a gratuitous overplus in a world already full to the brim.[86] There is nothing for it, therefore, but to

[81] But "she is not herself a substance, except relatively to consciousness. . . . She is a *mode* of substance, a trope or habit established in matter." *R.M.*, p. 140.

[82] ". . . The organ of intuition . . . governed by the laws of material life, in other words, by habit." *R.E.*, p. 37.

[83] *S.A.*, p. 185. Santayana's theory of psychology is the counterpart of his conception of the psyche. *vid. S.A.*, Chap. xxiv, *R.M.*, Chap. viii.

[84] ". . . By the psyche I understand a system of tropes, inherited or acquired, displayed by living bodies in their growth and behaviour." The psyche is "a habit in matter." *R.M.*, p. 139.

[85] *S.A.*, p. 284.

[86] "Can anything, inwardly considered, be more gratuitous than consciousness?" *S.A.*, p. 283.

think of consciousness as an epiphenomenon or ghostly addendum to bodily existence.

19. The exact place of spirit in the scheme of things is stated in the chapter on the psyche in *The Realm of Matter*. ". . . I will beg the reader to distinguish two levels of life in the human body, one of which I call *the spirit*, and the other *the psyche*. By spirit I understand the actual light of consciousness falling upon anything—the ultimate invisible emotional fruition of life in feeling and thought."[87]

Spirit, then, is no other than consciousness itself interpreted as a "level of life in the human body"—consciousness, that is to say, conceived not as mere awareness, but as "intent, expectation, belief and eagerness."[88] "Its peculiar sort of reality is to be intelligence in act."[89] As such, it resembles light—not, however, the light which is visible, but that which renders all else visible[90]—"a living light ready to fall upon things, as they are spread out in their weight and motion and variety, ready to be lighted up."[91] Even this, however, is not quite adequate. For if the light is living, it is more than light. The proper analogue is rather the power of seeing.[92] Spirit is active discrimination, marking the "differences of essence, of time, of place, of value."[93] It is obvious that there is nothing substantival, nothing personal and individual here. As Santayana says, "spirit is a category, not an individual being."[94] He further describes it as "unsubstantial and expressive," "essentially secondary,"[95] "the voice of something else,"[96] "life looking out of the window."[97] It "arises in man" upon occasion, and the occasions on which it does so are "the vicissitudes of his animal life."[98] Its manifestations are episodic and intermittent. In spirit

---

[87] *R.M.*, p. 139.

[88] *S.A.*, p. 275.

[89] *op. cit.*, p. 274.

[90] *op. cit.*, pp. 272, 274.

[91] *op. cit.*, p. 273.

[92] *op. cit.*, p. 272.

[93] *op. cit.*, p. 273.

[94] *op. cit.*, p. 275.

[95] "Spirit . . . is no substance, and has no interests." *op. cit.*, p. 148.

[96] *op. cit.*, p. 285. ". . . The most intellectual powers of spirit—attention, synthesis, perception—are voices loudly issuing from the heart of material existence, and proclaiming their origin there not only by their occasions and external connections, but by their inmost moral nature." *ibid.*, p. 281.

[97] *R.E.*, p. 10.

[98] *S.A.*, p. 276.

existence "becomes, so to speak, vocal and audible to itself. Not indeed in its entirety . . . but in snatches. At certain junctures animal life, properly a habit in matter, bursts as with a peal of bells into a new realm of being, into the realm of spirit."[99] *When* exactly this occurs, and under what occasions, are problems which Santayana seeks to solve with the aid of metaphor and along the lines which his initial assumptions have rendered inevitable. His contention is that in the original set of the organism there are predispositions which figure forth as biological tendency what later comes to light as consciousness. "We may presume that some slumbering sensibility exists in every living organism, as an echo or foretaste of its vital rhythms; and even when no assignable feeling comes to a head, if there is life at all, there is a sort of field of consciousness, or canvas spread for attention, ready to be occupied by eventual figures. . . . Thus sensations and ideas always follow upon organic reactions and express their quality; and intuition merely supplies a mental term for the animal reaction already at work unconsciously."[100]

It Is So Largely Sunk in Nature, That What Remains of It Cannot Be Spirit

20. From this summary and from these citations it is clear that the refusal to grant an independent status to the spiritual, and the determination to sink the life of mind in the physical, as it has already broken up the latter by dividing nature from her meanings, now breaks up the former by dividing the spiritual from itself. Thus in place of a single system of subjective forces, integrated in the unity and individuality of personal existence, we are presented with a psyche and a spirit, two modes of subjectivity which can neither be dissociated nor brought into intelligible relation. From one point of view, it is true, the difference is merely one of level. Psyche and spirit are successive revelations of the possibilities implicit in matter. But this account of them is not borne out by a detailed study of their respective characters. When viewed more closely, the serial order gives place to a relation of mutual tension. Spirit does not merely carry one step further the process inaugurated by the psyche. The psyche does not merely propagate itself in the new medium of consciousness. On the contrary it violates

[99] *R.M.*, p. 156.
[100] *R.M.*, pp. 156-7.

the sanctity of the spirit which it evokes. Immersed in the flux of matter, of which it is a trope, and infected with self-interest to the core, the psyche is all bias and selection, whereas disinterestedness and catholicity are of the very essence of the spirit. As Santayana puts it, ". . . in this animal faith, and even in the choice of one essence rather than another to be presented to intuition, spirit suffers violence, since spirit is inherently addressed to everything impartially and is always, in its own principle, ready to be omniscient and just."[101] Again, "my substantial self [that is, the psyche] and the spirit within me," so far from being identical, are really "the opposite poles of my being, and I am neither the one nor the other exclusively."[102]

21. From the anti-dualistic point of view this is a thoroughly unsatisfactory position, but there is no escape from it so long as the naturalistic attitude is maintained. A spiritual life that is no better than a predicament of bodily existence is unable to support the attributes of spirituality (consciousness and knowledge, for example), and in so far as these attributes are recognized, they refuse to accept the framework of fact provided for them. Thus once again fact and significance fall apart; and what might otherwise be conceived as one must perforce be conceived as two. In all that pertains to the conditions of its existence, its emergence in the stream of actual bodily events, the subject of experience becomes the psyche: in all that gives it its distinctive character as consciousness, perception, mind, intelligence it becomes the spirit. And if, as the writer asserts, spirit has a right to be explained, the right is one that can never be made good upon the premises. In order to get spirit out of nature it is necessary first of all to sink the spiritual in the natural; and if anything is to remain of the former, it can only be by modifying the concept of the latter in some such way as Santayana himself suggests. Thus the physical becomes miraculously pregnant with possibilities that become actualities only on the plane of the spiritual; and so the concepts of both nature and spirit are obscured. The one takes on an alien character of subjectivity, and the other loses that peculiar inwardness, that concentration around a centre, which is the essence of personality and selfhood. Even then there is a surplus of unabsorbed significance.

[101] *S.A.*, p. 214.
[102] *S.A.*, p. 278.

Consciousness, however disguised as "intent," "eagerness," "expectation," can neither be got rid of nor assimilated to the flux of animal existence, but remains winking at us like a bubble on the surface of life, to mark the travail of the psyche underneath. The moment we try to submerge it, the "light," which is all of being it is permitted to retain, is extinguished in the darkness of blind physiological process. Spirit cannot survive the scandal of its origin in the womb of the psyche; and if it is to be kept alive, it can only be by separating it from the matrix of a purely animal existence, and attaching it to the non-existent essences, which are its "native affinity," and which it is its specific function to discern.[103]

The purpose of this criticism is not to contest the proposition, which I take to have all the force of fact, that in some way very hard to understand the life of the spirit realizes itself under the conditions of bodily existence. My point is rather that this truth is rendered doubly obscure and in the end reduced to hopeless paradox by the efforts of the naturalist to render it irrefragable. The moment spirit is absorbed into nature and becomes an episode in the flux of material existence, that existence is divorced from the meanings, so necessary to it, which the essences supply; and the only way in which the contact can be reestablished is by an activity of apprehension whereby existence is transmuted back into essence.[104] But by the same activity spirit is released from the bond of matter, and itself passes over into a realm of being defined as the non-existent. Thus in order to establish its claim to existence spirit must lose its character as spirit; and in order to recover its character as spirit, it must sacrifice its claim to existence. The initial dualism of existence and essence has propagated itself in the further dualism of spirit and psyche.[105]

[103] "The native affinity of the mind to essence rather than to fact is mind itself, the very act of spirit or intellectual light." *R.E.*, p. 9.

[104] *R.E.*, p. 10.

[105] It is interesting to note that John Dewey, who is in so many ways closely in sympathy with Santayana, is fully alive to the conflict between the doctrine of essence and the doctrine of nature. Santayana, he tells us, "confounds his would-be disciples and confuses his critics by holding that nature is *truly* presented only in an esthetic contemplation of essences reached by physical science, an envisagement reached through a dialectic which 'is a transubstantiation of matter, a passage from existence to eternity.' This passage moreover is so utter that there is no road back. . . . The perception of genetic continuity between the dynamic flux of nature and an eternity of static ideal forms thus terminates in a sharp division, in reiteration of the old tradition." *Experience and Nature*, p. 58.

Other Examples of the Contemporary Tendency to Sink Mind in Nature. Whitehead

22. These unsatisfactory conclusions are the result of what, by an adaptation of Professor Alexander's well known phrase with regard to time, I have called the failure to take mind or spirit seriously. The attitude is widely reflected in the literature and philosophy of recent times. In writers who differ *toto coelo* in their general outlook upon life we find a point of contact in the common assumption that mind should not be treated in detachment from body or considered as having a nature of its own. The exact form of this prepossession varies, of course, with the author and the context. Where the problem is that of accounting for the appearance of mind in a world that is otherwise non-mental in its constitution, we have such typical solutions as Lloyd Morgan's theory of emergent evolution, and the cognate doctrine of Professor Alexander, for whom consciousness—or, generally speaking, "mentality"—is a quality of neural process which appears against a purely physical background at a certain level of development.[106] Professor Dewey, in his treatment of the same problem, adopts a similar point of view, and describes his argument as "an attempt to contribute to what has come to be called an 'emergent' theory of mind."[107] Professor Stout approaches the immemorial question of the relation of mind and body with the proviso that so far as the former is concerned, the reality with which we have to do—what actually exists—is always the *embodied* soul.[108] In the popular literature of the age human life is commonly presented in an aspect that is determined by a touchingly naïve faith in body-soul. This belief finds theoretical expression in a special literary mode—a quasi-philosophical *genre*—to which I am tempted to give the title of "anti-intellectual extravaganza." A striking example is D. H. Lawrence's *Fantasia of the Unconscious*,[109] with its basic conceptions of a pre-mental consciousness and a blood consciousness.[110] The tendency to deny an independent status to the spiritual is nowhere more strikingly manifested than in the fact of its appearance

[106] *Space, Time and Deity*, Book III, Chap. I, A.
[107] *Experience and Nature*, p. 271. *vid.* in general Chaps. VII and VIII.
[108] *Mind and Body, passim.*
[109] In particular Chaps. III and XIV.
[110] Mr. Lawrence can hardly be said to exemplify my observation about the failure to take mind seriously. On the contrary his *fear* of mind is a veritable obsession—an ever-present phobia of the most virulent character.

where we should least of all have expected it—in Dr. Temple's recent, finely reasoned defence of the Christian faith.[111] Here the writer begins his exposition by repudiating Cartesian dualism and accepting the current view of mind as a late product of evolution from non-mental factors. From the implications of this position, so obviously embarrassing to his eventual thesis,[112] he makes his escape by the device of a "dialectical transition," the effect of which is to show that mind cannot be represented as the end-term of an evolutionary process except upon the assumption that the world is mind-infested from the beginning. This conclusion, however, is still entirely in keeping with the modern tendency in its pan-psychic or immanentalist, as opposed to its materialistic, phase; and further dialectical operations are necessary before the spiritual can be placed in the position of original ascendancy which a theistic philosophy demands—in other words, before we can pass (in the Archbishop's phraseology) from "the immanence of the transcendent" to "the transcendence of the immanent."

23. Among representatives of the current attitude Professor Whitehead occupies a unique position. His monumental *Process and Reality* is the constructive masterpiece of the movement, and reveals with unequalled impressiveness the general character of a universe in which the mental and the physical are merely polar aspects of a reality that throughout all its phases remains indissolubly one. This great work, however, does not readily lend itself to the kind of examination which I am here attempting—partly because of its inherent difficulty, but chiefly because the writer presents his theme, somewhat in the manner of the creative artist, as a synthetic composition rather than a chain of reasonings. Considered in itself, *Process and Reality* is a modern example of metaphysical "dogmatism" in the Kantian sense of the term; but the preparatory labours, represented by the earlier *Principles of Natural Knowledge* and by *The Concept of Nature*, are definitely critical in their significance. In these epoch-making works the

---

[111] *Nature, Man and God.*

[112] Dr. Temple does not hesitate to describe his doctrine in its initial phase as virtually identical with the dialectical materialism of communistic theory. *op. cit.*, pp. 487-8. He differs from Karl Marx in maintaining that in the end dialectic is fatal to materialistic conclusions.

traditional categories of scientific thinking are scrutinized and in large part rejected as no longer commensurate either with the state of scientific knowledge or with the well instructed powers of human judgment. It is to these earlier books that we must look for a revelation of the train of thought by which, in Whitehead's system, the distinction of subjective and physical is worn away until in the end it loses all ontological importance, and disappears in a conception of reality as organism and process.

That there is progressive continuity of thinking throughout this whole development is a fact which is somewhat obscured by certain superficial evidences to the contrary. Thus Whitehead begins by affirming the realistic principle that nature may be treated as completely independent of the subjective processes by which we apprehend the outer world. From this it would be natural to expect that he would accord a similar independence to these subjective processes—the more so as he recognizes the truth that while the objects of science exist outside mind, the scientific knowledge of them exists in mind alone. That, beginning here, he should have ended where he does, by minimizing the distinction of physical and mental, and by permitting the physical to contract the character of subjectivity, is certainly noteworthy.

The explanation of this apparent change of front is to be found not in any inadvertence or any intellectual revolution, but in the very consistency of Whitehead's effort to render science more adequate to its own realistic ideals. In particular the old distinction between the genuinely independent world of mathematical properties and a mind-dependent world of sensory qualities must be done away with. The objective manifold which we call nature is one system and not two systems of being; and the problem is to correlate the data of sense, and generally speaking the whole objective content of our perceptual experience, not with our consciousness of the latter, but with those independent and imperceptible processes which for science constitute the continuity and indeed the being of the physically real. In this way the function of sustaining the perceptual character of things passes from the subject of experience to the independently existing world of natural events.

The result is a profound change in the concept of the subjective. The essence of the latter is no longer to be found, where it had been so long assumed to reside, in a perceptual consciousness of objects. Such consciousness is not primitive but derivative, and is altogether devoid of causal efficacy.[113] So far as the outer world of nature is concerned, it makes no difference whether any one is conscious of it or not. As for the inner life of the "experient subject," it is not in a clear perceptual awareness of things that its essential being consists. For Whitehead the *esse* of the subject is emphatically not *percipere* in the Berkeleian sense. On the contrary, we approach the principle of its being only when we invert the traditional procedure, and instead of beginning with presentational immediacy, and deducing causal efficacy from the latter, begin with causal efficacy as the basic experience upon which presentational immediacy is altogether dependent.[114] But causal efficacy does not stop short with the consciousness of it or even with the world of living things. Rather it goes beneath all such distinctions as the conscious and the unconscious, the animate and the inanimate. At this level these distinctions lose their significance. The *experience* of causation, therefore, is nothing but the *effectiveness* of causation. That is to say, the feeling is not one thing, and the effectiveness another. All is effectiveness, all feeling, all experience. Thus with the elimination of consciousness as an essential, that is, a definitory factor in the life of the subject, we pass to the conception of physical feelings, and to that of a universe in which the physical and the subjective have become mutually assimilated.[115]

[113] There are really two points involved. (1) Consciousness itself is derivative; and (2) among the modes of consciousness those characterized by the greatest clarity and distinctness—perceptual experience, for example—are a later development of a dim sense of inward dynamism. Thus, "the organic philosophy holds that consciousness only arises in a late derivative phase of complex integrations"; and again, "those elements of our experience which stand out clearly and distinctly in our consciousness are not its basic facts; they are the derivative modifications which arise in the process. For example, consciousness only dimly illuminates the prehensions in the mode of causal efficacy, because these prehensions are primitive elements in our experience. But prehensions in the mode of presentational immediacy are among those prehensions which we enjoy with the most vivid consciousness. These prehensions are late derivatives in the concrescence of an experient subject." *Process and Reality*, p. 226.

[114] *op. cit.*, p. 248.

[115] Whitehead does, however, recognize a distinction. In "inorganic actual occasions," we are told, "the two higher originative phases in the 'process,' namely, the 'supplemental' phase, and the 'mental' phase" are lost. *op. cit.*, p. 249.

Such, I take it, in brief outline, is the train of ideas which leads from the initial postulate of a natural world closed against mind to the conception of a reality which is at once subjective and physical. We cannot, however, rest content with such a summary account of the matter. I therefore propose to devote a chapter to the detailed discussion of this most significant movement of modern thought, with special reference to its initial phase in the *Principles of Natural Knowledge* and *The Concept of Nature*.

APPENDIX A (*See note 43, page* 60)

THE CONTEXTLESS CHARACTER OF SANTAYANA'S ESSENCES

It is true that Santayana speaks of the identity of an essence "in various contexts" (*S.A.*, p. 111); but the statement must be taken as referring not to essence as such, but to the adventitious circumstance of its appearance and reappearance in the alien medium of the flux. In this respect the context is like the identity and duration which "are not properly predicated of essence in its own realm," but are "superfluous epithets . . . , and almost insults, because they substitute a questionable for an unquestionable subsistence in the essence." *ibid.*, p. 112. cf. *R.M.*, p. 103, where the "essential context" of the essence is contrasted with the "contingent relations" of the flux. It is clear that in its "essential context" the essence is essentially contextless.

A glance at some of the instances adduced is instructive. The following examples are culled from *S.A.* and *R.E.*: Unity, plurality, number, the dyad, "those very high numbers . . . which nobody has ever thought of specifically"; Euclidean space in its simplicity or in the complexity which it reveals when analysed, the round square, the square and circle of Euclidean geometry, geometrical figures "fixed by intent" (!), the form of a hollow sphere, corneredness, the straightness that provokes one to exclamation when contemplating a palm tree, a Roman road or the horizon; "the space, matter, gravitation, time and laws of motion conceived by astronomers"; equations, definitions; "this colour of an after-image, this straight stick bent at the surface of the water"; sensory data and emotional states if properly insulated; colour, sound, touch, sights, contacts, tears, provocations, which are signs of the objects of which animals have a sensory or emotional experience; the properties of the sensory data, as loudness, dazzlingness; music (in its objective nature); pain, terror, shock: "those many forms of torment for which nature does not provide the requisite instrument, and which even hell has neglected to exemplify" (this last an essence which has no context of existence from which it must be separated by the sceptical reversion); "all the qualities of sensation despised by Platonism and all the types of change or relation neglected by that philosophy"; food or pure succulence, crescent, satellite, the temperatures or perspectives of anything; "all possible terms in mental discourse," the beautiful, the good, pure being; truth, which is "an essence involved in positing any fact, in remembering, expecting, or asserting anything"; "types of animal bodies or human institutions which may be arrested in thought"; the universe itself.

There Must Be, Yet Cannot Be, a "Realm" of Essence

I say, here, "mostly"; for it is evident that from this point of view they are not all on the same footing. The round square, for instance, and "those many forms of torment for which nature does not provide the requisite instrument" obviously constitute a class by themselves, and the problem of correlating them with the events of the natural world does not arise. It is different when we come to geometrical figures, the sensory data, types of animal body, and the laws of motion. Further complications arise when we admit the good, the true and the beautiful. Between these groups of essences there is such a profound discrepancy of character that we are constrained to ask what is to be gained by the mere act of assembling them under a single rubric such as *essence*. Is there any advantage in thinking of goodness as belonging to the same category which includes satellite and the square circle? The question leads to another: Whether is it more important to view the essences together in the light of what they have in common, or to recognize the characteristic differences that distinguish them from one another and divide them into groups? The answer must depend upon the principles that determine each procedure.

On one point we are left in no uncertainty. The bond of community among the essences is nothing but their intuitable character and the fact that in our apprehension of them they demand a non-believing attitude.[1] In order to appropriate their fine effluvia we must take them, as has been remarked, out of every context of life, of judgment and of purpose. They do not permit us to indulge our vital interests or our active propensities. Hence we find them everywhere: hence too one essence is just as good as another. It is so, however, only in respect of its formal character as essence: as *individual* essence it has its own identity which is altogether inalienable, and is marked by a certain "inward complexity" peculiar to itself.[2] From whatever point of view, therefore, we regard the subject, it is unhelpful and unmeaning to consider all the essences together. If we regard them in the light of the character that constitutes them essences, the element of difference is wanting. If we take them by themselves, it is so pronounced as to reduce the "realm of essence" to a "chaos." Being "infinitely various," this realm has no "frontiers," no "alternatives." It is not a "closed system" or indeed a

[1] *S.A.*, p. 93.
[2] *op. cit.*, p. 116.

system of any sort, but is perfect in its "catholicity"—"placid and safe and the same whatever may happen in earth or heaven."[3]

From this the answer to our first question is plain. There is no point of view from which essences can legitimately or profitably be regarded as constituting a class. Science, contrary to the author's assertion,[4] knows nothing of such uncorrelated miscellanies, and what is true of science is true of every other spiritual discipline. The conclusion is inescapable. Essences there may be—intuitable non-existents; but there is no authentic realm of essence. We do not, that is to say, add to our intuitive apprehension of the latter by thinking of them as constituting a class, or by viewing them in the light of what is common to them as essences.

But if essences are not to be thought of as constituting a class, it is no less certain that we cannot intuit them as individuals without seeing that they fall into certain classes based upon some principle of difference or resemblance. At the very least there is the fundamental cleavage between those which do and those which do not supply descriptions to the transient episodes of the flux. Of course from the standpoint of their common character as essences this is a fact of no significance; but we have seen that there is no significance in the fact that they have a common character; and surely it can hardly be questioned that the distinction I have pointed out is of real importance. There is all the difference in the world between intuiting a purely theoretical degree of torture in a non-existent hell and intuiting a law of gravitation in an actual world of moving bodies; and if the conception of essence reduces the two to a level, the result is merely to discredit the conception of essence. Indeed in certain aspects it is difficult to take the latter seriously. There is in it a suggestion of Goethe's Mephistopheles, the "universal humorist," as Coleridge calls him, who destroys all proportions and all perspectives. On the ground of sheer decorum it is necessary to recognize a difference of import between essences like crescent or succulence on the one hand, and good or beautiful on the other. All of these, it is true, supply descriptions to the flux, but they do so in very different ways, and they affect us in very different phases of our ex-

---

[3] *R.E.*, p. 82.

[4] Of course he is not thinking of all essences or of essences as such, but only of the intuitions which are "analytical and selective," in contrast to those which are "passive, aesthetic, and mystical." An imaginary game of chess is cited as a case in point. Such a game is an "object of exact science"—although, as Santayana admits, it is not really an object of *knowledge*, but is more in the nature of a day-dream. *R.E.*, p. 5. This in itself is sufficiently question-provoking. My point, however, is merely that in respect of its nature as essence, the game of chess loses its character as an object of science as soon as it associates itself with entities which are not such objects. In other words, it ceases to be an object of scientific interest when it becomes an essence.

perience. We are therefore faced with the alternatives of (1) recognizing the significance of the descriptive function and classifying the essences accordingly, or else (2) discrediting all those aspects of human experience and forms of spiritual activity which we distinguish as science, art, religion and the moral life.

In Santayana's philosophy neither of these courses is pursued with rigour and consistency. There is a constant passing from one to the other in a planless and aimless fashion. Such a procedure is inevitable from the outset. It is implicit in the dualistic presuppositions of the system, with its sceptical retreat to immediacy and its assertive movement through action and belief to practical achievement.

CHAPTER III

PHYSICAL AND SPIRITUAL IN MODERN PHILOSOPHY—WITH A
SPECIAL EXAMINATION OF PROFESSOR WHITEHEAD'S SYSTEM

Whitehead's Problem: to Avoid the Fallacy of Bifurcation

1. In the two books which we are about to examine, *The Prin-ciples of Natural Knowledge* and *The Concept of Nature*, the problem dealt with is that of reconciling the objective world of our ordinary perceptual experience with the strange and perplexing transcript of the latter by physical science—in other words, of bringing into intelligible relation the "familiar" and the "scientific" world of which Sir Arthur Eddington writes so amusingly in the Introduction to his Gifford Lectures. Whitehead's later work, *Process and Reality*, is much more comprehensive in its scope. It embodies what has always been the specific project of metaphysics—that, namely, of elucidating the nature of reality as a whole. *Process and Reality* is a speculative completion[1] of the train of thought which began on a different plane with the *Principles of Natural Knowledge*. Yet the conclusions of the later work are dependent upon premises supplied by the earlier, and must stand or fall with these.

2. From the beginning the reader is impressed by the extent to which this vast enterprise of thought is dominated by the constructive spirit of synthesis. Already in *The Concept of Nature* that spirit is revealed at work breaking down the barrier which divides the world of perceptual experience from the world of physics. That barrier is due to "vicious bifurcation,"[2] a species of fallacy with which "the modern natural philosophy is shot through and through."[3] "What I am essentially protesting against," we further read, "is the bifurcation of nature into two systems of reality, which, in so far as they are real, are real in different senses."[4] On the one hand is "the nature which is the fact apprehended in awareness," and which "holds within it the greenness of the trees,"

---

[1] With incidental emendations. *vid.*, e.g., the substitution of the notion of "extensive connection" for the earlier notion of "extensive abstraction" upon suggestions derived from certain articles by Professor de Laguna. *op. cit.*, pp. 407 *sq.*, 416 *sq.*

[2] *Concept of Nature* (hereafter *C.N.*), p. 187.

[3] *C.N.*, p. vi.

[4] *C.N.*, p. 30.

the song of the birds," and, generally speaking, the manifold deliverances of a sensory experience. On the other hand is "the nature which is the cause of awareness," and is identified with "the conjectural system of molecules and electrons which so affects the mind as to produce the awareness of apparent nature. The meeting point of these two natures is the mind, the causal nature being influent and the apparent nature being effluent."[5]

3. Now it cannot be denied that a vast amount of error and confusion has been introduced into philosophy by the theory which would reduce the world of our perceptual experience to the product of an external reality, whether definable in terms of electrical forces, or, as in the earlier form of the doctrine, in terms of the primary properties of matter (which are really the properties of Euclidean space[6]) acting upon our minds and causing them to generate the secondary or sensory properties. But the bifurcation is not limited to these particular historical forms. Santayana has certainly emancipated himself from the special fallacies which Whitehead exposes; yet we have seen how his thinking terminates in the irresolvable dualism of substance and essence; and we must ask whether a similar dualism is not the eventual issue of all Whitehead's efforts to evade just such a conclusion.

His Principle: to Include Sense Data in Nature, and Treat Nature as "Closed to Mind"

4. At the outset we encounter a principle which may be taken as definitory of the realistic standpoint of science in the interpretation of the outer world. ". . . Nature can be thought of as a closed system whose mutual relations do not require the expression of the fact that they are thought about."[7] This assuredly must be granted. In the scientific exploration of nature's forms and processes the consciousness of the observer is not among the data investigated; nor do the relations which it is his business to examine include the special relation which connects the data with his consciousness.

Whitehead, however, goes further. Beginning with the definition of nature as "that which we observe in perception through the

---

[5] C.N., p. 31. For the detail vid. Principles of Natural Knowledge (hereafter P.K.), pp. 90 (24.5) and 94 (25.2).
[6] Motion is sometimes added, as by Descartes and Locke—a further complication.
[7] C.N., p. 3.

senses," he remarks that "nature as disclosed in sense-perception is self-contained as against sense-awareness, in addition to being self-contained as against thought," and concludes with the observation: "I will also express this self-containedness of nature by saying that nature is closed to mind."[8]

Now while it is easy to accept the general principle that the outer world, as viewed by the sciences, is closed to all the mental processes, whether in the form of sensory awareness or in any other form, doubts and questions begin to arise as soon as we turn to the definition of nature that has just been given. In particular that definition contains the suggestion of a threat to the principle itself. What we "observe in perception through the senses" is an ambiguous phrase, and can only be made plain by a theory of perception which, unfortunately, can only be developed in a slow and piecemeal fashion. There is the familiar difference, for example, between *this green* and *this green leaf*.[9] In each case the object defines itself against the sensory awareness of it, and in this general sense may be said to be "closed to mind." But the phrase acquires a different meaning according as it is applied to *this green leaf* or to *this green*. The latter falls into a world of colours, the former into a world of botanical forms; and it is obvious that the concept of "closure against mind" does not mean the same thing in the two instances. Colours are closed to mind in the sense that they are among its objects and not among its states or processes. That is to say, they stand in a particular relation to one of its conscious modes. This, however, does not tell us anything about what they are in themselves, or whether they exist independently of the relation in question. Green leaves, on the contrary, are known to exist in organic relation to the trees that bear them, and hence in a context that invests them with a certain independence as actually existing members of a non-mental world. In other words, the characteristic fact about a colour is that it is seen (or at least, under the proper conditions, visible), while the characteristic fact about a green leaf is that it grows upon a tree; and the facts are of profoundly different import in so far as they help to define the sense

[8] *C.N.*, p. 4.

[9] In Whitehead's phraseology "sense-objects" and "perceptual objects," the latter including "physical objects." *P.K.*, Chap. VII; *C.N.*, Chap. VII.

in which the two kinds of object stereotype themselves against the minds that know them.[10]

5. It is, however, of the utmost importance for Whitehead's whole inquiry, actuated as it is by the desire to obtain a completely unified concept of nature, and to avoid the fallacy of bifurcation, that the distinction between the objectivity of the physically real, represented presumably by the green leaf, and what, with some hesitation, I shall call the immediate datum of sense, represented by the given *green*, should not be allowed to complicate the issue by suggesting that nature closes itself in two distinct ways against our consciousness of it. For this reason it is necessary that the sensa should be taken over into the flux of natural events and exhibited as ingredients in the latter rather than as terms in a subject-object relation. Of course Whitehead is far too deeply concerned about the distinction to permit it to become obscured in the general concept of objectivity.[11] His problem is to find a place for it within a system of nature defined in terms of a thoroughgoing realism. The solution depends upon the issue to a problem much more fundamental, of which, indeed, the difficulty referred to is a minor complication.

Nature as Flux; and "Objects," as the Factors in It Which "Do Not Pass"

6. That the time element is integral to the concept of nature has long been acknowledged both by scientists and by philosophers. But the discovery of this truth is the result of theoretical necessity, and its assimilation to the system of our everyday thinking has been retarded by a tradition, wrought into the fabric of our experience, whereby a certain priority has been assigned to the spatial over the temporal factor. This tradition has been promoted, if indeed it has not been definitely propagated, by a series of episodes in the history of science—for example, the triumph, in classical times, of the Democritean picture of the world as a distribution and re-dis-

[10] Whitehead's own words upon the distinction are worth noting: "Thus we distinguish between the qualities of events as in individual perception—namely, the sense-data of individuals—and the objective qualities of the actual events within the common nature which is the datum for apprehension." *P.K.*, pp. 78-9, and generally §§20.2 and 20.3. cf. *op. cit.*, p. 85, where the writer differentiates between what is "perceived" and what is "really perceived," and remarks that "it is only the incurable poverty of language which blurs the distinction." (*ibid.*, §23.5.)

[11] As we shall see, the "sense-object" appears in a "hierarchy" of objects as the simplest type. *P.K.*, p. 83; *C.N.*, p. 149.

tribution of atoms in a void, over the Heraclitean conception of a world-flux, in modern times the impression made upon the mind of Europe from the days of the scientific Renaissance by Copernicus' discovery of the "immensity" of the celestial spaces.[12] The spatial factor could not fail to make this impression—there was *so much of it*. Hence it was that the characteristic phenomenon of the natural world came to be conceived as a collocation of the contents of space displacing an earlier collocation, and itself displaced by a later. Of course these displacements were events in time; but the significance of an event was reduced to that of the relationship between a spatially filled *terminus a quo* and a spatially filled *terminus ad quem*. Thus the character of spatiality imparted to the event all the reality it could be said to possess, while the status of the temporal factor was that of a predicament. In Whitehead's words: "The ultimate fact embracing all nature is (in this traditional point of view) a distribution of material throughout all space at a durationless instant of time, and another such ultimate fact will be another distribution of the same material throughout the same space at another durationless instant of time."[13] This conception, with all its inherent difficulties, has continued to dominate our thinking as regards the macroscopic objects of perceptual experience; and the general tendency has been reinforced by the fact that such objects are in many cases not obviously in a state of perpetual change, but appear to maintain their identity unaffected by the flight of time and the changes that are going on around them.

Now the really fundamental problem for Whitehead is to show that the real fact, the actuality, behind the apparently static objects of perception is a process that goes on uninterruptedly because time is of the essence of "that which we observe in perception through the senses." In order to see the problem in its true light, however, it is necessary to clear away a possible misunderstanding implicit in our statement of it.

As I have just remarked, the point to be established is the existence of a process behind the fixity of appearance. But this is not to be taken as if it meant no more than the reduction of an apparently static to an actually moving system. Such reduction is

---

[12] *De Revolutionibus*, I, vi. Copernicus' disciple Giordano Bruno places the conception of a spatial infinity in the forefront of his system.

[13] *P.K.*, p. 2.

among the commonplaces of experience, as we realize every time a microscopic examination reveals the minute movements that underlie the immobility of a gross structure. Microscopic movements are certainly among the ingredients which a close scrutiny may sometimes detect in the macroscopic world. Apart altogether from this, however, is the much more important fact that even in their macroscopic aspect the objects of perception are elements (Whitehead would say *abstract* elements[14]) in a time-conditioned manifold, and are amenable to all the implications of this fact.

To take an illustration from Whitehead himself,[15] Cleopatra's Needle is an object of perceptual experience (the analogue—only partial—is *this green leaf* rather than *this green*) which, rightly understood, resolves itself into a phase in the universal "life" of nature, "the ether of events,"[16] characterized by extensity in all dimensions,[17] the temporal included, and hence into a system of happenings. Some of these are minute changes due to the action of the London atmosphere upon the fabric. Others are the electrical events which provide "situations" for the "scientific objects" we call molecules, atoms and electrons.[18] But the point of chief importance is that by the inclusion of the time factor, the structure itself considered as a whole becomes a complex event completely integrated on every side with other events, and maintaining its identity, however that is to be explained, by processes which, so far from isolating it in some backwater of existence, presuppose its continuity with other similar identities in the all-embracing flux. This is one side of the truth.

7. There is another side. If it is the case that nature is a universal process, the concept of process is one which cannot be taken as

---

[14] *C.N.*, p. 171.

[15] *C.N.*, p. 166.

[16] A concept which Whitehead substitutes for the traditional "ether of material," and which expresses the assumption "that something is going on everywhere and always." *P.K.*, p. 25; *C.N.*, p. 78.

[17] *P.K.*, p. 61.

[18] *P.K.*, pp. 66, 93 *sq.*; *C.N.*, pp. 170-1. Whitehead seems to me to be wrong in classifying molecules, etc., as objects rather than events. As this is one of the points on which the distinction, as he himself calls it, between objects and events breaks down, I shall reserve consideration of it for a later point in the text. Meanwhile I should like to remark that the electronic events which constitute the atoms cannot strictly be interpreted as minute changes in the fabric of the macroscopic object. Since the difficulties inherent in Bohr's theory became apparent, and led to such developments as Schrödinger's undulatory hypothesis, it is hardly possible to think of the atom merely as a microscopic constituent of matter.

absolute without compromising the very conditions which render human experience in certain of its most significant phases possible. It is therefore necessary to qualify the concept by adding such features as are necessary to account for the unmistakable deliverances of experience or for the applications of reason to the latter.[19] Above all, in a world consisting entirely of events no act of *recognition*, no "rational thought,"[20] could ever occur. "It is impossible to recognize an event,[21] because an event is essentially distinct from every other event.[22] But since the possibility of recognition can hardly be denied, we must provide an object for it, which shall be exempt from the peculiar disability to which events are subject. There must be non-transient elements in nature. To these Whitehead gives the name of *objects*. Objects are "factors in nature which do not pass."[23] He adds a definition of "recognition." This is "the awareness of an object as some factor not sharing in the passage of nature"—"an awareness of sameness."[24] In this it is not implied that in order to recognize an object we must have had previous acquaintance with it.[25] Recollection is not a necessary ingredient in recognition, and is not a *possible* ingredient in *primary recognition*. "The primary recognition of an object," we are told, "consists of the recognition of its permanence amid the partial events of the duration which is present"[26]—in other words, "within the

---

[19] *P.K.*, p. 74.

[20] *P.K.*, p. 64.

[21] Events are experienced by a mental act which Whitehead distinguishes from recognition as *apprehension*. ". . . We shall say that we 'apprehend' an event and 'recognize' an object. To apprehend an event is to be aware of its passage as happening in that of nature, which we each of us know as though it were common to all percipients. . . . We apprehend nature as continuous and we recognize it as atomic." *P.K.*, pp. 67, 70 *sq.*

[22] *C.N.*, p. 143; *P.K.*, p. 61.

[23] *C.N.*, pp. 124 *sq.*; *P.K.*, pp. 62 *sq.*

[24] The latter expression must be qualified by the observation that the awareness in question does not imply "an intellectual act of comparison accompanied with judgment. I use recognition," Whitehead explains, "for the non-intellectual relation of sense-awareness which connects the mind with a factor of nature without passage." *C.N.*, p. 143. The distinction of objects and events comes out further in the following: "An event is what it is, when it is, and where it is. Externality and extension are the marks of events; an event is there and not here or, here and not there, it is then and not now or, now and not then. . . ." *P.K.*, p. 62. ". . . The self-identical object maintains itself amid the flux of events: it is there and then, and it is here and now. . . ." *ibid.*, p. 63. We are also told that "the object is permanent, because (strictly speaking) it is without time and space." Hence the expression "eternal object" in *Process and Reality*.

[25] *P.K.*, p. 64.

[26] *P.K.*, p. 64.

specious present."[27] In addition to this there is "indefinite recognition" (or recollection), which is defined as "the awareness of other perceptions of the object as related to other events separate from the specious present, but without any precise designation of the events," and "definite recognition" (or memory), "which is an awareness of perception of the object as related to certain other definite events separate from the specious present."[28] It is easy to see why these three modes of recognition are supposed to be implied in the awareness of objects, of which the definitory characteristic is permanence.

The Kinds of Object Which Whitehead Recognizes

8. As for the *identity* of the permanent objects, Whitehead's account, while agreeing closely in substance, if not in form, with that of Santayana,[29] differs from the latter in restricting itself in the main to the class of objects which are alone significant in a philosophy of nature—those, namely, which are correlated with events in the natural world, or, in Whitehead's parlance, which are "situated" in these events.[30] There are three principal types, sense-objects, perceptual objects and scientific objects.[31] These "form an ascending hierarchy, of which each member presupposes the type below."[32]

9. Sense-objects are the rudimentary objective contents of sensory experience, specific colours, sounds, tastes and sensa of every sort.[33] It is important, however, to note that the object is not to be identified with the particular datum presented at any moment of time—the actual green or red or blue that appears for an instant and is gone for ever. On the contrary it is to be identified with *this*

---

[27] *P.K.*, p. 82.

[28] *P.K.*, p. 82.

[29] Whitehead recognizes "an indefinite number of types." *C.N.*, p. 149.

[30] *P.K.*, p. 67; *C.N.*, p. 149. In addition to these Whitehead recognizes objects which are the abstract product of comparison between "the recognized objects of one event"—or, generally speaking, objects which, though "not posited by sense-awareness," "may be known to the intellect"; e.g., "relations between objects and relations between relations." *C.N.*, pp. 125-6.

[31] The "percipient object," on which Whitehead touches rather lightly, and on which I shall have something to say later, is "situated" in the "percipient event"; and, although not expressly included in the three main types, conforms to the general description. We shall see that more depends upon the percipient object than is apparent from Whitehead's statement.

[32] *C.N.*, p. 149.

[33] *P.K.*, p. 83.

particular shade of green or red or blue, which appears and re-appears in any number of actual contexts. It is what we see when, in Whitehead's words, "we see redness here and the same redness there, redness then and the same redness now."[34] The particularity is not that of the event (which is unique), not that of *this time*, but that of *this shade*. Thus Cambridge blue is an object, but as such it is not "a particular patch of blue as seen during a particular second of time at a definite date. Such a patch is an event where Cambridge blue is situated."[35]

10. In contradistinction to sense-objects perceptual objects "are the 'things' which we see, touch, taste, and hear"—in a word, "the ordinary objects of common experience—chairs, tables, stones, trees."[36] They differ from the individual data of sense in complexity. "A perceptual object is recognized as an association of sense-objects in the same situation. The permanence of the asso-ciation is the object which is recognized."[37] A point of importance is that this definition covers delusions as well as "non-delusive" perceptual objects.[38] The distinction is obviously one of funda-mental significance. Whitehead's attempt to state it involves the theory of "perceptual judgment." The latter is not required for "primary recognition" (which is merely "the conveyance of a per-ceptual object by a sense-object"), but "supervenes" at an early stage and forms "an important ingredient in what may be termed 'completed recognition'." It is here that delusional objects become possible. "If the perceptual judgment is false, the perceptual ob-ject as perceived is a delusion."[39]

Strangely enough it is in the first instance as the negation of a delusion that the "physical object" is defined. "A non-delusive perceptual object will be called a 'physical object'."[40] In order to obtain a positive conception of the latter it is necessary to combine in thought the permanence characteristic of all objects and the complexity characteristic of those we call "perceptual," and to consider the permanence as characteristic of the complexity. Thus a particular association of sense-objects occurs in a single "situa-

[34] *P.K.*, p. 83.
[35] *C.N.*, p. 149.
[36] *P.K.*, p. 88.
[37] *loc. cit.*
[38] *P.K.*, p. 89.
[39] *loc. cit.*
[40] *P.K.*, p. 90.

tion," and we have a perceptual object. A second association of the identical sense-objects occurs in a second situation, and we have the same perceptual object. The operation may be repeated an indefinite number of times; and when we think of the various *associations* as constituting a single, self-identical group, the object defines itself as "physical." This is what I take Professor Whitehead to mean when he says: "So far as it is directly perceived in its various situations, a physical object is a group of associations of sense-objects, each association being perceived or perceivable by a percipient object with an appropriate percipient event as its locus."[41] I shall have to deal with the "percipient event" and the "percipient object" in my final review of Whitehead's realism. For the moment it will be enough to think of the percipient event as the event which occurs when anything is perceived, and of the percipient object as the permanent identity (according to Whitehead the unity of consciousness) which we recognize every time a percipient event takes place.

11. The concept of "scientific objects" rests upon that of "active conditioning events."[42] If I may express the matter in my own way, the idea seems to be this. Sense-objects reveal themselves from time to time as fixed identifiable presences in the general flux of nature. But their appearances are not haphazard or undetermined. We recognize them under conditions which admit of exact specification. Certain situations must arise before the act of recognition is possible. These situations belong to the determinate order of events in the physical world. It is obvious that there is a problem here. The actual experience of sensory or perceptual objects does not carry its explanation with it. When I become conscious of green or of the green leaf, I must ask how the experience is conditioned. But if the question means anything at all, it means that the conditions for which I am in search are conditions which apply not only to this particular experience, but to every experience of this type. In a word, the inquiry is immediately and necessarily transferred to the plane of the universal and hypothetical. This is implied in the nature of all objects as permanent identities. I am asking in effect: What are the universally operative conditions which must be presupposed if the object which I call

---

[41] *P.K.*, pp. 90-1.
[42] *P.K.*, p. 93, §25.1.

this shade of green or *this green leaf* or *Cleopatra's Needle* is to supervene at any moment in the endless lapse of natural events?

Does the Physical Explain the Perceptual (Nature) or Is There a Re-Bifurcation?

12. The value of Whitehead's magnificently bold and original reconstruction of the facts will depend to a large extent upon its effectiveness in providing a satisfactory answer to the question now before us; and that in turn will depend on the writer's success in circumventing the fallacy of bifurcation against which all his efforts are directed. In view of this it is a little ominous that he falls back here upon the very assumption in which all the errors of bifurcation have their origin—the assumption, namely, that the objects of sensory and perceptual experience are conditioned by *physical* objects. It is in physical objects that he finds "the links connecting nature as perceived with nature as conditioning its own perception."[43] The problem assumes a quite specific form. We must seek in the definitory character of physical objects, as already given, the key to those conditions, yet to be discovered, whereby nature generates a perception of itself.

In what way, then, do physical objects enable us to pass in thought from the conditioned world of perceptual experience to the universally operative conditions which that experience pre-supposes? It will be remembered that physical objects belong to the realm of the perceptual, of which presumably they constitute the main division.[44] Furthermore they represent, the upper *limit* of perceptual experience in the hierarchy of objects. We *perceive* physical objects; but we cannot pass from them to other objects of perception as we passed from sense-objects to perceptual. The next step is one which carries us beyond sensory experience altogether into the region of intellectual construction or scientific conjecture. The entities with which we shall here have to deal are hypothetical entities.

13. Before proceeding further I must be allowed to interpolate a remark which, while it may be regarded as parenthetical, is none-theless highly relevant both to Whitehead's argument and to that by which I hope to follow it up. The fact that the entities with which physical science is concerned are introduced hypothetically

---

[43] *P.K.*, p. 94.
[44] The other division is that of delusions.

is no reason why we should treat them with disrespect. If their concepts are the product of an inference from the facts, if the evidence for their existence is purely circumstantial, it need not on that account be assumed that they have no claim to credibility; and Whitehead himself quite rightly and most effectively protests against the tendency to dispose of molecules and electrons as no better than ingenious fictions.[45] Such a view, pushed too far, would be the end of all science. Of course it is a safe assumption that in the advance of natural knowledge every hypothesis will have to be recast and every conjecture emended; but if so, it will be only that they may make way for other conjectures better grounded than themselves; and throughout the whole process it will be necessary to add, at every stage, what I have called "the postulate of being," to the effect that whatever the hypothesis or the construct in use, the reference is always to *that which is*. It is not my intention, therefore, to countenance the tendency to discredit scientific objects on the ground that their concepts are the product of inference and artifice. My objections, as will appear in the appropriate place, have to do rather with Whitehead's interpretation of such entities as atoms and molecules. Our immediate business, however, is to complete the account of scientific objects; and again I shall crave permission to paraphrase Whitehead's admirable statement in the way best calculated to bring out the points I have in view.[46]

14. It will be remembered that a physical object is a group of associations, the individual members of an association being sense data. Let *abc* be such an association, appearing and reappearing in the successive situations, X, Y and Z. Since a, b and c are objects, they do not vary from one situation to another, but each by definition remains identical with itself through all possible vicissitudes of space and time. X, Y and Z, on the contrary, being events, are each of them unique, unprecedented and irrevocable.

---

[45] *C.N.*, pp. 45-6. *vid.* especially these words: "Do away with this elaborate machinery of a conceptual nature which consists of assertions about things which don't exist in order to convey truths about things which do exist. I am maintaining the obvious position that scientific laws, if they are true, are statements about entities which we obtain knowledge of as being in nature; and that, if the entities to which the statements refer are not to be found in nature, the statements about them have no relevance to any purely natural occurrence."

[46] For the passage on which the following statement is mainly based, *vid.* *P.K.*, pp. 93-5.

It must be added that every time the association occurs, *two* distinct events occur with it. One of these is that which has already been dwelt upon—namely, the *situation* in which the association of sensory elements emerges as a perceptual object. The other is the "percipient event"—that is to say, what happens when the life-process of the percipient is modified by the experience of perception. And finally along with the "percipient event" there goes the "percipient object," which is just the recognizable permanence, the self-identity of consciousness that underlies successive percipient events.

Now the transition from physical to scientific objects is effected in this way. The events which constitute the course of nature are infinite in number. Hence the association of the sense-objects, *a*, *b* and *c*, in the perceptual object *abc* is liable to occur any number of times. The possibility is ever present; and the physical object is just the association viewed as a permanent possibility. One way of describing this fact is that adopted by Whitehead when he speaks of the various associations as constituting a group. From this it appears that physical objects are identical with perceptual objects when the latter are thought about in a particular way and are thus, so to speak, authenticated. The essence of such authentication is the completed recognition of the object by a judgment. This I take to mean that we add to the perceptual recognition of an association (that, for example, which constitutes the unity and identity of a tree) a judgment to the effect that *this is a tree*. In so judging, we assume that this identical association of sensory elements will emerge as a perceptual object in the stream of events as often as the relevant situation occurs—provided only that along with this relevant (or "favourable") situation there is found a favourable "percipient event." That is to say, the judgment presupposes a concept of nature which includes the hypothesis of "active conditioning events" for all sorts of perceptible objects for which percipient events are forthcoming. The remainder of the problem is to determine the exact character of the "active conditioning events" upon which these possibilities depend. It is here that scientific objects must be taken into account.

15. These objects (atoms, for example, and electrons) are of course not themselves perceived. They are supplied by thought upon clues derived in the last resort from actual perceptual experience. But the procedure involved in following up the clues is

subject to certain principles which I venture to state thus. The starting-point is the existence of perceptual objects, and the motive is to find the causal explanation of the latter. In other words, we wish to ascertain how exactly the events of the natural world come to be the active conditions or determinants of the objects which we perceive through the senses. On further consideration we see that in so treating these objects we are interpreting them not merely as perceptual (which on the face of them they are) but as physical (which we judge them to be). That is to say, we are treating them from the standpoint not so much of their relation to ourselves, who perceive them, as of their relation to the manifold of nature, to which they belong. In Whitehead's phraseology, we are seeking to explain what we perceive by viewing it in the context of its characteristic situations rather than in that which connects it with the percipient event and the percipient object. This, however, we can do only by adding an act of judgment to the primary awareness whereby we accept the presentation as a given percept. In seeking the explanation of perceptual objects in the world of outer events we have therefore passed beyond the region of perceptual experience as such to the region of intellectual construction. The judgment which turns an object of experience into a physical object carries us immediately into the realm of scientific hypothesis; and the authentication of the judgment implies the validity of science. Everything then turns upon what science has to tell us, under the limitation imposed by its hypothetical character, about the nature of the world, and more particularly upon the question whether its deliverances fulfil the function for which they were designed—that, namely, of showing how events come to be the active conditions of perceptual objects. Is it possible to gather from an examination of scientific knowledge how far this end is achieved?

How Do "Scientific Objects" Enable Events to Condition the Physical Objects of Our Perception?

16. In the first place it should be noted that what, upon this theory, science has to explain is an *object*—the object of perceptual experience—and that the explanatory factor is an *event*—the "active conditioning event" which we ordinarily conceive as a

cause.[47] The question therefore narrows itself down to this: Can science help us to understand how an event can be the cause of a perceived object? Professor Whitehead answers that events become the cause of such objects through a relation in which they stand to the objects of scientific knowledge. To quote his exact words: "The characters of events in their capacity of active conditioning events for sense-objects are expressed by their relations to scientific objects."[48] This statement, however, is of little use until we understand how the expression "scientific objects" is to be interpreted. Nor does it help us to be told that scientific objects are molecules and electrons. What we really want to know is how exactly the relation to scientific objects (whatever these may be) can turn events into causes, and more specifically into the causes that are responsible for the physical objects of our perceptual experience. But so far the only information that seems to be available on that vital point is a statement to the effect that scientific objects are definable in terms of their ability to perform this service. "Scientific objects are not directly perceived, they are inferred by reason of their capacity to express these characters, namely, they express how it is that events are conditions. In other words, they express the causal character of events."[49]

17. Thus the argument seems to end in a circle. First we are referred to scientific objects for the explanation of which we are in search. And then, when we try to ascertain what these scientific objects are, we are informed that they define themselves by reference to the part they play in providing the explanation required. The only way out is to furnish sufficient detail of the relation of scientific objects to events to enable us to utilize this relationship in the attempt to explain how events come to condition perceptual objects. In this the first step is to ascertain how far into the changing world of nature, the ether of events, the relationship extends, and how it varies with the varying conditions. For the sake of sim-

[47] There are also events which are "passive" conditions. These are reducible to space and time, "presupposed as the setting within which the particular events occur." Whitehead adds: "But space and time are merely expressive of the relations of extension among the whole ether of events. Thus this presupposition of space and time really calls in all events of all nature as passive conditions for that particular perception of the sense-object." *P.K.*, p. 86. Like the distinction between the so-called "cause" and "conditions" in J. S. Mill's logic, the difference between active and passive conditions is one which cannot be rendered absolute. *vid.* Mill, *Logic*, Book III, Chap. v, §3.

[48] *P.K.*, p. 95.

[49] *loc. cit.*

plicity we shall confine ourselves to the electron, which, in the present state of human knowledge, may be taken to represent the "ultimate" scientific object.

The concepts required are two in number, *field* and *occupation*.

"Each scientific object has its special relation to each event in nature. Events as thus related to a definite electron are called the field of that object."[50] It is obvious that there can be no limits to a field either in space or in time. Every field comprises the sum-total of all events,[51] and one field differs from another only in respect of the electron to which it is related. In other words, the totality of events acquires a *distinct character* for each electron. Thus there will be a field for the electron A and a field for the electron B; and the difference between the two will be in the fact that certain characteristics of the universe of events are due to B and certain others to A.

The terms "occupied" and "unoccupied" apply to parts of the field—that is to say, to certain of the events of which the field is composed. An event is said to be "occupied" when its relation to a scientific object corresponds to that of a "situation" in regard to a physical object.[52] Thus if e is an event, and B a permanent character which the latter expresses, e is "occupied" by B. In relation to B all events which do not possess this character are "unoccupied." They are not on that account *uninfluenced*. On the contrary they "possess a definite character expressive of the reign of law in the creative advance of nature, i.e. in the passage of events,"[53] and this character they receive from the electrons which do not occupy them, as well as from that which does.[54] The definition of the electron follows. ". . . The electron," we are told, "is nothing else than the expression of certain permanent recognizable features in this creative advance."[55]

Clearly we are here considering the facts from two points of view. From one of these the electron is seen to stand related to the whole universe of events. From the other we regard it in relation to its situation, the event which it occupies. The first standpoint is that which more adequately expresses the concept of nature. The

[50] *loc. cit.*
[51] *P.K.*, p. 96.
[52] *P.K.*, p. 96; p. 166, §53.2.
[53] *P.K.*, p. 97.
[54] *ibid.*, §25.7.
[55] *loc. cit.*

second is that which bears more directly upon the problem with which we are dealing—the problem of explaining physical objects causally by relating them to their active conditioning events.

If I interpret Whitehead aright, the cause of any physical object is expressible in terms of the events occupied by the ultimate scientific objects which correspond to the physical object in question—that is, in the last analysis, the electrons. This means that in order to obtain a causal explanation of anything which we interpret as a physical object we must replace the obscure and relatively complex event which is the situation of that object by the relatively simple event which the electron occupies. Or, looking at the subject from the standpoint of the objects rather than of the events concerned, we must replace the physical by the scientific object. Of course it would be inaccurate to describe the electron as the cause of the physical object. The electron is itself an object: causes are events. But the electron is the permanent character of the event which it occupies, and may therefore be described as the "causal character" of the active conditioning event which is the real cause of the object we are trying to explain.[56]

The question comes to be how these replacements are effected; and the answer according to Whitehead is: by an act of simplification through the "method of extensive abstraction." Of this method it will be sufficient to say that its purpose is to remove the object from the vast and bewildering context of its spatio-temporal determinants, and that when its application is complete, "the result," in Whitehead's words, "is to separate off the temporal and spatial properties of events."[57] Thus, to quote our author again, "in terms of space and time (as derived by the method of extensive abstraction) the situation of a physical object shrinks into its spatial position at an instant together with its associated motion. Also an event occupied by an electron shrinks into the position at an instant of the electric charge forming its nucleus, together with its associated motion."[58] In this way it is possible to pass from the obscure and scientifically unmanageable object of experience to the concept of a system of electronic events localized in the atom and representing in simple schematic form the identical events in which the physical object is situated.

[56] *P.K.*, p. 183, §60.2.
[57] *P.K.*, p. 96, §25.5.
[58] *loc. cit.*, §25.6.

This is as near as I can come to Whitehead's meaning; and while the statement is far from complete, and is designed, as I have explained, to bring out only the points that are relevant to my argument, it is sufficient to furnish the material for an answer to the question whether Whitehead has succeeded in avoiding the fallacy of bifurcation. What we have to ask is whether it is possible to explain the objects of perception and of sense by referring them to the world of scientific objects, of which the electron is the ultimate and simplest, and to the events which the electron occupies.

Whitehead himself has furnished a valuable analysis and characterization of his method.[59] That method is admittedly based upon abstraction.[60] To this no exception can be taken. Molecules and electrons, with the events which they occupy, are assuredly abstractions from the reality which comprehends them;[61] but that does not mean that they are unreal.[62] We posit them hypothetically, but not as *entia rationis* or as pure logical constructions. The postulate of being is implied in all the sciences of nature, and the justification of the postulate is the authenticity of science itself. Mere abstractness then is not a fatal objection to causal explanation. The point upon which everything turns is the extent to which in any particular instance a concrete effect may be intelligibly attributed to an abstract cause. Whitehead's statement of the causal principle is in these words: "The origin of the concept of causation (in this application of the term) is now manifest. It is that of the part explaining the whole—or, avoiding this untechnical use of 'part' and 'whole,' it is that of some explaining all."[63] But this is not enough. Before the principle can be accepted, it is necessary to be more specific, and to state exactly *which* "all" and *which* "some" can be considered as standing in the relation of effect to cause. Now the answer to this question, it seems to me, is fatal to the whole contention.

It will be remembered that the purpose of this inquiry is to explain the objects of *sensory* and *perceptual* experience. In the last resort, then, these must be the effects which Whitehead designates the "whole" and "all." But if the argument proves anything, it

---

[59] *P.K.*, Chap. XVI on Causal Components.

[60] *P.K.*, pp. 188-9.

[61] *C.N.*, p. 171.

[62] ". . . The abstractions of science are entities which are truly in nature, though they have no meaning in isolation from nature." *C.N.*, p. 173.

[63] *P.K.*, p. 187.

proves that the ultimate scientific objects, the electrons and pro- tons (or, as we should say now, positrons) cannot be considered as furnishing the causal components of anything so remote from them in character as perceptual and sensory objects.[64] The relation of "some" and "all," "part" and "whole," "abstract" and "con- crete" does not accurately denote the relation of electronic events to colours or to things combining colour with other sensory properties.

This can be shown in different ways. For example, by inverting the method of extensive abstraction, which thereby becomes the method of extensive concretion, we reunite the spatial and tem- poral factors which the former method has separated, and thus obtain four-dimensional entities in space-time. But the method of concretion entirely fails to suggest a principle whereby its products acquire a sensory, as distinct from a purely formal (that is, a mathematical or logical) character.

Again, if y and z are two separate sense-objects (for example, a specific red and a specific green), we cannot be said to have dis- covered the cause of either if the active conditioning event is the same for each—if, that is to say, the *difference* between y and z is not in any way accounted for. But this is precisely what happens in certain cases when we attempt to explain perceptual objects by reference to scientific. One and the same set of electronic events becomes the cause of red, if the percipient is a person with normal vision, and the cause of green, if the percipient is colour-blind. From this it appears that the causal influence of these electronic events extends only to the spatio-temporal or mathematical prop- erties of the object. For the cause of the *sensory* properties we must look to the percipient event and perhaps to the percipient object as well. It is in the event as qualified by the fact of percipience, rather than in the event as qualified by the character of the "scientific object," that we find the cause of difference.

A more thorough scrutiny of the problem, however, reveals difficulties which go far beyond the mere *application* of the relevant conceptions, and affect the *validity* of the conceptions themselves. These difficulties may be summarized as follows:

---

[64] The point of my criticism is not that effects should resemble their causes, but that the specific respect in which colours (for example) differ from electrons, etc., is not represented by the distinction of *concrete* and *abstract*, *all* and *some*.

*For a "Bifurcation" Which Was Only a Challenge to Further
Thought, Whitehead Substitutes One That Is Irresolvable*

18. (a) As soon as we attempt to obtain an exact view of the
factors involved, causal explanation, in accordance with Whitehead's principles, is seen to be invalidated by the very defect which
he is most anxious to avoid. What we try to explain causally by
referring it to active conditioning events is the manifold of sensory
and perceptual objects which constitutes the natural world. This
statement, however, is not sufficiently explicit. Strictly speaking,
we have no right to assume that objects *as such* are causally determined at all. Objects are by nature (perhaps I should say, by
definition) eternal, according to Whitehead, and therefore, like the
Platonic ideas, neither call for nor admit of a causal explanation.
Indeed it would be the height of paradox to refer them in such a
connection to *events*: it would be to explain the intrinsically permanent by the intrinsically transient. It may further be taken for
granted that for reasons which are the reverse of those just stated
it would be absurd to think of events *as caused*. Events *qua* events
are, according to Whitehead, unique and individual. They happen
once and for all. But causality implies the recurrence of a common
character.[65] When we explain any phenomenon by reference to its
cause, the assumption is that there are other phenomena which resemble the former in certain significant respects. The causal explanation, therefore, begins by relegating the phenomenon to a
class based upon community of nature. From this, and from the
fact that *events* cannot conform to the conditions implied, it follows
that there can be no causal explanation of an event as conceived
by Whitehead.

In so far as the conception of causal relationship is at all possible,
it can only be by reformulating the problem of causal explanation.
This we may do as follows. When we resort to such a mode of
thought, what we seek to explain is not how certain objects come
to be the objects, and certain events the events, they are (in all
strictness objects never *come to be*, and events never *are*), but how
the objects we recognize in experience come to be situated in the
events we experience in apprehension. Now I do not say this is an
impossible procedure. Indeed I gladly acknowledge the extreme

---

[65] This is so, of course, even in theories which, like those of Hume and J. S. Mill,
admit the complete irrationality of causal connection.

freshness and suggestiveness inherent in Whitehead's method of stating the problem. But it cannot be denied that the method is seriously jeopardized from the outset by certain negations implicit in the concepts employed. Objects and events are conceived in negative relation to one another; and in so far as they embody the fundamental notions in the interpretation of nature, that interpretation begins with a duality which we do nothing to overcome by representing objects as *situated* in events and events as *occupied* by objects. The duality in fact is identical with that of essence and existence in Santayana's system; and the objections to the latter apply with equal force to Whitehead's philosophy of nature.

It is interesting to note that Whitehead is not at all behind Santayana in acknowledging this duality, and in pointing out the positive antagonism of the antithetical elements in his doctrine. In a paragraph headed "Duality of Nature" he writes: "There are two sides to nature, as it were, antagonistic the one to the other, and yet each essential. The one side is development in creative advance, the essential becomingness of nature. The other side is the permanence of things, the fact that nature can be recognized. Thus nature is always a newness relating to objects which are neither new nor old."[66]

We are thus forced to the conclusion that in attempting to avoid the fallacy of bifurcation by bringing the world of physics and the world of perceptual experience together on a purely naturalistic or non-subjective basis, Whitehead has merely succeeded in giving the offence a new form, and one which unfortunately invades the scientific explanation of nature as such. In place of an initial duality of actual perception and scientific thought—a duality which is no more than problematical, a challenge to further thinking—we have a duality which is admittedly fundamental and irresolvable, and which therefore leads to scientific dualism.

Some Inconvenient Corollaries of Whitehead's Distinction Between Object and Event

19. (b) The effects of this initial error come to light in two trains of thought which everywhere run counter to one another. On the one hand there is the train represented by the passage that has

[66] *P.K.*, p. 98, §26.1.

just been quoted. Object and event are diametrically opposed in character, and must not be confused.[67] In other passages they are so closely integrated that each depends on each for all that can be known or said of it. Let us take the two points of view in turn.

i. The difference between objects and events is so radical that it may be expressed as a difference in the modes of experience itself. Objects are experienced in the sense that they are recognized by the intellect;[68] whereas "events are lived through. . . . They are the medium within which our physical experience develops, or rather, they are themselves the development of that experience."[69] It should be noted that in the very process of bringing out the distinction of objects and events the distinction between *the event experienced* and *the experience of the event* is almost completely obliterated. Thus while Whitehead fully admits the difference between the experience which is the intellectual recognition of an object and the experience which is the empirical apprehension of an event, he allows the difference between the kind of event which we experience as a natural occurrence and the kind of event which is itself an experience of the latter to remain in obscurity.

ii. When it becomes necessary to emphasize the opposite side of the truth—the integration of event and object—serious difficulties arise. We are told that "there is no apprehension of external events apart from recognitions of sense-objects as related to them, and there is no recognition of sense-objects except as in relation to external events."[70] Again: "The apprehension of an event as the situation of a physical object is our most complete perception of the character of an event. It represents a fundamental perception of a primary law of nature. It is solely by means of physical objects that our knowledge of events as active conditions is obtained, whether as generating conditions or as transmitting conditions."[71]

Now it is undoubtedly true that a knowledge of the unique and transitory (that which never repeats itself) is rendered possible by the element of universality (that which does not pass). This is a principle of all knowability. But the principle is rendered inapplicable when the transient and the permanent are defined, as they

---

[67] *P.K.*, pp. 64-5.
[68] *P.K.*, p. 64, §15.3.
[69] *P.K.*, p. 63.
[70] *P.K.*, p. 83.
[71] *P.K.*, p. 90, §24.6.

are by Whitehead, in negative terms of one another, and when the events and the objects which embody them are represented as completely separate entities, constituting a fundamental and irresolvable duality in nature. So long as this is so, it is very difficult to attach a clear and definite meaning to the ideas of "situation" and "occupation." Not that these ideas are impossible in themselves. On the contrary they are supported by the whole trend of scientific thought in recent times. But in order to substantiate them upon theoretical grounds we must go back to our presuppositions, and modify the concept of each by relating it in a new and positive way to that of the other. The theoretical needs of the case would be met if it could be shown that the character of objectivity is attributable to events and that of temporality to objects. These conditions in turn are realizable if the essence of objectivity is not timelessness, but a relation to conscious processes—provided that relation is such that it comes and goes with the latter. Thus, events will be objects if anyone is conscious of them: they will have the definitory character of objectivity in so far as they are possible objects of experience in any of its aspects, cognitive, conative or affective. Conversely, objects will be events, or at least the time-conditioned functions of events, in so far as the relation involved is sustained by processes some of which are internal to the mind of the observer, and others characteristic of the external world. Once more, of course, this view implies the duality of nature and mind, and such complete redistribution of all the factors in the case as is necessitated by this duality.

How Can Sense-Objects Be Eternal?

20. (c) The distinction of object and event, as formulated by Whitehead, leads to certain collocations, under one head or the other, which are hardly less surprising than the collocation of entities in Santayana's realm of essences. That sense-objects like red or blue and scientific objects like electrons should appear together in the class of entities characterized by permanence or eternity is much too startling an innovation upon traditional modes of thought to be accepted on any but the most conclusive grounds. As a matter of fact, the principal ground upon which this strange collocation is made to rest resolves itself into the same distinction of event and object which we have just seen reason to

reject. The conception of a permanent character or eternal object, whether in the sensory realm or in that of science, is arrived at by an act of thought whereby we distinguish the *content* from the *instance*. A particular shade of red, for example, is an eternal object: every actual existence of it is an event. Symbolically expressed, the instances are a, a', a'', etc., the object is A. The former we experience or *live through* in an act of apprehension: the latter we recognize. Are these distinctions real? Is it possible to maintain them to the end?

On Whitehead's own admission we have no means of knowing a, a' and a'' except in so far as we recognize A in each of them. But if the recognition of A is all that is meant by the apprehension of a, a' and a'', it is difficult to see how any one of these events, as it reveals itself to us in experience, can differ from any other. Presumably then we must revise our statement in such a way as to allow for the difference between recognizing A in a and recognizing A in a' or a''. In other words, we must find a formula which will enable us to express the difference between a, a' and a'' as that between three separate instances of one and the same recognizable character. In terms of our symbolism, this means that the events in question, in so far as we have experience of them, are not a, a' and a'', but the a instance of A, the a' instance of A, and the a'' instance of A—or, more briefly, aA, $a'A$ and $a''A$. But in so far as event and object are still by definition fundamentally opposite in nature, the example given breaks up once more into three events and one object. And since all that is recognizable in an event is the object situated in it—since, that is to say, the object is the factor which enables us to identify the event, it is difficult to understand how in the case before us one event can be *recognizably different* from another.

It may be said that when different events supply a varying situation to a uniform object, they articulate themselves not by reference to the single object which we recognize in each of them, but by reference to features which are not thus uniform, and which, though not recognized, are still apprehensible in consciousness. Every event, in addition to the object which it shares with the other events, has a context that is exclusively its own. The only result of this mode of reasoning, however, is to drive the wedge still deeper between object and event. Everything must fall on one side or the other of a dividing line, which is absolutely fixed; and from this conclusion there is no escape so long as events are all *otherness* and objects all *sameness*.

As a matter of fact this extreme antithetical view of the difference in question seems irreconcilable with much that is valuable in Whitehead's theory. Events do not merely succeed one another in time: they do not merely define themselves *against* one another in virtue of their character of successiveness. They *enclose* one another, so that every event is related to some events as whole to part and to others as part to whole.[72] Moreover even in their succession they overlap,[73] and in view of this it is obvious that for every event there must be another which is all but identical with the former, the element of difference being infinitesimal. Thus the character of mutual exclusiveness, which is due to succession, is modified by the community of extension which is implied in the enclosure of one event by another.

And How Can They Have the Sameness Which Whitehead Must Attribute to Them?

21. As for the "sameness" which Whitehead ascribes to sense-objects, it will be admitted that there is something highly problematical in this. Of course if by "sameness" Whitehead means "self-identity in a single situation," there need be no difficulty over the concept. But it is not in this sense that we usually employ the word "same." Indeed *diversity* of situation is precisely what is needed to convert the conception of mere *identity* into the proper sense of *sameness*. But it is doubtful whether sameness in this sense is ever realized in sensory experience.

So far as primary recognition is concerned, we can say* without hesitation that the object (in some instances at least) may have about it a certain definiteness of self-identity.[74] It is what it is (this colour or that sound, and no other); and when the percipient event which enables it to emerge for a moment as an identifiable object

---

[72] "If an event *A* extends over an event *B*, then *B* is 'part of' *A*, and *A* is a 'whole' of which *B* is a part." *C.N.*, p. 75.

[73] This is among the new possibilities for which provision is made in *Process and Reality*, where Whitehead substitutes the more general conception of "extensive connection" for that of "extensive abstraction."

[*So it stands in the manuscript. The sense requires "we may admit. . . ."—Ed.]

[74] It is necessary to exercise some verbal caution here in view of the vagueness which may characterize *any* sensory experience, and which usually does characterize certain types of sensation—the kinaesthetic and the organic, for example.

has passed away, it does not lose its identity in that of something else, but is definitely displaced by a successor. Indeed there is a sense in which nothing that has ever been can ever lose its identity. But in this sense, which may be trivial in the extreme, and which is significant only from the standpoint of abstract logic,[75] the event which is its *situation*, and the percipient event as well, continue for all time to be the *events* they originally were. In any other sense than this it is in the highest degree questionable whether a sense-object, as actually given, can be said to retain its identity through a variety of occasions.

It would certainly be taking a great deal for granted to assume that the shade of red which we think we recognize (and do recognize for all practical purposes) as identical* with the shade which furnished its object to the first act of recognition is in the most absolute and unqualified sense one with the latter. What is most unmistakably true of the sensa is the fact that of all possible objects of cognition they are the most completely determined by the conditions, subjective and objective (but in either case transitory and occasional) which render them perceptible. On Whitehead's theory these conditions, which are a tangle of events, are in each instance unique and irrevocable; and the closeness of the integration that binds the object to its successive situations throws suspicion upon the act of mind which recognizes in the object, as presented for the second time, the identical object† which was presented at the first. Identification of course there is, and therefore identity; but the question remains whether the identity is that of the object considered in and for itself, and apart altogether from the nexus of circumstance in which it is enveloped. Is it really ever possible to assert with perfect confidence: "This is the identical shade of red which I saw yesterday?" And how could such a question ever be decided? Obviously only by comparing the object of yesterday's experience with the object of today's—that is to say, by comparing the object in one situation with the object in another. But situations are events; and events for Whitehead are never the same. In so far then as we *identify* the object as pre-

---

[75] It is part of my purpose to show that certain contents of experience, once they have become *past*, can acquire a new significance, and so a new identity, at a subsequent point of time.

[*"as identical," that is, "as *in ordinary parlance* identical."—Ed.]

[†"the identical object," that is, "the *literally* identical object."—Ed.]

sented for the second time, we must abstract each from the situation in which it occurs. In this case we do away with the comparison. For we cannot be said to compare objects which are in every respect identical. From this it appears (*a*) that we can establish identity only by comparison, and (*b*) that the act of comparison precludes completeness of identity.

22. Such embarrassments compel us to assume that there is something wrong with the presuppositions—in this case with the assumption that when we recognize an object of sense as *the same*, we are postulating an identity without difference. I would suggest that the source of the error is a wrong diagnosis of the primary act of recognition.

Primary recognition is presumably less simple than Whitehead's account of it would suggest. When I see a particular shade of red for the first time, I experience a sensory awareness of the object. But I cannot in any significant sense be said to *recognize* the latter until the sensory awareness of it has been supplemented or *complicated* by an act of identification.[76] That is to say, there is posited an ideal entity—say, *X*—which is the *identity* of the object presented in experience. The relation of the object to its identity is not itself a relation of identity. Rather it is like the relation between an ectype and its archetype. The latter is an ideal which the former exemplifies; and as a number of ectypes may be struck from a single original, so a number of sensory objects may exemplify an identical ideal. The various copies may be indistinguishable to the senses; but the *fact* which this circumstance expresses need be no more than a high degree of resemblance. So of the second and third instances of a sense-object. Their identity with one another must not be interpreted to mean that in the various instances there is only one object which appears and reappears with the appropriate event. It is much safer to say that there is a distinct object for each successive situation, but that the objects resemble one another so closely that the ideal identity of any one may be made available for the interpretation of any other.

[76] I am not here postulating a distinct and *subsequent* act, but a complication in the original act. Whether such a thing as perception (perhaps I should say *sensation*) without identification is possible is a psychological question which need not trouble us here. The assumption is that of a sensory object having a well defined identity of its own. Identification may therefore be taken for granted.

To this way of putting things it will be objected that it separates the object from its identity, and therefore introduces two factors where, as in Whitehead's theory, one is sufficient. The truth is rather that it shows how alone any object can claim to have an identity of its own and at the same time attain to actuality in a particular instance. In Whitehead's theory this particular patch of Cambridge blue is an event; this particular shade is an eternal object. My suggestion is that the shade and the instance are so completely integrated that I cannot recognize the former except as the shade *of the latter*. The blue is the cognizable content of the event which is its actual appearance in the flux of nature. This statement applies to the sensory awareness of the object taken in its immediacy as a particular presentation. My contention, however, is that when I *recognize* the presented object (even if the recognition is primary) as *this particular shade*, I have passed beyond the stage of sensory awareness as such. What I recognize is a universal element of which there may be other instances; and it is with the universal or ideal shade that I now identify the individual example.

A complete analysis of the situation would involve the following propositions: (i) There is a sensory awareness of this particular blue. (ii) The blue may therefore be identified with the object of awareness: it is that of which for the time being *I am aware*. But (iii) it is not so that I consciously identify the objects of my sensory experience. I identify them by considering their relation not to my momentary states of consciousness, but to one another in a universe of objects. In the case of colour any particular shade acquires the identity by which I recognize it through the position it occupies in a general scheme of colours. I recognize it as an instance of this particular shade. Thus (iv) the conceptions of object and instance acquire a certain complexity which in Whitehead's doctrine they do not possess. It is not merely a case of this unique and eternal object appearing and reappearing in a variety of unique and transitory situations or instances. Every situation has an object of its own—the immediate object of sensory awareness as such; and each of these objects is an instance of the eternal object which it serves to symbolize in human experience. In brief, between the eternal object and its situation-instance we must interpolate the object-instance, the immediate object of sense. It is through the latter that the "object" and the "event" combine.

Are Scientific Objects Eternal?

23. Passing now to scientific objects, I have already remarked how strange it is to find these figuring along with objects of sense in the general class of the eternal. Once more the source of the difficulty is to be found in the distinction which Whitehead draws between object and event. As a matter of fact in this case the distinction is very badly sustained. For example, molecules and electrons are both described as scientific objects; but they are not objects in precisely the same sense. The electron is the ultimate scientific object. That is to say, it is the simplest permanent character by which the event it occupies can at present be known. "Such ultimate scientific objects," says Whitehead, "embody what is ultimately permanent in nature."[77] They are "the objects whose relations in events are the unanalysable expression of the order of nature." The molecule is relatively complex. It is so in the sense that the character which it embodies requires for its expression a certain "rhythmic repetition" in the event which it occupies. ". . . The recognition in perception [of the objects corresponding in sensory experience to the scientific objects of which the electron is the simplest] requires the recurrence of the ways in which events pass. This involves the rhythmic repetition of the characters of events. This permanence of rhythmic repetition is the essential character of molecules, which are complex scientific objects. There is no such thing as a molecule at an instant. A molecule requires a minimum of duration in which to display its character."[78]

Now it seems to me that in view of these admissions there is something artificial and unreal in the conception of the molecule as an eternal object. Suppose, for example, that X is one duration and Y another. The contents of these durations are rhythmical processes, of which the elements are, in the first case a, b, c, and in the second a', b', c', the rhythm R being identical. R then is the identical molecule which occurs in the processes X (abc) and Y ($a'b'c'$). But when we consider the facts of which these formulae are the descriptions, would it not be more natural to identify the molecule with the event which exhibits this uniformity of rhythm rather than with the rhythm incidental to the event? An object which is so closely integrated with an event that it requires a

[77] *P.K.*, p. 98.
[78] *P.K.*, pp. 98-9.

specific duration for its actualization is surely best construed as a feature in the actualization itself.[79]

Although on somewhat different grounds, a similar conclusion would seem to apply to the case of the electron. Certainly in view of all that science has to tell us of the latter, it is difficult to conceive the electron in terms of anything but its own activity. If, as we are still for certain purposes entitled to do, we accept Bohr's model of the atom as a planetary system, no other conception seems possible but that of a circular movement round a nucleus; and if this quasi-pictorial representation is rejected as inadequate, the alternative would seem to be along the lines of Schrödinger's theory, in which the electron appears as a wave or as a centre of influence pervading the physical universe, and expressing itself in modifications of all that is going on throughout the system. It is very difficult to think of such modifications as induced by an entity defined in terms of permanence and unchangeability—indeed by anything short of an *agent*. A similar difficulty occurs if we consider the electron from the opposite point of view as itself subject to variation—as when, for example, under the influence of radiation, it "jumps" an orbit. A permanent character as such neither produces changes nor is itself susceptible of any. And indeed Whitehead's language at points suggests that he is alive to this aspect of the case. "Thus," he says, "in an event unoccupied by it an electron is discerned only as an agent[80] modifying the character of that event; whereas in an event occupied by it the electron is discerned as itself acted on, namely the character of that

[79] This is partly conceded by Whitehead in the concluding chapter of *P.K.*, where he deals with rhythms in relation to life. "Now a rhythm is recognizable and is so far an object. But it is more than an object; for it is an object formed of other objects interwoven upon the background of essential change. A rhythm involves a pattern and to that extent is always self-identical. But no rhythm can be a mere pattern; for the rhythmic quality depends equally upon the differences involved in each exhibition of the pattern. The essence of rhythm is the fusion of sameness and novelty," etc. *P.K.*, p. 198, §64.7.

[80] Whitehead has defined agency as "nothing else than relations between those entities which are among the ultimate data of science." On this I would remark (i) that while there may be conclusive reasons of a scientific nature for substituting the concept of relations for the concept of agency, it is difficult to see how the latter can be *identified* with relations; and (ii) that the relations in question have surely to do with *changes* that are going on everywhere, and not with the timeless forms that are assumed to characterize these changes. Thus in the passage before us it is stated that the electron modifies an *event* which it does not occupy. How can this be interpreted as a statement about the relation between changeless entities?

event governs the fate of the electron."[81] Surely an entity defined in terms of changelessness cannot be thought of as "acted upon" or as having a "fate."

The Reorientation We Propose

24. On all of these grounds it seems better to replace the conception of scientific objects by that of scientific (or, as I prefer to say, *physical*) events; and this is the first step in a process of simplification which extends to all the factors with which we have been dealing.

Thus the electronic events into which the physicist resolves the whole of the natural world will represent what I shall call the ultimately and absolutely physical—reality itself in that aspect which remains over when we abstract every vestige of anything that owes its existence to the presence of percipient organisms. From this point of view nature is a system of electrical events. To be such an event in space and time is the primary character of all modes of existence which are interpretable in terms of the purely physical. But the physical, thus defined, acquires the secondary character of the objective in so far as the events become the objects of scientific investigation. The reverse is the case with the data of sensory experience. The sensa may best be considered as primarily objects of consciousness; but they take their place in a world of physical events in virtue of the fact that they are conditioned by events, some of which are physical. It is my contention, already set forth tentatively, that the formula which expresses their ontological character is that which would represent them as functions of the physical in conjunction with the subjective conditions of perceptibility. By an extension of the same line of thought "perceptual" and "physical" objects (should the distinction be found of any significance) might be explained as functions of the same two ultimates—the physical and the subjective—where the conditions are more complex. The presupposition is once more a complete reorientation designed to bring the subjective factor into prominence as the ontological correlate of the purely physical mode of being.[82]

[81] *P.K.*, p. 97.

[82] It will be seen that my conception of physical events and of their functions is made to cover all that Whitehead includes under the headings of "sense-objects," "perceptual objects," "physical objects" and "scientific objects." The last-mentioned I

25. (d) After the amount of thought that has been devoted to the distinction of object and event, it is unnecessary to dwell at length upon the difficulty, incidental to the distinction as formulated by Whitehead, of explaining how the eternal objects come to characterize the events of nature. The crux of the difficulty is that the eternal object, which is timeless and changeless,[83] must somehow be thought of as repeating itself with each successive event of which it is the character. From another point of view it is the difficulty of seeing how events, whose nature it is to pass, can be characterized by objects, which by definition do not pass. The expression Whitehead uses to designate the strange conjunction is "ingression." But the term does not help us much. The word "ingression" suggests a process or movement whereby the eternal object invades the passing event and adds a meaning of its own to the meaning of the latter. But clearly no such movement occurs. So far as the eternal object is concerned, nothing ever *happens*. The ingression of the object is therefore not a vicissitude of the latter. Nor can it be construed as an event in the world of events, or as part of the event which sustains the ingression. Objects are the character which events contract while they transpire; but that character is not conveyed to or from them in any of the ways by which the events themselves come about and pass away.[84] By the term "ingression," therefore, we are to understand something highly abstract—what it means that an object or permanent character should be situated in an event, or what it means that an event should have a permanent character[85]—in brief, the relation between events and objects. "You may have noticed," writes Whitehead, "that I am using the term 'ingression' to denote the general relation of objects to events. The ingression of an object

identify with physical events, all the others with functions of these events under varying conditions. For the question of the existence of objects in a definitely physical mode *vid.* Appendix A to this chapter, p. 130.

[83] I ought in fairness to point out that Whitehead would not accept this characterization of objects. His theory permits us to speak of objects, but not of events, as changing. *P.K.*, p. 63. The point is really a verbal one. Objects change, but only in the sense that they are variously related to passing events. In themselves they are not subject to alteration. "On the other hand events do not change because change is the very essence of what events are. Moreover every event is irrevocably what it is. . . . Change in objects," Whitehead adds, "is no derogation from their permanence, and expresses their relation to the passage of events; whereas events are neither permanent nor do they change." *loc. cit.*

[84] *vid.* Appendix B, p. 133.

[85] i.e. a character which is identifiable as a universal.

into an event is the way the character of the event shapes itself in virtue of the being of the object. Namely the event is what it is, because the object is what it is;[86] and when I am thinking of this modification of the event by the object, I call the relation between the two 'the ingression of the object into the event'."[87] This is apparently to assert, what no one will dispute, that the events of nature are functions of nature's laws; but the truth of the proposition is obscured rather than clarified by the use of an expression which almost irresistibly suggests a passage out of the eternal into the time-conditioned manifold.

The Percipient Event

26. (e) A final criticism has to do with the part played by the percipient event and its correlate the percipient object. The impression these concepts convey is that of a somewhat hesitating and altogether inadequate admission that the concept of natural events with objects situated in them is insufficient to account for the world of sensory and perceptual experience. The doctrine of percipient events is an extreme example of what was said about the obscuration of the distinction of subjective and physical in contemporary philosophy. Indeed the conception owes whatever force it possesses to this obscuration. Its workability in Whitehead's system depends upon an oscillation of thought, whereby physiological processes are interpreted in terms of psychical states and psychical states in terms of physiological processes.

The starting-point is Whitehead's assumption that nature is knowable as a system of sensory objects. It is ultimately with these that we have to do; and if we are to avoid the fallacy of bifurcation, we must be careful not to formulate our problem as if the aim in view were to explain how a physical reality outside the mind can cause sensory impressions of itself to arise within consciousness. "Nature is nothing else than the deliverances of sense-awareness.

---

[86] Another way of saying that events are functions of objects. This will hold in some cases. In others I prefer to think of objects as functions of events taken in conjunction with certain conditions. What science, as I understand it, does is to remove the accompanying conditions (e.g., the sensitiveness of a percipient organism) and with the latter the character which the events contract in this conjunction. The residue is an actually existing world of physical events.

[87] C.N., p. 144.

We have no principles whatever to tell us what could stimulate mind towards sense-awareness."[88]

Such being the case, we must limit ourselves to the observation of what goes on in nature, of the characters which qualify the events we thus apprehend, and of the relations which obtain between the characters. "Our sole task is to exhibit in one system the characters and interrelations of all that is observed. Our attitude towards nature is purely 'behaviouristic,' so far as concerns the formulation of physical concepts."[89] In so far then as the fact of percipience must be taken into account, it must be treated like any other fact. That is to say, it is an event among events: it belongs to the system of nature; and just as in the external world events are characterized by the recognizable permanences which Whitehead calls objects, so it is in the world of percipient events. Hence the conception of the percipient object.

The problem before us is to ascertain how exactly the percipient event, with the associated object, comes into the general scheme of things. We must ask: What is the relation between nature as a whole and those elements of nature which we are here calling "percipient events"?

The outstanding truth about the natural world—the truth to which all our observations and all our comments must be adjusted —is that nature reveals itself to our experience as in a state of "activity" or "passage." "This passage of nature—or, in other words, its creative advance—is its fundamental characteristic."[90] We observe events or "active entities" which are "chunks in the life of nature."[91] Creative advance is therefore the very essence of what *existence* in the natural world connotes. It is within a system so conceived that a place must be found for percipient events; and the place assigned them is in the forefront of the movement. ". . . Perception," we read, "is always at the utmost point of creation."[92] As an event it is "here and now"; and this fact serves further to define its relation to the rest of nature. The characteristic of perceptual experience is the compresence of the "here

[88] *C.N.*, p. 185.
[89] *loc. cit.*
[90] *P.K.*, p. 14.
[91] *C.N.*, p. 185.
[92] *P.K,.* p. 14.

and now" with another event which is the world around us characterized as "there and now."[93]

So much may be granted. What we mean by perception certainly includes the awareness of another, caught in the advancing stream of events; and this awareness is itself part of the general advance.[94] The relation between the percipient advance and the advance of external nature is obviously therefore a fact of importance for the interpretation of the percipient event. But how exactly the relation is to be conceived is another question.

27. The striking thing about Whitehead's account is that while on the one hand he speaks as if we were dealing with two sets of events transpiring concurrently in the total system of nature,[95] on the other hand he keeps interpreting one set of these events in the light of a concept which is entirely absent from the other—the concept of knowledge. If we call the two series the a and the β series respectively, the former is the succession of events that constitutes the natural world of scientific investigation. Now we have seen that at the very beginning of his inquiry he expressly excludes the perceptions of the observer from among the data of such inquiry. Natural science, we are told, although "it is concerned with nature which is the terminus of sense-perception," "is not concerned with the sense-awareness itself."[96] But now, by including percipient events within the general concept of nature, Whitehead is entangled in the very procedure which he is anxious to avoid. If it were possible to treat these events without reference to that sense-awareness which is their essential character, or if it were possible to treat sense-awareness as nothing but a sequence of natural events (physiological changes, for example), the difficulties which arise at this point might have been averted; and indeed the second of the two courses suggested seems to represent the procedure which Whitehead has mostly in view. But to carry out this procedure consistently would be to imperil the concept of nature in that aspect which includes sensory and perceptual objects as genuine permanent characters in the flux of events.

---

[93] *loc. cit.*

[94] I attach great value to what Whitehead says about the "here *and now*." As we shall see, the distinction of past, present and future becomes applicable to the time of external events only through the identification of present time with that of percipience.

[95] *P.K.*, pp. 82-3, §22.3.

[96] *C.N.*, p. 4.

The following are the relevant points. (i) The existence of *mind* is frankly recognized in various contexts. For one thing it is the locus of science.[97] For another, it is to be identified with the percipient, but not with the percipient event.[98] That is to say, it is the mind that perceives. (ii) The mind's percipience takes the form of sensory awareness or "perceptual knowledge,"[99] a process in which "recollection and memory are the chief agents in producing a clear consciousness of a sense-object."[100] (iii) The "percipient event" must be sharply distinguished from the activity of sense-awareness and from knowledge. Sense-awareness is an act of mind: the percipient event is variously identified with the life of the body, a bodily state or the body itself. As such it belongs to the realm of nature.[101] (iv) The relation of inclusion within the natural world is not the only significant relation in which we find the percipient event. The latter is also related to the mind's awareness,[102] and in this connection it is described as "the medium relating [the mind of the observer] to the whole of nature."[103]

Of the various factors so far mentioned Whitehead is concerned (at least in the two works with which we have been dealing) only with percipient events. Mind and its awareness play no appreciable rôle in an inquiry devoted to the nature of the outer world, and conceived from the standpoint of what our author calls "homogeneous" thinking about nature.[104] To all of this no exception need be taken; but when we consider the actual part played by the percipient event, the clarity of Whitehead's exposition begins to be overclouded by a certain disturbing ambiguity. This can best be

[97] "Science is in the minds of men." *P.K.*, p. 10.

[98] "This event is not the mind, that is to say, not the percipient." *C.N.*, p. 107. From this it appears that Whitehead has evaded the necessity to which other thinkers (e.g., William James in the *Principles of Psychology*, *passim*) have succumbed, of having to represent mental states—here percipient events—as the subjects of other mental states—the percipient or knower.

[99] "Perception is an awareness of events, or happenings, forming a partially discerned complex within the background of a simultaneous whole of Nature." *P.K.*, p. 68.

[100] *P.K.*, p. 84. What Whitehead has in mind is that in primary recognition "the sense-object and the event do not clearly disentangle themselves."

[101] "This percipient event is roughly speaking the bodily life of the incarnate mind." *C.N.*, p. 107. The word "roughly" is explained as meaning that "the functions of the body shade off into those of other events in nature." Again: "The percipient event is the relevant bodily state of the observer." *C.N.*, p. 152. cf. pp. 154, 187.

[102] *P.K.*, p. 68.

[103] *P.K.*, p. 80.

[104] "What I mean is that we can think about nature without thinking about thought." *C.N.*, p. 3.

brought out by viewing the percipient event from the standpoint of the percipient object.

Formally speaking the latter is and can be nothing but the permanent character which we recognize in the percipient event—that is to say, the uniformity discernible in a flux of physiological process. The life of the body is an event or a chain of events, and like the external events which constitute the "life" of nature, it reports itself to our observation in the light of its own fixed principles or laws. These are the characters which do not pass, as the body itself passes, from one phase of its existence to another. Now while empirical investigation has revealed a certain correlation between the uniformly operating principles of the physiological life and the conscious states of mind, this fact is one which has no bearing on the interpretation of the natural world as such. The percipient event belongs to the realm of nature, and a place must be found for it in the latter. But the correlation with awareness is not among the facts which admit of treatment within the limits of our "homogeneous" thinking about nature. And yet there is evidence that for certain purposes Whitehead does make use of this correlation in an inquiry from which it should have been excluded. In defining the percipient object, for example, he most surprisingly abandons the physiological for the psychological point of view. "The percipient event is discerned as the locus of a recognizable permanence which is the 'percipient object.' This object is the unity of the awareness whose recognition leads to the classification of a train of percipient events as the natural life associated with one consciousness. . . . Owing to the temporal duration of the immediate present the self-knowledge of the percipient object is a knowledge of the unity of the consciousness within other parts of the immediate present."[105]

Thus the permanent character of bodily functions, the "quality" which gives a living organism its identity as *one*, is the unity of the mental processes—something which, on Whitehead's own account of it, rather suggests the Kantian unity of mind, the "I think" which accompanies all our representations.[106] Conversely the unity

[105] *P.K.*, p. 83.

[106] Except that the unity of mind, as I understand it, is not that of a timeless principle, whether the Kantian "I think" or the "object" of Whitehead, the view I intend to advocate is not badly expressed by the first part of the above sentence. In brief I shall present the phenomenon of life as a function of subjectivity in a physical structure. My

of mind differentiates itself (in a way quite alien to the Kantian conception) into a succession of events which are not mental, but physiological processes. The source of the error is a failure to apply the concepts of object and event with sufficient rigour. If the life of the body is a series of physiological events, the corresponding object can be no other than the principles or uniformities of physiological being. If there is an object* which is the unity of *consciousness*, the events in which that object is situated must be passing states of consciousness. To correlate the living body as an event with the mind as the permanent character of that event is to obliterate the distinction between the mental and the physical—a distinction which Whitehead by implication recognizes in so far as he begins by excluding mind from the investigation.[107]

28. Even so, from the standpoint of a naturalistic theory, there would be no great harm done if the interpretation of mind and body in terms of one another were not permitted to affect the doctrine of nature at critical points. Unfortunately the influence of this confusion is manifest in ways that are far from incidental and unimportant. For example, the natural world, which it is the business of science to explain, reveals itself to us as a manifold of sensory and perceptual objects. These are determined by their active conditioning events in the external world, but only upon the added condition that the appropriate percipient event is forthcoming. The percipient event must therefore cooperate with the external event in the genesis of those sense-objects which are the content of nature. Now when we look closely at this notion, we see that everything depends upon what exactly is meant by a percipient event. The physiological processes which have to do with sensory experience cannot in themselves throw any light upon the question as to how that experience is generated. What we know is that vibratory motions are transmitted from external objects to the body, and are there received and propagated inwards to a central organ evolved by nature for their reception. But the *fact* involved is merely the propagation of a movement from one medium to another. The series of events is somewhat analogous to

quarrel with Whitehead has to do not with his conclusion as to the relation of mind to the living body, but with his premisses.

[*"An object," apparently in deference to W.'s way of speaking. One thinks, of course, of the subject.—Ed.]

107 He quite rightly remarks that "this discussion of the percipient object leads us beyond the scope of this enquiry." *P.K.*, p. 83; cf. p. 195.

that which occurs when the wind imparts a motion to the sea, or when the ocean swell is prolonged in the ripples of some inland creek. In a word, so long as our attention is confined to the outer event and the repercussions of the latter in the living organism, we are still thinking about nature homogeneously. But there is no place in such homogeneous thinking for the data of sense as these reveal themselves to our experience in the form of colours and sounds, or as the qualities which we call hot and cold, hard and soft, rough and smooth, sweet and bitter. These qualities (or at least some of them) are, as we have seen, located by Whitehead in the outer world of external events. It is these events that provide the situations for the sense-objects. But they do not do so except through the mediation of the percipient event. As a bodily process, however, this event belongs to the same outer order of nature to which the "external" events belong, and as such it furnishes no key to the mysterious fact that vibratory movements in a medium devoid of sensory properties should acquire these properties through other vibratory movements in the living body. And in the absence of any light from this quarter, it is difficult to maintain the conception of sense-objects as *situated* in external events except in the sense that they are *objects of consciousness persisting in time*. In other words, they are objects which are also events and events which are also objects.[108]

That Whitehead thinks of them as situated in external events through some relation in which they stand to percipient events suggests that he is trying to accommodate an unmistakable fact of experience to the exigencies of his theory. The fact in question is that sense-objects *are perceived*, and that they are perceived as *outside the body*. That is to say, they are not experienced as physiological processes. It is therefore natural to think of them as having external situation, as being *there* rather than *here*. But to argue that their externality, their existence outside the body, is *conditioned* by the physiological processes that go on inside the body is surely unintelligible except on the assumption that there is more in the percipient event than mere physiological process. If such

---

[108] I need hardly point out that the word "object" is here employed in a sense quite different from that of Whitehead's usage, and connotes the correlate of conscious states.*

[*With this note, compare note 2, Appendix A, p. 131, below, and the full discussion in Chap. VIII.—Ed.]

process were all that is meant by such an event, then obviously we should have to invert Whitehead's conception, and argue that the percipient event is conditioned by the external, and not that the latter is in some way conditioned by the former. In order to give meaning to the contention that sensa are dependent upon a conjunction of the active conditioning event in the outer world and the percipient event in the living body, it is necessary to interpret the latter from the standpoint of its character as revealed not in the permanent qualities of physiological activity, but in the *percipient object*. That is to say, in so far as the percipient event is thought of as conditioning the permanent recurrences or recognizable character of events in the outer world, rather than as itself conditioned by such events, it is thought of as a mental function of percipience. Indeed it is only so that we have any right to represent it as a percipient event at all. Although therefore Whitehead denies that the discussion of the percipient object belongs to the inquiry into the principles of natural knowledge, he is really compelled to utilize the conception of this object in order to justify the use he makes of the percipient event.

Nature's "Creative Advance"

29. But this is not all. The concept of nature as an active movement or creative advance into the future is really unjustified except upon grounds which presuppose the interpretation of the percipient event in the light of its connection with the knowing process rather than as a mere physiological occurrence. This may be shown by an argument which involves the following steps:[109]

(i) Perceptual knowledge (in which I here include sensory awareness) is not the same thing as the percipient event, though it is rendered possible by the latter. (ii) The question must therefore be asked: What exactly is the form assumed by this perceptual knowledge, and how does it stand related to the percipient event? (iii) Whitehead's answer is that it "is always a knowledge of the relationship of the percipient event to something else in nature." This statement can hardly be taken at its face value. Surely when we are perceptually conscious of something in the world around us, what we perceive is not the relation between it and the physiological processes which go on in the sensory organs

---

[109] My statement is an attempt to arrange the matter of *P.K.*, p. 14, so as to bring out the implicit logic of the passage.

and elsewhere. Of all this the majority of men are blissfully un-
aware. The most that Whitehead can possibly have meant is that
our perceptual experience conveys a sense of the outwardness of its
own objects. A relation of externality is therefore implied; but it
would be too much to describe this relation as constituting what is
actually *known* in perception. (iv) The relation in question, however, appears to be more than a relation, for the knowledge of it
conveys a "sense of action." Thus Whitehead remarks: "The sense
of action is the direct knowledge of the percipient event as having
its very being in the formation of its natural relations. Knowledge
issues from this reciprocal insistence between this event and the
rest of nature, namely relations are perceived in the making and
because of the making." In other words, when we perceive something outside us, we feel that a relation *is being formed* or established between it and ourselves. We are aware of something *going
on here*, and also of the fact that nothing would be going on here
but for the relations between here and *there*. These relations are
therefore organic constituents of the percipient event; and that
event so far is nothing but their formation. Hence in relation to
our percipient events nature reveals itself to us as actively creative.[110]

In the passage before us Whitehead is trying to do two things.
He is trying (*a*) to prove the creative activity of nature, and (*b*) to
explain the nature of knowledge as determined by the solidarity of
the world in general with the percipient event. These two motives
are so interwoven in his statement that it is a matter of the
greatest difficulty to disentangle them. In fact they are not meant
to be disentangled; for in so far as they are taken separately, the
first proposition loses all force through abstraction from the second.
That is to say, if it were not for the fact that the interplay of the
living body and the environment produces a knowledge of both in
us, there would be no point in describing that interplay, and with

[110] The solidarity of the percipient event and the rest of nature is further elaborated
as follows. Nature as a whole assumes the character of a "now-present." But the "now-
present" "evidently refers to some relation; for 'now' is 'simultaneous with,' and
'present' is 'in the presence of' or 'presented to.' Thus 'now-present' refers to some relation between the duration and something else. This 'something else' is the event 'here-
present,' which is the definite connecting link between individual experienced knowledge and self-sufficient nature. The essential existence of the event 'here-present' is the
reason why perception is from within nature and is not an external survey. It is the
'percipient event.' The percipient event defines its associated duration, namely its
corresponding 'all nature'." *P.K.*, pp. 69-70.

it the part due to nature's external forces, as action, far less as creation.[111] For obviously the formation of a new relationship in a time-conditioned manifold of impersonal forces is not what we mean by action. And to describe the process by this term is merely to invest it in a mystical glamour. Physiological processes are just changes in the living body, and changes are events. As such, of course, they are not undetermined, but by adding the concept of determination to the concept of change we do not produce the concept of creative activity. Activity is the characteristic function of an agent, creation the characteristic function of a creator. In introducing knowledge as he does,[112] Whitehead is introducing activity in one of its most unmistakable forms; but it is the only form in which he has any right to interpret the notion of change as equivalent to that of action. Throughout his argument, therefore, the percipient event must be construed not merely as physiological change, but as physiological change sustaining, or sustained by, psychical process. It is only so that the former acquires the character of *activity*.

Unfortunately this construction is not possible in the simple and direct manner necessary for Whitehead's argument. By no possibility can "natural knowledge" be "exhibited" as "a self-knowledge enjoyed by an element of nature respecting its active relations with the whole of nature in its various aspects."[113] Natural knowledge, like every other form of knowledge, is the activity characteristic of a knower; and until the latter, the subject of an experience, has been demonstrated to be (what Locke thought it might possibly be) identical with the living body, it is pure dogmatism to assume identity.

30. Furthermore I venture to assert that the concept of knowledge cannot be made available for the purpose of validating the activist interpretation of nature, until justice has been done to what is most characteristic of knowledge itself—namely, the fact of consciousness. Consciousness is not, what it is so often assumed

---

[111] The principle involved is, I think, stated in *Process and Reality*. "It is the basis of any realistic philosophy, that in perception there is a disclosure of objectified data, which are known as having a community with the immediate experience for which they are data. This 'community' is a community of common activity involving mutual implication." *op. cit.*, p. 110.

[112] "The conception of knowledge as passive contemplation is too inadequate to meet the facts." *P.K.*, p. 14.

[113] *loc. cit.*

to be, a mere epiphenomenon or gratuity, something for which no place can be found within the framework of reality. Rather it is the most characteristic expression of spiritual energy—the only form of energy of which we have direct, because interior, experience. If the world-process as a whole is to be construed as activity and as a creative advance, it is to be expected that consciousness will play a central rôle in the exposition of that process. But in the great masterpiece in which Whitehead expounds his finished cosmology, *Process and Reality*, the contrary is the case. Throughout this work the writer seems to be labouring under what I can only describe as a constant *fear of consciousness*. He is never tired of warning us against the assumption that consciousness is a necessary ingredient in situations where we should be inclined to take it for granted. This is so, for example, in the case of feeling, which for Whitehead has a physical as well as a mental form, and, generally speaking, of experience as a whole.[114] To develop the consequences of these paradoxes would lead beyond the limits of a chapter already unduly prolonged. In place of further criticism I shall offer a theory conceived and developed from the opposite point of view. Meanwhile I have to make one observation of a very general character.

Recrudescence of Animism in Contemporary Thought

31. Such doctrines as those of Whitehead and Santayana are actuated by a definitely naturalistic motive. It is the purpose of their authors to exhibit reality and nature as one. In the process, as we have seen, they virtually ignore the cleavage of nature and spirit. Or, perhaps I should say, in tacitly acknowledging the distinction, they assume that in the total scheme of reality nature is almost everything and spirit next to nothing. The result is truly striking—although in a sense it is just what was to be expected. Having purged the concept of reality, as far as possible, of every

---

[114] e.g.: "Finally, in the cosmological scheme here outlined one implicit assumption of the philosophical tradition is repudiated. The assumption is that the basic elements of experience are to be described in terms of one, or all, of the three ingredients, consciousness, thought, sense-perception. . . . According to the philosophy of organism these three components are unessential elements in experience, either physical or mental. Any instance of experience is dipolar, whether that instance be God or an actual occasion of the world. The origination of God is from the mental pole, the origination of an actual occasion is from the physical pole; but in either case these elements, consciousness, thought, sense-perception, belong to the derivative 'impure' phases of the concrescence, if in any effective sense they enter at all." *Process and Reality*, pp. 49-50.

vestige of the non-natural[115] or spiritual, the philosophy of the
present era proceeds to reinterpret the natural in terms that are
saturated with suggestions of a spiritual significance. Thus if on
the one hand experience, feeling and purpose are characterized as
"physical,"[116] if there is talk of "satisfactions" from which consciousness is on principle excluded,[117] on the other it is remarkable
that the physical should be thought of as occurring in the form of
"experiences," "feelings," "purposes," and that nature should be
conceived as having a subjective "life" of her own. This is nothing
short of a return to primitive animism at the level of a highly
sophisticated culture.[118] Now the serious feature in the situation
becomes apparent if we remember that it was the break-up of
animism which enabled science to make its first beginnings, and
that the progress of scientific thinking ever since has been commensurate with the gradual elimination of the lingering residues
of the same primitive doctrine. There is something in this calculated to give us pause, and to make us ask whether a philosophical construction of reality which is ostensibly based on science, and
yet in its final issue reverses the attitude to which science owes all
the progress it has made, is likely to do justice to those aspects of
the truth which scientific thinking is best qualified to bring out.
The question is all the more serious in view of the fact that the
type of philosophy with which we have been dealing, should it

[115] I am not forgetting Whitehead's: "A percipient object is in some sense beyond
nature." *P.K.*, p. 195. The point of the remark is in the words "in some sense," the
implication being that the non-natural, when we are forced to recognize it, must be
assigned to a vague peripheral region beyond the all-but-universal embrace of the
natural. I would point out that as a matter of intellectual strategy the admission of the
non-natural to a minor place in a scheme of things conceived on a naturalistic basis is
open to more serious objection than the full recognition of the supernatural as central
and fundamental.

[116] *Process and Reality*, Part III. For "physical purposes" *vid.* pp. 390 *sq.*

[117] "No actual entity can be conscious of its own satisfaction." *op. cit.*, p. 118.

[118] The writings of Santayana and Whitehead abound in expressions which, if they
are taken at all seriously, can only be construed as animistic in their import. At times
the doctrine becomes explicit. For Whitehead "the difference between a living organism
and the inorganic environment is only a question of degree." *Process and Reality*, p. 252.
Santayana, while concluding a survey of the subject with the remark: "There is therefore no direct evidence of animation in nature," proceeds thus: "On reflection, however,
and by an indirect approach, I can see good reason for believing that some sort of
animation . . . pervades the organic world; because my psyche is animate. . . . I
would even suggest that all the substance of nature is ready to think, if circumstances
allow by presenting something to think about, and creating the appropriate organ."
S.A., pp. 249-50. "Reflective animism" would be a fair designation of modern philosophy in one of its phases.

prove inadequate as a generalization or sublimation of scientific knowledge, has no compensations to offer. A theory of being which would partly submerge the spiritual in the physical, and partly permit it to play as a faint irridescence on the surface of animal life, is unable to sustain the weight of all those disciplines—political and social adjustment, economics, art and religion—in which the spirit demands for itself a position of centrality and of pre-eminence over the conditions of a natural existence.

APPENDIX A (*See note* 82, *p.* 115)

The Existence of Objects in a Definitely Physical Mode

As a result of the highly speculative character of modern physics a curious paradox has arisen in the tendency (1) to substitute the concept of scientific laws for the concept of definitely identifiable physical entities, and (2) as a result of this to represent the outer world around us as partly subjective in character. A good example occurs in Chap. II of Eddington's *New Pathways in Science* (Cambridge, 1935). In answer to the question: "How should we now describe the physical universe or 'the universe as it is conceived in modern physics'?" the writer says: "I suppose that we ought to mean that conception or formulation which has been generally adopted as giving the most complete agreement with observation." Taken strictly, this statement would seem to mean that the "physical universe" is to be *identified* with the descriptive formula which represents the scientist's conception of it. But if so, nature becomes no better than an artefact of human minds. That this is really what is intended might well appear too unlikely to warrant a moment's serious consideration. And yet in the sequel we find that the difference between the description and the object described is treated as negligible. The line of thought is this. Bohr's theory of the atom as a planetary system has one serious defect. The behaviour of the electron cannot be brought within a single system of the laws of motion. In Eddington's words, "the older quantum theory which treated the electron as a particle succeeded up to a certain point. But it never got so far as to formulate a system of laws of motion which would cover the jumps of the electron from one orbit to another. It was a collection of strange empirical rules rather than a systematic theory." The new quantum theory inaugurated by Heisenberg in 1925, and developed by de Broglie and Schrödinger in the form of wave mechanics, is an attempt to remedy this specific deficiency. Now the characteristic feature of this new doctrine is that it knows nothing of individual wave motions in space and time. All the properties of the quanta are statistical properties, expressive of the fact which we call probability, and capable of being formulated in wave equations which have become "the basal laws of physics." *op. cit.*, p. 44. cf. Eddington's *Nature of the Physical World*, Chap. x on "The New Quantum Theory."

The situation is therefore this. We are confronted with two sets of factors, (1) the laws of wave mechanics, and (2) "the recurrences of sensory experience" which it is the professed aim of physics to explain and which are actually explained with a high degree of success by these laws. In the meantime the microscopic units of physical reality virtually disappear from sight. The laws of wave mechanics are not an *explanation of* the electrons and their erratic behaviour, but a *substitute for* them. And so the question arises: To what exactly do the laws apply? What are the independently existing entities of which the formulae of wave mechanics express the statistical nature? The answer is that nothing is known of any such entities—nothing, that is to say, but what is expressed in the formulae.

A drastic change of viewpoint has thus been achieved. In place of "contents" without satisfactory laws (as in Bohr's model), we have been given laws without any well defined "contents" (as in Schrödinger's theory). This is how Eddington puts it: ". . . It cannot be said that the content of the universe as it is conceived in modern physics consists of a number of particles called protons and electrons together with waves of radiation. It is no use assigning contents without laws governing them; and we have not succeeded in formulating a system of law on this basis." The "actual stuff of the universe as it is conceived in physics" is represented by the symbol of probability "ψ." Eddington adds: "We ought therefore to say that on the present view the content of the universe consists, not of particles, but of waves of ψ. But at the same time it must be realized that a universe composed of ψ waves necessarily contains a large subjective element"; and finally: "We must conclude . . . that 'the universe as it is conceived in modern physics' is not identical with what a philosopher would call 'the objective physical universe.'" If Eddington is right (and his way of putting things is typical[1]), the upshot of the matter is that in its ultimate structure the physical world is not physical at all.

Now while the philosopher has no right to dispute the detail of his science with the physicist, the questions which Eddington raises in the sentences last quoted are not scientific questions. They have to do with interpretation, and physics does not contain the key to their answer. Assuming that physical science in its profoundest phase consists of propositions of the type which Eddington has described for us, and that it includes no propositions relating the former to an "objective [i.e. I suppose, an *independently existing*[2]] physical universe," it does not seem to me to follow that the world to which these statistical propositions refer, the order of things within which the laws of wave mechanics hold good, can possibly be designated as in any sense or in any degree "subjective." We have still to consider the exact meaning (or meanings) of the latter term; but I take it that what the word is here meant to convey is just what Eddington has in mind when he denies the identity of

---

[1] cf. J. W. N. Sullivan, *Science: A New Outline*, p. 145.

[2] As will appear more fully later, this is not the sense in which I ordinarily understand the word "objective"; but I hope to show how this usage springs from the one which I recognize as fundamental.

the physicist's world with the "objective physical universe" of the philosopher. In other words, he is maintaining that all the physicist claims to know is the formulae which he has himself devised—presumably upon evidence—and that he has no evidence of a world existing in any way but that to which the formulae give expression. Precisely so. But surely the assumption is that these formulae have reference to something other than themselves and other than the mental processes by which we think them: surely the question of their truth is the question of their relation to an order of being outside men's minds. If so, the fact that we have no independent cognizance of the entities to which the laws of nature apply does not mean either that these entities do not exist at all, or that they exist, as the formulae themselves exist, and as Bertrand Russell has declared *things* to exist,[3] as mental constructs pure and simple. On the contrary, the constructs have the significance of scientific validity, as distinct from logical or imaginative merit, only upon the understanding that the mind has put nothing into them without the thought of a *de facto* world, the sphere of their application. In brief, the ultimate subject of predication is an independently existing universe of which the scientific equations are true. In relation to that universe the equations have a definitory significance. That is to say, the physically real may be defined as the subject of scientific truth, or as that which exists in the ways of which science is a description. I do not mean that all scientific propositions are existential in their force. Existence, as in the postulate of being, may have to be posited independently. But if so, there is nothing gratuitous in the postulate. The latter is necessary in order to turn logical and mathematical necessities into truths of nature.

I think we may go one step further. Granted that there is no such thing as an individual quantum behaving in space as physical particles are supposed to behave, granted that quanta truths are all statistical in their significance and expressive of averages, there must be a class of entities (other than the macroscopic objects of ordinary experience) to give support to these quanta truths. Of the individuals that compose the class we have no separate knowledge. Nonetheless we may have a perfectly distinct conception of what it means to be a unit of physical existence. Every such unit is definable in terms of its membership in the class of entities to which the laws of wave mechanics refer.

I shall have occasion further on to point out a significant anticipation (by Mr. Holt, in his book, *The Concept of Consciousness*) of the view that would reduce the physical world to its own laws—and the science of physics to a branch of logic.

[3] *Our Knowledge of the External World*, p. 89.

INGRESSION

I cannot help thinking that Whitehead's use of the term "ingression" (in itself so misleading) was prompted by a verbal circumstance. Of the two nouns derived from the Latin "ingredior," *ingression* and *ingredient*, the former retains, the latter has lost the original connotation as expressive of a movement. In its adjectival or participial use the word "ingredient" combines the two meanings. To be *ingredient* is either to be *in the act of entering into*, or to be *constitutive of* something. But a word is still wanted to give abstract expression to what "ingredient" expresses in the concrete—a word to denote not *a constituent*, but *what it means to be a constituent*. Such a word would be forthcoming if there were an abstract substantival equivalent of the participial "ingredient" in the second of its two senses. My conjecture is that it is primarily in this sense that "ingression" should be understood. This is rather borne out by the way in which the conception is introduced, and more particularly by the order of the expressions used—*ingredient* (noun), *ingredient* (participle) and *ingression*. "An object is an ingredient in the character of some event. In fact the character of an event is nothing but the objects which are ingredient in it and the ways in which these objects make their ingression into the event." *C.N.*, pp. 143-4.

CHAPTER IV

MIND AND SPACE

Is Mind Something in Space?

1. Among the considerations which in modern times have reinforced the mutual assimilation of physical and spiritual is one which has to do with the relation of mind to space. Powerful arguments have been advanced and cogent reasons given for attributing a spatial character to our conscious processes. If these reasons are valid and these arguments conclusive, the fundamental identity of the psychical and the physical will follow of its own accord. For each of the factors involved will be definable, in virtually the same terms, as events in space and time; and any differences which may reveal themselves to closer inspection will have no ontological significance. They will not be differences in the modality of being, but will have their origin in the fact that there may be different systems of being with the same modality. The problem of the spatial in relation to the psychical is therefore one which affects the very foundations of our inquiry; and upon the solution to it depends the possibility of further progress.

2. In the *Essay concerning Human Understanding* John Locke remarks of his soul that it is something which travels with the body in the coach or on horseback from Oxford to London.[1] From this we see that Locke attributes position and change of position, both spatial characters, to the spiritual part of our being. Furthermore the soul's position in space is identified with that of the body and of nothing else. The argument is that "every one finds in himself, that his soul can think, will and operate on his body in the place where that is; but cannot operate on a body, or in a place an hundred miles distant from it." Thus Locke denies *actio in distans* to the soul, but upon grounds which imply that the latter possesses a spatial nature; and the evidence he advances in support of his contention is set forth in the form of a simple appeal to the universal consciousness of mankind. "Every one finds" that it is so.[2]

---

[1] *op. cit.*, Book II, Chap. XXIII, §20.

[2] Locke's views on the relation of mind to space are in complete accord with his conclusion that there is no theoretical objection to assuming that the power of thought may be directly vested in corporeal substance.

3. Professor Alexander maintains the spatiality of psychical process on the evidence of personal experience. "Mind," he asserts, "enjoys itself spatially, or is extensive, in the same sense as it is successive and endures in enjoyed time."[3] Its activities may be felt as movements in the body, like that of Tennyson's "great thought," which "strikes along the brain and flushes all the cheek." Somewhat surprisingly, it is to "the higher acts of mind, imagination, or desire, or thinking" that Alexander ascribes the clearest sense of position and direction in space.

4. There are really two main lines of argument by which those who maintain the spatiality of consciousness enforce their conclusion. In the first place there is the psychological line, which is illustrated by my references to John Locke and to Professor Alexander. These writers claim that it is possible by introspection to detect certain unmistakably spatial properties in our conscious states. The second type of argument is epistemological. Its exponents try to prove that unless our mental processes were spatial we could not know space by means of them. I shall begin with the epistemological argument.

This has been worked out with the utmost skill by Mr. E. B. Holt in his important but somewhat neglected work, *The Concept of Consciousness*. In what follows I shall use Mr. Holt's book as a text, but I shall permit the argument to develop, if need be, beyond the limits of mere commentary.

Criticism of the Epistemological Argument for This Position, on the Assumption of a Distinction between States and Objects of Consciousness

5. To state the matter as briefly as possible, the writer attempts to show that the denial of a spatial character to our subjective states is merely a corollary to the fallacy of representative perception. Thus, we are conscious of space; this means that we have "ideas" of it. So much may be taken as universally admitted. The question is: How are these ideas to be understood? What is the relation between them and the space of which they are the consciousness?

[3] *Space, Time and Deity*, Vol. I, p. 97. *vid.* the whole passage to p. 101. Especially striking is the description of mind as "streaked" and as "spread out or voluminous in its enjoyment."

The answer given is that if they are not themselves in space, they must somehow *represent* or *stand for* that which is. But this, the writer maintains, is precisely what they cannot do, so long as they are not themselves in space. The justice of this conclusion, it is assumed, will be apparent as soon as we ask the question: How could non-spatial ideas possibly represent their spatial objects? Certainly not "as an analytic equation represents an extended curve";[4] nor yet "as any symbol represents the thing symbolized." For, we are told, in the case of actual perception "it is *spatial* space and not a subjective symbol that we started with." The conclusion is that spatial sensations (a somewhat question-begging expression) are themselves extended, and that "ideas of space are spatial ideas."[5]

As regards this specific argument, it may be pointed out in the first place that it involves an *ignoratio elenchi*. The doctrine under consideration is that which maintains the non-spatial character of consciousness: the doctrine actually rebutted is "the representative theory of knowledge."[6] That these two are identical cannot be taken for granted, any more than that the "representative theory," as our author also appears to think, is the essence of idealism.[7] The truth is that idealism in its most developed forms combines the rejection of spatial ideas with that of representationism.

[4] As a matter of fact it is only the *order* of the curve that is represented, and both the equation and the figure are instances of order. This is Mr. Holt's own observation, and it rather spoils the contrast he here assumes between ideas and equations as representatives of space.

[5] *The Concept of Consciousness* (hereafter *C.C.*), pp. 144-6. The writer further remarks that "consciousness is extended in both space and time: in space as spatial objects are extended, consciousness being actually such parts of the objects as are perceived, i.e. such parts as are consciousness." *op. cit.*, pp. 210-11. The question might be asked: If consciousness is to be identified with objects perceived, with what is the perception of these objects to be identified? The only possible answer is: With the consciousness of them. Thus, as for Hume, there is no difference between perceiving objects and being the objects perceived.

[6] *C.C.*, p. 141.

[7] Representationism is actually attributed to Berkeley! (*C.C.*, p. 140.) It is surprising how persistent the critics of idealism have been in their assumption that this doctrine is identical with Berkeleianism. *vid. op. cit.*, Chap. VI. The baselessness of the assumption has been once more exposed by Clifford Barrett in an article "Is Idealism Realism? A Reply in Terms of Objective Idealism," *Journal of Philosophy*, August 3, 1933. To crown this edifice of misunderstanding, Berkeley's idealism, to which Mr. Holt opposes his theory of spatial ideas, is the one form of idealistic theory in which the spatiality of ideas is freely granted.

6. It is clear that the problem, as it has come to shape itself in Mr. Holt's argument, demands a careful inquiry into the relationship of ideas to their objects in the spatial world. That inquiry is necessarily rendered somewhat complicated by the variety of entities which may stand in the relation of object to our consciousness of them,[8] as well as by certain ambiguities in the use of the word "idea."

If, for example, as realists of a certain school assume, there are objects which exist independently, and yet can be known directly, their objectivity, which is merely their relation to a mind, has no bearing upon their ontological character. They are not mind-conditioned, but mind-indifferent. In this case the factors involved are three in number—x, the independent real; y, my consciousness of x; and z, the relation of objectivity which connects y with x, and invests the latter with the purely adventitious character of "object." Here then my "idea" of the object in question can be no other than my consciousness of it—hence a subjective activity or state.

7. On the other hand, the object may belong to a class which I shall describe hereafter as "subjectively conditioned."[9] This class, with which I shall have to deal at length, includes "mental" images, concepts and intellectual constructions of all sorts, ideal entities like the contents of true propositions, which, while they have an independent *validity*, have no existence apart from the mind that thinks them. To this category of the "subjectively conditioned" likewise belong those ideas which the historical exponents of representative perceptionism interpolate between our consciousness and the outer world.[10] Where the object is thus mind-

---

[8] For a more detailed discussion of objects *vid.* Chap. vi, 9-20. An additional source of difficulty is to be found in the fact that the word "representation" (Vorstellung) is highly ambiguous. Sometimes it means "what is presented to the mind," and therefore "the object of consciousness as such"; at other times it is the substantival equivalent of the verb "to represent," and consequently connotes the mental activity of sustaining an object in consciousness. It is also used to express the relation between the mind and its object—a relation which might be described in some such phrase as "symbolic substitution or reference."

[9] I do not attribute a belief in these exclusively to the idealist, because everyone who recognizes the existence of mind or spirit is bound to acknowledge *some* objects as belonging to this class. What is peculiar to the idealist is that for him *all* objects are in some way mind-determined. [cf. Chap. vi, 12-20, pp. 226-35.—Ed.]

[10] I have not thought it necessary to discuss the historical doctrine in detail, as the theory which Mr. Holt attacks is much more comprehensive in its scope. What I have

dependent, it is commonly and quite appropriately described as an "idea." "Object" and "idea," therefore, here coincide, while both differentiate themselves from "idea" in the subjective sense of "conscious state or process."

8. The whole question of representation must be viewed in the light of these distinctions. In the first case, "my idea of the object" is my consciousness of it—that is to say, the identity of my subjective state stereotyping itself against the independently real, and yet in such a way that even in its subjectivity it owes something to the real which is its object. Can this be fairly considered a case of representation? Only in one sense. If my consciousness of the real may be described as an *activity of presenting*, or as a subjective operation whereby the mind establishes the relation of objectivity between itself and another, the word "representation" may quite appropriately be employed as an abstract substantival expression of the event. In the same way "action" is the substantival equivalent of the verb "to act." So far then as the subjective term is concerned, "representation" is just a name for a certain inner activity of my consciousness in relation to an independently existing reality, and in actual usage the name is applied indifferently to the relation and to the activity.

Now provided instances of the relation I have described actually occur—provided there is such a thing as being directly conscious of the independently existing—there seems no reason for denying the possibility of having ideas of space which do not partake of the spatial character of their objects. The assumption is that consciousness and the object of consciousness are ontologically distinct entities. It is therefore not necessary (indeed, on this hypothesis it is not *possible*) that they should resemble one another in *every* respect; and it is difficult to think of *any* respect (save that of their common temporal character) in which a state of consciousness is *bound* to resemble the reality that stands to it in the relation of objectivity.[11] The amalgam that holds them together is not resemblance, but the uniqueness of their mutual relationship. *y* is

to say about the latter will embrace any points in the former which are relevant to our problem.

[11] The diversity of being to which ontological independence is attributable is indicated by the fact that the real may occur in any of the original modalities. Thus *x* may be a physical existent or a subjective system (person). Of course such systems, although they *exist* subjectively, may contract the relation of objectivity and may be quite unaffected by the fact.

specifically the object of x, and x specifically the consciousness of y; but this does not in the least suggest a community of nature between these terms. To argue that because x is my consciousness (and in that sense my *idea*) of a line five feet in length, the idea must itself be extended, is like arguing that my idea of red must be a red idea. Obviously such an assertion is meaningless so long as we continue to recognize the distinction between being conscious of an object and being an object of consciousness. In so far then as Mr. Holt maintains that my ideas of space are spatial ideas, he is by implication denying the distinction in question—a conclusion from which in the end he does not shrink.

9. We have not, however, reached the point at which we are prepared to deal with such an extreme position. So far we have considered only one of the senses of the word "representation," that, namely, in which it is synonymous with the presentative activity of consciousness in relation to the real. It has just been pointed out that in this sense of the term the "representation" of space cannot be intelligibly described as spatial. But what of the case in which the representation is not of the independently existing, but of the kind of object which I have called "subjectively conditioned"? The crux of the question is the fact that such mind-dependent objects frequently have a spatial character. Visual imagery is the most obvious illustration. Is it legitimate to argue that since "mental" images of visible objects have a space of their own, the subjective activity of representing them must also be something that goes on in space?

The answer is that even when the space in question is not independent of our mental processes, even when it is the creation of an active visual imagination, there is still no meaning in describing the latter as in any sense a spatial activity. Our acts of representation, of ideation, do not exist in imagined, any more than they do in physical space. We are conscious of our images, as we are conscious of their prototypes in the outer world; but in neither case is the extension which characterizes the objective factor attributable to the subjective. My conclusion therefore is that if by "ideas" and "representations" we mean our mental states and processes as distinct from their objects, to describe them as spatial is to have recourse to a form of words entirely wanting in significance, and that irrespective of the question whether the object is conceived to exist independently of mind or to be dependent upon the latter for its existence.

10. To this the opponents* of representationism would themselves agree. They would do so on the ground that the doctrine which I have outlined is not "representationism" as they understand it. For them, as for Mr. Holt, to "represent" is not "to be conscious of," but to symbolize, to stand for, to be a fitting substitute; and clearly a subjective activity cannot *represent* its object in this sense. A state of consciousness is not to be explained as a symbol interposed between consciousness and that of which we are conscious, and the process of presenting does not mean standing in place of something else. If ideas are to represent their objects in the sense of symbolizing them, they must be suited by nature to the symbolic function, and this means one thing and one thing only. The ideas in question must themselves be objects. Here then we[12] pass from the subjectivist interpretation of ideas and representations, and adopt the standpoint of the naturalist who, although he speaks of ideas as subjective, does not mean the expression to be taken seriously. What he is really thinking of is not a state of mind, but a symbolic object *provided by mind* as a substitute for an independent reality in the world of physical space.

Representation in what (incidentally) I take to be the commonly accepted meaning of the term will thus be a function not of the subject, but of a certain type of object, the mind-conditioned; and a "representative idea" will be not an object *as represented*, but rather an object as *representing*—in brief, a symbol specially prepared by consciousness for its own use, and designed to stand between its subjective processes and the independently real.

Now my contention is that we are bound to recognize the existence of representative ideas of this type. Images are employed

[*"The opponents." The sense seems to be that the opponents, if one directs their attention to subjective activity, will not claim that the representationist was wrong in denying spatial character to *that*. He does not in fact trouble to deny spatial character to that—taking it for obvious. But, it is urged, he cannot, as he tries to do, deny spatial character to idea as *object*, even as mind-conditioned object. It is on this last assertion that the author proceeds to take issue. If the representationist denies the *necessary* spatiality of idea as (mind-conditioned) object—even when the idea is of something physical—then thus far he is right. To be symbolical of the spatial an idea does not *require* to be itself spatial.—Ed.]

[12] In the second of the two cases with which I have dealt, that in which the object is mind-conditioned, it is quite in keeping with ordinary usage to refer to the latter as an *idea* or *representation*.

as substitutes for concepts, and concepts are made to represent all *conceivable* entities. To the free acknowledgment of these possibilities no exception can be taken on the ground that the idea is subjective, and therefore unfit for the symbolic function. Both the symbol and the symbolized are now objective; and in theory at least any object may be chosen to symbolize any other.

But for this very reason it is a mistake to argue, as Mr. Holt does, that the ideas which represent the world of space must themselves have a spatial character. As a matter of fact some of them do. My "mental" image of Flodden Field, for example, has a space of its own and quite elaborate spatial contents and properties. It has a foreground which is occupied by a field of waving wheat, and in the middle of this is a sizable battle monument. It has also a background in which the most prominent feature is the spatial mass of Branxton Hill. But the space of my imagination is quite distinct from that of the actual battlefield. The one belongs to the order of being which I call physical: the other, which is mind-conditioned, does not;[13] and to claim that the latter must necessarily have spatial properties if it is to represent the former is to misconstrue the symbolic function altogether. My image is necessarily spatial, not because it stands for an extended original, but because it is a visual image; and there are other objects of a purely mathematical or conceptual nature which, although they have no spatial properties, may serve equally well to symbolize the position and extent of Flodden Field.

To sum up briefly. If by "ideas" we mean states of mind, the latter, in the only sense in which they can be described as representative, are emphatically non-spatial. If, on the other hand, we mean mind-conditioned objects of consciousness, it is not at all necessary that these should be spatial before they can represent the contents of the spatial world.[14]

[13] In a complete statement these observations would of course require some qualification. The actual battle was not a purely physical event (although physical events were mixed up with it), and the portion of space which differentiates itself as Flodden Field is therefore determined and characterized by properties many of which are mind-conditioned. Some of them indeed are very like the properties of imaginary space. These considerations, however, are of little account. What really matters is the fact that the space of the battlefield includes physical events. That is to say, it is the kind of space in which such events actually occur. It is otherwise with the space of imagination.

[14] I must point out here (what is only too obvious) that the number of my ideas which are taken to "represent" the spatial manifold is strictly limited. The argument from representationism therefore carries us only a short way. Mr. Holt does not fail to

Is the Epistemological Argument Strengthened if the Distinction between States and Objects of Consciousness Is Denied?

11. The discussion so far has been based upon assumptions of my own choosing—in particular the assumption that states of consciousness and objects of consciousness are always distinguishable,[15] and in some cases (as where the object is an independently existing real) may even be ontologically distinct. All of this Mr. Holt (and, generally speaking, the writers whom I designate naturalists) would refuse to admit. Now in justice to those whose views are so fundamentally opposed to my own it is only right that I should reverse my foregoing procedure and should treat my presuppositions (from which incidentally Mr. Holt has been arguing with a view to their overthrow) as definitely *sub judice*. I therefore propose to meet my opponents on ground, not of my own, but of their selecting. In this I shall be but following Mr. Holt's example. For in order to make good the spatiality of ideas, he has taken his stand on the "representative theory of knowledge," which he believes to be responsible for the opposite view, and has deduced his conclusion from the breakdown of this theory. The analogous procedure will be to begin where he ends, by eliminating from the argument every vestige of that subjectivity (and with it the distinction of subjective and objective) which up to the present I have assumed, and which is precisely what the naturalists deny.

Let us suppose then that there is no such thing as a "subjective activity of presentation," and that it contributes nothing to the explanation of my ideas to think of them either as conscious states or as the objects of such states. On this view all ideas are alike: they are just what they are—neutral entities, neither objective nor subjective—and that is the end of the matter. Naturally along with the subjective and the "subjectively conditioned" the distinction between what I have called "physical" space and every other kind of space—that of images, for example, and that of objects seen in a mirror—will disappear, and we shall recognize only one *kind* of space—the kind that Mr. Holt calls "spatial." Of course there will still be different systems of this. To take Mr.

recognize the fact that "one's knowledge contains a vast number of items that are not spatial." *C.C.*, p. 241.

[15] I do not mean that every state of consciousness has an object (that this is not so is a main feature in my completed theory), but that there *are* experiences in which the distinction of subjective and objective is fundamental. [cf. Chap. VII, 7, pp. 261 *f.*—Ed.]

Holt's own illustration, there will be the space-system of a distant town, and that of the "neutral" ideas which constitute my "mental" image or "knowledge" of the latter.[16] These systems, however, will differ in quite another way than that which I assumed when I distinguished the spatial system of my imagination from that of the physical world. The difference, that is to say, will not be metaphysical. Modalities of being will not be involved. Any distinctions which remain will be merely such as are presupposed in every attempt to ascertain and to describe the exact position of an object or group of objects in a spatial manifold the relations of which we are trying to explore. The assumption, I suppose, is that every position is definable by reference to a number of terms outside itself. These, when taken along with the position in question, constitute a spatial system. But since the terms may be variously chosen, the object may be considered as occupying more than one position at a time—that is to say, as belonging to more than one system of definitory points.[17] This is not to deny that space is one. The complete coordination of all possible systems is an ideal, interpretable, if need be, as the oneness and universality of space.

12. Such are the concepts with which we are left to work out all the problems that arise from the spatial structure of the world of our experience. To test the adequacy of the theory with which we are dealing it will be sufficient to consider one such problem. Where exactly must I locate my "knowledge" of a place that is spatially remote—say a distant town? Mr. Holt has set forth what he conceives to be the conditions of the question with subtle ingenuity,[18] and his explanation has been in part approved by Professor Alexander.[19] To put the matter briefly, this piece of knowledge, this "knowledge-mass" is in neither of the two positions which on first thoughts would seem to exhaust the possibilities of the case. That is to say, considered in itself it is neither within the head of the

---

[16] Unfortunately there seems no escape from the terminology of the subject-object superstition. Too much should not be made of this, any more than of the linguistic necessity that compelled Hume to have recourse to personal pronouns and possessive adjectives.

[17] C.C., pp. 233-4.

[18] C.C., Chap. xii on "Memory, Imagination, and Thought."

[19] Space, Time and Deity, Vol. I, p. 99, footnote. Alexander differs from Mr. Holt by persisting in the belief that "the image of a town belongs to the actual place of the actual town."

knower nor yet in the spot where the actual town is situated.[20] The truth is that nothing has position *in itself*. Hence all attempts to locate the "knowledge-mass" must wait upon the discovery of the appropriate external frame of reference. The question therefore is: With what points or terms in space outside the "knowledge-mass" can the latter be coordinated into a single spatial system? The answer is furnished by an analysis of the knowledge of place.

13. In the instance before us this knowledge, we are given to understand, will ordinarily consist of fragmentary glimpses of the buildings, streets, etc., of which the "actual" town consists.[21] These "features," taken in their entirety, do not constitute the town; but that is merely because of their fragmentariness. They are cross-sections or intercepts of an original, defined by the differential responses of the nervous system;[22] and between them they constitute our image or knowledge of the object, as distinguished from the object itself. It appears, therefore, that the difference between the actual town and my knowledge of it is merely the difference between a whole and a part, or, to be more exact, between a complete and an incomplete assortment of particulars, with whatever variation this may imply in the relations involved. Thus "the expression 'knowledge-mass' means that portion of the actual town that is also in the conscious cross-section of some knower, and means it as a member of such conscious manifold."[23] In the light of this explanation we are able to give a more precise meaning than has hitherto been possible to the concept of "representation," by defining the symbolic function which is the essence of the latter. The underlying condition—and indeed "the only meaning that 'representation' has," is partial identity.[24] This occurs when a number of particulars appear as constituents in more than one system. Representation, then, depends upon the element of identity; but it is obvious that the identity cannot be complete, as in that case there would be only one system, and not two or more.

When the systems in question are space and our consciousness of space respectively, the latter is able to *represent* the former only in

[20] *C.C.*, p. 231.
[21] *C.C.*, pp. 231-2.
[22] *C.C.*, Chap. XII.
[23] *C.C.*, p. 233.
[24] *C.C.*, p. 238.

so far as it is identical with it.[25] Apparently the identity is limited to the relations involved. As an example of what is meant the writer instances a "true map," which he defines as "a scheme of spatial relations that is identical with relations that exist, along with much else, in the greater region that is mapped."[26]

The implications of this illustration are noteworthy, and must be drawn out in more detail.

If a Selection from the Object Is to represent the Object, Then the Rejected Distinction Must Be Reintroduced

14. In the first place, while what is said about maps in relation to their geographical originals is not only intelligible but indisputable, it is not so easy to see that it applies (as on naturalistic theory it is bound to do) to our *consciousness* of the object represented, when taken in relation to the actuality of that object. Thus on this view a person's geographical knowledge of New Jersey and a map of New Jersey are the same kind of thing—except, I presume, that the knowledge is in most cases less accurate and complete than the map. In brief, we are here dealing with two maps, a bad one, in which there is perhaps much pictorial detail, but only vague intimations of proportion and direction, and a good one, in which proportion and direction are everything. Beyond each of these there is the actual territory which is known as New Jersey, and which, in a measure, they both represent.

Now the question arises: If my consciousness of New Jersey, geographically considered, is literally a bad map of that state, and if there exists a good map of the same, how is my knowledge or consciousness *of the latter* to be interpreted? Clearly in the light of the now familiar principle that my consciousness of any object *is* that object in a particular context. Thus my knowledge of the good map is just the good map itself in the context of the objects that constitute my experience in general. But since these objects are largely irrelevant to the map in that essential aspect which constitutes it a "true" representation of its original, it must lose some-

---

[25] *C.C.*, p. 237.

[26] *C.C.*, p. 237. In the next page it is pointed out that the map represents relations, but not magnitudes. But surely magnitudes go with relations. If not, what is meant by describing a map as having a scale of half an inch to the mile? Does not the distance of half an inch on the one represent a distance of one mile on the other?

what in completeness and accuracy through the unfortunate circumstance that I have become conscious of it.[27]

Entities, it will be observed, are multiplying around us. First
there is the geographical area or spatial system called the State of
New Jersey. Then there is my knowledge of the latter, which is a
selection from the contents of that spatial system, made on practical principles and occurring within the more comprehensive system of my experience. In the third place there is the official map
of the state, which hangs on a wall in the Capitol at Trenton, and
of which, when I look at it, I have a distinct and separate consciousness. This last, as I have explained, must be identified with the
map itself, but with that map as mutilated and transferred from
its native environment into one determined by the vital necessities
and selective responses of a particular human body. The total
spectacle presented is that of an original manifold of space, from
which, by successive displacements and intercepts, a variety of
more or less imperfect replicas—my consciousness of the manifold,
the map of it, my consciousness of the map—has been struck off
by an agency which, in the last analysis, is always resolvable into
the selective activity of nervous systems.

Such are the basic notions to which we must have recourse if we
are to give a genuinely naturalistic account of the facts we should
ordinarily describe as "making" or "consulting" a map, "comparing the map with our memories of the original," or "correcting or
reviving our memories" by a similar act of comparison. Let us in
conclusion consider the naturalistic transcript of these familiar
processes. Once more the problem has to do with the nature of
representation.*

15. Upon naturalist assumptions my mental images of a distant
or absent locality represent the locality in exactly the same way as
a map. We have a spatial system characterized by a certain
partial schematic identity with each of two further spatial systems, in relation to which it may be designated "the actual locality" and "the original." Suppose now for the moment we con-

---

[27] This of course will be explained or condoned on the ground that it is the natural
consequence of the process whereby the nervous system selects the features best calculated to serve the interests of the organism. My practical need is usually not for a
complete and perfect map, but only for one which will tell me what I want to know at
the moment—for instance how to find my way home at night.

[*It will be observed that in the three next following sections the author is writing
throughout from the "naturalist" point of view. He then goes on to criticism.—Ed.]

fine our attention to the actual locality and to the map, without taking into account the system of "mental" representations. Is there any sense in which, under these conditions, the map can be said with significance to *represent* the locality? The assumption is that no one is conscious of either, but that between the two systems there is a relation such that if certain terms in the one constitute a particular geometrical formation, certain terms in the other will constitute a similar formation.[28] In this sense the map *resembles* the original, and representation, as for Hume, is nothing but resemblance.[29]

16. Now it is upon the conception of resemblance or similarity that the issue turns. Resemblance has been defined as "partial identity," and, so understood, has been taken as equivalent to representation. But it is obvious that this is not exactly what is meant. There are numberless instances in which two or more systems overlap or partially coincide, but in which we should never think of one system, at least *on that ground*, as *representing* another.[30] Thus the individual known to history as James I of England and VI of Scotland belongs to a series definable as the line of Scottish kings, and to another series definable as the succession of English monarchs; but it would be difficult to find a sense or a context in which, because in his person and in that of his Stuart successors the two series coincide, the line from Scotland would naturally be considered to *represent* the line from England or the latter the former. The note G may occur in various bugle calls; but each call *represents*, not another call which resembles it to this extent,[31] but

[28] "Similarity is partial identity: and similars are completely identical in those respects in which they are similar." *C.C.*, p. 148.

[29] Holt speaks of "the absurd impasse of declaring that the idea which represents is not even like the thing which is represented" (*C.C.*, p. 237), and declares emphatically for the opposite view. Thus on the ground that resemblance or "partial identity" is "the only meaning that 'representation' has," he does not hesitate to assert that the idea of red is a red idea. *C.C.*, p. 238. cf. p. 148.

[30] I say "on that ground" in order to make room for the truth already stated, that *anything* may be taken to represent anything else. The implication of this assertion is of course entirely opposed to the naturalist doctrine we are examining; for in the absence of resemblance the representative function has its origin in the *fiat* of some conscious intelligence.

[31] The statement would hold good if what were in question were not a single note but a complete phrase. In a world so given to music as ours many combinations of notes must recur over and over again in distinct compositions, and under certain conditions any one of these may recall certain others; but if so, the fact is of purely psychological significance. It does not point to a relation of mutual representation between the compositions concerned.

a phase of military routine having no discernible resemblance to a musical *motif*. Clearly the conception of partial identity must be further qualified before it can yield a reason for interpreting resemblance as representation.

17. The further qualification is to be found in the *logical* nature of the assumed identity.[32] This is particularly obvious in the example we have been considering—that of the map in relation to its original—for except in their logical aspect, the aspect in which they lose their particularity as actually existing spatial systems, the spatial properties of the map and of the geographical area do not count at all.

This may easily be shown. *North* on the map is not necessarily *in the north*;[33] and the line that joins it to the cartographical south does not necessarily coincide with any terrestrial meridian. All that matters is that it should be at right angles to another line joining the cartographical east and west, and that the cardinal points should bear a certain well-defined relation to one another. For the rest they may occupy any position whatever in space according to the position of the map; and the latter may be indefinitely rotated, so that the north point may occupy successively every position in the compass. Thus, although, as Mr. Holt maintains, positions are determined by relations, the relations here in question are independent of any positions which may exemplify them either on the map or on the surface of the earth. But in this case we are obviously dealing with a set of relations in the abstract —a logical scheme of relations which, however frequently and variously it may be exemplified in the world of actual spaces, must in itself be taken as absolutely one. That is to say, while north, south, east and west may be anywhere, the relation that at once connects and differentiates them is unalterably the same, and that wherever they may be. Thus from the only point of view which has any relevance to our problem, the map and the original cease to be two objects, and dissolve alike into the unity of an abstract relational identity.

[32] This Holt acknowledges of the relation between the distant locality and the knowledge-mass which represents it (*C.C.*, p. 233); and of course the same holds of the relation between the "true" map and its original. In each case it is the "scheme of spatial relations" (that is to say, the relations themselves considered in their logical aspect) that must be taken into account. *vid. ibid.*, p. 237.

[33] Hence the necessity, for certain purposes, of *setting* the map.

18. This conclusion is incompatible with the presuppositions of our problem. In defining representation as *partial* identity, the naturalist assumes the twofoldness or manifoldness of representative and represented. He therefore recognizes that in the actual world, where countries or distant towns as well as maps and "mental" images are supposed to exist, a unique and self-identical relation may somehow be found reduplicated in a variety of concrete instances.[34] Thus north and south are not merely definable as opposite to each other in the scheme of relations which also includes the oppositeness of east and west: they are definable as the relative positions of the north and south poles, of Edinburgh and London, and of the "ideas" which in my "knowledge-mass" represent these geographically determinate positions. How is this possible? Only by bringing into consideration the aspects in which these various spatial systems *differ*—that is to say, the existential contexts which impart a manifoldness of character to the most inveterate of self-identities.

It thus appears that reduplication or repetition is as essential as identity to the concept of representation. Y can represent X only in so far as there is identity of nature between the two; but then again there must be at least *two* terms before this possibility can arise. A map is not a map unless it has an original,[35] and unless the original is distinct from the map. The existence of a spatial manifold of the type we call "geographical" is the precondition under which alone another spatial manifold acquires the character of a cartographic reproduction.

19. But this is far from being a complete statement of the conditions involved. Maps are not things which occur of their own accord, and which we merely discover and take for granted. The geographical system does not produce a duplicate of itself by some miracle of spontaneous generation; and even if it did, the product would not be a map. The representative function, which is the definitory feature, implies a selective process whereby certain traits in a geographical system are first reduced to abstract terms in a relational scheme, and then, having lost their particularity,

[34] The "repetition of identicals" is empirically guaranteed. "We do experience repetitions and correspondences, and they play an important part in cognition." *C.C.*, p. 238.

[35] The original, I suppose, may be an imagined territory, as in Stevenson's map of Treasure Island.

are replaced by certain traits in another system of space, the cartographic, which reproduces the schematic arrangement of the first.

Now there is only one way in which such displacement and replacement can occur. It must be *decreed, posited, understood*. The formula of representation is an invariable: "Let it be." But such a decretal precondition can be conceived only as a function. The question is: Of what? Assuredly of neither of the spatial systems considered in itself, but of the being, whatever its nature, for which the duplicate has the significance of its prototype. That being, on Mr. Holt's view, is no other than the human body in one of its most characteristic aspects—the aspect in which, by means of a special apparatus (the nervous system) it evinces a certain differentiated responsiveness to the world around it, and thereby imparts to individual "features" in that world a significance and a distinctiveness which they did not possess before. The features thus selected, since they occur in a context supplied by the selective activity of the organism, constitute a system which is distinct at once from that of any geographical area and that of the corresponding map. It is the system of "mental" images by which (however these images are produced—whether physiologically or subjectively) human beings reproduce, in a medium of their own, the forms of things around them; and (what is of special importance for us here) all the modes and possibilities of representation, including that by which a map represents a geographical area, have their origin in this initial act of mental reproduction. Thus from the standpoint of its meaning, which is its representative function, the map implies a spatial system which is existentially distinct alike from itself and from its original, but is formally identical with both—a system defined by the discriminatory action of the human body, to whose neural responses is due the selection of features necessary to give a cartographic diagram the significance of a map. The condition presupposed in all such instances of representation is therefore no other than the representative function itself, as characteristic of the human organism. That any system of *objects* should represent any other is due to the fact that human beings have the power to reproduce any manifold of objects in the ideal form of a representative system. The initial exercise of this power, since it precedes all other applications of it, I shall call "primary representation."

Now this concept, which has its origin in the necessary requirements of the naturalistic theory, is really at variance with that
theory. If representation is reducible to partial—that is, logical—
identity, there is no reason in the world why one particular type
of representative system should stand out by itself as the precondition of all others. Hence there is no place for primary representation in the very doctrine that depends upon the latter for its
validity and completion. The full force of these remarks will be
apparent when the exact nature of primary representation has been
made clear.

The system of spatial and spatially related images which constitutes my knowledge of a distant town may once more serve the
purposes of illustration. It is not difficult to show that Mr. Holt's
explanation of the "knowledge-mass" by reference to the conditions under which it is generated cannot be sustained. It will be
remembered that the writer describes our knowledge of this absent
object, the distant town, as "defined"—that is, intercepted from
the original manifold—by the selective responses of the nervous
system. But surely the result of such physiological discrimination,
in so far as it has to do with the *object of response* rather than with
the responsive organism, could only be to break up the former into
a plurality of distinct objectives, each definable as the end-point
in its own specific reflex. That these objectives should be organized together into anything remotely resembling the town they
are supposed to represent, that they should reproduce the spatial
relations of the original manifold with a degree of exactitude
amounting to identity, is a suggestion so improbable that it may
safely be disregarded. The spatial pattern of the "knowledge-
mass" could indeed with as good reason be assumed to reflect the
structure of the nervous system, to whose selective energies it owes
its existence. The distant town would then be represented by the
(doubtless vague and schematic) image of a brain and a spinal
column, deformed and complicated by further patterns derived
from the organs of sense. This is hardly in keeping with the assumption that a representation must resemble its prototype.

20. These difficulties are traceable to an inadequate conception
of experience. For the naturalist experience is merely an ordered
series or organized system of objects—a specific *run* or dimension
of "neutral" contents in a world where the possibilities of dimensional arrangement are infinite. Such dimensions may cross and

recross one another in all sorts of ways. Where they intersect we find a content common to more than one of them, and thereby the condition is realized upon which the possibility of representation is supposed to depend. The supposition is not justified. Representation as between series of objects which partially coincide is possible only upon the further condition that each of these series is covered by the same system of experience. In terms of our previous illustration, it is only as an object of experience that a piece of territory can be represented by a map, and it is only as an object of experience that a map can represent that piece of territory. But if so, experience can no longer be identified with a series of objects cutting across other series, as these in turn cut across still further non-experiential systems. For this conception furnishes no explanation of the all-important fact that experience is in all cases necessary to representation. It follows that experience is not a name for one of the intersecting dimensions into which the contents of the "neutral mosaic" fall. It is not a name for anything in the relations of object *qua* object *to* object. Rather it is a precondition under which certain possibilities of objective relationship —among others those included in the representation of one object by another—arise. We must therefore seek for this precondition beyond the realm of the objective altogether. This compels us to reinstate the supposedly discredited conception of a subjective mode of being, with its characteristic manifestation of consciousness.

21. The reintroduction of this factor, which for the naturalist is no better than a metaphysical gratuity foisted upon the argument in defiance of the law of parsimony, immediately results in a marked simplification and clarification of the situation.

We have seen that the naturalistic idea of representation as between objective systems can be rendered thinkable only upon the assumption that each of the systems in question is traversed by a third—the system of experience. In this way experience is made to intervene between the original and the symbolic representation. In other words, we are constrained to postulate a third system of objects in order that the remaining two may sustain the assumed relation. This comes dangerously near to that very complication which for the naturalist is the damning defect of the "representative theory of knowledge." A further difficulty arises when we consider the relation of primary to other forms of representation.

If a map can represent a geographical area only in so far as there exists an experiential system which represents both, it would seem to follow that the conditions of representation vary, and that the word "representation" must itself be understood in different senses. In one instance the mediation of the experiential system is presupposed, in the other it is excluded by the conditions of the case.

All of these complications disappear with the recognition of consciousness and the interpretation of experience as subjective. It is true (as I have had repeated occasion to remark) that by thus distinguishing experience from the system of its objects we sacrifice the apparent advantage of assuming that in the end all being is modally homogeneous. But for this seemingly uneconomical procedure there is compensation in the fact that it enables us to overcome the further distinction, forced upon us by the logic of the naturalist position, between primary and other forms of representation. Upon the subjectivist view of experience it is no longer necessary to assume that if one system of objects is to represent another, each must first be independently represented by a third. All that is required is that the representative and the represented should be objects of one and the same consciousness—that is to say, should stand in a special relationship (familiar, but not definable) to a single subjective system. Granted this relationship, any object or system of objects (under conditions of which practical convenience is the sole principle) may represent or stand for any other, simply and directly, and without compelling us to have recourse to the obscure notion of resemblance, or to make matters even worse by defining the latter as logical identity repeating itself in a plurality of existential forms. Thus the map represents the territory without the intervention of "mental" images, but not without my consciousness of each. My experience of a distant town is not the system of spatial images which sometimes "represent" the latter to me, but the system of my conscious states (a subjective and non-spatial system), which have the actual locality for their object. Whether or not this object shall be accompanied in my consciousness by images of itself is largely a question of psychical endowment; and in this respect individuals differ enormously.[36] One thing is certain. In no case do the images constitute my *knowledge* of their independently existing prototypes.

[36] The capacity for eidetic imagery appears to vary with the age of the subject.

To *know* the distant town does not mean to have a "mental" picture of it. The ability to conjure up such pictures may enrich my aesthetic experience. Except in naturalistic theories, its epistemological significance is rudimentary.

Mind Not Epistemologically *Shown to Be in Space*

22. I conclude then that my knowledge, my experience, of space is not to be identified with any system of spatial images. The recognition of consciousness and of subjectivity in general as a distinct modality of being at once disentangles it from the network of considerations which have led certain philosophers, on epistemological grounds, to ascribe a spatial character to it. That a non-spatial mind should be capable of knowing a world in space, and this by means of non-spatial, subjective processes, is indeed a mystery; but no light is thrown upon the problem by the assumption that mind exists in space. The truth is that the mystery is not primarily that of space and its relation to the non-spatial, but that of mind and its relation to the object of knowledge. What I deprecate is the procedure, so characteristic of modern philosophy, which would demolish the problem at a single stroke by turning objects into minds. To put the matter otherwise, it is no more unreasonable to begin by frankly acknowledging the duality of consciousness and space than to obscure the nature of both by first reducing consciousness as a whole to the manifold of its own objects, and then representing certain of these as the consciousness or knowledge of others.

The Strong Point of Alexander's Psychological *Argument for Spatial Characteristics in Mind: Body Feelings* Are *Cognitive*

23. The second argument in favour of the view that minds and their states have spatial properties is, as I have pointed out, the psychological. The appeal is now to the verifiable facts of experience. Professor Alexander has described in graphic phrase what he assumes to be the spatial character of his own mental activities. The latter, as we have seen, are "spread out," "voluminous," "streaked": they have "position and direction." In this they resemble certain of their own objects. But there is a difference between the space of mind and the space of the outer world. The

latter is "contemplated," the former "enjoyed" space.[37] These expressions indicate two distinguishable modes of experience. In the one case we observe the spatial properties of objects around us: in the other we appreciate the spatiality of our own conscious states. Enjoyed space is one with the enjoyment of it. In this way enjoyment, which is just experience itself conceived in the context of its subjectivity rather than in relation to its object, reveals its spatial character.

24. That Alexander has drawn attention to a significant distinction is beyond dispute. Space is experienced not only as an object of contemplative awareness, or as an observable relation between the contents of an objective manifold, but in another way as well— a way which, for the moment, I shall content myself with describing as non-contemplative. I cannot, however, accept Alexander's account of our non-contemplative spatial experience. As the difference between us has to do with our respective interpretations of what we are agreed in regarding as identifiable matter of fact, I shall try to indicate where and how exactly the element of fact comes in. If I can trust the intimations of my own experience, it comes in at two points: (1) The consciousness of our own bodies includes a feeling of their spatiality (we actually *feel* our bodies *in space*); and (2) just as we are able to reproduce the objective space of contemplative awareness in imagination, so we are able to evoke an imaginative counterpart of felt space. These, I think, are the facts which lend colour to Alexander's doctrine of "enjoyed" space as the space of our mental processes. Of the two, the first is obviously basic. For this reason I shall take it for granted. My starting-point, then, is the willing acknowledgment of an obscure but thoroughly familiar and potent mode of consciousness, which is variously known to psychologists as "general" or "common sensibility," "coenaesthesis," "Gemeingefühl," "Gemeinempfindung," "Gefühlsempfindung," "Gemeingefühlsempfindung," but to which, in the special context of our problem, I shall give the name of "body-feeling."[38]

---

[37] The two, according to Alexander, "belong experientially to one space." *Space, Time and Deity*, Vol. I, p. 98.

[38] *vid.* Appendix A, p. 174.

25. By *body-feeling* I mean the rudimentary consciousness we all have of our own bodies.[39] It should be obvious that these living structures are not revealed to us in the first instance as definite and definitely identifiable objects of observation. We learn so to view them at a more advanced stage of the mental life, and even then it is not normally as *objects* that we experience the bodies which we claim as *our own*. The latter announce themselves through vague, though sometimes intense, mental states which I can only designate "feelings" or "sensations."[40] These must be distinguished from other entities to which the name of "feeling" is commonly applied—the sensation of touch, for example,[41] or the emotional ingredient in all our conscious states, both the general pleasure-pain condition and the highly specialized affective component in the individual instincts. Body-feelings may of course be pleasant or painful: they may include the mode of consciousness known to some psychologists as "affect"; but their essential character is to be found in something else.

The conception is undoubtedly difficult and elusive. I shall try to render it as definite and complete as may be by viewing it in a variety of contexts and approaching it successively from different angles.

26. To begin with, assuming the familiar psychological distinction of a cognitive, an affective and a conative aspect in all our mental processes, I assign body-feeling to the category of conscious states in which the cognitive aspect prevails over the other two.[42]

[39] Professor Alexander might with some appearance of reason object to my tracing back the experience of enjoyed space to this source. For, as I have already pointed out, it is not in the rudimentary forms of awareness, but more particularly in "the higher acts of mind," that he finds the spatiality of consciousness most pronounced. My point, however, is not that body-feeling occurs only when our experience is at the rudimentary level, but that this rudimentary form of spatial awareness may accompany my experience at any level of development. That it should be more pronounced (in the experience of some) in the higher mental activities might be explained on the ground that for refined natures and developed intellects these activities are the most *exciting*, and are therefore apt to reflect themselves most noticeably in bodily *excitation*. I shall return to the point.

[40] Though ill-defined, these feelings, as Sir John H. Parsons remarks of hunger and thirst, and of the sense of position and change of position, must have a very high survival value. *An Introduction to the Theory of Perception*, pp. 10, 239.

[41] Although, as we shall see, touch includes coenaesthetic experience.

[42] I intend this statement to hold good even where the feeling is a violent pain. For while in this case the affective aspect may be most prominent in the consciousness of the subject, it is only in virtue of its significance as a revelation of the body (e.g., in respect of position, direction and extensity) that a pain is definable as "*body*-feeling."

Whatever be its conative conditions and its emotional accompaniments, it is in its modality as an informative state of mind, a being conscious *of something*, that its significance lies. At the same time its epistemological value is of the lowest. While body-feeling is a way of *knowing*, as *knowledge* it has about it something nebulous and inchoate.[43] Hence it takes its place in the class of rudimentary cognitions—a class which also includes the more generally recognized forms of sensation, but at a stage of development prior to that at which the latter become elaborated in a definitely perceptual experience.[44]

The Problem of Distinguishing Body Feelings or "General Sensibility," from the Special Senses. They Are differently Cognitive

27. The next step is to determine the exact position of body-feeling within the category to which I have assigned it. This involves the question of its relation to the sensations in general and in detail. Among the writers who have attempted a systematic exposition of the subject there is a tendency to treat "general sensibility" as a comprehensive term for all the obscurer and less frequently recognized sensations—those, for example, to which the designations "kinaesthetic" and "organic" have been applied, with a somewhat indefinite variety of subordinate types.[45] We are here in a region which has not yet been satisfactorily explored, and much uncertainty remains as to the number and nature of the sensations involved.[46] This, however, is a matter of lesser impor-

---

[43] That is to say, *if taken in and by itself*. I wish to make this clear because, as a matter of fact, we learn to bring the vague feeling of our corporeality into contexts of interpretation which invest it with the value of a *sign*. It may thus acquire a high degree of cognitive significance. Thus certain forms of tonality (the exhilaration or the malaise, whether general or localized, of which we are conscious when we feel "well" or "ill") may have great diagnostic value. It is worth noting the remarkable expression in the New Testament story of the woman with the issue of blood. ". . . And she felt in her body [literally, "*knew with her body*"—ἔγνω τῷ σώματι] that she was healed." Mark v. 29.

[44] This is the aspect of body-feeling which justifies the application of the term "sensation," "Empfindung."

[45] A list of these will be found in Titchener's *Text-Book of Psychology*, §§38-59. In the former class are included the muscular, tendinous, articular, ampullar and vestibular senses, the two latter (i.e. dizziness and the sense of rectilinear movement, particularly in a vertical direction) having their supposed seat in the cristae and maculae of the semi-circular canals. Among organic sensations Titchener recognizes those which we associate with the different abdominal organs.

[46] *vid.* Appendix B, p. 175.

tance, in so far as the expression "general sensibility" has nothing to do with a *collection* or a *generalization* of instances. It is not as covering a plurality of distinct types, but as connoting a certain property of *commonness* in every member of a group,[47] that the words "common" and "general" are to be understood.[48]

On the other hand there is something to be learned from any representative list (whether more extended or more restricted) of the "common" senses—something which brings together unmistakably these obscure, yet *distinct* and identifiable forms of sensibility, and stereotypes them against certain other forms, which, in Cartesian parlance, are not only distinct but *clear*. The latter forms, sight, hearing, taste, smell and (in certain of its aspects) touch, quite obviously constitute a class by themselves; and this is a fact which at once supplies at least a negative differentia for the senses we designate "general" and "common." The question we have to ask is this: What is it in the five familiar "senses," recognized from time immemorial, that so sharply distinguishes them from the many others which we have been led to think of as senses at all only by recent advances in physiology and psychology? It is not merely that the former found their way into the tradition of our thinking at an earlier stage. Rather the cleavage has to do with a generic difference both in the *conditioning* and in the *outcome* as a form of experience (or, generally speaking, in what I shall call the "modality") of the sensory function as such.[49] We are

[47] Thus we may not only speak of a "general sense," but we may describe a variety of individual senses as "general." This view also precludes the interpretation of body-feeling as a summation or product of component sensations (although of course it may have its components), as a "panoramic background" (Parsons, *op. cit.*, p. 31), and as a total feeling of the body. "Commonness" does not mean totality. If there is a feeling of the body as a whole, it is an *instance* of body-feeling; but so are the feelings of individual parts.

[48] In recent years there has been a tendency "to abandon the numerous sense modalities once posited in this connection, such as cutaneous sensitivity, kinaesthesis, joint sense, muscle sense, and to unite these modalities into one sense department recognizing pressure, warmth, cold, etc. as 'qualities' of the modality." John P. Nafe, "The Psychology of Felt Experience," *American Journal of Psychology*, Vol. XXXIX, p. 367.

[49] The term "Modalität" was introduced by Helmholtz (*Handbuch d. physiol. Optik*, 1894, S. 584) to denote the specific character that marks off the sensations of one organ from those of another, in contradistinction to the differences of *quality* that characterize the sensations of a single organ. vid. J. B. Haycraft, *The Sense of Taste*, in Schäfer's *Text-Book of Physiology*, Vol. II, pp. 1242 sq. In applying the term to the sensory function as such I am merely extending its application from the specific differences which distinguish any one sense from any other to a more general difference which divides the senses as a whole into two inclusive groups.

dealing with a principle of discrimination so fundamental that in relation to it the whole of our sensory experience falls naturally on one side or the other of a single dividing line.

28. The attempt to define this line has led to considerable misunderstanding. For example, there has been a marked tendency to assume that the "common" may be distinguished from the "special" type of sensation in virtue of a certain *subjectivity* peculiar to the former.[50] This is of course entirely misleading. All our experience is subjective, and the latter property cannot be treated as differentiating one mode of sensitivity from another. Again the suggestion that the distinction may be traced to the difference between peripheral and internal excitation is untenable. It may be that, as Sir Charles Sherrington points out in his account of "total common sensation,"[51] "stimuli exciting the apparatus of the special senses, visual and auditory, under ordinary circumstances give but little towards 'common sensation'," whereas "the sensations that arise in internal organs and viscera . . . contribute a great deal"; but it would be an error to make serious use of this distinction in the attempt to differentiate general from special sensibility, and to conclude, as the writer does, that coenaesthesis is "built" of what, following Herbert Spencer,[52] he calls "entoperipheral" in contradistinction to "epiperipheral feelings." The difference is not that between internal and surface sensations;[53] and the best corrective to this simple and misleading dichotomy is Sherrington's own invaluable analysis of the nervous system with reference to the important factor of receptivity.

In his *Integrative Action of the Nervous System* Sherrington has shown that neural activity, as developed on the basis of the reflex arc, implies a set of organs which, in relation to the stimulus, he calls "receptors," but which, morphologically speaking, should be included along with the *conductor* and *effector* organs in the physiological structure of the arc itself.[54] So regarded, receptors are really "initiating organs." As elements in neural structures they fall into

---

[50] Wundt, *Physiologische Psychologie*, 1902-1903, Vol. II, p. 42; O. Funke, *Der Tastsinn u. die Gemeingefühle*, in Hermann's *Handbuch der Physiologie*, Vol. II, p. 302.
[51] *Cutaneous Sensations* in Schäfer's *Text-Book*, Vol. II, p. 970 (Edinburgh, 1900).
[52] *Principles of Psychology*, Vol. I, pp. 166 and 250 (London, 1881).
[53] cf. O. Külpe, *Grundriss d. Psychologie* (English tr. *Outlines*), pp. 140-1.
[54] *op. cit.*, p. 7.

three classes according to the "field" of their activity. There are "two primary distributions of the receptor organs," one on the surface and one in the depth of the organism. This gives us the distinction of *extero-* and *proprio-ceptive* fields.[55] But the former is subdivided into two further fields, one of which (designated *extero-ceptive* in a narrower sense) "is coextensive with the so-called *external* surface of the animal," while the other, the *intero-ceptive*, though still in contact with the environment, is "deeply recessed" and "partly screened by the organism itself." The reference is to the so-called "internal" surface, which is "usually alimentary in function." This threefold classification does something to obscure the simplicity and directness of the contrast between surface and interior excitation; but the significance of the contrast, thus impaired, is completely destroyed by a fact to which Sherrington also draws attention, namely the neurological solidarity of the *extero-* and *proprio-ceptive* fields. Thus "reflexes arising from proprio-ceptive organs come . . . to be habitually attached and appended to certain reflexes excited by extero-ceptive organs. The reaction of the animal to stimulation of one of its extero-ceptors excites certain tissues, and the activity thus produced in these latter tissues excites in them their receptors, which are *proprio-ceptors.*"[56] The writer goes on to cite the flexion reflex, and points out that in this case "the receptive field includes not only reflex-arcs arising in the surface field, but reflex-arcs arising in the depth of the limb."

In view of these facts it is no longer possible, without further qualification, to distinguish sensations according as they are peripherally or internally initiated. But apart from this particular objection, I hope to show that even where the sensation is unmistakably peripheral, as in surface pressure, it cannot, on that ground alone, be relegated to the category of "special," and excluded from that of "general" sensibility.[57]

[55] *op. cit.*, p. 130.
[56] *op. cit.*, p. 130.
[57] Wundt had drawn attention to a fact which is capable of different interpretations, but which may, I think, fairly be taken to support the view that emphasizes the solidarity of peripheral and central excitability. In the case of sensations like muscular exhaustion, hunger, thirst, and breathlessness, the occasion may be located in the peripheral nerve-spread, but the real source is in the nerve-centres. *Physiol. Psych.*, Vol II, p. 43.

The First Point of Contrast: the Body Feelings Are Cognitive of the Organism

29. The real point of the contrast, as I see it, is this. The "special" senses have each a specific type of object, other than the body itself or the bodily organ or the receptors affected— colour in the case of the eye, sound and savour in that of the ear and the organ of taste respectively. I presume the sense of smell belongs to the same category, and must be explained by reference to similar factors. What is characteristic of this group of senses is that in the first place they are all associated with "distance receptors" or "receptors which react to *objects* at a distance,"[58] and in the second place, that these receptors, "acting as sense-organs, initiate sensations having the psychical quality called projicience."[59] This latter is the spontaneous reference of the sensations to the external objects in which the stimuli have their source.[60] Such reference is either entirely wanting in the mode of general sensibility, or else, where it is present, as in surface pressure, it reveals itself as only one aspect in a sensory experience from which, in another aspect, external reference is absent.[61] However this fact and the fact to which, in the case of the special senses, it stands opposed are to be interpreted, we have here a differentia which can hardly be less than decisive in its significance. The common senses have nothing corresponding to the highly specialized, extra-organic objects of sight, hearing, taste and smell, which announce themselves not as properties or conditions of the receptors or organs affected, but as conditions of the environment or qualities

[58] Sherrington, *op. cit.*, p. 324.

[59] *loc. cit.*

[60] There is some obscurity in Sherrington's account of smell and its relation to its object. The organs involved are recognized as distance-receptors, and the consciousness of odours is classed with that of light and sound as characterized by projicience. Presumably the field, like that of the taste organs (*vid. op. cit.*, p. 317), is intero-ceptive. And yet the property of projicience is denied to sensations having intero-ceptive fields. *op. cit.*, p. 324. The contradiction is quite explicit in Parsons' *Theory of Perception*, where we find "the common chemical sense" of "olfaction" expressly referred to the group of intero-ceptors (p. 10), while the writer follows Sherrington both in denying projicience to the class of sensations thus marked off, and in according it to smell (p. 24).

[61] If, e.g., I pass my hand lightly over the smooth surface of a table, I am conscious of two things, only one of which is external to my body—viz., (1) the table, and (2) a series of cutaneous sensations. Surface pressure is an anomalous case, and will have to be dealt with by itself.

of extraneous bodies. Whether this circumstance is to be described, as Weber describes it, by denying all *objects* to the common senses,[62] and identifying the latter with changes in our state of sensitiveness,[63] is a question which can be answered only by reference to a more general context of interpretation than that supplied by physiological psychology. What is unmistakable is the absence of all reference to anything outside the organism.

30. But what of the organism itself in relation to the various forms of general sensibility? Is it not the case that these differentiations of experience direct our attention to the bodies which we think of as our own, just as the special senses do to objects other than our bodies? The suggestion is surely one which we are bound in some sense to accept. I say "in some sense," because the exact nature of the connection between our living bodies and the sensory awareness of them is so far exceedingly obscure. As I have just indicated in a general way, we are not yet in a position either to assert or to deny that in such instances as hunger and thirst, cutaneous irritation, muscular strain and "heartburn," the bodily elements involved are to be construed as *objects* of the experience.[64] But that the experience includes what I shall call a *reference* to certain parts of the body or to the body as a whole is too obvious to be questioned. However ignorant I may be of its structure and functions, however blind to the real nature of what is taking place within it, it is of my body (though perhaps not of it alone) that I am conscious, when I experience any of the general sensations. This is a fact which stands out in such vivid contrast to its counterpart in the other group of sensory experiences, that I propose to stereotype it (in an expression suggested by Sherrington's classification of the receptors) as "proprio-sensitivity." The special senses, on the contrary, which direct the mind to something beyond the body— something which in this relation takes on the indisputable character of objectivity—may be designated "hetero-sensitive."

---

[62] *Der Tastsinn und das Gemeingefühl*, Ostwald's *Klassiker*, pp. 563, note, and 495.

[63] "Änderungen unseres Empfindungszustandes," *op. cit.*, p. 563. cf. O. Funke, "Veränderte Zustände des Bewusstseins," *Physiol. d. Hautempfindungen*, in Hermann's *Handbuch*, Vol. II, p. 301.

[64] I have of course already agreed that in body-feeling the spatial factor is not an object *of contemplation*. The question which remains is whether it would be appropriate to represent the body as *an object of feeling*.

*The Main Contrast: the Special Sense in Which Body Feelings Are
Cognitive of the Organism: Their Loci Are not Definable by
Reference to Points in Public Space*

31. It will be observed that the distinction, as thus formulated,
is entirely dependent on the non-subjective factors in the case. The
difference is that between a reference to the living body, viewed
from the standpoint of its owner, and a reference to its environment. But obviously such a context of relations, though thoroughly
relevant, is unable to provide the proper setting for a genuinely
philosophical insight into the nature of body-feeling as such. For
this we must have recourse to a totally different point of view. We
must place the experience of body-feeling in the context of its
native subjectivity; and it is in this setting that we must seek the
answer to our question as to the connection between such feeling
and our sense of space.

32. As I have assumed throughout, "body-feeling" is not a state
of the body, but a state of consciousness, a way of knowing these
bodies of ours. In other words, the concept is not that of something
physical, qualified by the fact that it is felt, but that of something
subjective, qualified by a physiological condition. The relation
involved may be expressed by saying that the feeling in question
is a consciousness *of* the body. It is not so, however, in the sense in
which seeing is a consciousness of colour, hearing of sound, or
touch of the smooth, hard surface of an external object. The difference turns upon the distinguishing characteristics of proprio-sensitivity in its spatial aspect, of which there are three: (1) the direct
and immediate reference of the space-term to our consciousness of
it, (2) the isolation of the body, as a spatial system, from every
frame of reference other than itself, and (3) the total absence of
those lines of implication which lead inevitably from the individual's private space-experience to an independently existing public
space. It will be convenient to begin with the second of these considerations. The first and the third go together, and may be disposed of later as aspects of the same truth.

33. That it is possible to have an experience of spatial systems
in complete detachment from that of the physical world around us
is at once apparent from the case of scenes depicted in a painting
or reflected in a mirror. These are of course related to the world of
physical space, but not in a spatial sense—that is, in the way in

which one object within the latter is related to another. To take a simple illustration: a person, let us suppose, is standing in front of a mirror, but at a distance of five feet from its surface. Under these circumstances the figure in the glass will appear at a similar distance from the reflected foreground. It would not on that account be correct to describe the two figures as ten feet apart. Nothing seen in the mirror has any assignable distance from anything seen outside it. The reflecting surface is not a plane interposed between a number of physical objects on the one hand and their simulacra on the other: rather it divides the real objects in front of it from the real objects behind it; and the reflections have no place in either class. Their spatial relations, therefore, constitute a system which is cut off entirely from that of real space. The same is true of a pictorial representation.

There is therefore no a priori difficulty, no theoretical impossibility, in thinking of the living body as an exclusive spatial system out of all spatial relation to the space of the actual world. In point of fact it is precisely so that we experience it. When we refer the body-feelings to a locus in the organism, that locus is not definable by reference to points outside the body: it is not *near* any one of the latter, nor *far from* any other: there is no position in the environment which it ever approaches or from which it ever recedes. In brief, we cannot find or even imagine a frame of reference which includes at once the loci of our coenaesthetic sensations and points in public space.

34. Among these sensations there is a group (of which surface pressure and temperature may be taken as the type) that might at first sight appear to offer an exception to this statement. Thus, to repeat our former illustration, when we lay the palm of the hand upon the surface of a smoothly polished table, we experience a double sensory impression, first of the table itself, and secondly of the hand. Now the temptation is to refer the two impressions to a single locus, definable as the plane of contact between the palm and the table. The palm, it will be said, is experienced exactly where the surface of the table is experienced and vice versa. In support of this view it might be further pointed out that the function of touch is largely that of identifying the positions, shapes and sizes of objects in the outer world by the sensations they produce

in us, and that this result is achieved by placing portions of our bodies where these objects are.[65]

This is a highly misleading account of the matter; and it is due in large part, I think, to the fact that through constant association we have come to read the one experience in the light of the other. The tendency to assimilate the space of *touching* to that of *the object touched* is doubtless reinforced by the concentration of our interest and attention upon the latter. Whatever the explanation of this error, the fact is that the position, size and shape of the object are not really experienced in the body, by which in this case is meant the skin, any more than colour is experienced in the eye or sound in the ear. So far as its relation on the one hand to the outer world, and on the other to our consciousness, is concerned, the skin is a specialized organ of sense. Its function (or, to be exact, the function of the cutaneous receptors localized in it) is to reveal the presence of external objects. This is one thing: the proprio-sensitivity of the receptor organs is another. The two experiences are indeed closely correlated. As allied forms of sensation they have presumably been evolved together—or, perhaps I should say, the perception of the tactual object through the cutaneous receptor has been evolved from a primitive touch-consciousness akin to body-feeling. But once the differentiation has occurred, the essence of the dual experience is that the thing felt is referred as an object to the outward system of observed space, the cutaneous sensation to the felt space of the organism. It is only for certain limited purposes that we tend to identify these two. For the rest they define themselves against one another, but not as contiguous portions of a single homogeneous extension. The surface of the body, as located by tactual feeling, is like the surface of the mirror in relation to the objects reflected in it—that is to say, it is not a plane dividing the space of the organism from surrounding space. All the points of reference which serve to define it *as felt* lie within the body, and there is no felt space beyond. The surface of the table, on the other hand, is like that of the mirror in relation to the physical world. It is to this world that the mirror belongs; and it has no connections of a spatial character with any other. For a similar reason the table's surface cannot be thought of as occupying

---

[65] The case of a blind man "feeling" his way about by means of a stick would be an extension of the same process by mechanical means, kinaesthetic sensation, which generally accompanies active tactual experience, taking the place of surface pressure.

the same position in space to which, by feeling, we refer the palm of the hand.

35. That in spite of this impossibility we do habitually refer the two surfaces for certain purposes, whether theoretical or practical, to an identical position (definable as the plane in which they coincide) is a procedure that admits of justification upon one ground alone. There must be some sense in which it is possible to view the body and the table in the same order of space. Now obviously an inanimate object cannot be transferred to the space of feeling. But the living body, which we feel in a space of its own, can *also* be experienced as an object of observation in the public space which contains the table. The isolation of the organism is thus overcome, but at the expense of one whole phase in our experience of it. So long as we recognize the coenaesthetic consciousness of our bodies in any one of its numerous forms, the space with which we have perforce to deal is a space apart from that of the physical world, and definable as the system of all the loci to which our body-feelings directly refer.[66]

The Reference Which Body Feelings Have, Even to Body Space, Does Not Give Them Interpunctual Organization or Make Them Spatial

36. The conception of "reference," to which I have repeatedly had recourse, calls for explanation. In the physical world every position is determined by the relation in which it stands to certain coordinates (fixed for the purpose) in a frame of *reference*. These relations are strictly inter-objective; and objectivity, in accordance with the concept of the physical, may here be construed as implying independence.[67] Should any particular position become an object of consciousness, this fact has no bearing upon its spatial determinateness. The relation of object to subject becomes an experience of space only in so far as it is mediated by a relation of object to object, maintained in complete independence of the other relation. The same thing holds good not only of physical space as such, but of those spatial systems which, like that seen in a mirror or a picture, are subjectively conditioned. That is to say, while the space in question exists only for the mind of the spectator, it ar-

---

[66] cf. the remarks of Ward beginning: "In the concrete, the body is the origin or datum to which all positions are referred." *Psychological Principles*, 1918, pp. 144 *sq.*

[67] By this of course is not meant absoluteness of position, but non-relativity to mind.

ticulates itself in a way that is determined by the reference of every point to every other in the objective manifold presented, rather than by the common reference of all points to a conscious subject.[68]

It is otherwise with the space of coenaesthesis. The latter is a mode of experience in which we refer our conscious states directly to positions in the organism. *Reference* then in this case is the immediate relation of the living body, in its spatial character, to the coenaesthetic consciousness of it. The point which must be emphasized is the directness of the relation. This is the characteristic of felt space which decides the question whether or not the bodily correlate of coenaesthetic experience can be properly designated the *object* of body-feeling. Doubtless the question is to some extent a verbal one; but I would point out that while the essence of objectivity (as we shall see later) is the relation to a *subject*, the general assumption is that the entity so related defines itself within a plurality of similar entities, against which the subject stands out in the attitude of detachment so well described by Professor Alexander as contemplation. Where the subjective attitude is *feeling*, the non-subjective correlate in its turn detaches itself, in the first instance, more or less completely from all contexts save that which unites it to the mind of the percipient. This does not mean that the correlate of general sensibility is necessarily simple and atomic, but only that in its complexity it comes before the mind as something entire and integral, and that its differentiations reveal themselves not as particulars to be observed along with the relations between them, but as qualifications in the end-term of the experience itself. In view of this important difference it seems to me advisable to reserve the word "object" for the correlate of our contemplative awareness.[69]

37. I return to the conception of *reference*, defined as the relation of body-space to body-feeling. This relation differs profoundly from that which serves to determine the spatial identity of objects; and with the change in the relation there goes a no less radical change in the conditions by which the spatial articulateness of the

[68] The difference between an independently existing and a subjectively conditioned spatial manifold is one of ontological status rather than of form or structure.

[69] This statement is subject to one important modification. Everything that is or can be thought of is capable of entering into the relationship of objectivity. In certain contexts (for example, the context of this theoretical discussion) the spatial correlate of body-feeling necessarily becomes an object. It does so, however, not as the correlate of body-feeling, but as the subject of discourse.

body is determined. All positions are now fixed, not as terms in a relation which binds them to one another independently of the relation in which they stand to consciousness, but as the immediate relata of a partially differentiated, yet relatively primitive sensitivity.

The error which I am trying to expose, the error of attributing spatiality to our mental states, may be corrected in theory by a strict attention to the fact of *reference*. But in practice this has been rendered difficult by a constitutional tendency *to refer our sensations themselves* to the positions in the organism *to which they refer*. Thus we locate our aches and pains more or less definitely in almost every region of the body; and we describe and classify them (in terms which, either directly or by implication, convey a reference of space) as sharp, piercing, shooting, splitting, throbbing, spreading, massive, diffused, voluminous. Cutaneous irritation in its various forms, pressure, temperature, muscular and articular sensation are all assigned to special areas supposed for the time being to be affected. These areas may differ both in position and in extent; and the difference has been recognized by psychologists, in their conceptions of local signature and extensity, as applying to the sensations as such. In this the psychologists are merely drawing attention to certain distinguishable features in the data. Only, it should be clearly understood that extensity and local sign, in so far as they are differentiating properties of *sensation*, are not spatial differences. Thus local sign is not definable as "place felt," but as "a feeling of place"; and the difference between two local signs is not that between one part of the body and another part, but that between *feeling the first* and *feeling the second*. In like manner extensity is not spatial extent, but a subjective quality which varies, it may be, in some cases with the volume of the object, but more strictly speaking, and more generally, with the area of the body affected by the stimulus. To put the matter briefly, just as felt space is the non-psychical correlate of body-feeling, extensity and local sign are qualities of body-feeling in its aspect of psychical correlate to felt space.

It should be noted that extensity, like the space of coenaesthetic sensation, is not the product of interpunctual organization. The sense of "voluminousness" is an altogether integral experience. That is to say, it is not a compound of many feelings, nor a way of feeling many things together, but a massive kind of feeling or a way of feeling one thing *massively*. The absence of an interpunctual system is no less characteristic of local signature. The latter is not the *selection*, but the *feeling*, of a point. In both cases the rule of coenaesthetic space-experience is correlation without objective coordinates.

38. The foregoing discussion, it will be remembered, had its origin in my attempt to deal with the second distinguishing characteristic of proprio-sensitivity as a consciousness of space, namely, the relegation of the living body to a spatial system of its own. In the course of its unfolding, however, the argument has brought out in detail the characteristic which I placed first in order—that is to say, the direct reference of the space-term to our coenaesthetic consciousness. Of this no more need here be said. All that remains is to show how the third characteristic—the inconvertibility of felt space into public space—is implied in the first.

So long as we take our stand within the limits of body-feeling as such, and do not pass to the point of view from which the body appears as an object among objects, the spatial reference is always to a uniquely existing organism, the immediate correlate of a no less uniquely existing subject-self or conscious personality. It follows that the space of coenaesthetic experience must always be completely private to the individual. By no possibility can any one system of such space be synthesized with any other, or be made to appear as a differentiation within a homogeneous continuum of extension. If we try to view it in this way, it loses its character as the non-subjective correlate of body-feeling, and becomes a configuration in the public space of observational experience. Doubtless there is a profound significance in the very possibility of thus passing from one mode of experience to another; and the subject (though in another connection) will have to engage our attention at a later stage. For the present our business is to place the distinction beyond the range of that confusion which, as I have suggested, is responsible for the doctrine that enjoyed space is mental and that the mind has spatial properties.

Is Spatiality of Mental States a Deliverance of Mature Experience?

39. It is my contention that the only *de facto* psychological evidence we can have for the spatial interpretation of mental processes is derived from the immediate reference of our coenaesthetic experience to loci and to areas in the organism. But to in-

terpret this experience so is to misconstrue it altogether. The space of proprio-sensitivity, though felt rather than observed, enjoyed rather than contemplated, is nonetheless the space of the living body, and not the space of the mind. The question might be allowed to rest here; but before passing from it altogether, I should like to dispose of two objections to the view I have advanced.

The first is one upon which I have already touched. Proprio-sensitivity is obviously a primitive mode of consciousness. But Professor Alexander, as I have had occasion more than once to notice, affirms that the spatiality of mind is most pronounced in its higher activities. My suggestion as to how this difficulty may be met calls for a little elaboration.

It will hardly be questioned that all our mental processes (the more highly refined and sublimated, as well as the most rudimentary) have their physiological concomitants, and that the more advanced these processes become in complexity and in spiritual significance, the more active and complicated is the cerebration which they imply. At the lower levels of control our ideas and feelings tend to reflect themselves in changes of respiration and circulation, and to work themselves out in mimetic action, or at least to find an egress in facial expression, in gesture, and, generally speaking, in gross bodily movement. Where the inhibitions that come with training and sophistication have neutralized the tendency to spontaneous discharge through the motor mechanisms, or where the mental processes involved are too delicate and rarefied for overt physiological self-expression, it still remains true that thought and emotion continue to register in subtle changes within the organism as a whole. These changes are in many cases beyond the range of clear consciousness; but they frequently give rise to vague though unmistakable sensations. The intense cerebration that accompanies hard thinking can be distinctly felt. It can even be approximately located, very much as we locate muscular strain. Successful mental effort reports itself not merely in the satisfaction that attends achievement (a pleasure which has its origin in the activity of the subjective system as such), but also in a pervasive exhilaration which is quite distinct from this pleasure, and can only be construed as a psychical repercussion of animal effectiveness. Under other conditions the attendant body-feeling may take the form of acute malaise, ending in sickness and collapse. Of this

we have a striking example in the account which Dorothy Wordsworth has given of her brother's sufferings in periods of heightened
poetic activity.[70] Such experiences are of course as exceptional as
the efforts that called them forth. But they are merely extreme
instances of the sensitivity of the organism to the higher activities
of the mind.

The precise point to which I wish to draw attention is the fact
that when subtle bodily changes thus reflect the energies of spirit,
these changes may in turn be reflected back into consciousness in
the form of body-feelings with the inevitable reference to space.
This of itself would seem a sufficient explanation of the apparently
spatial character of the mental processes in question. But if it is
thought that something is still wanting to a complete elucidation
of the mystery, I would suggest that it is to be found in the
second of the two facts of which I made special mention at the beginning of the inquiry—the fact, namely, that the mental powers
are frequently associated in their exercise with the activity of the
spatial imagination.

I am not thinking of the propensity (sufficiently attested by
experience) to accompany our highest intellectual flights (even in
the sphere of abstract thinking) with visual imagery. The activity
which I have in mind is the imaginative counterpart of a *feeling*,
rather than a *contemplative* space-consciousness. When the feeling
of space is thus subjectively initiated, it enters the main stream of
our mental activity with the apparent force of an adjectival qualification. In this way our thoughts, desires and emotions may contract the illusory aspect of position, direction and volume in space.
That these characters should seem to *qualify* the dominant mental
activity is doubtless due to the difference of intensity, explicitness
and relevancy between the main stream of consciousness and the
vague space-feeling which has filtered through from its source in
the imagination.

The Difficulty of "Referred" Pain

40. The second objection has to do with the phenomenon known
as allocheiria or allaesthesia, the reference of sensations to a part
of the body other than that affected by the stimulus or by a

[70] cf. *William Wordsworth* by George McLean Harper, Vol. I, p. 411; Vol. II, pp.
26-7.

lesion.[71] "Referred pain" is a familiar instance of this.[72] An allied phenomenon, "das Phantomglied," is the propensity of persons with an amputated limb to experience sensations in the missing member.[73] These possibilities would seem to discredit the view that the spatial reference implied in local signature is necessarily to definite positions in the body. Where there is a doubt as to what these positions are, or where the element of illusion enters into the experience, felt place, it will be argued, cannot be limited to bodily place, because the point of reference is not the point of stimulation, and is even found in some cases to lie outside the organism altogether.

The contention rests upon an error I have been at some pains to dispel. When it is said that the body is stimulated at one point, and the sensation located at another, the underlying assumption is that of a single interpunctual system within which the difference arises. But of the two positions here in question only one belongs to such a system. The spatial identity of the other is defined by the relation in which it stands to the coenaesthetic consciousness of the subject. We have therefore no right to assert difference in the sense intended, any more than in a previous instance, and under a similar erroneous presupposition, we had a right to assert coincidence. As the place of touching and the place touched cannot be described as *one*, so now the point of stimulation and the point of reference in body-feeling cannot (in the ordinary sense of such a proposition) be described as *two*.

An identical criticism applies to the statement that in the case of the "Phantomglied" the point of reference lies outside the organism. The idea is that since an amputated member is one which has been removed from the body, any sensation felt in the member must be felt outside the body, and therefore at a point in circumambient space. But the whole of my argument assumes that external space cannot be felt. The objection as stated involves a

[71] The term "allocheiria" (other-handedness), in accordance with its etymologica' sense, is sometimes limited to cases in which the sensation is referred to the opposite side of the body. *vid.* Osler and McCrae, *A System of Medicine*, London, 1910, Vol. VII, *Diseases of the Nervous System*, pp. 30, 283, 694.

[72] Sir James Mackenzie, *Symptoms and their Interpretation*, London, 1909, pp. 27-8; 38; 51 *sq.*; Chap. IX, p. 97. Also, *The Future of Medicine*, London, 1919, Part II, Chap. II, pp. 66 *sq.*

[73] A. Pitres, "Étude sur les sensations illusoires des amputés," in *Annales Médico-Psychologiques*, Paris 1897, pp. 5-19 and 177-92, gives a bibliography.

false analysis of the facts. It is not correct to speak of a sensation as located in an amputated limb or in the portion of surrounding space which such a limb would normally occupy. Where then is the point of reference assumed in this mode of experience?

The answer is contained in my definition of felt space as "the system of all the loci to which our body-feelings directly refer." The sensations with which we are here dealing belong to the class of body-feelings, and their points of reference are among the loci which contribute to the space of the body as felt. As experienced, therefore, the "Phantomglied" is a part of the body. From this standpoint the fact that a member has been removed by amputation is an irrelevant circumstance—although of course it acquires the significance of a physical event when we pass from the system of points which constitute the correlatives of body-feeling to the interpunctual system of coordinates in objective space. So long as these two are not confused, there need be no difficulty in the thought that the point to which the feelings in question are referred is situated in the body. This conclusion at once implies, and serves to reinforce, my contention that the limits of the body felt must not be conceived to coincide with those of the body which we experience as an object in a manifold of objects.

To sum up the general import of this chapter—the psychological and the epistemological argument for the spatiality of mind and its processes are alike untenable. If in spite of this it is still maintained that the psychical has spatial properties, it can only be on the ground that mind and body are in the end identical. This is a proposition which we have found independent reasons for rejecting.

APPENDIX A (*See note 38, page* 155)

The Terms for Body Feeling

There is no general accord or consistency in the use of the terms listed on page 155. "Gemeingefühl" and "Gemeinempfindung" (or "Gemeinge-fühlsempfindung") are sometimes treated as interchangeable. (*vid.* E. H. Weber, *Der Tastsinn und das Gemeingefühl*, in Wagner's *Handwörterbuch der Physiologie* (1846), III ,2, S. 562 *sq.*; republished, Ostwald's *Klassiker der exakten Wissenschaften*, No .149, Leipzig, 1905.) Sometimes they are distinguished. (*vid.* Wundt, *Physiologische Psychologie*, 5th ed., Leipzig, 1902-1903, I, 352; II, 356-7. F. E. O. Schultze, "Über Organempfind-ungen und Körpergefühle (Dynamien)," in *Archiv für Gesamte Psychologie*, 1908.) For this latter writer the distinction is so elusive as to be practically inapplicable. Theoretically it is expressed thus: "If I have a *sensation* in my head or elsewhere, it remains a *sensation* in my head or elsewhere. If on the other hand I have a *feeling* localized in my head, my whole body seems to be pervaded by a sense of pleasure, sadness, etc., as the case may be." (*op. cit.*, p. 200.) On the tendency to identify Gefühl and Empfindung, characteristic of Weber and Johannes Müller, *vid.* Wundt, *op. cit.*, Vol. II, pp. 346 and 366. For Wundt, as for others, the distinction rests on that of subjective state and objective content. O. Külpe rejects the expression "common feeling" in favour of "common sensation" (*Grundriss der Psychologie*, §23, English tr. p. 146), but retains the former ("Gemeingefühl") as a name for the general sus-ceptibility of the individual to pleasure and pain, in contradistinction to "Einzelgefühl"—the susceptibility which goes with specific sensory stimulus. (*vid. Vorlesungen über Psychologie*, Leipzig, 1920, p. 232.)

APPENDIX B (*See note* 46, *page* 157)

THE SENSATIONS INVOLVED IN GENERAL SENSIBILITY

A characteristic enumeration is that of O. Funke in Hermann's *Handbuch der Physiologie*. Under the collective title of "Gefühlsempfindungen" this writer brings together all the forms of sensibility which do not depend upon the peripheral organs of sight, hearing, smell and taste. (cf. Schultze, *Arch. für d. Ges. Psy.*, 1908, p. 155.) This "negative category" is composed of the sensations of "bodily" pain, tickling, shivering, sensual pleasure (Wollust), hunger, thirst, pressure, temperature, muscular sense or strain (Anstrengungsgefühl) and tired feeling. (*op. cit.*, III, Part II, p. 292.) Additions to the list can easily be made—e.g., joint-sensation (Gelenkgefühl, Titchener's articular sense), nausea, various forms of cutaneous irritability, itching, tingling, pricking, pins and needles, goose flesh (Jucken, Kriebeln, Ameisenlaufen), with the sensations due to change in the action of the heart and the respiratory organs, breathlessness and palpitation. (*vid*. Wundt, *Phys. Psy.*, Vol. II, pp. 42 *sq*.; Külpe, *Outlines*, §23.) What Titchener calls the ampullar and vestibular senses are sometimes combined in the generalized conception of a "static sense" (a consciousness of the "orientation" of the body as a whole), for which the organ is the vestibule and the semi-circular canals of the labyrinth. (Külpe, *op. cit.*, p. 149; Parsons, *Theory of Perception*, p. 239.) The expression "static sense" is obviously unsuited to vertigo induced by rotation. (*vid*. the article by the Editor, "Die Lage-, Bewegungs- und Widerstandsempfindungen," in Nagel's *Handbuch der Physiologie des Menschen* (1905), Vol. III, p. 735.)

CHAPTER V

THE MODALITY OF SPIRIT: SUBJECTS AND SYSTEMS OF EXPERIENCE

Methodological Effectiveness as Criterion of Success in Philosophical Inquiry

1. The point of view from which I wish to develop my theme has been indicated by my attitude to the tendency, characteristic of present-day thinking, to minimize the distinction of nature and spirit. This tendency, which, in its various forms, may be described as naturalistic, terminates in a position closely akin to animism.* My own position may be designated anti-animistic and non-naturalist. It is my object to restore a heightened consciousness of the duality which until recently has more or less dominated the history of modern philosophy since Descartes.

If an outlook so determined is necessarily dualistic, then I must accept the appellation. But I do so under a proviso which I have already stated, namely this: the epithet must be taken as the adjectival equivalent of "duality" and not of "dualism."[1] Let me be more explicit. We have seen that in any attempt to deal with the nature of things comprehensively being must be brought in as a postulate.[2] We may argue *from* it, but not to it.[3] The question, however, remains whether being should be postulated once only or more than once. If, as I believe, the answer is that the postulate must be repeated (and this is what is meant by recognizing certain modalities as original), it by no means follows that reality must be

[*The author's allusion, of course, is to the way in which, in animism, spirit and matter are confounded.—Ed.]

[1] Presumably the difference is clear. Duality is a *fact* for thought to deal with: dualism is a way of dealing with the fact—in brief it is a *theory*. My point is that it may not be the only theory available.

[2] cf. Professor Kemp Smith's remark in criticism of Descartes' *cogito ergo sum*, that "we never need to prove existence, since we can never get away from it, but only to define it." *Studies in the Cartesian Philosophy*, p. 51.

[3] I may be permitted to refer to my own observation, in a review of Dr. Temple's *Nature, Man and God*, to the effect that every argument *to* God's existence is an argument *from* His existence. *The Oxford Magazine*, December 6, 1934. Of course there is such a thing as advancing (and accepting or rejecting) *evidence* for the existence of particular entities—the American continent, the planet Neptune, the Ewe-speaking tribes of Africa. This is quite a different matter. The existence for which it is reasonable to seek evidence *presupposes* the existence (our own, for example, or that of the world) which we have to postulate because we cannot prove it in any of the ordinary ways.

thought of in a pluralistic sense. Before the question of monism versus dualism or pluralism can be settled, it is necessary to view the postulate of being in the light of the concept of system. There is at least no a priori objection to the theory that while the *modes* of being are two or more, the *system* of being may be one. Indeed it is quite conceivable that one and the same order of reality may express itself in several mutually irreducible modes of being. To say so is merely to recognize the possibility that the sum-total of things may be not a mere plurality, but a heterogeneous system.[4]

2. In the constructive effort to which I now proceed the general conduct of my argument will be governed by a recognition of the possibilities to which I have drawn attention. I shall not assume that metaphysical inquiry must necessarily be inspired by the ideal of an ontological monism. Nor shall I consider it incumbent upon me to work towards such a conclusion. My guiding principle throughout will be nothing more pretentious than a strict regard for methodological effectiveness. By this I mean coherent thinking concentrated at the points where the human mind has become most acutely conscious of its problems. These points are mostly to be found within the continuity of a living tradition[5]—what I shall call a tradition of understanding. Science in general represents one such tradition. So in a more limited sense does each of the special sciences. The same thing is true of religion as a whole, and, with the necessary qualifications, of each of the historically evolved religions. It is my assumption that wherever there exists a tradition of understanding, methodological effectiveness is a key to the solution of any philosophical questions that may arise.

In the sphere of science, for example, there is the question which I raised in the opening chapter: Is the realm of nature to be conceived as a single comprehensive system? Have we a right to the notion of a physical universe? The answer, in accordance with the principle I have just stated, is in the affirmative. That is to say, in the presuppositions which enable science to define its attitude to its own problems and to the world, as well as in the conclusions successively and temporarily arrived at in the course of its history,

[4] On similar grounds C. Stumpf does not hesitate to accept the charge of dualism. He writes: "Ich kann darin nichts so Fürchterliches finden, solange nur die Einheit des Zusammenwirkens und der obersten Gesetze gewahrt bleibt." *Leib und Seele*, Inaugural Address to the International Congress of Psychology at Munich in 1896.

[5] Whether and how far progressive or liable to change is a special problem.

there are considerations of weight which point with remarkable consistency to the view that the natural world is one. This view therefore derives support both from a study of the necessary preconceptions by which scientific investigation is conditioned, and from a knowledge of results achieved. A monism thus restricted to the ends of scientific knowledge is methodologically effective: that is to say, it is a satisfactory way of thinking about nature. On the other hand, as I have tried to show in the three preceding chapters, an ontological monism based on the obscuration of modal differences and the reduction of nature and spirit to what Mr. Holt very happily calls a "neutral mosaic" is methodologically ineffective: it is an unsatisfactory way of thinking about reality. The use which I intend to make of the concepts of function and system, and the application of these concepts under conditions determined by the postulate of being will find their justification, if at all, in considerations of methodology.

Being and Its Modalities—Subjective, Physical, Psycho-physical and Derivative

3. As a beginning I postulate being. I postulate it in as many modes as experience compels us to acknowledge. This may well appear an egregiously obscure assertion. It is obviously impossible upon empirical grounds (and in the end there are no others available) to specify exactly and exhaustively the number and the nature of the forms which it is possible for existence to assume. As a result of our preliminary inquiry, however, and of its negative conclusions, we are in a position to state the supreme principle by which empirical investigation must be guided in its pursuit of the fundamental modalities.

From the standpoint of methodological effectiveness it has been found a serious error to postulate any mode of being upon the assumption that the distinction of subjective and non-subjective or physical is of no account. That is to say, there is no being to which that distinction is utterly irrelevant: there is no being whose modality does not require for its expression some reference, direct or indirect, to the distinction in question. To specify a mode of existence is therefore by implication to affirm the mutual irreducibility of the subjective and its ontological opposite. The problem in each instance has to do with the precise nature of the reference to the basic antithesis.

There are two initial possibilities. We may postulate being either in the spiritual or in the physical mode. In other words we may assume that it is possible to exist in a way that may be described as spiritual but not as physical, or else in a way that may be described as physical but not as spiritual. In any being so defined—that is, defined as "spiritual" *or* as "physical"—the reference to the underlying antithesis expresses only the relationship of disjunction. Nothing that exists in the one mode can possibly exist in the other. Where the relationship is thus disjunctive, the mode in question is clearly original and homogeneous.

4. The remaining possibilities are easily gathered from a consideration of the initial two. In the first place the mutual disjunction of the original modes does not preclude their compresence in the world of actual existences. Though by their intrinsic nature for ever distinct, they may quite well occur together. As a matter of experience they do so in two ways. In one of these the relation between them is conjunctive; in the other it is functional.

5. If the physical and the spiritual stand in functional relation, they constitute a single system of being which cannot be described as either definitely spiritual or definitely physical, but must be designated psycho-physical. The psycho-physical mode is that in which human beings, or, generally speaking, embodied spirits exist. It is a question whether the latter class does not include the lower animals as well, and indeed all living things. Where the relationship involved is functional, the mode is composite and heterogeneous; but there is nothing in the bare conception of composite modality to indicate whether the latter is original or derivative. In finite beings with transient natures it may be derivative. The union of the psychical and the physical in the embodied soul may be a mere episode in the existence of the two former. If, on the other hand, as I have suggested may be the case, it is the nature of reality to express itself in two or more mutually irreducible modes of being, it may be that these modes exist in functional relation and constitute a system from the first. In this case their union will be a primordial fact, coeval with the existence of the modes themselves.

6. The final instance is that in which existence presupposes a relationship of *conjunction* between the two original modalities. Of this relationship the mode in question is a function. I am thinking of a large and ill-defined class of entities which includes the "data"

of sense and a vast and miscellaneous plurality of values. The mode which thus depends upon a conjunction of originals is obviously to be described as "derivative."

I should add that these descriptions must be taken throughout in a generic sense. Within each of the modalities mentioned existence occurs in a variety of minor forms, for the knowledge of which we are dependent upon experience. There is the difference, for example, between existing in any modality as a system and existing in the same modality as an element or member of a system. In the case of the derivative mode, the types of value, so far as our insight into them extends, may be considered indefinite in number.

7. From this account of the matter it will be seen that the postulate of being not only admits, but actually requires, an expression of modality in one or other of its generic forms. If anything *is*, it must exist either (1) in the spiritual sense, (2) in the physical sense, or (3) in a sense determined by the compresence of the physical with the spiritual, whether functionally or conjunctively, in the total scheme of things. Our problem from this point on is the detailed exploration of the modalities from a point of view which I shall describe as "critico-empirical."*

The meaning of this last expression is as follows. As I have already remarked, our knowledge of the modes is derived in the last resort from our experience of them. But the experience to which, in an inquiry like this, we have recourse must be developed experience. It must have reached the stage of symbolic expression in words and propositions. I shall take it for granted, for example, that the science of physics, which is the growing record of man's most cultivated experience of the outer world of spatio-temporal events, is the best available medium for the study of the physical mode of being. We have no such developed body of doctrine upon the spiritual mode. But here too man's mind has been at work upon the data: here too human experience in a more or less developed form has left its record in the words we use and the thoughts we commonly entertain about the inner life of conscious beings. It is my belief that a considerable insight into the spiritual mode of existence may be obtained from a study and a purgation of the language that has grown up spontaneously around the theme. My

[*It may be permissible to draw the reader's especial attention to this paragraph, as a rapidly drawn silhouette of the total picture, of which the author intended all his philosophical utterances to be the filling in.—Ed.]

account of the spiritual will therefore, to an extent which at first may appear extravagant, be made to depend upon linguistic considerations.*

In the theoretical treatment of the two unmistakably original modalities it will be difficult to isolate questions having to do primarily with the spiritual from questions having to do primarily with the physical. Even in their mutual negativity the modes are bound together by numberless relations; and the difficulty of keeping them apart for purposes of examination has been aggravated by the general misunderstanding of the relations involved. Moreover there are special problems—for example that which has to do with the meaning and nature of selfhood—which involve an equal reference to the two modes. It is hardly possible to attain an adequate conception of subject-selfhood without considering the relation of selfhood in general to the non-subjective. For these reasons I shall have from time to time to anticipate conclusions to be established at a later point. A certain amount of repetition will also be unavoidable. But with these qualifications I shall try to keep together what I have to say of the physical, the spiritual, the psycho-physical and the derivative modalities. The present chapter and those which immediately follow will be devoted primarily to the exposition of the spiritual mode of being. Our first task will be a review of the verbal forms in which man has tried to express his consciousness of the latter.

What Subjective Being or "Spirit" Is Taken to Be, as Revealed in Human Language

8. I shall begin with a group of expressions which, in certain of their usages, are more or less synonymous, in others more or less distinct. My contention is that the elements of meaning which these expressions have in common are more fundamental than those in which they differ. As a matter of fact the differences have to do largely with certain variations in linguistic practice and in doctrinal belief. These are not without their importance; but more important is the fact that the variations referred to do not reflect themselves except in superficial ways in the denotation of the terms involved. It is to one and the same class of entities that we

[*The author's linguistic researches were of long duration and upon an extensive scale. Only the refined precipitate of them, so to speak, is embodied in the text. He seems to have felt the affinity of philology and philosophy profoundly.—Ed.]

refer when we use the words "I," "you," "mind," "soul," "spirit," "person," "subject," "ego," "agent," "conscious being."[6]

9. The first question would naturally be: To what class of entities? But before proceeding to this I should like to dispose of the differences to which I have alluded as being of minor importance.[7]

In actual usage the words "mind" and "soul" differ from "subject," "person," "agent" and "conscious being" in that we commonly represent the former as possessions, whereas we identify ourselves with the latter. I *have* a soul and a mind, but I *am* a subject, an agent, a person.[8]

The significance of this is presumably to be found in the fact that the words "mind" and "soul," while, like the other terms, they express what is essential to our spiritual nature, do so under certain qualifications. "Mind," for example, commonly suggests the intellectual or cognitive aspect of consciousness as contrasted with the affective and the conative. If we speak of *"my* mind," the reason is doubtless that the power to think and to know defines itself in our experience within the unity of a subjective system which we feel to be more comprehensive and concrete. Mind is only *a part* of what *we are*, and as such it *belongs* to the whole—that is, *to us*. Hence we look upon it as a possession. In the case of the soul the explanation is at once analogous and different. The soul is the spiritual self-identity of the individual, the veritable self. But it is the self viewed in the light of a profoundly disturbing predicament —its alternative association with and dissociation from the body. It is usually as *embodied souls* that we think of ourselves; and when for special purposes we segregate one of the normally associated factors in thought, that factor assumes the character of a component in our psycho-physical selfhood, and hence of something we possess. That is why we speak of *"my* body," *"my* soul."

[6] Ward, who, unlike some psychologists, insists upon the "subject of experience," identifies "ego," "subject" and "self," but remarks that the "psychological concept of a self or subject . . . is . . . by no means identical with the metaphysical concept of a soul." *Psychological Principles*, 1918, p. 35. In justification of my usage I would merely remark that the "concept of a soul" (except in so far as this is viewed in the light of some dogma) is no more metaphysical than that of a subject or self. The truth is that all the concepts involved are metaphysical or psychological according to the treatment of them.

[7] Personal pronouns, which are the supreme, as they are the original, expression of man's conscious subjectivity, will have to be left out. In a philosophical discussion what exists subjectively must be treated objectively, and this implies the displacement of pronouns by substantives.

[8] On the word "person" *vid*. Appendix A to this chapter, p. 212.

These considerations point to important truths; but for the exact expression of the latter we require a special terminology. I shall treat the terms "mind" and "soul" as referring quite simply to being in the subjective form, and therefore as equivalent to one another and to the various expressions I have enumerated. On special occasions my choice of phraseology will be determined by the needs of the context.

10. Certain of the terms under consideration refer to the spiritual individual, others to the individual and also to the mode of his being—subjectivity as such. To the first class belong the words "ego," "person," "subject," "agent," and, in most contexts, "conscious being." "Mind," "soul" and "spirit" are employed either in the concrete to denote the subject-self, or in the abstract as a name for subject-selfhood, or for some quality connected with the latter.

In the second group, however, linguistic usage varies. By "soul," for example, we do not *ordinarily* mean the mode of being, the subjectivity, of individual souls. Indeed there is perhaps only one connection in which the word would naturally bear the abstract sense; and here the two meanings virtually coalesce. In pantheistic and pan-psychic theories the same expression denotes the psychic individuality of the world and the metaphysical nature of the world as psychic. Apart from this, the term in its abstract application varies in its significance. Sometimes it connotes what we call "soulfulness," sometimes concentrated effort, sometimes humanity. We speak of a person throwing his whole *soul* into a piece of work, or of his conduct as showing a want of *soul*. Similarly a musical performance might be described as *lacking in soul*. These statements convey judgments of value, and express our approval or disapproval rather than our sense of the presence or absence of subjectivity in the individual.

In "mind" and "spirit" abstract and concrete reflect one another much more exactly. Indeed the two senses in each case approximate so closely that it is sometimes difficult to distinguish them. In the early history of philosophy words for "mind" make their appearance in a cosmological context as an expression of man's consciousness that things do not happen in *any* way, but in determinate ways. In this aspect the idea is of course highly abstract. But even as a universally diffused cosmic principle mind is not assimilated to the manifoldness of the world. On the contrary it asserts its inviolable self-identity against the mutually immersed forms of nature. Thus it acquires at least as much of concrete individuality as is implied in a well sustained identity of its own. The νοῦς of Anaxagoras (not yet conceived in a definitely immaterial sense) is at once the omnipresent element of order, intellect, design in the universe, and the profoundly insulated being which concentrates that element in itself.[9] Something of the same duality of connotation is traceable in the Aristotelian νόησις, the mind which, as νόησις νοήσεως, is at once subject and object, and in both capacities is the concrete embodiment of intellectuality. Of the two words, νοῦς and νόησις, regarded from the standpoint of linguistic form, the first is naturally the more concrete, the second the more abstract; but in each case the abstract significance tends to prevail over the concrete. This, I think, is also true of the English "mind," and of certain foreign equivalents like the French "esprit" and the German "Gemut." Mind then as the essence of mental existence, rather than as the mentally *existent*, is what we tend to think of when we hear this word; and this is an added reason for representing our minds as something which we own rather than as something which we *are*.

11. It is only when we come to the word "spirit" that we find it practically impossible to differentiate between the claims of the concrete and the abstract. The meanings appear to be perfectly poised. It is so in English: it is so with the German "Geist" and the Greek πνεῦμα, the latter of which combines the meanings of ψυχή, the concrete, individual, living soul, and ζωή (in the New Testament sense of the term), the soul's life. This twofold eligibility is among the numerous advantages which the word "spirit" possesses above all possible alternatives.

To sum up on this point, there are cases in which the concrete and the abstract stereotype themselves against one another in distinct verbal forms—"person, personality"; "agent, agency";

[9] Contrast the two statements, (1): "Mind is infinite and autonomous, and is mixed with nothing, but is alone and altogether by itself (μόνος αὐτὸς ἐφ' ἑαυτοῦ)," and (2): "Mind, which is eternal, is assuredly there where everything else is (ὁ δὲ νοῦς, ὅς ἀ <εἰ> ἐστι, τὸ κάρτα καὶ νῦν ἐστιν ἵνα καὶ τὰ ἄλλα πάντα)." Diels' reading, followed by Burnet, *Early Greek Philosophy*, 3rd ed., p. 260. The two points of view come together in the statement: ἐν παντὶ παντὸς μοῖρα ἔνεστι πλὴν νοῦ, ἔστιν οἷσι δὲ καὶ νοῦς ἔνι.

"subject, subjectivity."[10] A second group is composed of words like "soul," "mind" and "spirit," which may be either concrete or abstract. Of these "soul" is primarily concrete. In the abstract it becomes ambiguous, and it is only in exceptional contexts that abstract and concrete are correlates of one another. In "mind," on the contrary, the abstract tends to outweigh the concrete signification. The two are evenly balanced in "spirit"; and here, as incidentally in the case of "mind," the provision of the required abstraction by a double use of the same word leaves room for a second abstract term ("spirituality") derived not from the concrete substantive but from the corresponding adjective. This last circumstance suggests certain points of considerable importance.

12. It would be natural to suppose that in the class of words with which we are dealing the adjective would take its meaning from the corresponding noun—that "mental," for example, would ordinarily mean "pertaining to mind," "spiritual" "pertaining to spirit," etc. As a matter of fact we must take into account not only the substantive to which the adjectival form is cognate, but also the substantive to which it is attached. Thus it is not merely to the being, states, predicaments and processes of mind or spirit that we apply the terms "mental" or "spiritual." We attach these expressions to the *objects* of mind as well, to entities which, like Wordsworth's "works that came from mind and spirit" (that is, books),[11] are the *product* of spiritual activity; and we attach them generally speaking to anything which, irrespective of its intrinsic nature, is capable of entering into certain kinds of relationship with consciousness. The epithet "subjective" is frequently applied to phenomena because of the part which mind is made to play in their explanation. Among the objects of our sensory experience— for example, colours and sounds, or trees and mountains—there are some which, although they may reveal themselves to us, as in eidetic imagery, with all the vividness of ordinary percepts, we discredit as illusions, and stigmatize as "mental" or "subjective." But it is clear that they are not mental in the sense of being states of mind, or subjective in the sense of being subjective processes. What we must mean, therefore, is that the phenomena in question,

[10] It can hardly escape notice that the abstractions belonging to this group are strikingly ambiguous. In "ego" we have a concrete with no corresponding abstract— "egoism" and "egotism" having a different meaning.

[11] *Miscellaneous Sonnets*, III, 38.

while they are *objects of experience* rather than experiences, are *subjectively conditioned.* When a similar explanation is given of the sensa and percepts which we do not discredit as delusional, but accept as authentic, the result is the theory known as *subjective* idealism. Here the qualifying epithet connotes a special feature in the interpretation not of the subject, but of the objective world. Berkeley's system is on the whole an exposition of nature rather than of spirit.[12] It deals principally with the ideas of which the *world* consists, and these are *objects* of consciousness organized in uniform collocations and sequences.[13] The attribute "subjective" therefore does not describe the modality of the ideas, but only the fact of their complete ontological dependence upon the spiritual mode of being. As applied to the system of Bishop Berkeley, it may be taken to summarize the doctrine that the objects of which the outer world consists are the *work* of minds.[14]

From these examples it is clear that the adjectival expressions with which we are dealing take their meaning partly from the

[12] I am thinking of the doctrine of the *Principles* rather than of the later suggestions of mysticism in the *Siris.*

[13] *vid.* Appendix B, p. 213.

[14] In his *Theory of Mind as Pure Act* Giovanni Gentile has criticized Berkeley on the ground that he represents human thinking as "conditioned by the divine thinking," and so reproduces "in the case of human thinking the same situation as that in which mind is confronted with matter, that is with nature, regarded as ancient philosophy regarded it, a presupposition of thought, a reality to which nothing is added by the development of thought." Thus "from Berkeley's standpoint thinking, strictly, is not anything. Because in so far as the thinking thinks, what it thinks is already thought"— viz., by God. English tr., pp. 3-4. There is truth in these strictures. But Berkeley's error is more than that of replacing the activity of the human mind by the creativity of the divine. God certainly is represented as providing the natural world which man perceives. Man's perception, therefore, as Gentile remarks, adds nothing new to what is already there. But apart altogether from this, Berkeley has no adequate conception of the finite spirit as subject of an experience. A mode of being which defines itself in terms of percipient activity, whether volitional or otherwise, is wanting in that inwardness of nature, that permanency, continuity and depth which are the essence of subjective selfhood. Nor is the lack made good by the recognition of the "powers" which Berkeley calls "will" and "understanding," and of the fact that we have a "*notion* of soul, spirit and the operations of the mind, such as willing, loving, hating—inasmuch as we know or understand the meaning of these words." (*Princs.*, 27, added in later editions.) The fundamental reason why for Berkeley thinking "is not anything" is that except in a verbal sense he fails to provide a *thinker*—in other words, to show that individual acts of perception are coordinated (along with a great many other mental processes and conditions) into the unity of a subjective system, as their objects are coordinated (by divine decree) into the system of nature. The explicit elimination of the conscious subject by his naturalistic successors is the inevitable sequel to Berkeley's theory, which posits a soul without a self.

nouns from which they are derived and partly from the contexts in which they are applied. In the latter case the ultimate reference is of course to the original source of significance. Thus when such adjectives as "mental," "subjective" or "personal" are applied to entities other than minds and their states, we may be sure that the justification is to be found in some relation supposed to exist between these entities and the spiritual mode of being. In all of this there is great danger of confusion. There is paradox in the fact that expressions specially designed to distinguish the subjects of experience and their constituent activities or predicaments from the objects of experience and their characteristics are frequently annexed to the latter and withheld from the former. Thus we discern "spiritual" quality in a combination of sounds, that is, in a piece of music, and we miss it in the character of the composer. Of course in this instance the adjective has acquired a normative coloration. This is a fresh complication, and it is aggravated by the fact that the normative significance is propagated from the adjective to the derivative substantive. In one of its most characteristic uses the word "spirituality" is a term of distinction. And so of "personality." It is obvious that these abstractions are direct derivatives not of the original substantives "spirit" and "person," but of the corresponding adjectives. The effect is striking. It is possible for a spirit to be lacking in "spirituality" and a person in "personality." Normative significance is present also in the term "subjectivity." Only, here the implication is rather that of reproach—the kind of reproach that attaches, for example, in the writings of Irving Babbitt[15] and Paul Elmer More,[16] to the sentimental romanticism, the lawless ego-centricity of which Rousseau is the reputed head and front, and which comes out in surprisingly different forms and in writers so varied as Chateaubriand and Diderot, Blake and Byron, Walt Whitman and Emerson, Newman and Huxley, Carlyle and Walter Pater, Nietzsche and Fiona Macleod.[17]

13. In a discussion like the present it is important that we should not be misled by the vagaries of linguistic usage. The following

---

[15] vid. Rousseau and Romanticism.

[16] The various volumes of Shelburne Essays, in particular Vol. VIII, The Drift of Romanticism.

[17] A powerful indictment of the modern era as a whole, on the ground of excessive subjectivism and the decay of "objective structures" in each of the main departments of human activity, will be found in G. P. Adams, Idealism and the Modern Age.

observations are designed to limit the possibilities of error. I have pointed out that words like "personality," "subjectivity," "spirituality" are not always the exact abstract equivalents of the concrete forms—"person," "subject," "spirit"—with which, through the corresponding adjectives, they are connected. In the interest of consistency, however, I intend to employ both the adjectives in question and the derivative abstractions in the sense which they receive from the original concrete expressions. Any departure from this rule, necessitated by certain types of context, will be restricted as far as possible to the adjectives, where misunderstanding can always be avoided by noting the substantives to which they are applied. The principle involved is that apart from this necessity the meaning should be determined by that of the noun which supplies the verbal derivation. Thus the adjective "mental" will be employed in the sense in which it applies to mind itself and to the states or processes of mind, rather than in that which it bears when applied to the objects or products of mental activity. And so of "spiritual," "subjective," "personal" in relation to the relevant substantives. The derivative abstractions will take their meaning from the adjectives.

As for the special advantages which I claim for the use of the word "spirit," let me recapitulate and complete what I have to say on the point. In relation to the various possibilities of conscious experience, cognitive, affective and conative, "spirit" is catholic and impartial. Moreover the word is used indifferently in the abstract and the concrete sense. Like the Greek πνεῦμα it is equally applicable to the individual, as when we speak of "*a* spirit," "*the* Holy Spirit," and to the mode of being characteristic of the concrete exemplar as in the proposition: πνεῦμα ὁ θεός.[18] Furthermore it is peculiarly adapted by use and wont to draw attention to the existence of something in man which differentiates itself from his body within the unity of the psycho-physical system that holds the two together. In contrast to the terms "subject," "agent," "ego," it does not conjure up any such conception as that of Kant's unknown noumenal self—a conception which would immediately bring our inquiry to a close. *Spirit*, unlike the noumenal ego, does not discourage, but rather invites, inspection. Finally, the term is free from the objection to which the phrase "conscious

18 For a note on the New Testament use of the word *vid*. Appendix C.

being" is exposed, namely, its unfitness to express the nature of an entity which, so far as we at present know to the contrary, may quite well include unconscious as well as conscious states among the predicaments of its existence.

Spirit as a System of Experiences

14. It is now possible to proceed to the fundamental problem of defining the kind of being for which the word "spirit" seems to be the most appropriate expression. What is spirit, and what does it mean to be *a* spirit or a spiritual being?

The definitory characteristic is best brought out by the word "experience."[19] If there is any mode of being which differentiates itself from every other as experience differentiates itself from all else, that mode of being may be characterized as "spiritual," and the individual that sustains the qualification, as a spirit, and, in certain limiting contexts, as a person.

15. The latter part of this assertion suggests a further question. In what sense can a concrete individual be said to *sustain the character* of spirituality? The question has to do with the relation between experience as such and what we commonly call "the subject of experience." Now the point upon which everything turns is our ability at once to maintain the distinction and to prevent its rendering the relationship unintelligible. The special danger to be avoided is that of separating the subject from the successive contingencies that give a content to its existence, and relegating the subject to the position of an unknown support or hidden principle of synthesis. But this is precisely the fate in store for it if we think of the relation between it and its experience in a superficial or external way. On the other hand it would be no less fatal to its character as an *individual* to identify it too directly and literally with the endlessly variable, incessantly dissolving particularity of its moment-to-moment predicaments. The subject is not resolvable into the mere plurality and sequence of its own states. Our problem therefore is to reconcile the indefinite manifoldness of experience and the indefeasible oneness of the self-identical ego.

16. The difficulty is not peculiar to the case with which we are dealing. It has its analogue in the conditions by which the life of organisms is determined. Living things maintain their identity

[19] cf. Ward, *Psych. Princs.*, pp. 39, note 2, and 40.

over a vast range of variety in what, metaphorically speaking, we might call "biological experiences." Life is a flux: living things are relatively permanent structures. Where the "life" in question is mere biological subsistence, however, the problem of correlating the two is rendered comparatively easy by the fact that the organism is a spatial system as well as an ordered sequence of events in time. This enables it to maintain an overt and ostensible identity of appearance, while the metabolic changes go on unseen within it. The identity of the individual is thus brought home to the senses and the imagination as the identity of the body. There is much that is questionable in this, and the analogy from the biological sphere is to be treated with the utmost suspicion. Nonetheless it may help us, by way both of comparison and of contrast, to a realization of the concept for which we are seeking.

17. The point is that the changes which go on in the living body are related to one another as determinant and determined in a sequence of functionally related biological events. Between them therefore they constitute a variety of systems, and these are in turn so correlated as to constitute a single comprehensive system— the continuity of a life ordered as one and defining itself against a vast plurality of similarly ordered systems. We are here in the region of the four-dimensional. Living organisms are not only ordered processes in time: as bodily structures they occupy space. What is of fundamental importance, however, is not that the bodily parts should be thought of as organized together into a completely integrated whole, but that the integration of the body should be viewed in the light of the functional relations which mark the ordered sequence of vital changes. In brief, we must realize that the crux of organization is process, and we must interpret the concept of organism as the functional integration of events in the unity of a system that is temporal through and through.

18. Applying this to the case of mind or spirit in relation to experience, we note to begin with that the spatial factor is absent. As I have tried to show, the mind and its experiences do not occupy space. They have their relation to the latter; but that relation would not be correctly described by attributing a spatial character to the spiritual. Experience is not a content of space; space is an object of experience or a relation between such objects: otherwise

it is a system of all the terms which furnish points of reference to our consciousness of the living body.[20]

Such being the case, if we think of the mind as an organism, we must do so without the aid of the familiar spatial dimensions. The identity of a spirit is not brought home to the visual imagination, like that of a biological structure, by the mental picture of a familiar body. The concept of system must be applied to the continuity of a temporal process as such—a process of which the differentiations are not organs but events. We can gain no insight into the relation we are investigating by considering it in the light of any other relation—that, for example, which connects experiences with their objects, or persons with the physical conditions of life. In each of these cases the relation is that of the subjective to the non-subjective. But that with which we are concerned is the relation of the subjective in one aspect and the subjective in another: the difference involved is that between the individual experiences which stand in certain functional relations to one another and the single comprehensive system which the functionally related experiences constitute and presuppose. This provides a preliminary notion of spirit in the concrete. To obtain such a notion it is only necessary to bring together the concept of experience and the concept of system and to define the latter in terms of the former. A spiritual being or a spirit is a subjective system or a system of experiences.

Difficulties of thus Finding System in the Subjective: Can a System Be a Subject?

19. The objections which this view, upon first thoughts, can hardly fail to suggest fall into two classes. Both have to do with the concept of system when applied to the subjective as such.

First, it will be said that this concept is obviously intended to express the nature of the being which we usually describe as a "conscious *subject*," but that a *system of experience* is not exactly what we mean by a *subject of experience*. Even if we admit that conscious states may be functionally related, and so may constitute a system, the subject to whom they are ascribed and even *imputed*—the subject who in some instances is held responsible for them—is more than the *system* of these states. A person, for ex-

---

[20] To bring out the difference prepositionally, what we must say is not that experience is *in* space, but that there is an experience *of* space.

ample, is the self to which a plurality of experiences belong. We say that they are *his*, but we do not think of *him* as in any sense reducible to *them*. The subject can even in a sense repudiate his experiences. He can refuse to *identify* himself with certain passages in his subjective history: he can disown his past and dissociate himself from elements in the present of his inner life. This is a possibility of which the Founder of Christianity was wont to take advantage when He addressed Himself, over the head of those experiences which we call men's sins, to the core of personality within the agent. If there is anything in such a procedure, it would seem to show that personality—the being of the subject—defines itself (at least in some cases) *against*, and not *in terms of*, its own subjective contents, and that we cannot dispose of our subjective self-identity by resolving it into the organized totality of our experiences. In support of this contention it may be argued that in the concept of a system there is something adventitious and artificial. The definitory factor is a mere relation: the terms involved, which in this case are individual experiences, must be presupposed. But this is to invert the natural order of thought. We do not begin by recognizing the existence of mental states and then proceed to think them together. We begin by recognizing the existence of the conscious subject, and we assume the mental states as predicaments of his being.

20. A second set of difficulties has its source in the attempt to apply the concept of system to the time-conditioned manifold of subjective events. Exact definition is the essence of system. When, however, we are dealing with a sequence of events in time, and more particularly with one from which the spatial factor is wanting, the only possible boundaries are a beginning and an end. But here there is no means of fixing either. Exactitude of definition is therefore out of the question. Which is the subject's first experience, and which the last? Even if we eliminate such theoretical possibilities as antenatal existence and survival after death, the question remains unanswerable. How, where and when the sequence or continuum of experience originates, whether at the moment of birth, or in the prenatal stage, we have no means of determining with precision; and, on the other hand, so long as the individual remains alive, the ordered sequence of his experiences is incomplete.[21] In

[21] In the end, even where the spatial factor is included, as in physical systems or in the universal "system of nature," similar difficulties arise over the time element.

other words, it is only at the moment when (assuming the non-survival hypothesis) the system ceases to be, that we are in a position to describe it as a single system. In any case the organized totality of subjective events which constitutes the life of a person differs indefinitely, both in range and in integration, from one individual to another. Can our definition be said to apply indifferently to the most highly developed character and to the child who dies in infancy?[22]

21. The second set of objections can be adequately dealt with only when we have considered the structure and characteristics of subjective time. For the moment it will be enough to point out that it is symptomatic of a subjective system to transform all the meanings of time, interpretable in terms of sequence, into new meanings, interpretable in terms of synthesis. Thus the indeterminacy of mere consecutiveness and duration gives place to the uniformity of a scheme in which the identity of a life-process is defined and stereotyped, not by reference to the vague and indeterminable outward limits of life, but centrally, by reference to that point of concentration which we call the present. Of course the present is for ever changing, and in that sense it too is indefinable; but it is so only if we regard it abstractly from the standpoint which it itself displaces. Present time, as we shall see, is not merely a division in a series which begins with the past and looks to a future. It has an identity which is determined on quite other grounds than that of an indefinitely variable temporal position. In brief, it is definable as a function of spiritual activity, whereby the distinction of *before* and *after*, characteristic of mere succession, acquires the significance of past, present and future; and wherever the function occurs, we are entitled to postulate a well defined and strictly self-identical system of subjective events. Thus the objection based upon the necessary indefiniteness of time disappears of its own accord. Rightly understood, the procedure is not that of "applying the conception of system to a time-conditioned manifold," but that of showing how the time of subjective events inevitably manifests those functional relations which compel us to postulate a system.

---

[22] The theological difficulties as to the eventual destiny of the latter, revealed, e.g., in a treatise like St. Augustine's *De Peccatorum Meritis et Remissione*, are the reflection, in another medium, of problems which, since they have to do with a mode of being and with its implications, are also metaphysical.

A System of Experiences Can Be a Subject

22. As regards the first group of criticisms, all the alleged differences that distinguish a *subject* from a *system* of experiences can be seen to have nothing in them, if we only keep sufficiently in mind what it means to be a system *of experiences*. For one thing, the latter are not isolated events. They do not come into existence independently of the functional relation between them. In so far as they are posited, that relation is posited with them and as their precondition. Functional dependence is of the essence of their being. If y is an experience, therefore, the implication is that there must be another experience x, of which y is a function;[23] and in accordance with a principle stated in the opening chapter, this fact must be interpreted as meaning that x and y between them constitute a system. The fundamental truth about y, then, is not that it is a function of x (although this is true), but that it defines itself within the unity of the system xy, and that it is a function of the latter. In the order of being the system assuredly precedes its individuated contents.

These statements, however, are quite general: they apply to every kind of system, and do not in themselves make it perfectly clear that a system and a subject of experience are necessarily one and the same thing. This truth implies certain additional considerations. We think of a subject as *sustaining activities*—those, for example, which we designate knowing, thinking, feeling, desiring and willing. The propositions which best express the nature of such a being are propositions that involve the use of active verbs and imply the existence of an *agent*. On the contrary we do not so readily think of a system as *acting*, even when its constituents are

[23] Of course the expression "an experience" must not be taken to connote a perfectly defined, atomic individual; and the *course* of experience must not be construed as a succession of such individuals. There are no absolute units of experience. In the psychical realm change is all-pervasive. But the flux is not uniform and featureless. There is a decided want of smoothness in it. Identifiable phases occur within the uneven flow of mental events. My point is merely that when we seek to single out any such identity and to stereotype it as "an experience," the truth upon which we strike is that the phases of the continuum vary together, and that so far the continuum itself may be regarded as a system of concomitant variations.—Incidentally it seems to me that Ward in his "presentation continuum" theory and William McDougall in his denial of distinct "ideas" (*Outline of Psychology*) have both gone too far in their attempt to discredit the atomic view.

activities.[24] It would seem then that there is a very appreciable difference between being a system of activities and being an active system or agent. The point I wish to make is that in the present instance, where the activities in question are psychical, there is no such difference. The being to which a number of functionally related experiences are attributable as *its activities* can be no other than the subjective system which these experiences between them constitute.

23. As evidence of this I offer the following observations. Granted the view that our mental states are really psychical activities, and are not to be identified, as they are by the naturalist, with their own objects, the question arises: Whose activities are they?—or (if this way of putting the question seems to prejudice the answer): What is the being to which, as subject, the activities are attributable as experiences? The answer is expressible in a couple of dichotomies. The first is as follows. Either (*a*) the activities must be assigned to a subject other than themselves, or else (*b*) there is no need to assume any such subject. By the latter alternative I do not mean that a subject or agent is denied, but that the character of subject is ascribed to the activity as such.

On this view (*b*), not only are our mental processes represented as psychical operations, but they are represented as themselves *performing these operations*. The psychological writings of William James abound in expressions which can only be so construed. We are told that "the same reality can be *cognized* by an endless number of *psychic states*," and that the "*feelings* from our viscera and other dimly felt organs . . . may be very vague *cognizers* of the same realities which other *conscious states* cognize and name exactly."[25] Again James remarks: "We may explain how one bit of thought can come to judge other bits to belong to the same ego with itself."[26] "Each pulse of cognitive consciousness," he says, "each Thought, dies away and is replaced by another. The other, among the things it knows, knows its own predecessor, and finding it 'warm,' in the way we have described, greets it, saying: 'Thou art *mine*, and part of the same self with me'."[27] These statements

---

[24] The reason for this is presumably that there are many types of non-active systems, some of these, like their contents, pure abstractions or *entia rationis*.

[25] *Principles of Psychology*, Vol. I, pp. 173-4. Italics mine.

[26] p. 331.

[27] p. 339.

are a little puzzling, because the author appears at one and the same time to represent the momentary state or "pulse" of consciousness as itself the knower, the judge, the subject of experience, and to recognize an "ego" or "self" as over and above the momentary state. But James has left us in no uncertainty as to his meaning. In the end agent and activity are one. "The passing Thought then seems to be the Thinker."[28] "And yet turn we must, with the confession that our 'Thought'—a cognitive phenomenal event in time—is, if it exist at all, itself the only Thinker which the facts require."[29] "*If the passing thought be the directly verifiable existent which no school has hitherto doubted it to be, then that thought is itself the thinker*, and psychology need not look beyond."[30]

This whole way of representing the matter is based upon a confusion. It is quite true that a particular mental process, y, may be defined as a knowledge of another mental process, x, or, indeed, as a knowledge of anything at all. In other words, some states of the mind are identifiable with the activity of knowing an object. Others again are identifiable with an activity of thinking, willing, desiring, etc. But the fact that y is the psychical operation, say, of knowing x does not mean that x is known to y or that y *knows* x. The direct opposite is the case. y cannot possibly know x, and x cannot possibly be known to y, and that for the very reason that y *is* the knowledge of x and is definable as an activity of knowing. Activities do not act—although, when we think of them, we are bound to assign them to beings that do. To represent a mental process as at once a psychical performance and a performer is out of the question.

24. The remaining alternative, that the subject of psychical action is other than the activity in question, also embraces two possibilities. Either (a) the subject must be thought as existing independently of the activities assigned to it; or (b) the activities and the subject must somehow be thought together.

(a) The former view involves the irresolvable difficulties of a Kantian noumenal ego. On these I shall not dwell at length. But I should like to point out that the objections to an ego so conceived are not confined to the general theoretical considerations which tell against the unknowable thing-in-itself in relation to its appear-

[28] p. 342.
[29] p. 369.
[30] p. 401.

ances. My point is that the subjective states or activities, which differentiate the empirical from the transcendental self, are not appearances at all. That is to say, they are not *objects*, but *instances*, of experience, and for that reason it cannot be assumed (as it is by Kant) that they define themselves against the noumenal ego as appearances define themselves against the thing-in-itself. If subjective processes are to be distinguished in the modality of their being from the subjects that sustain them, it must be on very different grounds from those on which thinkers like Kant have tried to distinguish the phenomenal and the real.[31]

(b) The only possible conclusion would seem to be that the subject and the activities of the subject must be thought together. This does not mean that they are identical. It means that every time we think of a mental event as occurring, we must think of a subject as acting. The latter is an implicate or presupposition of the former. Our problem is the identification of the active subject under the conditions of this statement.

25. The fact upon which everything depends is this. Not only does every activity imply what I have called an "active subject," but the very notion of an active subject implies *a plurality of activities*. These relate themselves to the agent as an indefinitely variable manifold to an invariable unity. The relation between action and agent, however, is only one of the relations involved. The other is the relation of action to action. If the latter is ignored, the subjective events fall apart, and the manifold assumes the aspect of a mere plurality, in which the individuals flash out for a moment in their singleness and disappear for ever. In this case the subject which every mental action implies must be postulated separately for each. But a subject so postulated is a meaningless addition to the event as such, and may safely be eliminated. The final result is the "neutral mosaic," to which the very notion of the subjective, for want of a counterpart, has become irrelevant.

To avoid a conclusion so completely opposed to the hypothesis on which we are working we must think of the subjective activities

---

[31] The difficulties of Kant's theory come to a head in the *Critique of Practical Reason*. Behind them all is an inadequate conception of experience. In the first *Critique* the latter is defined as "a knowledge of objects" ("eine Erkenntniss der Gegenstände," Introduction). It is therefore primarily to the objective manifold that the designation "empirical" applies. And yet in the second *Critique* the *empirical* is taken as a matter of course to be identical with the *subjective*. From the standpoint of the absoluteness of moral law, the two appear to occupy the same ground.

as mutually correlated from the beginning—that is, as related to one another in ways that are not adventitious and inconsequential, but are definitely determinative; and we must think of the subject as the implicate of these activities, not in their singleness, but in their determinative interconnection. Thus the subject remains indefeasibly one, whatever the variety of its activities, and however extended the latter in time. As for the relation between the events in question, it is apparent from the description that this is functional in character; but if so, these must be thought of as constituting a system which, with each addition to its contents, will reassert its unity and self-identity. The concept of a *subject*, and the concept of a *system*, of experience have now been brought face to face. The question is whether there is any point in keeping up the distinction.

The answer must surely be in the negative. All the demands of theory which the former was designed to meet are satisfied by the latter. Thus the concept of a subjective system or system of subjective events effectively stereotypes the permanent self-identity of selfhood or personality against the flux, the variability and the indefiniteness of experience. It secures us in that sense of possessiveness which characterizes our self-consciousness in relation to the empirical content of the inner life. The constituents of a subjective system may be said, with all the meaning of which the phrase is capable, to "belong to" the system that includes them. Above all, and as a precondition of the statement that has just been made, a system of subjective activities can be quite appropriately represented in the character in which we commonly view the subject—namely, as an agent. If an activity of thinking or knowing takes place, and if this fact calls for expression through an active verb—"X is thinking," "X knows"—what could be more natural than to think of the agent as one with the system of experiences that furnishes all the conditions by which the existence and the identity of the event in question are determined? On this view the vague notion of a subject, which is otherwise little better than a point of reference, acquires a definite content. I therefore conclude with the suggestion, based on methodological advantage, that the concept of a system be substituted for that of a subject, or, to be more exact, that the word "subject," which is indispensable for certain purposes, be interpreted as equivalent to "subjective system" or "system of experience." In so far as any difference of meaning remains, it amounts merely to this. A system of experience is the unity of our mental activities when viewed in the light of their functional relations to one another: a subject of experience is this same system when viewed in the light of its relation to any particular activity.

Experience to Be Defined by Reference to Consciousness. The Attempt to Derive Consciousness Not Satisfactory. Holt

26. The next step is to determine the meaning of a word which I have been using freely, and which I have included in the definition of spirit—the word "experience." In this case the statement as to meaning must be taken as an exposition of the truth about the entity to which the word refers.

By experience I understand a mode of being which defines itself by reference to a certain unique and unanalyzable possibility—the possibility of *being conscious*. All conscious states belong to some system of experience: every system of experience has an ontological and structural character of the type which comes most distinctively into view in conscious beings.

These statements are once more at variance with the general trend of modern thought. For the tendency has been to magnify experience and to deprecate consciousness. The concept of experience has been developed without much regard for consciousness. Prominence has been given to such considerations as the active adaptation to environment, whether in the biological or the social sense, continuity, organization, selection, spontaneity.[32] Now without disputing the value or relevance of these notions, I would point out that before they can be made available for the definition of experience, they must be brought severally and collectively to bear upon the mode of being which I have tried to indicate, in a totally different way.

To take a concrete illustration. Professor Dewey refers to the "life and experience" of an amoeba, and the conditions he mentions as indispensable are "some continuity in time in its activity" and "some adaptation to its environment in space." Now such conditions are interpretable in two senses. They may be taken as purely physiological in their significance, or they may be taken in a sense which implies the recognition of an ultra-physiological

[32] The writings of Professor Dewey may be taken as representative. *vid.*, e.g., *Reconstruction in Philosophy*, pp. 90-1.

mode of being—a psychical mode to which conscious states belong. The question has been dealt with by Professor H. S. Jennings in his masterly work upon the behaviour of the lower organisms. After a minute study of the amoeba, the paramecium and other infusoria, Jennings concludes that the activity of these elementary forms of life is "of the character which we should 'naturally' expect and appreciate if they did have conscious states," and that to the question whether their behaviour is "of such a character that it does not suggest to the observer the existence of consciousness" a negative answer must be returned.[33] Now for the modern writers to whom I have alluded the answer to the question propounded by Dr. Jennings has no bearing whatever on the definition of experience. These writers would have no hesitation in attributing experience to the paramecium and the amoeba irrespective of any such consideration. The one feature of importance (and in view of some of their statements even it appears to be of no importance whatever) would be the evidence of adaptation and selection in the movements whereby, for example, the amoeba follows up and ingests a euglena cyst,[34] or the paramecium reverses its reactions in passing from one chemical medium to another.[35] My contention, on the contrary, is that the presence or absence of consciousness, in whatever form and measure, or of a type of activity to which consciousness is the only reliable clue, is a fact of decisive import, and that upon it depends our right to interpret the movements in question as constituting the "experience" of the organism.[36]

27. In the attempt to obtain a concept of the spiritual mode of being I have advanced two propositions. Spirit has been defined in terms of experience, and the notion of experience has been singled out and set apart from all else by the part which consciousness plays in it. On this last point I have been intentionally vague, for a reason which will become apparent as we proceed. For the moment my point should be sufficiently intelligible. What I main-

---

[33] *Behaviour of the Lower Organisms*, p. 336.

[34] *vid.* Jennings' fascinating account of this operation, *op. cit.*, pp. 12-19.

[35] *ibid.*, pp. 47 *sq.*

[36] This of course is not to be taken as meaning that these movements are consciously selected and deliberately directed to chosen ends. Such an assumption would be just as unwarranted with regard to a large part of our human behaviour. And yet unless it were possible to connect our bodily activities at some point with at least an obscure awareness of them—unless "body-feeling" were in some degree present—we should hardly think of them as contributing to our *experience*.

tain is that whenever anything is recognized as *experience*, whether in the form of a conscious state or not, the idea of consciousness is needed to give significance to the act of identification. Before attempting to render the implied relationship more definite, I must say something about the interpretation of consciousness as such.

I agree with Professor Dewey that consciousness is indefinable. Mr. Holt takes the opposite view, and as his treatment of the question, like his treatment of mental space, raises issues that are too fundamental to be ignored, we shall have to consider what he has to say on this subject also.

28. The starting-point is the concept of being itself. "That which all things are is not a feature or property by which some things are distinguished from others."[37] In other words, since *everything is*, the fact of existence can throw no light upon the special character of anything. As the all-inclusive category, being is at once fundamental and simple. It must stand indifferently behind all distinctions, including that of real and unreal, true and untrue, subjective and objective, mental and physical. It must go deeper even than the gulf that divides contradictory propositions. Whatever is more highly specialized than mere existence, whatever is distinguished as a *this* from a *that*, must find a place for itself within the sphere to which all such differences are irrelevant. And then the problem comes to be that of locating the entity in question within the said sphere. The determining factor in each instance is the distance of anything from the fundamental simplicity of being.

The bearing of this upon the interpretation of consciousness appears in the following disjunctive statement. "The fact is that either consciousness is a complex entity, not fundamental but definable in terms of simpler entities that are not consciousness, in which case unconsciousness can also be a complex entity in the system; or else consciousness is fundamental and simple, is opposed by no negative category of unconsciousness, and can in no wise become the subject of further discourse."[38] Of the alternatives presented, Mr. Holt is of course compelled by all the principles of his thinking to accept the complexity and to reject the simplicity of consciousness. For him, therefore, the definition of consciousness

[37] *The Concept of Consciousness*, p. 20.
[38] *op. cit.*, p. 73.

is a feasible proposition. A place must be found for this as for other entities in the sum-total of existence.

Short of being itself, all things consist of simple entities in varying degrees of composition.[39] They constitute classes which may be viewed in hierarchic order; and since the distinction of subjective and its opposite is not permitted to invade the fundamental category of being, the world assumes the aspect of that "neutral mosaic" to which I have repeatedly referred. Within this mosaic the physical and the mental appear as distinct aggregates of neutrals.[40] In the end, and in respect of their being, all entities meet on a dead level of simple givenness, where they can be dealt with only by the science of logic. Thus the entities of the physicist (that is, his masses, motions and electrons) are really and literally reducible to the laws, equations or logical concepts which are his explanation of them,[41] and the physical world becomes an artefact of logic. So also does the mental. To take an extreme example, the volitions of conscious subjects are merely more complex and specialized instances of what we encounter in the relation of propositions to their own terms.

29. In accordance with these general considerations the problem of placing consciousness in the "simple-to-complex series of *being*" is solved by a logical process whereby from a set of terms and propositions, specially designed for the purpose, "a system is deducible that contains such an entity or class of entities, as we familiarly know under the name of consciousness or mind."[42] When the process is complete, it appears that consciousness is reducible, as we have already seen, to a "neutral cross-section outside of the nervous system, and composed of the neutral elements of physical and non-physical objects to which the nervous system is responding by some specific response. This neutral cross-section," we are further told, "coincides exactly with the list of objects

[39] The conception of simplicity here can hardly be the same as in the case of being. The latter is simple because it is all-comprehensive and therefore lacking in specific character. Presumably distinguishables are simple when they represent the limit of specification, the units of particularity.

[40] *op. cit.*, Chap. VIII.

[41] It is interesting to note that Mr. Holt here anticipates a view which has since become prevalent among the physicists themselves. For my observations on the point *vid.* Appendix A to Chap. III.

[42] *op. cit.*, p. 166.

of which we say that we are conscious." Not only so. It is identified with our awareness of these objects. As Mr. Holt says: "It is the manifold of our sensations, perceptions and ideas: it is consciousness."[43]

30. My criticism of this conclusion goes back to the principles upon which it rests.

In the first place Mr. Holt's account of *being* as at once fundamental and simple is open to objection. If being is *simple* in the sense intended (that is, devoid of all special or distinguishing properties), it is no better than the last of all abstractions—das Sein, τὸ εἶναι, conceptualized existence—and in this aspect there is nothing *fundamental* about it. As an all-inclusive category it does not really go *behind* or *beneath* the differences that divide its own specific manifestations. It is merely distilled from them by thought. On the other hand in so far as being is genuinely *fundamental*— that is, actually determinative of these manifestations—there is no reason in the world why it should be considered *simple*. We are here in the realm of concrete existence—das Seiende, τὸ ὄν—and all the arguments that have been advanced against any theory that would minimize the distinction of physical and spiritual point to the view that being in all its derivative forms goes back to at least two ultimate and mutually irreducible roots. Mr. Holt's position amounts to a repudiation of the original modalities; and the difference between it and my own is that I maintain (upon grounds of methodological advantage) what he would deny— namely, that there are ways of being which are *at once* fundamental *and* special.

31. In the interpretation of consciousness this initial difference of viewpoint bears fruit in a further twofold antithesis. On the one hand being is represented as simple, and for that reason indefinable, whereas consciousness is actually *defined* as a cross-section of the neutral mosaic. On the other, the rejection of neutrality permits the definition of being in terms of its own modal peculiarities, while consciousness remains indefinable because the mode to which it belongs, and which would have to supply the generic concept, itself requires for its definition a reference to the possibility of consciousness.

[43] *op. cit.*, p. 182.

There Is Such a Thing as Unconscious *Experience*

32. The question that really calls for consideration therefore is not: "What is consciousness?" but "What is the relation between consciousness and experience? What is the nature of the 'reference' to the former, which, as I have just said, the latter requires for its definition?"—To begin with, the two are not identical: they are not equivalents. Experience includes unconscious as well as conscious states, and this fact lends a certain colour to the contention that consciousness is of little account.[44] If unconscious states of being are rightly included in the concept of experience, it seems natural to conclude that so far as that concept is concerned, consciousness itself and the distinction between it and the opposite condition are of no definitory value.

33. The inference, however, would hardly be warranted until a further complication has been duly considered. If there are states of being which, *although* unconscious, we do not hesitate to call experiences, there are others which, *because* they are unconscious, we should not call experiences. There is therefore a problem of differentiating the unconsciousness which is not experience from that which is. In ordinary practice and apart from contexts of speculation we have no difficulty in identifying the former. Inanimate objects, for example, appear to exist and to undergo changes. They have states or modes of being, and these are presumably unconscious; yet it would never occur to us to think of them as the unconscious *experiences* of the objects concerned. Indeed no one but a philosopher (unless it were a savage or a child), would be likely to approve the remark of Professor Dewey in an early work, that a stick or a stone, because it "exists and undergoes changes," "has experiences."[45] I have already dwelt upon Professor Whitehead's view that consciousness is "unessential" to experience and that the latter occurs in a "physical" as well as in a "mental" form. In direct contradiction of all such suggestions I contend that no experience can possibly be physical, and that the

---

[44] Of course with the refusal to recognize the modal distinctiveness of consciousness the antithesis of conscious and unconscious loses all its force. Again cf. Holt, *op. cit.*, p. 202. Mr. Holt regards subconscious mental processes as nothing but "conscious processes which elude the individuals' introspection and reflection." Can it be seriously maintained (as this statement seems to imply) that the distinction of conscious and subconscious is identical with that of reflective and unreflective states of mind?

[45] *Psychology*, p. 2.

concept of experience cannot cover unconscious states of being to which the designation "mental" is inapplicable.

Such being the case, it follows that consciousness must stand in opposition, (1) to states of being which are unconscious yet mental, and (2) to states which are unconscious and non-mental. In the first case the opposites define themselves against one another as subordinate modes within the comprehensive modality of experience or spirit: in the second they stand opposed as everything within the spiritual mode is opposed to everything outside it.* This statement, however, is far from satisfactory, and until it is itself cleared up, it can only serve to render the modalities involved obscure. In particular it is difficult to see why in certain cases unconsciousness† should be classified along with consciousness in common opposition to the unconscious, or why, looking at the situation from another point of view, a simple and obvious antithesis should be complicated by opposing the unconscious in one of its phases,‡ not only to consciousness, but to the unconscious as well.

34. The difficulty can best be met by viewing these modal differences in the light of certain truths having to do with the systematic organization of the modes. These truths, like the knowledge of the modes themselves, rest upon an empirical basis. To put the matter roughly, there is a way of being unconscious which we experience in ourselves as a periodic or occasional contingency of our existence as conscious subjects; and there is another way which, upon the evidence, we judge to be the permanent condition of things around us in the world of space. In more exact language, the unconscious states which we classify with consciousness as a phase of experience reveal themselves in a context which shows that they belong to the same system to which our conscious states belong, and that that system, in its conscious and unconscious phases, must be conceived as modally homogeneous. That is what the word "mental," when applied to the unconscious, must be taken to mean—namely, compresence with consciousness in the unity of a homogeneous subjective system. Between the unconscious and the conscious states of the mind there is a continuity of

[*See the diagram, p. 215 below.—Ed.]
[†CD in the diagram.—Ed.]
[‡DB in the diagram.—Ed.]

being which is no less pronounced than is the discontinuity of all
our mental states alike with the outer world.

Unconsciousness as a Characteristic Human Experience

35. I have remarked that the evidence upon which these conclusions rest is that of experience itself. But how, it will be asked,
can there be an *experience* of the unconscious, and how can such an
experience enable us to differentiate between separate modes of the
latter? Above all, how can we hope, upon empirical grounds, to
justify the paradox of arguing that there is such a thing as the experience *of being unconscious*? Is not unconsciousness the limit of
negation, rather than one of the modes, of experience? A complete
answer to these questions would imply (1) a clear conception or
the difference between the subjective and the objective, and (2) a
developed theory of the self and of the consciousness that goes with
it—self-consciousness in its various forms. But even in the absence
of such a conception and of such a theory* it is possible, I think, to
indicate, if not to develop, the precise points involved in a really
adequate answer.

Obviously a state of absolute unconsciousness, taken in and by
itself, is not an experience at all, and cannot be interpreted as such.
But states of unconsciousness do not occur in and by themselves:
they occur, as I have suggested, in contexts and under conditions
which are at least to some extent ascertainable. Now my contention is that when this circumstance is taken into account, there are
found to be states of unconsciousness (those we attribute to ourselves and to beings like ourselves) which are so intimately contextual with our conscious states that the latter owe their subjective content, which is their identity, to them. What I mean
is specifically this. Suppose U is a state of unconsciousness,
and C a state of consciousness. Under the circumstances here assumed the identity of C is definitely determined by that of U. In
other words, C is definable as "what it feels like to be so far forth
unconscious," or as "this particular experience of what unconsciousness means to a conscious being."[46] Such experiences are ex-

[*The theory is the theme of Chaps. vi and vii, below.—Ed.]

[46] The expression "so far forth," as will appear from the illustrations I shall give, is
designed to indicate certain limiting conditions under which alone the unconscious becomes an experience. For example, we experience unconsciousness as a state of mind
contemporaneous with consciousness, when we are trying to induce a certain state of

ceedingly common. Indeed they are of daily occurrence in the normal life of every man and woman. But it is obvious that there could be no such thing as an experience of *what it means to be unconscious* unless unconsciousness were itself *an experience*. To revert once more to our basic concepts—in the instance before us C is a function of U. Hence C and U together constitute the system CU; and it is of this that C, in the end, is really a function. Finally (and this is the point upon which everything turns) the subjective homogeneity of the system is guaranteed by the fact that on no other basis could C sustain the identity expressed in its definition. U must be an experience, if C is to be the experience of U. This is tantamount to saying that C is what it is because CU is a subjective system in which conscious and unconscious states are experienced together.[47]

To sum up—there is such a thing as consciously experiencing what it means to be unconscious. Unconsciousness, therefore, may exist as an experience; but it can only so exist in the experience of a conscious subject. It is this last qualification that differentiates the mode of the unconscious which must be designated "mental" from that which cannot be so described. The states of being which we find, and the changes which occur, in the inanimate world may be functionally related to one another, and so may constitute a system: they may be related to our consciousness of them as its objects. But there is no place for any such state in a homogeneous system of experience.

36. It should now be apparent why in the definition of experience it is necessary to make special mention of the part played by consciousness, while merely noticing the presence of unconscious states. Consciousness is necessary in order to give the character of experience or subjectivity to unconsciousness. The principle involved may be formulated thus: A state of being from which consciousness is absent must be reckoned an experience, and therefore a subjective condition, if there is a second state which is the

consciousness to appear. Otherwise the two opposite conditions may be experienced successively, but still within the continuity of a single experience.

[47] Professor Dewey, contrasting consciousness and mind, remarks: "Mind is contextual and persistent; consciousness is focal and transitive." (*Experience and Nature*, p. 303.) I agree. Only, I would add that our conscious states, concentrated as they are at special points, and divided from one another by intervals of unawareness, are nonetheless wrought, along with these episodes, into the very fabric of our minds, with all the exactitude of functional relationship. They are among the elements which sustain the "contextual" structure of the subjective system.

consciousness of what it means to be the first. In the light of this, the exact nature of the "reference" to consciousness which is necessary for the definition of experience is apparent. Experience is the mode of being which includes conscious states, and in which all other states are organized together with consciousness in homogeneous systems that are modally identical with the latter.

37. I have referred to certain "circumstances" as presupposed in all that I have said about the unconscious in relation to experience. These are nothing but the contingencies of experience itself, when seen in their contexts as characteristic predicaments of human life. Let me conclude this chapter with one or two illustrations.

Consider, for example, what is implied in the everyday experience of trying to remember something we have forgotten. This experience has two inseparable aspects. (1) It is a conative effort directed to an ideal end—the reinstatement of a certain condition of mind or the recall of a certain object. (2) It is also the subjective predicament of *having forgotten something*. From the second point of view trying to remember is an actual experience of what it is to be *unconscious* with regard either to a past condition of the subject or to an objective item of knowledge which the subject once included in his repertory. It is in fact the activity of appropriating to the self and subjectively realizing how a particular state of unconsciousness affects the whole system of our spiritual being. In our preoccupation with the end to be achieved, or with the object we are trying to recall, we are prone to overlook the true nature of the situation as a predicament of subject-selfhood. But if the struggle is sufficiently prolonged, and becomes sufficiently acute, the sense of mental vacancy is brought home to us with all the poignancy of an experience. Our minds are forced back upon themselves. We feel intensely what it is to be without the special mode of consciousness we desire; and our centre of attention changes, say, from the whereabouts of a missing key, to the train of experiences or subjective events which preceded the loss of the latter. We try to reconstruct a section of our past history up to the point at which it becomes a blank, and we do so in the hope that the blank will acquire a content through its continuity with its own antecedents. In this way a heightened self-consciousness is promoted by a sense of obliviscence or a limited unconsciousness felt as a deprivation.[48] To put the matter paradoxically, to be *uncon-scious* to this extent and under these conditions is among the ways in which it is possible to become acutely *conscious* of the self.[49]

In the instance with which we have been dealing consciousness and unconsciousness are compresent in a single experience which sustains both conditions simultaneously. In other cases there is a time difference between the unconsciousness to which we adjust ourselves in consciousness, and the conscious activity of self-adjustment; but no difference of principle is involved. Fighting down unconsciousness in the form of sleep is an example of what I have in mind. It is as a predicament of the self, and not as a mere negation or cancellation of our subjectivity, that we envisage the creeping tide of oblivion and grapple with its quelling power. The Arctic explorer, overcome by a snowstorm, and wrestling des-perately with the drowsiness that assails him, bends all his efforts to avert the onfall of complete unconsciousness. He does so because he knows that if he permits himself to fall asleep, he will never waken up alive. But while he dreads the first moment of oblivion as the precursor of death, it is as a *phase of life* (and therefore some-thing still within his power) that he sets himself to combat it. The unconsciousness of the living is one thing, that of the dead is quite another; and the difference between the two is that between a special plight of the conscious subject—a fluctuation in the con-tinuity of an experience that remains intact—and a change so radical as to render the very existence of the spiritual system a matter of speculation.

The struggle to avert unconsciousness has its counterpart in the struggle to induce it. When the sufferer from insomnia woos the priceless boon of sleep, the nescience he craves is not extinction or temporary non-existence, but a state of being to which, although it takes the negative form of *un*consciousness, he assigns a positive value (that of *rest*, for example) in the total economy of his sub-jective existence. For him a dreamless sleep is contextual with the

---

[48] The Aristotelian στέρησις as contrasted with mere nothingness.

[49] I might once more draw attention to the fact that verbs for remembering and for-getting commonly have a reflexive or semi-reflexive form (like the Latin deponents), and govern the genitive case. The significance of this, as I have already pointed out, is that in their primary aspect these verbs connote an involuted state of the self—an activity or experience of the subject in relation to its own inner life—and the reference to an object is secondary and indirect. The modern English idiom—an active transitive verb with a direct accusative—is inappropriate and misleading.

experience that encloses it. He savours it through the penumbra by which the core of utter forgetfulnes is enveloped, and the experience within which it falls as an interlude is profoundly modified thereby.

38. As a final argument for the interpretation of unconsciousness as experience, let me add a thoroughly familiar fact of psychological significance—a fact which may be stated objectively, and, in its obscurer phases, verified by methods of indirect observation. Consciousness does not normally alternate with unconsciousness by any process of instantaneous and complete mutual displacement; nor do these opposites confront one another with the absoluteness of two perfectly defined identities in which the grade is given with the fact. There is a total absence of the "all-or-nothing" character in both. Consciousness admits of infinite gradations, and its states shade away by imperceptible degrees into other states of greater or of lesser intensity. In such transitions there is neither gain nor loss of mental character.[50] The fundamental modality is unaltered by any variations which imply a reference to it in their definition. Thus a low degree of consciousness is a fact of the mental or spiritual order just as much as is a high degree of consciousness; and when the lower limit, the so-called "threshold" is reached, the mental character is perpetuated in a further series of states which follow one another continuously in a descending scale. There is such a thing as a *lighter*, and there is such a thing as a *deeper* hypnosis. It is possible to be *altogether* unconscious, and yet to be so only in *a slight degree*. It is also possible to be completely unconscious without ceasing to be extremely active in a mental sense. Such activity as goes on "beneath" the threshold, since it is subjective in character, and has repercussions throughout the subjective system as a whole, cannot possibly be excluded from the concept of experience.

39. As for the relation between successive grades either of consciousness or of the unconscious, there could be no more unmistakable example of functional variation in the world of empirically discoverable events. The distance from the threshold, whether above it or below, increases and diminishes with conditions which are to a large extent known and are presumably altogether know-

---

[50] This must not be taken to imply that there is no such thing as a greater or lesser fullness of spiritual *being*. Such differences define themselves within a modality that remains identical.

able. These conditions may be either subjective or psycho-phys-ical.[51] Among them are interest, attention and the strength of the stimulus—factors which, in their actual operation, are crossed and complicated in numberless ways. In particular the determinant, before it can produce its characteristic result, is liable to modification by a factor which I shall call the sensitiveness of the psycho-physical organism to the vital significance of the occasion. A typical example is that of the mother who sleeps through an inferno of irrelevant noises, but awakes at once upon the faintest stirring of the infant in the cot at her side. Here the grade of auditory sensitiveness is a function of the stimulus as qualified, not by its strength, but by its meaning. Or perhaps I should say that the response is functionally dependent upon the strength of the stimulus taken in conjunction with a certain initial adjustment of the organism to its vital interests.

40. So far I have tried to bring out the nature of spiritual being by reference to the concepts of experience, system and consciousness. The next step will be to view our theme from the standpoint of the distinction between subjective and objective and of the concept of selfhood.[52]

[51] Whether they are ever purely physical is a question we are not yet in a position to deal with. The answer to it depends on the nature of the relation (1) between the physical conditions of being in general and the life of organisms, and (2) between bodily life and subjective systems.

[52] For a diagrammatic summary of the basic modal differences in their mutual relationship *vid*. Appendix D, p. 215.

APPENDIX A *(See note 8, page 182)*

THE WORD "PERSON"

Sometimes, it is true, the word "person" is employed in the sense of a possession, as when we speak of "my person," "his person." But in this case the meaning is highly restricted. By a perfectly intelligible anomaly "person" is the term used to denote both the spiritual principle with which we identify our inner selves, and the visible emblem of spiritual being, the *body* which we claim as our own. It is a circumstance of note that whereas primitive languages abound in expressions for spirit, soul or self, it is only at an advanced stage of development that a verbal symbol is evolved for the expression of spirit in the specifically human form. Greek and Latin of the classical period have no word which corresponds exactly to the English "person," no word for "personality" or the German "Persönlichkeit." Equally remarkable is the fact that when the need for some such term began to be felt, the word that drifted into use was the Latin "persona" (Greek πρόσωπον, a face), which in its original usage connotes, not the deeply seated inner life of the conscious subject, but something preeminently overt and superficial, an actor's mask.

APPENDIX B (*See note* 13, *page* 186)

BERKELEY AND CONTEMPORARY PHILOSOPHY

It is not surprising that in modern times a position in some respects akin to Berkeley's should have been adopted both by scientists and philosophic interpreters of science. These thinkers mostly resemble Berkeley in rejecting a world of substances or independent things-in-themselves, and in reducing nature to a complex of sensa. They differ from him in denying an ontologically independent subject of experience, and in identifying the conscious self with some character in the sense complex—e.g., continuity and relative permanence in the related data. Although he would have rejected this latter feature, Berkeley himself prepared the way for it by his failure to furnish a circumstantial content to the subject of experience as such—or indeed any content at all except the general activity of perception, the definitory *percipere* that accompanies the definitory *percipi*. This modern tendency is exemplified in the work of Ernst Mach (*Die Analyse der Empfindungen, Populär-wissenschaftliche Vorlesungen*) and Richard Avenarius (*Kritik der reinen Erfahrung, Der menschliche Weltbegriff*). Max Verworn adopts the Berkeleian doctrine as modified by Mach (subjectivism without a subject) in the opening chapter of his *Allgemeine Physiologie* (English tr. by F. S. Lee, 1899, pp. 34-8). Among English thinkers it will be sufficient to mention Karl Pearson, Lloyd Morgan and Bertrand Russell, who concur in reducing external objects or "things" to a *construct* (Russell, "a mere logical construction") of sensory impressions. (*vid.* Pearson, *The Grammar of Science*, 3rd ed., Part I, p. 41; Morgan, *Animal Life and Intelligence*, p. 312; Russell, *Our Knowledge of the External World*, p. 89.) A phenomenological view of nature, based on Kant's *Critique*, underlies the physics of Helmholtz, and, in more recent times, the biological teaching of J. Von Uexküll, *Theoretical Biology*, 1906.

APPENDIX C (*See note* 18, *page* 188)

THE NEW TESTAMENT USE OF THE WORD "SPIRIT"

In New Testament usage the concrete and the abstract are poles between which the meaning varies with the context. It is a fact worth noting that in each of the four Gospels, as also in the Acts of the Apostles and in Paul's Epistle to the Romans, the word πνεῦμα is introduced for the first time without the article—"holy spirit" or "spirit of holiness" rather than "*the* Holy Spirit." *vid*. Matt. i. 18; Mark i. 8; Luke i. 15; John i. 33; Acts i. 2; Rom. i. 4. Spirit has many aspects. It is a medium in which one is baptized, a generative principle (Matt. i. 18, 20; John iii. 5; v. 8), a power, suggestive of *mana*, that comes upon the individual, and in which he goes from strength to strength. In another aspect it is a *content* of life, something with which the subject may be filled, as he is filled with faith or grace. The Spirit of the Father becomes a power of speech, the secret of prophetic utterance, as where David, ἐν πνεύματι, calls Christ Lord (Matt. xxii. 43). By God's spirit (ἐν πνεύματι θεοῦ) devils are cast out. In certain contexts the term acquires what is virtually a normative connotation. There is a spirit of life, a spirit of bondage, a spirit of sonship or adoption. Spirit ranges itself alongside truth in the ideal of a genuinely spiritualized worship (John iv. 23-4). It stands opposed to the "letter," to the "flesh." The supreme alternatives of life are summed up in the antitheses: κατὰ σάρκα . . . κατὰ πνεῦμα· ἐν πνεύματι, οὐ γράμματι.

APPENDIX D (*See note 52, page* 211)

(*See note 52, page* 211)

CONSCIOUS AND UNCONSCIOUS—A DIAGRAMMATIC REPRESENTATION

The various factors involved in an inventory of being from the standpoint of its fundamental modes may be seen at a glance from the following diagram:

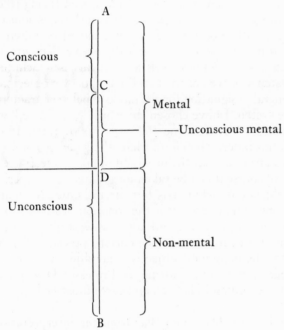

AB = being in general (all states).
AC = conscious states of being, all mental or spiritual.
CB = unconscious states of being, mental and non-mental.
AD = mental states of being, conscious and unconscious.
DB = non-mental states of being, all unconscious.
CD = unconscious mental states.

The division AD (mental, conscious and unconscious) covers what I understand by experience.

CHAPTER VI

SUBJECT-OBJECT AND SELF

The Subjective Mode of Being Exists in Systems Which Constitute Subjects or Persons

1. The points which throughout I have been trying to establish are that our subjective states, among which the conscious instances are revealed with a peculiar directness, should be taken together as constituting a system of dynamically active elements, and that every such system defines itself against all else, including other similar systems, as well as the manifold of its own objects.

As a general designation for the mode of being characteristic of a subjective system I have chosen the word "experience," which for various reasons seems to me the most appropriate. It is of the utmost importance, therefore, that the concept of experience should be kept free from the intrusion of non-subjective elements; and while of course it can be taken for granted that experience as a whole could not be what it is but for the objective manifold of which, in one of its phases, it is the consciousness, and to which it is the continuous reaction and progressive adjustment, nothing but confusion can result from the current practice of decrying or ignoring the distinction of subjective and objective,* or of physical and psychical, and from insisting, as Professor Dewey habitually does, that everything in heaven and earth must be included in the concept.[1]

It should be further noted that from the interpretation of experience as identical with the subjective in general it follows that the antithesis of rational and empirical, so deeply rooted in the

[* "Objective" is apparently being used here for the *non-subjective* objective. The subjective *qua* known is object-to-consciousness, and thus is itself part of the objective. Cf. 11, p. 226 below.—Ed.]

[1] e.g., *Experience and Nature*, p. 24. Good examples of the treatment of the body-mind relation (Dewey of course denies that there is any *problem* here, *op. cit.*, p. 255) are to be found, pp. 261, 272 and 285. "The distinction," so one passage runs, "between physical, psycho-physical, and mental is . . . one of increasing complexity and intimacy of interaction among natural events." And again: "In the hyphenated phrase body-mind, 'body' designates the continued and conserved, the registered and cumulative operation of factors continuous with the rest of nature, inanimate as well as animate; while 'mind' designates the characters and consequences which are differential, indicative of features which emerge when 'body' is engaged in a wider, more complex and interdependent situation."

hilosophical tradition, sinks to a level of relative insignificance. Certainly experience, in the comprehensive sense in which the term is here used, is not to be defined as the opposite of reason. On the contrary, the characteristic activity of reason, which is thinking, is one of the most revealing possibilities of experience.

Finally, the term cannot be restricted to those usages which would identify experience with certain of its own contingencies or with any ideals that are implicit in it. For example, it is not necessary that experience should be exciting or highly variegated or the product of accumulation and development; in the sense of the youth who will go in quest of experience, as if he himself were not already compact of the same. We often discriminate between men as experienced and *in*experienced without reflecting that for a subject to be altogether wanting in experience would be to be altogether non-existent. These modes of expression are both intelligible and legitimate; but they depend for their import upon the recognition of an initial subjectivity which underlies all such differences and possibilities.

2. The crucial points in my argument so far are these:

(a) In any attempt to characterize reality as a whole, or to explore the possibilities of being in the light of its most significant distinctions, it is important to realize that there is a form of being, the subjective or spiritual, which reveals itself (in so far as it does so affirmatively, and not merely as the opposite of another form) in a way that is altogether self-definitory. We cannot really say what spirit *is* except in terms which imply the character of spirituality. If there is a mode of being to which this character does not apply (and I think it may be assumed that there is), then the first step in any metaphysical inquiry must be to make sure that these two are not confounded.

(b) The spiritual mode of being occurs in organized systems, each of which must be conceived as existing substantivally. The character which we express by such terms as "subjective" and "spiritual" is not directly attributable to reality as such, whether as the deeply hidden inner principle of things or as a surface manifestation. Subjectivity in the strict sense is the definitory property and modal peculiarity of subjects or systems of experience, and of the states, predicaments and processes which constitute the content of the latter. If there is a sense in which the expression may be

extended to other modes of being, it is because of some significan
relation in which they stand to the experience of conscious sub
jects.

(c) In defining the nature of a subjective system in terms of ex
perience, it is essential that the element of consciousness be intro
duced at the right place and in the right way. The difference be
tween being conscious and being unconscious within the limits o
a subjective system is one thing: that between being conscious an
being unconscious in general is another. When we pass from th
first to the second difference, we are passing from an order of realit
which is altogether subjective, and therefore homogeneous, to on
which is heterogeneous because partly non-subjective. The uncon
scious states of a conscious being must therefore be construed i
quite a different way from the unconscious states of a physica
entity. Their relation to consciousness, whether actual or potentia
is part of their nature. But for this relation they would not b
what they are. Thus consciousness acquires the force of a de
finitory principle. There is nothing secondary or adventitious abou
it. If in the order of time it is relatively late in making its appear
ance, this fact must be placed in subordination to the deeper trut
that metaphysically speaking, the progress out of the unconsciou
can throw no light upon the nature of consciousness until tha
progress has been itself construed in the light of its final manifesta
tion.[2]

Such Systems or Persons May Be Embodied. Questions Concernin the Animal Body

3. Several points remain to be elucidated. One of these has to d
with the connection between the concept "person" and the concep
"man." These two are not identical. The word "man" connote
not merely the spiritual mode of being, but also the possession of
well defined type of animal body. Man occupies a distinctive plac
in the biological realm, and to that place he is confined by his cor
poreal nature. The concept of the body must therefore be com

---

[2] In dealing with the relation of Nature to Mind the Archbishop of York find
Nature prior in the order of time and Mind in the order of reality. The two points o
view, he further argues, can be harmonized by a dialectical transition from the one t
the other. (vid. Nature, Man and God, Chap. v.) To my way of thinking the solutio
must come rather from a searching analysis of the properties of time in relation to th
spiritual and the physical.

bined with that of the spirit in the concept of humanity.[3] But no such reference to man's body is implied in the concept of personality. Thus a person may be conceived as retaining his identity in the absence of bodily structure or throughout a series of reincarnations. From early times the notion has been prevalent of nonhuman forms of personal existence. Whether such forms actually occur, or are merely the product of the mythopoeic fancy, is a problem which need not trouble us here. The theoretical possibility, taken in conjunction with the reasons which have led us to postulate distinct modalities, is sufficient to exclude all reference to the human body from the definition of personality, and to render such reference indispensable in the definition of man. Among the factors which contribute to the concept of humanity, therefore, we must include a certain continuity of physical life, a certain biological self-identity, which has no part in the definition of personal existence.[4]

4. From this it will be clear that in refusing to include the human body in the concept of personal existence I am not in any way detracting from the truth, so often insisted upon, that man exists and is known to us only as an embodied soul. On the contrary, that truth acquires a peculiar significance from the recognition of the fact that man's body belongs to the realm of nature,[5] while his soul belongs to the fundamentally different realm of spirit. This way of looking at the subject implies no real change in the factors recognized. In each case we are dealing with a human body and a human mind. Only, from the one point of view we say: body + soul = personality; from the other: humanity = personality + a certain type of body. It must be admitted, however, that the implications (particularly the ethical implications) involved in the two ways of stating the relation may be profoundly divergent. In

---

[3] So Wordsworth's "Phantom of Delight" was not merely "a Spirit," but "a Woman too!" Of course the distinction which the poet has in mind is subtler than that of body and spirit, but it implies the latter distinction. In "Woman *too*" body combines with spirit to give a context to the finer modality of spirit as such.

[4] John Locke was thoroughly alive to the distinction. *vid. Essay*, Book II, Chap. XXVII, §§8-28. This is not to say that his conception of personality or personal self-identity as "the sameness of a rational being," or a continuity of consciousness, is in all respects the equivalent of that here offered. cf. *A Defence of Mr. Locke's Opinion concerning Personal Identity*. Certainly if Locke is adequately represented by his apologist, the author of the last-named treatise, I cannot agree at all. For personality, as there depicted, appears as a mixed mode and an abstraction.

[5] On the concept of nature as I understand it *vid.* Appendix A, p. 250.

the one instance the concept of personality includes that of bodily existence, and the type of moral achievement is apt to be found in successful adjustment to environment. In the other, personality is left free to define the moral end in terms of spiritual attainment, and without immediate reference to bodily effectiveness.[6]

5. The difficulty with regard to the human body suggests another problem. If a person is a subjective system, or a system including conscious states but excluding bodily structure, does it not follow that the lower animals, on the psychical side of their being, must rank as persons? That they are endowed with consciousness will hardly be denied; and if so, their conscious states, for the same reasons that hold in the case of human beings, must be thought of as organized together into the unity characteristic of a subjective system, and quite distinct from that of the body.[7]

Now this is a view which it is much more difficult to substantiate in the case of the lower animals than in that of man. The subjective life of the animals, we assume, can at the utmost be a life of impulse. That is to say, the psychical elements involved are unmistakably correlated with their physiological conditions: that they are correlated with one another (in any sense but that of temporal sequence) is far from clear. In other words, there is abundant evidence that the psychical and physiological factors combine to constitute a system which may be characterized either (a) as heterogeneous or psycho-physical, or (b)—if the mental element is reduced to the status of an epiphenomenon, and so rendered of no account—as definitely physiological (and in that sense homogeneous); but it is by no means so obvious that the psychical factors, taken in themselves, can be reckoned together as constituting a homogeneous system of spiritual events. Hence the uncertainty we feel in ascribing a soul to the lower animals. On the other hand, if we admit the fact of consciousness at all, we seem bound to provide for it by postulating a subjective system. In the end we are confronted with the following dilemma. If the brute creation is conceived as endowed with any degree of sentience, then in accordance with the general principle we have

[6] In this connection I would point out that the warring opposites involved in moral effort and moral conflict are never body and soul as such (flesh and spirit in the literal sense), but two phases of the spiritual life which differ from one another in accordance with certain differences in their relation to the bodily factor.

[7] For the relation of philosophy to the interpretation of animal life *vid.* Appendix B, p. 251.

assumed, we must posit a systematically organized experience, conscious and unconscious, for every individual involved. If in the case of any individual or of any species we feel unable to take this step, we thereby cast doubt upon our right to think of human beings as subjective systems or persons.

The traditional solution would be to discriminate between the human and the animal mind on the ground that the former contains, whereas the latter excludes, the capacity for general or "free" ideas. Upon this view the presence or absence of that capacity, rather than of consciousness as such, is the condition upon which the distinction between the personal and impersonal mode of being depends. Animals are conscious beings to which the power of ideation, as distinct from mere sentience, has been denied.

Without raising the question how far this theory is tenable, or the distinction on which it rests legitimate, I would point out that it fails to clear up the difficulties involved, and that there are considerations of a different character which, although they still leave much to be explained, go more directly to the root of the matter. Chief among these is the following. It will be agreed that the reason why we refuse to attribute personality, in the fullest sense, to *any* of the lower animals, and even in a qualified sense to most of them, is one with the reason which leads us to deny *responsibility* to the whole realm of living things beneath the level of mankind. Now the condition upon which a conscious being acquires the character of responsibility is that its conscious states should not be completely absorbed in their momentary external objects, but that it should be capable of the kind of experience which we call self-consciousness. A deficiency in this capacity is interpretable as an absence of that character by which persons are distinguished from sub-personal forms of being.[8] The differentia of personality within the genus of the subjective is therefore the capacity for self-conscious experience. For the rest, this type of experience depends

[8] A word of explanation is necessary here. By "self-consciousness" in the present context I mean what is commonly understood by that term—that is to say, a special way of being conscious, distinguishable from all others by the fact that its object is just the self which sustains the consciousness in question. As we shall see later, this is not the only sense in which the term may be understood. There is a form of self-conscious experience, to which I shall give the name of "primary," and which is presupposed in that most commonly recognized. "Primary" self-consciousness is an implicate, rather than a species, of awareness, and as such must be attributed to all subjects of experience, whether persons or not. For this reason it need not here be taken into account.

upon the relation in which the contents of a subjective system stand to their own temporal conditions. Self-consciousness develops within the continuity of an extensive, as distinct from a momentary *present*; and it varies in completeness with the degree to which the contextuality of earlier with later is appreciated and exploited by the conscious subject. The lower animals differ from human beings in that their pasts and their futures are altogether or largely meaningless, and indeed non-existent, for them. At each moment in their history they are confined to an awareness in which, if the evidence of their behaviour may be trusted, body-feeling preponderates over all else. Their life-history will therefore be the story of successive absorptions into body-feeling. In other words, it will resolve itself into a series of experiences which pass completely from their grasp with the physiological adjustments that accompany them. It is here that we perceive the fundamental contrast between the lower animals and man. The differentiating fact about our human experience is that its successive occasions do not vanish with their incitements, but organize themselves into systems which continue to shed the light of consciousness upon them as they recede in time. Not mere succession, therefore, but *inclusion* is here the characteristic relationship. Our momentary experiences individuate themselves within the unity of a comprehensive experience. The consciousness of this is a consciousness of our subjective self-identity, and it is the principle at once of responsibility and of personal existence. So interpreted, personality would seem to be restricted to members of the human race, and to any beings that share with man the capacity for self-consciousness.

6. The distinction involved is sufficiently important to justify the restriction; and I intend to comply with usage. But I would point out that systems of experience to which we refuse the higher status are nonetheless identical in their modality with systems which enjoy the latter, and that from the standpoint of their ontological nature, the lower animals, in so far as they are endowed with consciousness at all, must take their place along with persons as a concrete embodiment of the subjective mode of being.

The situation is the same if for "person" and "personal" we substitute the words "spirit" and "spiritual." We do not ordinarily think of "brute-beasts" as spirits, or describe the mode of their being as "spirituality"; but here again the difference is not one of modality: rather it has to do with the principle or degree of organization involved. We reserve the name of "spirit" for certain types of subjective system—the human and perhaps the superhuman. Modally speaking, animals and angels resemble one another, and both resemble men.[9]

The Term "Subjective" Connotes a Modality of Being; the Term "Objective" a Relation between Any Mode of Being and Consciousness

7. In the course of the discussion it has become clear that spirit must be viewed in two distinct contexts. We must consider it from the standpoint of what it is in itself. Here a number of distinctions are seen to be of vital importance—for example, the distinction of human and animal intelligence, and, in close connection with this, the distinction of consciousness and self-consciousness. On the other hand there are aspects of the spiritual or subjective that can best be brought out by considering the latter from the standpoint of the contrast which its modality as a whole presents to any other aspect of the real. Among the antithetical relations which thus come into view is that of the subjective mode as such to its natural opposite, the physical. The contrast is here ontological in its significance, and it is altogether fundamental. Nonetheless it may be strangely unilluminating. The reason for this is that before we can hope to utilize the distinction between the two ultimate modes of being in the interpretation of either, we must have a fairly developed concept of both. This science can provide for the physical. For a deeper understanding of the spiritual we must scrutinize the internal distinctions to which I have referred. Above all, the relation of conscious and self-conscious is of importance for a knowledge of spirit. With this we shall have to deal in the next chapter.

---

[9] The point of these remarks is doubtless more obvious in the case of the higher species, where the evidences of consciousness are fairly conclusive, than in that of the lower organisms, where the evidence seems to point in the opposite direction. The question therefore arises whether in the total and permanent absence of conscious experience we have a right to assume the presence of anything which might be described as subjectivity. If the subjective mode of being is identifiable by reference to conscious states alone, and if unconscious states are interpretable as subjective only if they can be seen to stand in functional relations to the former, the lower organisms would seem to be entirely excluded. The effect of this admission (which, in the absence of conclusive evidence, we are not bound to make) upon our general argument cannot be rendered apparent until we have considered the nature of life (in the sense of biological subsistence) in relation to spirit.

8. For the present we must consider certain concepts which are presupposed in a treatment of self-consciousness. In particular the concept of objectivity, and the relation of objective to subjective, call for careful attention. As regards the latter relation I would point out that it is neither internal to the spiritual mode as such, nor yet expressive of a difference between that mode and any other. The sheer anomaly, the uniqueness, of its significance is a measure of its importance. It is further clear that in order to deal effectively with self-consciousness we must have some notion of what is meant by "self." Hence we must add a discussion of self-hood to that of subjective and objective, as a preparation for an attempt to apply the concept of self-consciousness to the interpretation of spiritual being. In the order of inquiry, therefore, the following topics will come up successively for consideration: (a) the relation of subjective and objective, (b) the concept of "self," and (c) the distinction (and the relation) of conscious and self-conscious. The present chapter will be devoted to the first two of these topics, the following chapter to the third.

9. As we have seen, the term "subjective," in its primary and fundamental significance, connotes a *modality of being*.[10] In other words, when, in this fundamental sense, we speak of anything as "subjective," we are making a statement about *the way in which it exists*. Every experience exists subjectively: so does every system of experience. Such a system is commonly known as a "subject": its constituent experiences are conceived as its states.

10. The term "objective," on the other hand, connotes not a modality of being, but a relation. When we speak of anything as objective, we are not affirming existence at all, but are stating a connection, prepositional or adverbial between a certain entity and our consciousness of it. Existence, it is true, may be implied: it may indeed in some cases be the fact to which the objectivity of anything is supposed to point. But if so, certain other conditions must be assumed: it is only when these are present that objectivity may be taken as evidence of any specific mode of being.

---

[10] This is the precise point on which I differ with Mr. Holt. For him being defined as subjective (mental) or physical is, logically speaking, posterior to being as such. The general precedes the special. In my theory the logical gives place to the ontological point of view, and certain *modes of being* (of which subjectivity is one) are given at the very outset along with being itself.

As to the precise nature of the relationship in question, so far at least as its general character is concerned, we are here confronted with another indefinable. All we can say of it is that it gives meaning to the prepositional element in the phrase "conscious *of*."[11] The terms between which the relation holds are a state of consciousness on the one hand, and, on the other, an entity expressed by the substantive which the preposition governs. Both in a grammatical and in a logical sense the reference is to an "object." Hence the relation involved is that between a state of consciousness—the *in-term*—and an object of consciousness—the *out-term*. Of these the last-mentioned, whatever its ontological status, owes its identity *as an object* to the relation in which it stands, and therefore to the existence of a conscious subject, which renders that relation possible. Logically speaking, the concept of an object presupposes the concept of objectivity. The latter is required for the definition of the former.[12] I should add that the word "objectivity" not only expresses the nature of the relation between the in- and the out-term, but may also signify the characteristic property of the latter—"what it means to be the out-term in the relationship of which the in-term is a state of consciousness."*

It will hardly escape notice that this way of dealing with the various factors in the case involves a drastic reversal of the usual procedure. The objective is commonly identified with the substantival, the ontologically independent, the self-validating,[13] the absolute and non-relational, while the subjective suggests relations of a highly variable type, with the dependence and insecurity which such relations imply. The effect of this latter view, when worked out to its logical conclusions, is to reduce consciousness to an epiphenomenon or a relation, and the world to a "neutral mosaic," while the subject of experience disappears in a stereotyped association of its own "objects." Subjectivity without a subject, objectivity without a correlate to give it meaning—such are the characteristic products of a mode of thought which leaves us with logic but without a world.

[11] The indefinability of the relation obviously accrues to it from that of the term (consciousness) upon which it depends for its meaning.

[12] Hence those who refuse to recognize a subject, and reduce consciousness to a selection of neutral entities have no right to use the word "object."

[*It is this passage I have had in mind in the use I have made of the word "objective" in the *Analysis*.—Ed.]

[13] We speak, e.g., of the *objectivity* of moral standards and principles.

*Entities Are Classifiable in Accordance with Their Degree of
Dependence upon, or Indifference to the Relation of
Objectivity*

11. The transfer of ontological significance from the object to
the subject has an important consequence, to which I must draw
attention. An object of consciousness may exist in any of the modalities without exception. It may exist subjectively, as when we
introspect our mental states, and thereby bring them into the relationship which turns them into objects of observation. It may
exist as ideals or as qualities exist. It may exist, as physical entities
are supposed to exist, independently and substantivally. When we
describe it as an "object," we leave all questions of modality open.
The term will consequently cover the whole range of being,
whether mental or non-mental, in so far as the definitory condition
is fulfilled.*

12. From this it follows that objectivity can be treated as a
generic concept to which the modes of being supply specific types.
Conversely, the modalities, with all that differentiates them from
one another, may be brought together and viewed from the common standpoint of their relation to our consciousness. When we so
consider the possibilities of existence, we obtain an orderly conspectus of the varieties of the objective. This statement, however,
is too simple. That they are all alike, whether actually or potentially, related to the consciousness of some subject, is not merely a
character which the modes of being have in common: the *sig-*

[*It is important that the reader should try to have the architecture of the system
somewhat specially in focus at this point; keeping before him the respective places
given to the physical, the spiritual and the perceptual (or "nature," which carries the
realm of values).

Nature and its superstructure, this whole world of sensory properties and of values,
arises out of the *mere compresence* of spiritual and physical. Life, on the other hand,
implies the possibility of an organic or functional relation between the two. Account is
also to be taken (cf., e.g., section 16 (b), p. 230, below) of the fact that that *conjunctive*
contact with the physical on which the perceptual, etc., depend (and which is ultimately
mysterious to us) can apparently only be made by spirit, on condition of its prior entry
into the *organic or functional* relationship. In other words, it is for the *embodied* spirit
that "nature" exists. What, then, precisely, is life? Plainly, some such adaptedness of
the physical, as fits it to mediate this all-fructifying presence of spirit to its "other," in
which the sacramental aspect of the universe emerges. Does this throw any light upon
the otherwise perplexing difficulty we have in accounting for life satisfactorily on
mechanical principles? Can the vehicle of spirit be a mechanism? It will be seen that
for the author it "vibrates in spirit time." But its pulse does not synchronize with that
of the spirit. Hence the task of moralization.—Ed.]

nificance of the relation differs with the nature of the mode. In some cases the object owes nothing to our consciousness of it— nothing, that is to say, except its formal character as an object or out-term. The modality of the entity in question is quite independent of its objectivity. In other instances the modality and even the being of the entity are determined by the relation. Here objectivity is not only a logical prius of the formal character which constitutes the out-term an object: it has all the force of an ontological precondition.

13. The following is an attempt at classification from the point of view which I have just indicated. To begin with, we must recognize two main divisions, comprising: (1) the entities which are entirely independent of the relation in which they may stand to some system of experience, and (2) the entities which are not thus independent. Each of these classes admits of further, and in the end, perhaps, indefinitely extended subdivision.

(1) Although they are all alike characterized by ontological independence, the members of the first group may differ profoundly in their modality. There is, for example, (a) the subjective or mental mode which has been considered at length, and (b) an independently existing non-subjective or physical mode.

(a) As regards the former, it is evident that subjective states and systems may themselves enter into the relationship which invests them with the character of objectivity. We may introspect our conscious processes and observe those of others indirectly. We may think about ourselves and about our fellow-mortals as subjects or systems of experience. In each case we convert an entity which exists subjectively into an object of consciousness by placing it in a peculiar relation, and one which, in certain circumstances, may have no effect whatever upon its ontological character.[14] It is not as objects of observation or of thought that mental states actually occur, it is not so that they *exist*, and it is not so that in the first instance (and most characteristically) they reveal themselves to

---

[14] It is, however, important to note (and I shall have occasion in the next chapter to develop the point at length) that subjective states may, under *other* circumstances, be profoundly modified by becoming objects of attention. Consciousness, for example, may thereby be converted into self-consciousness, or (to be more exact) self-consciousness in one form may be converted into self-consciousness in another form. My point is that any such changes are mere variations in a modality which remains throughout inviolably subjective.

those whose mental states they are.[15] As for subjects or persons, they are the systems of these states, and they exist in the same way as the latter—that is to say, subjectively.

14. (b) The non-subjective, independent mode of being will be considered in due course. For the moment it is sufficient to notice that while by definition it is entirely unaffected by the relation of objectivity, that relation is nonetheless highly characteristic of it. It is only as an object of experience that the independently existing non-subjective reveals itself to us. The question that must be held over has to do with its precise identity. This much may be stated in advance. We are here in the realm of the eternally impassive which furnishes its subject-matter to the science of physics—what I shall call the utterly and absolutely physical. When we experience the entities which belong to that realm (and this we can only do by thinking them), they do not enter into our minds or acquire a mental aspect; and so long as we confine ourselves to the thinking attitude which alone is appropriate to the purely physical, the latter does not acquire properties or furnish a locus to meanings which are in any way dependent upon the presence of a subjective factor.

The Mind-Dependent Entities—Those that Are Non-Mental, Those that Are Mental and Those that Are Ambiguous

15. (2) We must further recognize entities which, whether mental or non-mental, owe at least something to the relationship in which they stand to mind. This relationship is a condition of their being. It helps them to their identity; but it does so in different ways and in different degrees. The following are the main divisions of this class: (i) states of mind which, although they are modally unaffected, are nonetheless liable to alteration, within the limits of their subjectivity, by the fact that they are experienced objectively as well as subjectively—in brief, mental processes which are functions of self-consciousness; and (ii) non-mental entities which are determined in part or in whole by our awareness of them. The former type is of such importance for our inquiry that I shall

---

[15] The failure to recognize this truth has played havoc with philosophy and psychology. A characteristic example of the confusion which flows from this source is furnished by Locke in his definition of an idea as "whatsoever the mind perceives in itself." *Essay*, Book II, Chap. VIII, §8. cf. Chap. IX, §1. Throughout Locke confounds the sensa with sensations and vice versa.

have to devote most of Chapter VII to the treatment of it.[16] For the present I shall content myself with noting its place in the general classification, and shall proceed to a consideration of (ii) the modes of being which are at once non-mental and mind-dependent. These also fall into a variety of groups.

16. (a) There are those which, although dependent upon consciousness for any ontological status they may possess, are not in the power of mind or at the mercy of the subjective processes which constitute them what they are. On the contrary, they impose themselves upon the consciousness that evokes them, and they do so with a coercive force that is purely their own. If we think them at all, we must do so in ways that *they* dictate. It is as if, like some malignant spirit, they made use of our minds in order to obtain the power which enables them to get the better of us. The objects of which I am thinking are exemplified by the timeless truths of mathematics,[17] and generally speaking by all truth, and indeed by all matter of fact—in brief, by *everything that is the case* and is expressible in a noun clause, in so far as it furnishes a content to the act of judgment.

This duality, this character of being mind-dependent, yet mind-coercive, is in even historical truths. "Caesar crossed the Rubicon." This is an event of history, and as such it belongs to the temporal order, and has a time and an existence of its own. But when I say: "It is a fact," or, "It is the case" that Caesar crossed the Rubicon, I lift the event out of its historical context and give it the significance of an eternal truth.[18] As an object of judgment it is dependent upon the minds that think it, and yet, like mathe-

[16] It will be seen that the independence of the physical differs from that of the subjective. The former is altogether unaffected by consciousness. In the case of the latter self-consciousness may make a profound difference to our mental processes: it may alter both their quality and their intensity. What remains unaltered is their basic modality. The objects of reflective self-consciousness continue to exist subjectively.

[17] The coercive character of these truths seems to be largely responsible for the extent to which they have been represented as independent of our subjectivity. The fact that they are discoveries and not fabrications is taken to mean that mind contributes nothing to them. But objective structural necessity is one thing, and existence is another. There is no theoretical difficulty in conceiving a realm which has no existence except as an object of thought, and yet is so organized as to impose upon the mind the principles in accordance with which the latter must think it.

[18] This, I think, is all that is valid in the contention of those who maintain that the past is eternal and changeless. It is only in a special relation of detachment from its setting in the flux that it acquires this character, and the relation is specifically that which turns the event into an object of mental affirmation. The implied condition is subjective.

matical truth, it dominates these minds in the very processes by which they sustain it in consciousness. That Caesar crossed the Rubicon is something that may be thought; but when we think it, we must think the event referred to *as an event of history*.

Other examples of these mind-dependent, mind-coercive objects are to be found in the standards of value which determine our moral and aesthetic judgments, and in such concepts as: "The sum of the series $0 + 1 + 2 + 3 + 4 \ldots$ to infinity." There is nothing subjective in objects like these, and yet in their very objectivity they depend upon the act of mind by which we posit them. This type of object may best be described by the word "ideal."[19]

(b) A second group of objects, profoundly different from those with which I have been dealing, yet no less definitely mind-conditioned, is to be found in the sensory properties of things—Whitehead's sense-objects. These too impose themselves on the mind under conditions which are empirically ascertainable, although we cannot profess to understand them. The fundamental condition is a complex relation between the mind, the living body and an independently existing physical reality.[*]

(c) Mental constructions and creations of all sorts, including the images which we conjure up at will, or which come unbidden in moments of dreamy idleness or of emotional excitement, belong to a special category. They are *objects* of consciousness, and therefore in the strict sense of the term non-mental. Yet they owe their existence entirely to the inner working of the psycho-physical organism, and in this the mental factor (at least in some cases) plays the dominant rôle. Hence the objects of constructive intelligence and sensory imagination, unlike ideal objects and objects of perceptual experience, may be relatively non-coercive in their force. In extreme instances, and in spite of physiological conditions which are beyond our control, the mind appears to have the power of indefinite initiative, conception, execution.

17. In this classification there are certain types of object for which it is impossible at present to find a place. I have said nothing about organic structures or living bodies, or about the class of

---

[19] For the perplexing problem of the relation between timeless truths and existence *vid.* Appendix C, p. 252.

[*The mind gets into that "conjunctive" relation to the physical, which conditions the perceptual, through having first entered into "functional" relation with the body.— Ed.]

entities which we commonly designate "things." The latter, in the absence of a more searching examination, may be taken as roughly equivalent to Whitehead's "perceptual" and "physical" objects—although it is only right to add that any differences in our respective theories and definitions may have an effect upon our classification of entities.[20]

The reason for this omission of things and of living bodies is that the modality of both types of being presents a problem with which we are not yet in a position to deal.* That organic structures belong to the physical world need hardly be questioned. It is certainly there that they have their locus. But that their properties are determined exclusively by the conditions of physical existence as such cannot at this point be safely assumed. To say the least, it cannot be taken for granted that so highly specialized a phenomenon as life is adequately explained as a function of the physical. The modality of its being can be determined only after a more detailed inquiry into the mutual relationship of the original modalities. The same is true of things. But here further difficulties arise with regard to boundaries, definition and identity. Is a chair or a table one thing or many things? Or, to do justice to its nature, must we say that it is in some degree both? Is water a thing? If so, does the designation fit the object as it fits a raindrop or a hailstone? Does the term apply with equal force to air and to the movement of air which we call wind, to fire and to the wood or coal which the fire consumes? And what of such exactly measurable and even marketable commodities as that referred to in the advertisements to which Professor Tait has drawn attention: "Spare Power to Let?"[21] These questions too must be left to answer themselves in the light of a general theory which has still to be developed.

18. From this account of the varieties of objectivity and from what has been said about the relation of the subjective and the objective it is clear that the latter distinction is not identical with

---

[20] To take a single example, I am unable to include delusional objects in the class of which the characteristic contents are "the ordinary objects of common experience—chairs, tables, stones, trees." Delusional objects in my scheme would naturally fall into the group of mental creations, and into that portion of the group where the freedom and initiative of the mental factor is most of all restricted by the activity of the physiological—in other words, where the coercive power of the mentally conditioned object is at a maximum.

[*cf. Chap. xii, 10 ff., pp. 359 ff.—Ed.]

[21] Watson, *A Text-Book of Physics*, p. 1.

that of the spiritual and the physical. The subjective and the spiritual are one and the same: not so the physical and the objective. Since the relation of objectivity is universal in its scope, and may be acquired by anything whatever irrespective of its modality, the spiritual and the physical will define themselves against one another within the concept of the objective; and each of them will define itself as modally independent against the class of objects that depend for their existence upon some sort of relation to the independent modes.

19. A further point is this. While the physical and the spiritual are mutually independent modes of being, and while, as has just been asserted, they differentiate themselves as such within the generic concept of the objective, it would not be natural in practice to define each of them in turn by reference to this fact. Thus we should never dream of defining the spiritual as the objective which exists independently of the physical. Where consciousness and systems of being including conscious states are concerned, the generic character of objectivity, which rests upon a relation, is far too casual and adventitious to draw attention to the essential nature of the existent. On the other hand, it would be quite reasonable to define the physical as the objective which exists independently of mind. In the latter case the relationship of objectivity may be utilized to a much greater extent than in the former in the attempt at a philosophical account of the nature of being. I shall return to this point when we come to the exposition of the physical.

The Meaning of "Self," as Revealed by Language

20. In the course of this discussion I have had frequent occasion to speak of self-consciousness and of self-conscious experience. We have seen that a capacity for the latter is what distinguishes the specifically human (and superhuman) type of subjectivity from that of the lower animals. In so far as it is legitimate to discriminate between the inner life of the brute creation and that of the human race, and to restrict the prerogative of personality, with all the higher possibilities of spiritual existence, to the latter, the difference turns upon the relation of experience to selfhood. Hence, as I have pointed out, some notion of what is meant by "self" is necessary to this phase of our inquiry.

The word "self" is something of a linguistic mystery, its ultimate etymology being lost in darkness.[22] What seems to be fairly well established is the original pronominal force of the expression. This is retained in Gothic and Scandinavian, while the adjectival use in the sense of "same," which occurs at a certain period in English, is derivative.[23] As a matter of fact the notion of "sameness," which is still expressed by the German "selb," is basic in the pronominal as well as in the adjectival usage. *Self* is just the *sameness*, the *oneness*, the *identity* of some individual; and when we use the word, we signify our desire that there should be no mistake about the exact object of reference. But if so, the reference must be to something with an identity sufficiently real to render it a matter of importance that there *should* be no mistake about it. Hence selfhood is most naturally attributable, not to transient appearances or phases of the flux, but to entities which are capable of sustaining a more or less permanent and substantival character.

On closer consideration it is seen that even among pronouns the word "self" is chiefly notable as stressing the latter notion. As this is one of those cases in which a philosophical question is inseparably associated with a linguistic, it is worth while pausing to get the verbal form into its true perspective.

Upon one point there should be no misunderstanding. Pronouns are not, as the name suggests and as tradition has it,[24] substitutes

---

[22] The identical form occurs in Anglo-Saxon, in Old German and in Old Frisian, while cognate forms abound in Gothic, Scandinavian and allied languages. Presumably it connects with the pronominal stem *se-*, Sanskrit *sva*, "one's own self," Latin *se*, Goth. *s-ik*, Ger. *sich*. (Skeat, *Etymological Dictionary*; Murray, *New English Dictionary*; Stratmann, *A Dictionary of the Old English Language*). Skeat traces the various related forms to a Teut. base SELBA, self, which he explains as possibly = SE-LIB-A: Goth. *laiba*, "a remnant." If this conjecture is correct, the original meaning would be "left to oneself."

[23] ". . . The sense of 'same,' found in Eng. and the other W. Ger. languages, was developed from this in collocations where the notion of identity implied by a demonstrative was emphasized by the addition of *self* (thus the O.E. *se selfa man þe* may be rendered either 'the *very* man who' or 'the same man who')." *N.E.D.* The disappearance of the adjectival sense (*self-same*) from English is symptomatic of the force inherent in the original pronominal usage. Of course we still employ the adjectival form in the compound "self-same"; but here the two verbal elements are virtually synonymous; and the effect of their conjunction is that of reduplication for emphasis. Or perhaps "self" may here be taken as adverbial in force (*self-same=very same*). In German the meaning varies with the case—*selb-*, nom. and acc. = "same"; *selbst*, gen. = "self." Contrast der*selbe*, den*selb*en, das*selbe* with *Selbst*bewusstsein, *Selbst*entsagung, *Selbst*bildnis.

[24] Lat. *pro nomine*, Gk. ἀντωνυμία.

for nouns. They do not ordinarily stand for, represent or presuppose the latter. The traditional view has indeed survived until comparatively recent times, and we find that it is countenanced by such authorities as Reisig and Henry Sweet.[25] But as Otto Jespersen remarks, it is difficult to see for what substantives the pronouns "I" and "you," "nobody" and the interrogative "who" could be the substitutes.[26] Among parts of speech the pronoun belongs to the class which, so far as can be gathered from the evidence, goes back to the rudiments of vocal self-expression. Hence the obscurity in which its origin is involved. It cannot be traced to anything beyond itself, because the idea which it is designed to convey, or, to be more exact, the spiritual impulse of which it is the release, is aboriginal. When the human mind first sought to vent itself in a common currency of conventional sound-symbols, the pronoun appeared in the earliest issue from the mint of speech.[27] But even at this stage there would inevitably be a certain difference of motive and function between the personal and the demonstrative forms. In the first of these the purpose is to symbolize the subjectivity of the speaker, the listener or the person referred to; in the second, to point out the object upon which it is desired to concentrate attention.[28] But in both instances the underlying need is primitive, and its satisfaction requires a definitely originative, though not a definitely reflective act of consciousness. Pronouns belong to a preconceptual phase of conscious experience.[29] There is no vestige of anything descriptive about them;

[25] *A New English Grammar*, §196.

[26] *The Philosophy of Grammar*, 1924, p. 82.

[27] Michel Bréal goes so far as to place pronouns definitely before nouns in the order of development. "The part of speech which must have been first distinguished from all others is in my view the pronoun. I believe this category more primitive that that of the noun, because it demands less inventiveness, is more instinctive, and lends itself more easily to the commentary of gesture." *Essai de Sémantique*, Paris, 1897. This conjecture (in itself a speculative one) receives a certain reinforcement from a study of the pronoun in relation to the verb. For example, that vast repository of linguistic information, Friedrich Müller's *Grundriss der Sprachwissenschaft* (3 vols., Vienna, 1876 *sq.*) reveals the fact that in a large proportion of primitive languages the pronouns or pronominal elements are constantly requisitioned in order to create verbs out of roots, to differentiate verbs from nouns, and to enable the verb to develop inflectional forms. This shows that the pronoun must have been already available.

[28] The close connection between demonstrative pronouns and adverbs ("this" and "here," "that" and "there") is obvious.

[29] cf. Steinthal-Misteli. ". . . Pronouns are almost universally distinguished from the coarser concept-roots by their volatile forms. . . . There are underived demonstrative elements which, like the 'ei,' 'i' in the verb 'to go,' defy all attempts to explain

they have no connotation of their own (except such as is implied by their inflections), and the entities to which they refer are so indefinitely variable that endless possibilities of misunderstanding may arise in the attempt to identify them.

It is this very circumstance that gives rise to the need for pronouns of emphasis or fixation. These are as elemental as the forms which they are meant to reinforce. But while this is so, while in their origin they are unmistakably pronouns, and not nouns or substitutes for nouns, nonetheless since it is their function to draw attention to identities, the notion of identity tends to acquire the force of a definite connotation in these forms of speech: they come to *mean* that identity which it is their business to point out. When this stage is reached, when they begin to signify that principle in anything which makes it what it is, they cease to be mere pronouns and become nouns. It is so that the pronominal becomes the substantival "self," the "self" which is one with the soul[30] or personality, and which figures so prominently in the language of philosophy. It is so that a connotationless verbal auxiliary enters the region of the conceptual, and takes its place with breath (prâna), seed and soul as an expression of being, viewed from the inside.[31]

21. From this brief survey it will be seen that the word "self," while generally expressing our consciousness of identity, may vary indefinitely in its significance and in the range of its application. The extremes are represented on the one hand by the vague and early pronominal, on the other by the late and explicitly substan-

them. *Charakteristik der Hauptsächlichsten Typen des Sprachbaues*, 1893, pp. 8-9. (A work by H. Steinthal, 1861, recast by Franz Misteli.)

[30] If St. Mark's version of Christ's question about gaining the whole world and losing one's soul is compared with that of St. Luke, it will be seen that the one uses the word "soul" (ψυχήν), the other "self" (ἑαυτόν) Mark viii. 36; Luke ix. 25.

[31] "The concept of self, alone among the pronouns, because of its forcefulness, requires for its expression a pronouncedly substantival and sensory form of speech. This is so even in the Indo-European languages, and indeed some such form is traceable in our 'selbst' and in the Finnish *itse*, of which the derivation is unknown. cf. Sanskrit *ātman-* (Ved. *tman-*) 'breath,' 'soul,' and Magyar *mag-*, i.e. 'seed,' 'grain.' Apart from this the word *itse* betrays its substantival character through the addition to it of a possessive suffix, *itse- -lle -ni*, 'mir selbst,' i.e. mein(*ni*)em(-lle) selbst. The adjectival 'selbst' (Indo-Germ. *svo* and *sevo-*) is also frequently replaced in German by the word 'eigen' ('own') and in Sanskrit by *nigâ*, which means 'native,' while in modern Greek it is restored to life in the phrase ἰδικός μου, etc. The Arabic *nafsum*, 'soul' for 'self,' might also be mentioned, e.g., in the expression bi *anfusi-hā* (-*him*) = 'through oneself'." Steinthal-Misteli, *op. cit.*, p. 9.

tival usage. In the initial stages of linguistic development the pronoun may signify little more than a momentary focus of attention; and of this practically connotationless use there are survivals (or at least analogues) in modern idiom. "Self" is still employed in contexts from which the idea of substantival selfhood is entirely absent. Indeed it is easy to think of cases in which the word or its equivalent has become so completely merged in a purely conventional formula as to be reduced almost to meaninglessness.[32] At the other extreme it has come to acquire the full force of a definite philosophical concept.

Selfhood Is the Identity of an Existing System Which Is Individual, Autonomous and Superior to Its Vicissitudes

22. In this latter significance the notion of selfhood has to do, not with identity in general, but with the identity peculiar to systems. Even this qualification, however, is insufficient to indicate the precise definitory characteristic. There are systems which we should not think of designating "selves." We must therefore try to discriminate between those to which the character of selfhood is strictly attributable and those to which it is not.

In the first place it is not attributable to the type which we have taken as our original model of a system. Where the definitory functional relations are mathematical, and the implied system is an artefact of logic, the idea of selfhood is quite irrelevant. At the very least the postulate of being must go with anything for which the character of a self may be claimed. The substantival use of the word, therefore, presupposes a certain ontological status in the system to which it is applied.

23. This condition is clearly fulfilled in the two independent modes of being—the physical and the subjective. Hence we shall have to put the question with reference to each of these in turn. That is to say, we shall have to ask whether (a) a physical system

---

[32] A characteristic example is that in which the reflexive form is devoid of reflexive significance and is used to convey a contingency or to express the passive voice. cf. "Il libro non se trova," "cela se dit," "cette robe se porte." (Diez, *Grammatik der Romanischen Sprachen*, Vol. III, p. 192; Vendryes, *Le Langage*, p. 122.) F. Brunst distinguishes pronominal from reflexive verbs, and gives the following examples of each: (1) "La fillette *se regarda* dans la glace et *se trouva* changée," (2) "Après cette événement, sa fortune *se trouva* changée." *La Pensée et la Langue*, Paris, 1922, p. 297. An instance of this conventionalized usage in German would be the familiar: "Das versteht sich von selbst."

and (b) a subjective system *as such* must be thought of as constituting a self.

As regards the former I have dwelt upon the evidences of systematic organization throughout the realm of nature. These evidences extend all the way from the atom to the solar system; and
the progress that has been made in establishing the chemical
solidarity and the physical continuity of the terrestrial and celestial regions supports the conception of the spatio-temporal
manifold as a single systematically ordered whole. But when all
has been said, the prevalence of system in the physical world
throws no light upon the question whether system in this case
implies selfhood. So far as our argument goes, it is quite conceivable that nature's rule might be: "System everywhere, but not a
trace of self."

24. In the case of (b) subjective systems or systems of experience
linguistic practice has already prepared us for the theoretical
identification of selfhood and system; but the identification has
still to be explained and demonstrated in detail. We shall also have
to ask whether the character of selfhood is attributable to the dependent modes—that is, to the group of actually-existing, mind-
conditioned objects of experience, and to the class of modally uncertain entities including living bodies and "things."

25. The first step is to ascertain by reference to what, the
varieties of being are judged to satisfy or to fall short of selfhood.
What then does it mean to be a self? So far as can be gathered from
what appears to be the universal intention of language and the
universal understanding of mankind, a system may be thought
of as a self under the following conditions. (1) It must exist, and
it must be an individual. (2) Its existence and its identity must not
be conceived as determined solely by a relation or set of relations
to anything outside the system. In other words, a self can never be
a mere function of something else. (3) The identity of the system
as a self is not represented by its definitory character as a system—
that is, by the functional relation which exists between its contents.
There is more in selfhood than the solidarity that comes of mutual
determination. xy is not a self because $y = F(x)$, and because this
equation rests upon the basic proposition $y = F(xy)$. (4) The exact
point of the distinction between system and self is this. In the one
case we have the unity of a functionally related manifold stereotyping itself against the variety of its contents as the identity of a

system: in the other the identity of a system stereotyping itself against the variety of its contents and of the relations, external and internal, which constitute its vicissitudes.

Generally speaking, a self is characterized by the complexity, the heterogeneity, the variability and the conflicting character of its constituents. That these, in spite of seeming mutual irrelevance and mutual incompatibility, acquire the force of determinant and determined, so that the character of a system is maintained under the most unfavourable conditions, is a circumstance so striking that it leads us to express the identity in question by means of a pronoun of emphasis and fixation. The very notion of selfhood has its origin in the urgent practical need to assert identity where identity is felt to be in some way challenged. The challenge may come in different forms. The most significant of these is the fact of change. Vicissitude is the incitement to the assertion of selfhood; hence it is of the essence of selfhood. This cannot be said of other types of system—even when these (as is frequently the case) consist of events, and are definable as the organized totality of the latter. The atom and the solar system are examples of what I mean. Changes in the form of events (gravitational and electronic) are the very stuff of which these systems are composed. Yet the characteristic processes to which the solar system (for instance) owes its identity could hardly be described as its vicissitudes. On the contrary we think of these processes as chiefly notable for their uniformity. And so of the atom. A very slight departure from this uniformity would mean, in the one case, the destruction of the solar system, in the other a change of identity—say the displacement of an element by its isotope. What is peculiar to a self is its capacity to survive vicissitudes which in any other type of structure would be destructive of identity. There is about a self a degree of flexibility which is quite unique—a flexibility that can only be explained on the assumption of a central energy of organization sufficiently potent to subdue to itself, and so to unify, an indefinitely variable mass of material. It is not enough to recognize (as we have already done) the priority of the system to its individuated contents. We must add to this an original synthetic activity as the principle of the system itself.

To What Modes of Being Selfhood May Be Attributed

26. These are highly generalized statements. They are made, as I have explained, under the assumption, to which linguistic practice is the cue, that the type of selfhood is the subjective system. Material evidence is furnished by the endless variety of the experiences which provide a content to the spiritual mode of being. All the properties which I have attributed to the constituents of a self are attributable to the experiences of a conscious subject. At the same time the subjectivity of the system expresses itself in a power of synthesis generated from within, and subduing the most diverse incidents and predicaments to the indefeasible unity of subject-selfhood. A more explicit rendering of this truth will have to await the detailed treatment of self-consciousness and spirit-time. For the moment the inquiry will be confined to the question whether the postulates of selfhood are realized in any other form.

With regard to the mind-conditioned modes there is no difficulty whatever. In so far as their being is determined by the relation in which they stand to consciousness, they fail to comply with the second of the conditions by which the constitution of a self is determined. If in any sense it is possible to speak of them as selves, their identity as such must accrue to them from the mental processes whereby they become the objects of experience. That is to say, it must be a purely putative selfhood, which, strictly speaking, is no selfhood at all.

The case of "things" and of living bodies is more difficult. Of the latter all I can say is this. If the secret of life is found exclusively in the facts of physics and chemistry, if organic structures are modally homogeneous with their atomic constituents and with the physical conditions of their existence—in brief, if *living bodies are no more than bodies*—the question whether they are to be considered selves is the question whether selfhood is attributable to the physical mode of being, and more specifically to physical systems as such. If, on the contrary, living bodies are bodies *and something more*, it is theoretically possible that even should the purely physical prove to be incapable of sustaining the attributes of selfhood, the latter may accrue to organic structures in respect of this overplus. Pending a theory of life and a concept of the latter, the problem of selfhood in the biological sphere must be postponed.

27. The nature of "things," though obscure, is perhaps less bafflingly elusive. This much at least may be asserted with some measure of assurance. Thinghood as such does not necessarily imply selfhood. If there are things which are selves (a hypothesis which, as we shall see, can hardly be substantiated) there are others which, even on a cursory acquaintance, are seen to preclude any such suggestion. Of course so long as the very identity of individual specimens—the line of demarcation which separates one thing from another—is open to question, it might seem presumptuous to offer any opinion on this much more fundamental issue. The problem, however, is really one of general principles, and the following observations, pointing as they do to a quite definite conclusion, will hold good even in the absence of any solution to problems of lesser importance.

"Things" are among the objects of experience which lay compulsion upon the mind that knows them. But the compulsion is of a different type from any of those that have been so far noticed. It is not like the compulsion of truth or that of the sensory properties. Truths about "things" remain while the things change. The sensory properties change while the things remain the same. The specific form of the compulsion appears in the fact that in the case of things the mind is *constrained* to treat a shifting manifold as one. Every *thing* is a definite concrescence of objective elements, some of which may be objects of sense, others objects of thought, while others again engage the conative strains and the emotional interests. But this is not an adequate statement of the case. What has really to be explained is why such and such a concrescence should ever occur, why this or that specific conjunction of sensory and other elements should constrain us to regard it as a unitary whole clearly and unambiguously articulated against a background of universal nature.

This is one of those questions that do not admit of a one-sided answer. If it is the unity of the object that constrains the mind, it is through the mind's reaction that that unity defines itself in our experience. That is to say, we know which among the numberless possible conjunctions of objective elements are to be accounted things by the effect of the latter *upon us*. And (what is no less significant) that effect is frequently, perhaps always, in some degree determined by our purposes, interests and points of view. In the case of artefacts the thinghood in each instance is the product of

actual constructive effort. It is *we* who decide what particular con-
crescences shall affect us in the way desired; and having made our
decision, or conceived our plan, in advance, we forthwith take the
steps required to give effect to it. But even where this is not so,
even where we are dealing with "natural" objects, it lies with us in
large measure to decide where the dividing lines shall fall. This
must not be construed to mean that these lines may fall anywhere
we please, but rather that the boundary which separates objects
from one another and fixes the limits of their respective thinghood
is determined by the nature of these objects in relation to our
minds and (in some cases at least) to our bodies. There are objects
which are "things" because they are fitted to the human hand or
foot. The existence of such a hand or foot, therefore, and of the
sensations, tactual and kinaesthetic, suggestive of action, which go
with the possession of the organ, has the force of a determinant in
relation to the objects in question. Nevertheless the fitness is not
that of the determinant, but that of the *thing*. As a matter of fact
there is a double concrescence, an objective and a subjective, and
each is the counterpart of each—on the one hand a concentration
of subjective energy into an act of selective discrimination, on the
other a convergence of objective elements into a non-subjective
equivalent. In spite of numberless ambiguous and uncertain instances, there are many "things" which define themselves with precision in our experience. They do so because they provoke the
powers within us to coordinated reaction. Their identity is that of
the counterthrust to the combined subjective and physiological
forces which unite, where they are constrained to converge, in the
directed activity of the psycho-physical organism.

But an identity thus established by reference to *our* activities,
however directed and concentrated, is not what we mean by a self.
So far the organizing principle in the system which we call the
thing is our interest rather than anything internal to the system as
such.

Are "Things" Ever Selves? The Case for Crystals

28. To this it may be objected that while generally speaking what
I have said is true, there are certain crucial instances in which the
above analysis is quite inadequate. An extreme case is that of
crystals. Short of living bodies crystals represent the limit of
organization in the physical world. Presumably they are to be

classified as things. Yet it would be absurd to say of them, as of other "things," that they are organized by our interest in them. On the contrary they are products of nature's impersonal forces, and their structure is emphatically their own. If there is any case at all for the identification of thinghood with selfhood, crystals undoubtedly furnish the best available evidence.*

29. The problem is again one of identities. We have to ask what crystals *are*, and how far the scientific methods by which they are known enable us to penetrate to the secret of their inner nature. It is only when analysis has revealed the type of structure with which we have here to do that we shall be in a position to raise the question of selfhood.

There are two ways in which the identity of a crystal may be determined. One of these is mathematical, the other physico-chemical.

(a) To ordinary macroscopic observation what is most obvious about the crystalline form is the geometrical regularity of the pattern, and, in particular, of the plane faces presented to the view. A closer consideration, aided by instruments like the goniometer, reveals less obvious but more significant facts. In any crystal of the same chemical constitution for example, the size of the faces may change with the growth of the whole, and their shape with the development of adjacent faces, but the interfacial angle remains constant.[33] This is a purely geometrical circumstance, and contributes an important element to the mathematical concept.

In the same way, when we come to the question of classification, the factors which count may be epitomized in the mathematical notion of "symmetry." Thus crystals differ according as they do or do not possess a "centre of symmetry,"[34] and more especially according to the planes and axes of symmetry around which they are built or may be made to rotate.[35] On the basis of these differ-

[*"Thinghood" = *inorganic* thinghood. The sense seems to be: things are things because selected and set up as things (partly); but the crystal sets itself up; and still more, the living plant or animal.—Ed.]

[33] A fact discovered in 1669 by Nicolaus Steno in the case of quartz. Guglielmini (d. 1710) established the constancy of the angles as a fundamental law of crystals.

[34] Defined as having the property "that all straight lines that can be drawn through it will pass through a pair of similar points, lying on opposite sides of the centre of symmetry, and at the same distance from it." Evans and Davies, *Elementary Crystallography*, 1924, p. 9.

[35] In the case of axes the point is this. When a crystal is rotated about a line of symmetry, similar faces and edges will be brought into the original position at regular in-

ences all possible crystals are divided into thirty-two classes and seven systems or "styles of architecture."[36]

The next step is to interpret these superficial characters in terms of interior structure. So far the point of view is still mathematical. We note, to begin with, the homogeneity of the solid body. By this is meant that "every point is similarly situated with regard to the points surrounding it."[37] The conception is obviously symbolic, a point being taken to represent an assumed structural unit and its position in space. All such units in a crystal are alike. In every such structure (to quote Sir William Bragg) "there must be an innumerable number of points such that if an observer, capable of taking up a position within the crystal and of noting the details of his surroundings, could be translated from any one of these points to any other, he would find no change in the outlook in any given direction in space."[38]

So long as the subject remained on the mathematical plane of development, the exact nature of the fundamental structure[39] was matter of conjecture; and the same can be said of the earlier theoretical attempts to construe the mathematical concept in physical and chemical terms.[40] It is natural, therefore, that until the stage of experimental verification was reached, the best results should have been obtained by ignoring the physical question of structure and concentrating upon the mathematical conception of unitary elements as constituting a "point-system."[41] This phase culminated in the space-lattices of Bravais, in which the units are conceived as arranged netwise in planes representing the seven systems, and in the sixty-five regular point-systems of Sohncke,

tervals fixed for each type of structure. Thus if the crystal must be rotated through a half-turn (180°) to reach the stated position, the line of symmetry is called a digonal axis of symmetry, with a cyclic number ii. Where a quarter-turn (90°) or a sixth-turn (60°) is sufficient, the line of symmetry is said to be tetragonal or hexagonal, with a cyclic number of iv or vi, as the case may be.

[36] Six if the trigonal (rhombohedral) system is identified with the hexagonal. A system is a set of classes having similar axes. vid. *Physical Chemistry*, edited Hugh S. Taylor, Vol. I, Chap. v, "The Solid State of Aggregation," by R. N. Peace, p. 149.

[37] Sir William Beale, *Introduction to Crystallography*, 1915, p. 114. "In the space lattice, the environment about every point is the same as that about every other point in the system." (A. W. Stewart, *Some Physico-Chemical Themes*, 1922, p. 226.) By the word "point" is meant a point of reference (centre or otherwise) fixing the locus of structural units.

[38] *An Introduction to Crystal Analysis*, pp. 7-9. In the cubical crystal of common salt, e.g., each atom of sodium represents the centre of an octohedron, of which the six angles

which are "homogeneous assemblages of points symmetrically and identically arranged about axes of symmetry," and expressing "the number of ways in which symmetrical repetition can occur."[42] From the mathematical point of view it was found possible to identify "all the possible types of homogeneous structures possessing the essential attributes of crystals." These are two hundred and thirty in number, and all of them "conform to the conditions of symmetry of one or other of the thirty-two classes."[43]

In all of this there is no suggestion of selfhood as I have defined it. So far as the mathematical identity of crystals is concerned, the latter are wanting in that flexibility and variability, that capacity for vicissitude which we have seen to be of the essence of a system which is also a self. Where the definitory properties are geometrical forms and metrically exact relations, individuality is lost in conformity to type.

are occupied by six atoms of chlorine. Similarly each chlorine atom is surrounded by six sodium atoms arranged in the same way. Thus:

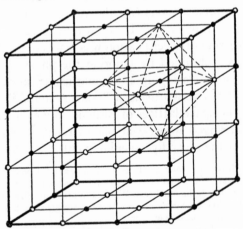

Black discs represent sodium, circles chlorine atoms. The diagram is taken from *The Structure of Atoms* by A. Stock, English tr. by S. Sugden, *vid.* pp. 55-6.

[39] The "Fundamentalbereich" of Schönflies.

[40] Typical constructs are the "molecules intégrantes" of the Abbé Hauy, the "polyhèdres" of Bravais and the fourteen-walled cell, the tetrakaidecahedron of Lord Kelvin. *vid.* A. E. H. Tutton, *Crystals*, p. 112; *The Natural History of Crystals*, p. 86.

[41] Tutton, *Crystals*, p. 113; *Nat. Hist.*, pp. 93-4.

[42] Tutton, *Nat. Hist.*, pp. 94-6.

[43] *op. cit.*, p. 86. cf. Bragg, *op. cit.*, Chap. IV.

30. (b) Passing now from the mathematical to the physico-chemical point of view, we notice certain characteristics which at first sight might seem to indicate the capacity, symptomatic of selfhood, for incurring vicissitudes and at the same time overcoming the effects of these by what I have called "a central energy of organization." Solubility, spontaneous regeneration, reproduction by kinds, growth by proliferation are among the mysterious capacities, which have seemed to many to invest crystals with a semblance of life. This view is reinforced by the discovery of a radical structure, the unit cell, which provides the pattern upon which the crystal is built up by repetition. If it should turn out that the concept of a self is here applicable at all, the *principle* of selfhood in the crystal is to be looked for in the cell-body. The question is one which has to do with the composition of the latter.

The unit cell is an aggregation of atoms in which the molecular arrangement of the latter is modified (perhaps I should say, *complicated*) by a further principle of organization. To take the most obvious illustration, the sodium and chlorine atoms in rock salt are no longer simply paired. To quote Sir William Bragg, "each atom of the one kind . . . is similarly related to the six atoms of the other kind which are its immediate neighbours, and no one of the six can be considered as its special partner. If we adopt the common view of what happens when sodium and chlorine atoms are assembled together we must consider each sodium atom to be positively charged, having parted with one electron, and each chlorine atom to be negatively charged, having taken to itself an extra electron. The positive atom will naturally gather round itself negative atoms, and vice versa: the structure we have found is the result. Each positive has six negatives as nearest neighbours; each negative, six positives."[44]

The structure referred to as thus conditioned is in the form of a cubical cell with alternate atoms of sodium and chlorine;[45] and the arrangement of these atoms in the cell-body gives the unit of pattern for the relevant space-lattice. The latter thus acquires the character of an actual, physically existing, three-dimensional grid or trellis. And so of every other crystal. The necessary empirical verification was furnished for the first time by von Laue and his associates Friedrich and Knipping in their epoch-making experi-

[44] *An Introduction to Crystal Analysis*, p. 53.
[45] The general form of the lattice is shown in Note 38. The subjoined figure is a

ment of 1912. For our purposes it will be sufficient to note that in this experiment a crystal functions as a three-dimensional diffraction grating breaking up a pencil of X-rays, and so projecting on to a photographic plate a pattern which depicts the structure of the interior of the crystal.[46] The demonstration presupposes certain correspondences between the wave-motion of the X-rays and the interior texture of the crystalline substance. There must be regularity in both, and there must be a certain commensurateness in the order of magnitude between the fineness of the meshes in the atomic net and the wave-length of the X-rays. Given these conditions, of which the "Laue effect" is the result, we have in this experiment an ocular proof of the presumed atomic structure of the crystal. To quote Professor Rinne: "In this way the space-lattice idea of crystallography became the starting-point of an extraordinary development of physical science; for not only the

representation of the individual cell-body.

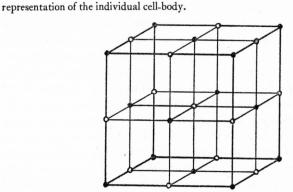

In order to render the concept intelligible I quote from the article by Dr. Peace already referred to. "The elementary cell has a chlorine atom at each cube corner and one at the centre of each face. Since each atom at a cube corner is also associated with seven other cubes, only 1/8 of its mass can be associated with the cube considered. But there are eight such atoms. Hence these altogether contribute the mass of one atom to the unit cell. Each atom in a cube face is associated with the adjacent cube and hence contributes only half its mass to the cube in question. The six such atoms altogether contribute the mass of three atoms to the cube. The total mass of chlorine to be associated with the unit cell is therefore equal to that of four chlorine atoms. Similarly it can be shown that four sodium atoms are to be associated with the cell. We may therefore say that the cell contains four molecules of sodium chloride." *Physical Chemistry*, ed. H. S. Taylor, Vol. I, pp. 158-9.

[46] *vid.* Tutton, *Nat. Hist.*, Chap. xii. Bragg gives a detailed explanation: *X-Rays and Crystal Structure*, 1915, and *Crystal Analysis*, 1928, Chap. i.

nature of X-rays as wave phenomena,[47] but also the actuality of the atom was experimentally proved, once and for all, by the Laue effect. The existence of atoms is as certain now as that of the macrocosm of the starry heavens. Laue's experiment may with justice be described as a solemn deposition of nature concerning its most intimate structure."[48]

31. Here then we have a conception of the crystal as an aggregation of atoms ordered in accordance with a unitary pattern endlessly reiterated. All the characteristic changes to which the structure is amenable, and which, at first sight, seem interpretable as its vicissitudes, are reducible either to an extension of the crystalline form by the addition of unit cell to unit cell, or else to the loss of that form through disorganization and a return to the amorphous condition. When the true nature of the process involved is understood, it is realized that in neither case can the event be rightly assigned to the crystal as a vicissitude—something that *happens to* the structure and, while appearing to threaten its destruction, is really becoming assimilated to its identity. For example, the disorganization of the space-lattice is not an *episode* in the "life" of the crystal. It is the break-up of the special aggregation to which the crystal owed its existence. In like manner the reverse process, so often described as "growth," is not to be interpreted upon any biological analogy as the enlargement, by internal differentiation, of a self-identical organism. On the contrary the identity of the structure, so far from being presupposed as the actual subject and implied condition of the process in question, must in the case of crystals be regarded as a derivative product of the activity of aggregation. In brief, the atoms do not organize themselves within the crystal: the crystal is the system which the atoms between them constitute when a certain alteration occurs in their spatial relations. Hence, as I have pointed out, it would be a mistake to represent growth or proliferation as an event in which the crystal is involved: it is an event in which atoms are involved when in accordance with the laws of electrical action more of them become organized in the form which we call crystalline.

[47] It was in order to prove this that the experiment was originally undertaken. The much more important result, the actual discovery of the arrangement of the atoms in the interior planes of the crystal, was an accidental by-product.

[48] *Crystals and the Fine Structure of Matter*, pp. 12-13. English tr. by Walter S. Stiles, 1924.

32. If this is a fair statement of the case, we seem as far as ever from the conditions of true selfhood. Beginning with the macroscopic properties of the crystal, which are mathematical relations, we have sought the secret of these properties in the spatial ordering of the atoms. It is from the standpoint of minute structure (leptology)[49] that the morphological identity of crystals must be studied; and this brings us sooner or later to the electronic events of the purely physical world. In this world, as we have seen, the prevalence of system is no guarantee of selfhood; and the uniformity, the repetitiousness, monotony and rigid adherence to type which everywhere characterize the scientifically authenticated processes of nature all point to the conclusion that we have here to do with reality in the aspect of external form or outward relatedness rather than in that of inner constitution and substantival self-identity. A consideration of crystals only serves to reinforce this view. It is true that they have a nature and identity of their own; but the identity of a crystal, when it is seen to be that of a diffraction grating, assuredly does not suggest the definitory properties of selfhood.

The Condition of Selfhood Is Consciousness; and Consciousness Is of Self

33. The situation now is that we have found ourselves unable to accord the character of a self (i) to the physical mode of being and to the systems into which the latter is organized, (ii) to the mind-conditioned modes, (iii) to "things," whether conceived as mind-conditioned or as endowed (like crystals) with a nature of their own. Living bodies constitute a class by themselves; and upon them we shall meanwhile have to suspend judgment. There remain subjective systems, which appear to fulfil all the conditions implied in the general concept. If so—if, that is to say, "selfhood" is conceived as the peculiar property of subjective systems—then, since experience is the veritable stuff of which such systems are composed, the property of selfhood must be realizable only in the medium of experience. And since, again, consciousness is of the essence of the latter, it follows that selfhood and consciousness must in some sense occur together. To be more explicit, every homogeneous system of being which includes conscious states must

---

[49] Professor Rinne substitutes this term for the more usual "stereochemistry" on the ground that the latter is not sufficiently comprehensive.

be a self, and every self must be a homogeneous system of which the characteristic content is consciousness. It is possible to go one step further still. Consciousness is not merely implied in selfhood; it is specifically the condition that enables a subjective system to survive its own vicissitudes and to reassert its identity by claiming the latter as contributory experiences.

34. Finally, the question arises whether the consciousness which is *a condition of selfhood* must not at the same time be *a consciousness of self*. It is of course customary to distinguish "self-consciousness" from mere awareness. The assumption is that the latter is possible without the former. If such is the case, if there is an awareness which is in no sense an experience of selfhood, we shall have to think of this awareness as completely absorbed in its object. But in this case, so far as I can see, the distinction between the consciousness of an object and the object of consciousness will fade away, as with Hume and his naturalistic successors, into the sheer manifoldness of the neutral mosaic. Thus the admission of a difference between *mere* consciousness and *self*-consciousness, if read in the light of its own implications, is fatal to the former, and is therefore self-refuting. The inference is that consciousness in all its manifestations must have about it in some degree the character of *self*-consciousness. This thesis is of fundamental importance, and calls for a detailed exposition.

APPENDIX A (See note 5, page 219)

The Realm of Nature

In one of its applications the word "natural" may be considered synonymous with "physical." This, however, is to restrict the usage unduly. When we speak of the natural world or of "nature," we usually mean more than the purely intelligible entities of physical science. Along with the latter we include the objects of perceptual experience, construed in that aspect which places them in antithetical relation to the subjective or spiritual. In other contexts the natural is opposed to the "unnatural"—a usage which presupposes a norm and the possibility of deviating from the latter. So understood the epithet "natural," as well as its negative "unnatural," may be applied to the subjective states themselves as well as to the artificial products of human endeavour. Much more significant from the standpoint of exact inquiry is the fact that apart altogether from this normative usage, and in spite of the antithesis of natural and spiritual, the spiritual is actually sometimes thought of as having a formal aspect or phenomenology of which the word "natural" is the only adequate designation. There is such a thing as the *natural history* of the spiritual. When we think of man's subjective life, not as it exists in itself or for him, but as a possible object of observation, it takes its place with its ontological opposites, the physical and the perceptual, as an ordered manifold, and as such it has a "nature" of its own. It will be noted, however, that the term applies to the physical as a mode of being, and to the spiritual as sustaining the relational character of objectivity.

Of these various usages the one which seems to me most available for philosophical purposes and most in keeping with ordinary linguistic practice is that which comprises the world of perceptual objects and the physical mode of being. I do not mean that the term should be thought of as applying indifferently to either of these. As I have said, by the "natural" or the "realm of nature" we usually mean more than the purely physical. We also mean more than the objects of sense as such— the so-called "sensa." And we certainly do not mean the mechanical addition of the two. The inference would seem to be that when we speak of the natural world we are thinking the physical and the sensory together. I take the term "natural" to connote an independently-existing, non-subjective order of reality conceived (under conditions yet to be examined) as furnishing a locus and a base to what we ordinarily regard as the sensory properties of things.

PHILOSOPHY AND THE INTERPRETATION OF ANIMAL LIFE

The attitude of different thinkers to the lower animals can sometimes be taken as roughly diagnostic of their philosophical outlook. To those for whom reason is the supreme principle not only of consciousness but of reality there is a great gulf fixed between humanity and the "brutes." Descartes and Spinoza are extreme instances, the former with his reduction of animal life to automatism, the latter with his frankly reasoned plea that no consideration should be given to the feelings of the sub-human species (*Eth.* IV, Prop. xxxvii, schol. 1). Fichte's view is also characteristic. An animal is primarily a body, and as such it is more specifically "a mobile system of plant-souls," differentiating itself from man in that its principle of motion is not free-will but natural determination. (*Sätze zur Erläuterung des Wesens der Thiere*, 1799 or 1800, Werke, XI, pp. 362 *sq.*) For Hegel also there is a great distance (although at the same time there is continuity) between the power to think, in the strict sense of the term, and all the modes of consciousness or representation that fall short of the Begriff. No less symptomatic (though in an opposite sense) is the affinity of human life to animal life in the teaching of Schopenhauer. Here the displacement of reason by the darkly moving power of impulse which Schopenhauer called "will" brings man and the animals together in a metaphysical sense. Something of the same sort is true of Oriental philosophy in those phases which fall short of extreme mysticism.

APPENDIX C (*See note* 19, *page* 230)

TIMELESS TRUTHS AND EXISTENCE

With regard to a certain class of mind-conditioned objects—those, viz., which I have described in the phrases "timeless truth," "matter of fact," "what is the case"—a special difficulty arises.

I have rejected the distinction of being and existence—*das Sein* and *das Dasein*. Except in the form of existence in time, being does not seem to me to occur at all. Obviously then it is impossible to attribute existence in any of its modalities to timeless truths as such. But if so, there would seem to be no place, in a classification *by modes*, for the entities to which I have referred.

On the other hand it will be remembered that we are here dealing not with different ways of existing, but with different types of *object*. We are trying to classify the latter in accordance with modal distinctions. Now while it must be granted that a timeless truth *which is not an object of consciousness* is devoid alike of existence and modality, the same cannot be said of *an object which happens to be a timeless truth*. Such an object is definable as the out-term in a relation to which a conscious process in some mind—i.e. an actual subjective event—furnishes the in-term; and it exists in time so long as the relation, "for consciousness," is sustained by the latter.

This solution to the problem, however, produces a fresh crop of difficulties. Apparently we are forced to conclude: (1) that the non-existent—here a timeless truth—can enter into occasional relationship with a time-conditioned existent in the form of a conscious state, (2) that this relationship, which is its objectivity, has somehow the power to transmute the intrinsically non-existent into an existent, and (3) as a corollary of these two propositions, that that which, from its very nature, for ever *is not* can *come to be* and *cease to be* with the fluctuating relations into which from time to time it enters. In brief, the argument amounts to this, that a relation between an existent and a non-existent can cause the non-existent to exist.

The source of all this confusion is imperfect analysis and the resulting identification (without the necessary qualifications) of one thing with another. To take a concrete instance, "that $2 + 2 = 4$" is an expression which may stand in two distinct types of context. These may be symbolized by the words: (1) "It is the case," and (2) "I judge, affirm, believe." The question for us is whether in this instance *what I believe or mentally affirm* is identical with *what is the case*.

That the two cannot be altogether identical would seem to follow from the fact that the former may vary with my varying mental attitude. I may or may not affirm it: I may affirm it today and deny it tomorrow. In this way the object comes and goes with my consciousness of it. What is the case is immune from all such changes. This at least is one aspect of the truth. "That $2 + 2 = 4$," defined as the content of my judgment, is one thing: "that $2 + 2 = 4$," defined as *what is the case* is another. It is however no less clear that what in this instance I affirm and what is the case do in some sense coincide. This is no less unmistakably an aspect of the truth. Our problem therefore has to do with the exact relation, involving, as it apparently does, both difference and identity, between the object of affirmation and the fact considered by itself. In what sense are these one, in what sense two?[1]

They are one in the sense that the expression "that $2 + 2 = 4$" *refers* to the same fact, whether it *denotes* what I am thinking or what is timelessly true. This property of "referring to the same fact" I shall call "identity of reference," and I would add that the latter property is attributable not only to the expression as such, but also to the object of my consciousness. That is to say, *what I affirm now* is identical in every particular with *what is true in any case*, except that the act of affirmation is necessary to the former and irrelevant to the latter.

The complementary aspect of the situation is that identity of reference is accompanied by diversity of denotation. In other words, the expression "that $2 + 2 = 4$" *denotes* in the one case the object of my judgment, and in the other the fact or timeless truth to which both the expression and the object refer. From this it follows that in the case of a timeless truth denotation and reference are the same thing, whereas in the case of an object of judgment they are not. The object has elements of identity over and above its reference. A timeless truth (we might say) has no definitory property except that of being the truth it is; whereas the object of judgment has both the property of being such an object and that of referring to a timeless truth.

Now the point I wish to make is this. When we think of a person A as being aware that such and such is the case or that so-and-so is true, it would not be correct to describe T, the truth in question, as *acquiring* the character of an object, O, through *entering into* the relation of objectivity with a subjective event in A's mind. T cannot *enter into* such a relation for the very good reason that T does not exist. In order to explain what has happened, therefore, we must begin at the other end

---

[1] When the case is that of a historical event an additional complication occurs. Analysis reveals three distinguishable factors: (1) the event itself, (2) the fact that the event occurred (a timeless truth), and (3) the object of my consciousness when I affirm the fact. Here (2) and (3), though distinguishable, are identical in the qualified sense explained in the text. In the same qualified sense each of them is identical with (1). Thus it is possible to say with significance and truth, but not without a certain qualification, that the event *is* my object.

with the entity O which constitutes the momentary object of A's awareness. But when we do so, we remember that O not only has the identity of A's object, but has also the property of referring to an eternal truth, T. That T is non-existent does not affect the possibility of a *reference* to it. Reference may actually be (and frequently is) to what is *not* the case, and therefore to what is eternally *untrue*. It is just as easy to *think* the latter, where non-existence goes without saying, as to think the former, where verity may be mistaken for existence.

The total situation therefore amounts to this. "That $2 + 2 = 4$" is something that may exist as an object of mind, but only in relation to the mind of which it is the object. When this is the case, the object has reference to something else—something which cannot be said to exist at all, but is nonetheless eternally true. To speak of the latter as itself the object of consciousness is quite legitimate, and may be looked upon as an abbreviated expression of the fact that an object of consciousness exists having as a definitory property (i.e. a mark of its identity) the reference to an eternal truth. In this way we overcome the difficulty of having to think of a non-existent as acquiring existence through a relation to consciousness.

With regard to the question of mind-dependence, what we must ask is whether anything could be *the case* if there were no such thing as being conscious of the fact—e.g. whether the expression "that $2 + 2 = 4$" could be characterized as an eternal truth if it could not also be characterized as an object of thought. The answer would seem to be that if there were no such thing as *being judged to be the case*, there could be no such thing as *being the case*. For to be the case or to be an eternal truth means to be the state of affairs *referred to* when the expression "that $2 + 2 = 4$" has the value of a true proposition. The concept of a true proposition is therefore presupposed in the concept of eternal truth. But a proposition is nothing at all if it is not an object of judgment.

The case of historical events is closely analogous to that of mathematical facts—although, as I have pointed out, there is here a special complication. The proposition "Caesar crossed the Rubicon" refers to an historical event, which is not an eternal truth, and is accordingly independent of anyone's consciousness of it. On the other hand, in the expression "*that* Caesar crossed the Rubicon" the reference is to an eternal truth, and the context of conditions is fundamentally different. Before it can *be the case that* an event *occurred* in past time, the event must be *thought* in a time which is not that of its occurrence. It is only through its aspect as an object of judgment that the time-conditioned can be despoiled of its particularity and can be made to assume the character of "what is the case."

CHAPTER VII

CONSCIOUSNESS AND SELF-CONSCIOUSNESS

Consciousness of an Object Is Necessarily Also an Experience of What It Means to Be a Subject

1. It is only when we come to the subjective mode of being and to the type of system into which consciousness enters as a component, that selfhood declares itself unmistakably. From its very nature such a system is necessarily defined by reference to states and processes which are internal to it. As for the relations in which it is involved, the most characteristic of these are at the same time *experiences*, and therefore the very stuff of which subjective systems are made. This is the principle and guarantee of that flexibility which enables a self to live through and to live down a degree and a variety of change that would be destructive to the identity of any other type of system. By internalizing these changes through the agency of consciousness, by converting relations into contents, or—to be more exact—by acquiring contents which also function as relations, a subjective system retrieves its losses and secures its gains in despite of all that time can do, and thereby maintains its identity intact in the maelstrom of events. What time takes from it in one phase of its subjectivity it recovers in another. Of this possibility the subtle interplay of consciousness and self-consciousness[1] is the underlying principle. It would hardly be too much to say that the identity of a subjective system is dependent upon this interplay, and that *self-consciousness* might therefore be represented as the principle of *self-identity*.[2]

[1] This phrase must be read in the light of the theory which I am about to develop. For the moment it is bound to suggest confusion. If, as I have indicated, all consciousness *is* self-consciousness, what is the sense of referring to an *interplay* between the two?

[2] From what was said in the last chapter it is obvious that this statement applies primarily to *persons*. The case of the lower animals, which presents difficulties in every context, will have to be considered once more in the proper place. Meanwhile it is worth noting that the identity of persons has always been felt to call for a highly specialized form of recognition. Of this the institution of proper names is evidence. In the first instance these were not attached, as labels are attached, extrinsically to their objects. They were no mere badges of *identification*, but were themselves pregnant with the *actual identity* which they served to symbolize. Hence the very word for "name" became a synonym for "self." cf. the usage in New Testament Greek, e.g., Acts xv. 14,

2. I have dwelt upon the fundamental character of the relation between selfhood and consciousness. This relation is two-sided. Consciousness, which is at once the condition and the diagnostic sign of subjectivity, is necessary to the existence of a self:[3] selfhood is no less necessary to the existence of conscious states. Every instance of the latter, every manifestation of what we mean by "being conscious," presupposes a subjective system within which, by virtue of the functional relation, the possibility arises. But there is more than this implied. Not only does every instance of consciousness *presuppose* a self: every instance *reveals* a self as well. In brief, there is no consciousness which is not in some sense a consciousness of selfhood. Our immediate task is the exposition and defence of this proposition.*

3. Throughout the history of philosophy in the western world there has been a general tendency to assume that by experience we must understand a consciousness of objects.[4] Objects and our awareness of them have been conceived as correlative to one another. Now it is assuredly the case that a consciousness of objects is among the characteristic forms or aspects of experience: *some* of our experience assumes this aspect. What has not been sufficiently realized is the fact that a consciousness of objects, like every other form of consciousness, is necessarily an *experience* of what it means to be the subjective system within which such a consciousness occurs.

where God is represented as visiting the Gentiles "to take out of them a people for his name"—τῷ ὀνόματι αὐτοῦ—i.e. for Himself.

[For further observations upon the nature of animals, see sections 28-30, pp. 283-6, below.—Ed.]

[3] Hence the prevalence of verbal expressions (not to be taken too literally) which imply a loss of selfhood or identity during unconsciousness, and represent the return to the conscious state as a *coming to oneself*—i.e. a reversion to the condition of self-identity. cf. Acts xii. 11, καὶ ὁ Πέτρος ἐν ἑαυτῷ γενόμενος, "and when Peter was come to himself." The "when he came to himself" (εἰς ἑαυτὸν . . . ἐλθών) of Luke xv. 17 refers to the recovery of a higher as against a lower type of self-consciousness.

[*On the showing of the next two sections, consciousness of object cannot possibly *not* be also consciousness of self. The argument is subtle but this is the burden of it.— Ed.]

[4] This is at the bottom of the whole empirical movement, and is closely connected with the false antithesis of rationalism and empiricism. Rationalism interprets the relation of the conscious subject to his "ideas" as that of a thinking subject to its modifications or modes. Locke represents these ideas as objects of observation exposed to the consciousness of the subject. From the latter point of view experience is just the activity, as knowledge is the fruit, of such observation. I have already drawn attention to Kant's definition of experience as "a knowledge of objects."

The starting-point in my argument is a reaffirmation of the ontological priority of the system to its own subjective constituents. These constituents are of course experiences, whether conscious or otherwise, in functional relation to one another. From this it may be concluded that wherever conscious states exist the reality that comes to light is the selfhood of a subjective system.

4. Now my contention is that in so far as the experience, to which the existence of a self furnishes a necessary precondition, is *a state of consciousness*, the latter must necessarily be *a conscious experience of the self*. This can best be brought out by considering the alternative hypothesis. Suppose C is a conscious state within the system S, but that it is not *a consciousness of S*. Of what then is it the consciousness? Presumably of its object O, or else—should the affective or conative element predominate—of an emotion or a mental activity. For purposes of this discussion the two last may be taken together and represented by any typical instance of either—say, then, by "Feeling." The total situation is therefore this. C, a state of consciousness in the subjective system S, is not the consciousness of S, but of an object O, or of a feeling F.

To take the second possibility first, it is obvious that any feeling and the consciousness of it are one and indistinguishable. Since, therefore, F is identical with C, there is no point in describing C as the consciousness *of F*. The idea of a prepositional relationship does not occur. All that can be said about C is that it is a quite specific state of awareness, and that it is the revelation of nothing but itself. But if so, it obviously cannot reveal the identity of the subjective system to which it belongs, or indeed the fact that it belongs to any such system. In the language of subjectivity, F is not *experienced* as *my* feeling, *your* feeling, *his* or *her* feeling. It is just *feeling*—feeling pure and simple. The question instantly arises whether in this case it can be thought of as *experienced* at all. The answer is that an experience so completely restricted to itself, could not possibly be *felt*, and that it therefore could not be a *conscious* experience. This, however, is opposed to the hypothesis.

The only way out of the *impasse* is to assume that a consciousness of the system to which it belongs is given with every emotion and with every conative condition. The identity of every such subjective event defines itself for consciousness within the comprehensive identity of a subject-self.

The remaining possibility is that in which to the question: "Of what is C the consciousness?" we answer: "Of its object O and of nothing else." As I have just remarked, between a feeling and the consciousness of it there is no difference whatever. The consciousness of an object, on the contrary, differs from an object of consciousness as the terms in a relation differ from one another. The factors in the situation are therefore in this instance (1) a subjective system S, (2) a state of consciousness C within the latter, (3) an object O, and (4) a unique relationship of objectivity between O and C. The question I wish to put is whether it is possible that C should be a consciousness of O without at the same time being a consciousness of S.

To this I should reply as follows. The fact that C has an object neither adds to nor detracts from its modal character as a conscious state. Every such state, metaphysically speaking, is a subjective event, and has its locus in a system of similar events. In this respect, however, it does not differ from an unconscious state of mind. Its identity as a specific state *of consciousness* is expressible by reference not to its ontological status or to its position in the system S, but solely to its object. That is to say, the *differentia* of C in the class of subjective events which constitute the system S is its character as a revelation of O.

Let us see what this implies. To be an object, as we know, is to be the out-term in a relationship of which the in-term is a state of consciousness. So far as the identity of the out-term is concerned, this relationship to consciousness is constitutive. In other words, since anything whatever *becomes* an object because of the relation in which it stands to awareness, an object actually *is* what it is *revealed to be*. Revelation is of the essence of its nature. But we have seen that upon the present hypothesis the defining characteristic of consciousness as such is no other than the revelation of its object—that is to say, the relation to an out-term, to which the in-term owes its identity. From this it follows that the in-term disappears into, and becomes one with its own definitory relation to the out-term. But if so, the relation itself disappears with one of the two terms required for its support. Hence the *revelation* upon which the object depends for its identity can no longer be interpreted as a *relation between* the latter and consciousness. Consciousness and the relation alike have been absorbed into the *revelation of the object*, which must now be construed as identical with the object itself. Thus of the various factors in the case only the subjective system and the object remain, but under the circumstances the latter can no longer sustain its character as object. It is a neutral content in a manifold from which the distinction of subjective and objective has been thought away.

This conclusion, which involves all the difficulties of the neutral mosaic, is the direct result of assuming that it is possible to be conscious of an object and of nothing more. The inference is that no such consciousness is possible. But if so, it becomes evident that along with the consciousness of every object there must go a certain awareness of the subjective system to which the conscious state in question belongs. Thus an experience which is on the face of it the awareness of an object is, less obviously, but to the analytic reason no less veritably, a conscious experience of what it means to be a subject. In the very act whereby experience reveals the out-term in the subject-object relation, it itself stands revealed as a reality of the subjective order. All consciousness is self-consciousness.[5]

Primary and Secondary Self-Consciousness

5. It remains only to ask: What form does this self-consciousness assume in the actual experience of the subject? What does it mean to be aware of the *self* as well as of the feelings and the objects that come and go with the perpetually changing circumstances of life? The answer is that the conscious subject is aware of a sustained— or, under certain conditions, a *recurrent*—identity of being, which underlies the successive phases of his experience. However varied and disjointed, however bewildering and incoherent, however intermittent and inconsecutive, that experience may be, it differentiates itself within a unity of organized feelings which remains one

---

[5] Among the thinkers who have had some inkling of this truth is Locke. "Every act of sensation, when duly considered, gives us an equal view of both parts of nature, the corporeal and spiritual. For whilst I know, by seeing and hearing, &c., that there is some corporeal being without me, the object of that sensation; I do more certainly know, that there is some spiritual being within me, that sees and hears." *Essay*, Book II, Chap. XXIII, §15. cf. Book IV, Chap. IX, §3. On this point *vid*. Green's Introduction to Hume's *Treatise*, Vol. I, p. 122. Fichte avails himself of the same truth in his introduction of the ego. "Think . . . any object, e.g., the wall in front of you, your writing desk. In so doing you assuredly assume a thinking being, who is yourself. You become immediately conscious of thinking in this thinking of yours." *Das System der Sittenlehre*, I, §1, p. 18, Werke, Berlin, 1845. cf. *Die Anweisung zum seligen Leben*, Lecture III. (English tr. *The Way Towards the Blessed Life*, pp. 41-2.)

with itself through all its vicissitudes, and passes unbroken across the gulf of sleep, the vacant interspaces of forgetfulness and the blank of pathological oblivion. There is no normal experience that is not charged with this brooding sense of self-identity. It follows us to the brink of the unconscious, and meets us at the threshold of returning sentience. It is not something which we discover *in ourselves* by a centripetal movement of the mind, but something that *discovers itself to us* in the very process by which, regardless of our subjectivity and inattentive to its symptoms, we issue from the inner citadel of our selfhood to meet the challenge of an outer world. It is in the sally of the spirit into the realm of the natural that the consciousness of the objective first reveals its inner secret as a consciousness of self.

From these observations it should be evident that what is intended is not self-consciousness in the reflective or introspective sense, but something prior to this and more fundamental,[6] something which introspective self-consciousness presupposes as a condition. Before we can be self-conscious in the later sense we must be self-conscious in the earlier. It would seem then that there are different types of self-consciousness. The failure to observe the various distinctions involved has been responsible for untold error and confusion in the history of philosophy and psychology.[7] We must therefore try to get these distinctions as exact as possible.

6. The modes of self-consciousness or ways of being self-conscious are two in number. (a) There is the mode which has been considered at length, and which may be characterized as primary. It is primary in the sense that, as has been explained, it is implied in the fact of consciousness as such. Another way of expressing the same truth would be to say that it is impossible to be conscious at all and not at the same time to experience the self as subject. It is in this sense that the principle, "all consciousness is self-conscious-

---

[6] Not necessarily more important.

[7] Those who have recognized the truth of the principle that consciousness implies an awareness of self have frequently falsified their own insight by overlooking the difference which I am stressing, and identifying self-consciousness in general with the introspective variety. The following are the words of an expert. "Consciousness will be the capacity of the subject to be aware of his thoughts as thoughts; the conscious person will be one who is not merely engaged in a mental reaction but is aware of that reaction as of something taking place within himself. . . . Conscious mental processes will be such as are actively introspected or are dependent for their nature on that kind of examination. . . ." Dr. J. T. MacCurdy, *Common Principles in Psychology and Physiology*, Cambridge, 1928, p. 49.

ness," is to be understood. (b) There is the mode which is usually described as reflective or introspective, and which, in contradistinction to the former, may be designated secondary. It is so in the sense that it presupposes the primary mode.

The distinction may be brought out as follows. In the introspective mode the self as subject confronts the self as object. The composite expression "self-consciousness" may therefore in this case be expanded into "the subject's consciousness of self, where the element of selfhood is governed by the element of consciousness as a noun is governed by a preposition or as an accusative is governed by an active verb." No such articulation divides the continuity of primary self-consciousness, which is subjective through and through.[8] Articulation there certainly is; but the mode of it is expressible as "subject-subject" and not as "subject-object."[9]

7. This statement of the distinction between what I have called "the modes of self-consciousness" is however much too simple and abstract. In actual experience the modes shade off in all sorts of subtle ways into one another. Primary and secondary self-consciousness may be present in infinitely varying degrees. For example, our attention may be completely or almost completely absorbed in the contemplation of an object or event in the outer world. In this case secondary self-consciousness will be altogether or almost altogether in abeyance, while primary will be present with a degree of intensity measurable by the degree of our concentration on the object. That is to say, our consciousness of what it means to be a subject, engrossed in this particular activity of observation, will be vivid and acute in proportion to the intent-

---

[8] For the linguistic expression of this truth in French *vid.* Appendix to this chapter, p. 287.

[9] So expressed, the view I am advocating is free from the objections usually brought against the doctrine that consciousness and self-consciousness are one. This would apply, for example, to Professor Ward's remarks in *Psychological Principles*, pp. 371 *sq.* Ward limits self-consciousness to the secondary form. Taking $S \, p \, O$ to represent the subject's consciousness of an object ("external perception"), and using the letters I and M for the I and the Me respectively, he symbolizes "internal perception or reflection" by the formula $Ip \begin{cases} M \\ p \\ O \end{cases}$ (the I perceives the Me in the act of perceiving an external object). This has no application to primary self-consciousness, of which the formula would be: $Ip \begin{cases} I \\ p \\ O \end{cases}$ (the I perceives itself *as subject* in the act of perceiving any object).

ness of our preoccupation. At any moment, however, our absorption in the object may be diminished, and a certain amount of our mental energy may be diverted in the direction of our own mental processes. If so, secondary self-consciousness will bulk appreciably in the total experience, but without necessarily detracting from primary. The change will be that involved in the transfer of attention from one object to another.

A further possibility is that of a profound preoccupation with our own inner state for the time being. This implies a great increase in the intensity of our secondary self-consciousness. But again the primary may remain unaltered. In brief, the subjective revelation of the self to itself is generally speaking independent of variations in the object of attention. Primary self-consciousness fluctuates with the intensity of our awareness irrespective of the direction of our attention and of its distribution among the possible objects of experience. Indeed there is no need to assume the presence of objects at all. The emotions, for example, may be exceedingly acute even in the absence of a definitely assignable object.[10] In this realm of experience intensity and indeterminateness frequently go together. The vague malaise of unadjusted youth acquires an added poignancy through the sheer inability to fasten it upon anything specific. Here primary self-consciousness is at a maximum: secondary may be present in any degree whatever.

How Self-Consciousness Constitutes Selfhood—Not by Having Its Past and Future States Presented to It, But by Its Power of Really Being in Them. Introspection Involves This

8. Above all, the relations involved can be rendered clear and exact only when the whole subject has been reviewed in the light of the time-factor. Time is of the essence of selfhood.* The concept of a self as a system determined by its inner constitution must be interpreted with special reference to the sequence of its predicaments. In particular the fact of sequence itself and the differences

[10] Though of course it must be recognized that acute emotion, like "bodily" pain, especially if prolonged, is apt to turn the self into an object of introspective regard. Hence the morbid interest in themselves which we frequently find in confirmed invalids.

[*It will be observed, in connection with the general subject of time, that the author is hardly interested in the question whether time is "unreal." Assuming it as real, he is interested simply in disclosing its nature.—Ed.]

which every sequence implies must be subordinated to the idea of sameness or identity which we have seen to be embedded in the original meaning of the word. A self, as I have insisted, is a system which appropriates *to itself* its own successive vicissitudes, and so internalizes them that while they serve to diversify its contents, they are powerless to dissolve its unity. Hence it is necessary to think of the past and future states or experiences of the conscious subject as the internal differentiations of a spiritual system which includes all its pasts and futures in a way that is not adequately represented by saying that it remembers the former and anticipates the latter. In the analysis of selfhood everything depends upon the interpretation of this statement. The question must therefore be considered—if necessary, at considerable length.

9. A convenient starting-point is furnished by the controversy over introspection. There has been a general failure to appreciate the exact points at issue, and the discredit into which the introspective method in psychology has fallen is the natural outcome of this failure. A brief consideration of the subject from this point of view will prepare the way for the restatement which is my eventual object. The ground is so familiar that I shall hasten over it as quickly as possible.

As is well known, the very possibility of introspection has been disputed for reasons which have been clearly set forth by Auguste Comte.[11] We cannot, so the contention runs, introspect ourselves, because in this case the subject and the object of observation are one, and in order to achieve our end we should have to perform the impossible operation of dividing ourselves in two. In other words, the very act of introspection displaces the mental state which is its object. So long as that state persists, therefore, it is incompatible with the attempt to observe it; and the moment the work of observation begins, the state of mind to which it is directed ceases to exist.

---

[11] *Cours de Philosophie Positive*, I, 34-8. For convenience I have made use of William James' restatement and discussion, *Principles of Psychology*, Vol. I, pp. 188 *sq*. Comte's objections apply particularly to the strictly intellectual processes. He admits the possibility of observing the "passions," on the thoroughly confused ground that "the anatomical organs of passion are distinct from those whose function is observation." (As if the difficulty were that while the brain could hardly be expected to observe the brain, it might have no difficulty in noticing the viscera!) But he denies that such observations as we can make in this region can have much scientific value, and in any case they are restricted to the weaker manifestations of passion.

To this it has been replied, for example by J. S. Mill,[12] that Comte has overlooked the fact of memory. Introspection is possible because we possess the power to observe our mental states the moment after they have occurred—a fact which has been generalized in the principle that all introspection is retrospection.

10. This is really the point upon which everything turns. Memory is one of the most question-provoking (and question-begging) of our spiritual endowments. To begin with, there is the length of time involved. Clearly what the advocates of introspection have in mind is our ability to recall the mental states which have just elapsed. Introspection as they understand it consists in laying hold upon the flying skirts of our subjective processes at the moment when they are passing from the immediacy of present experience. It is maintained not only that this is possible, but that retrospection, so understood, has distinct advantages over the witness of contemporaneous self-consciousness. "Thus," to quote Professor Stout, "introspection, when it is directly concerned with a mental operation that is in itself more or less absorbing, can proceed only by taking a series of transient side-glimpses," whereas "by calling up a process in memory immediately after it is over we are often able to notice much that escaped us when it was actually going on."[13] This may perhaps be granted; but if the value of the method is increased when the "transient side-glimpses" are supplemented by momentary *backward* glances, the question arises whether the advantage would not be still further enhanced by extending the retrospective survey over appreciable stretches of time. The suggestion contains the germs of a difficult problem. If introspection is to be interpreted as meaning retrospection, how far can retrospection be *re*interpreted in terms of genuinely *introspective* observation?

The principle involved would seem to be this. If the mental processes which we are investigating are separated by a considerable interval from the act of observing them, the latter act would normally be considered a case of memory pure and simple—retrospection and no more: if they are continuous with the act of observation, the element of memory is interpretable as introspection. But in either case the purpose is to obtain a view of some mental state or operation, which thereby becomes isolated (very much as

[12] *Auguste Comte and Positivism*, 3rd ed., 1882, p. 64.
[13] *A Manual of Psychology*, 4th ed., revised by C. A. Mace, p. 43.

chemical element becomes isolated) by the very act of mind that
turns it into a distinguishable object of attention.

Introspection then, as a method of psychological investigation,
has been made to rest in actual practice upon the supposed possibility of isolating our mental states for purposes of observation.
Now it is obvious that a mental state thus isolated does not constitute a *self*, and that a succession of observations brought to bear
upon a series of such states cannot strictly be described as a form
of *self*-consciousness. The self is a subjective system, and stands
subjectively revealed as such. The states we contemplate under
the conditions described are *objects* of observation to which we
direct our attention successively, dwelling for a moment upon each
and passing on the moment after to the next. Hume was so far
right when he declared in a passage which has become classical,[14]
that he could never "catch" *himself* without a perception, and
could never *observe* anything but the perception.[15] The truth is that
the introspective method as ordinarily understood has no light to
throw upon the subject-self as such—the self, that is to say, in its
aspect of sustained and permanent subjectivity. Its specific function is rather to break up that self into a manifold of "states," and
to bring the subjective into the special relation required to invest
it with the character of objectivity. Hence the modern intro-
spectionist, whose method Hume anticipates, is justified in char-
acterizing his investigation in the phrase: "psychology without a
soul."

11. By secondary *self*-consciousness, in so far as this implies a
genuine awareness of the self, I mean something more than introspection as understood by Hume and by certain psychologists of
later date. Let me try, by the aid of an illustration, to explain
wherein my conception differs from theirs.

I am (let it be supposed) contemplating a certain object of the
outer world—for example, a botanical specimen which I am trying
to identify. My mental state is one of complete preoccupation with
the object in question. No part of my attention is directed to the
subjective processes of observation and thought which are going
on within me. Secondary self-consciousness is in abeyance. On the

---

[14] *Treatise*, Part IV, sect. vi, Green and Grose, Vol. I, p. 534.
[15] The first of these propositions would have been more accurately expressed if Hume
had said that he could never catch himself *except in the form of* a perception. As it is, the
second proposition furnishes the necessary commentary on the first.

other hand primary self-consciousness is at a maximum. That is to say, I am having a very intense experience of what it means to be a conscious subject completely absorbed in an object of scientific curiosity. So thorough is my preoccupation, that I fail to notice the arrival of a second person on the scene, until the sound of his voice breaks in upon my preoccupation with the familiar question "What are you doing?" Instantly my attention is diverted from what a moment before had been an object of exclusive interest, to the subjective processes by which that interest had been sustained. I am now conscious not only of the botanical specimen, but of *myself* as actively interested in the latter. In this way a state of secondary self-consciousness is superimposed upon a state of primary. Such is the contingency which we are called upon to analyze.

12. To begin with the earlier of my two states, the factors involved are (1) an object of interest, and (2) an act of observation brought to bear upon the former. The subsequent state differs from this in that the activity of observing the object has now itself entered into the relation of objectivity: it has itself become an object of interest. It would not, however, be correct to describe the change that has taken place merely as the transition from one object to another. Along with this we must recognize a number of transformations or displacements which are fundamentally different in character from that which we experience, say, in passing from picture to picture in a gallery or in turning over the pages of an illustrated journal. For in the case before us the second object is really the activity of observing the first, and therefore a consciousness of the first object must be included in our consciousness of the second.[16] Moreover the second object, unlike the first, *exists* subjectively and not physically. Hence the relation of objectivity into which it has entered, and in virtue of which we designate it an *object*, is much less characteristic of it than of the other. As has been pointed out, it is not normally as objects of observation that our subjective states report themselves to us. These considerations must be borne in mind in the further interpretation of secondary self-consciousness in relation to primary. In this, one step of great importance remains to be taken.

[16] cf. Stout, *op. cit.*, pp. 3 *sq.*, and Ward's formula of self-consciousness, with my variation upon the latter, note 9 to this chapter.

Our illustration has revealed two objects, and two acts or states, of consciousness. These may be designated O^1, O^2; S^1 and S^2 respectively. Thus O^1 is a botanical specimen, S^1 the subjective activity of contemplating it: O^2 is what S^1 becomes when it in turn is made an object of contemplative interest. Finally S^2 is definable as "the act of contemplating S^1." Now the point that has just been emphasized is that S^1 does not cease to be, what it intrinsically is, a subjective state or activity of consciousness when, as a result of a relation which it has contracted, it assumes the character of O^2. Not only so, but the identity of O^2 with S^1 is what gives the former its identity as an object of the conscious state S^2. In other words, S^2 is the contemplative awareness of S^1, the latter being considered as an actually existing state of consciousness having O^1 as its object.

Now the pivot upon which everything turns is the relation between S^2 and O^2. If the latter were merely an object of contemplation, there would be nothing to distinguish the present instance from any other. But when the object, considered in itself, is a subjective state, and is contemplated as such, the fact of its objectivity (which is a relation or a character indicative of a relation) naturally subordinates itself to the fact of its subjectivity (which is its ontological status). Other types of object are known only in this relation: the subjective mode of being can be known thus only after it has become known in another way peculiar to itself.

13. Since then the objective contemplation of our mental states implies an understanding that these states exist subjectively, it follows that they do not define themselves individually and successively by reference to the individual and successive acts of mind whereby we turn them into objects of observation. That is to say, they are not to be identified merely as O^2, O^3 and O^4, the objects of three distinct acts of introspection. The circumstance that they are thus introspected is of too superficial an import to be employed as a principle of identification. Where the identity of mental states is concerned, the decisive consideration is not that S^1 takes on the character of O^2, but that O^2 is recognized as S^1. This means that it defines itself not by reference to S^2, the act of introspection, but within the unity of a certain subjective system, of which S^1 and S^2 alike are members. So understood, the introspective consciousness of S^1 is seen to involve something far more comprehensive than the direct knowledge of O^2. This something is

the knowledge of a whole system of being which is differentiated as S^1, S^2, S^3 . . . S^n. It is only when we recognize the fact that a consciousness of the individual contents implies a consciousness of the system to which they belong that the objective observation of our mental states as they occur may be classed as a form of *self*-consciousness—the form to which I have given the designation "secondary."

Introspection, however, a Very Imperfect Illustration of the Self-Consciousness Which Constitutes Selfhood. Synoptic Secondary Self-Consciousness

14. Our analysis is, however, far from complete. The foregoing statement has been concerned chiefly with introspection in the narrowest sense of the term. Now while we have seen reason to reject the familiar atomistic interpretation of this process, and to insist that even in its most restricted application introspection is a revelation of the *self*, there is something to be said for those whose view we have refused to accept. Introspection in this sense is an attempt to observe the self specifically from the standpoint of its individuated contents. To be still more exact, it is an attempt to obtain a distinct view of these contents in all their particularity and apart from any question as to their ontological standing. Isolation is therefore incidental to the method by which, in Hume's phrase, we "catch ourselves." The contents assume the aspect of atomic individuals, not because they exist in this form, but because we take them one by one. But this is a highly artificial procedure; and while it may be necessary for certain limited purposes, it does violence to an aspect of the conscious self much more fundamental than that to which it calls attention.

As we have seen, time is of the essence of subjectivity. Now this is not merely a statement as to the way in which our mental states are divided from one another. Successiveness is not the sole, or even the most characteristic, property of the time in which they have their being. Not only is there a time *between* them, there is a time *which they occupy*, a time of their duration; and these times are so completely continuous that it is only by an artificial act of abstraction that they can be thought of as distinct. And so of their subjective contents. In brief, our mental states are themselves extensive processes, or more exactly, distinguishable phases[17] in a single process, and the fact of vicissitude is not extraneous to them, but is of their innermost texture. It is obvious, therefore, that an introspective examination, working towards the limit of a mental atomism, must be supplemented by another mode of secondary self-consciousness working in the opposite direction. Here the ideal will be not that of isolating the units of consciousness—that is to say, the simplest and briefest mental states which permit of being *observed* as one—but that of extending the context of experience until the outermost limits of what may be interpreted as one are reached. The operation is the opposite of that described by Professor Stout as "taking a series of transient side-glimpses." What we try to obtain is not a succession of cinematographic presentations, but a conspectus. Our object is to see the individuated experiences unfolding themselves as the articulations of an experience which retains its unity and self-identity throughout. In this the range of our observations may vary indefinitely. We may review the experience of an hour or of the past week. We may sweep our own past history to the furthest horizon of memory. We may in some sense pass our lives in review. In each case it is the self we are observing, and the operation comes within the scope of secondary self-consciousness. As we contemplate the complex structure in its successive phases, we realize that it is one and the same being which meets us in each, and that that being is subjective in nature. Thus the experiences are all "mine," and the substantive entity to which the possessive adjective points is designated "I" and "me."

How Is Synoptic Self-Consciousness Possible? A Sceptical View

15. It would seem then that secondary self-consciousness takes two directions according as consciousness is turned upon a momentary state of the conscious subject or upon a synoptic view of the temporally extensive self. For the former type, in accordance with the tradition, the name "introspection" may be reserved: the name "reflection" will serve to designate the latter. The postulate of subject-selfhood is presupposed in both; but within the limits of this assumption the content to be examined presents itself in

[17] Objectively distinguishable, that is. Subjectively they are *distinct*, but not in any atomistic sense. We experience differences within a continuum. This is an instance in which Hegel's insistence on the relativity of the continuous and the discrete is particularly apposite.

the one case as a momentary experience, in the other as a more or less extended phase of life.

Secondary self-consciousness in the synoptic sense is subject to a difficulty from which at first sight introspection appears to be free. As a matter of fact, the difficulty affects both types alike,* and a clearing up of the whole situation is essential to an understanding of self-consciousness in general.

Superficially expressed, the difficulty to which I refer is one that has to do with memory. In the attempt to obtain a synoptic view of the self as a continuum of successive experiences we are compelled (so it would seem) at every point to have recourse to recollection in some form. The *self* which constitutes the object of secondary self-*consciousness* is almost altogether (perhaps quite so) a *remembered* self. But our memories are notoriously defective, and at the best they can give us a somewhat imperfect rendering of our past history. Thus the very power which was evoked to render the introspective type of secondary self-consciousness effectual is now seen to render the reflective type precarious. From this point of view, to all appearance the difference is merely one of time and of the disabilities which time brings with it. The retrospection which accompanies introspective self-examination extends only to the immediate past, where owing to the proximity of its object memory can hardly be at fault. Reflective self-consciousness, on the other hand, implies a memory of events which may extend over years, and may be divided from one another by long periods of oblivion. Hence the possibilities of error are indefinite.

16. Such an explanation does not go to the root of the matter. For one thing, there is no exact and authentic correlation between the reliability of our memories and the length of time they cover. Our recollection of passages in early youth, as old people frequently testify, may be very exact and detailed, whereas, for want of con-

[*"The difficulty affects both types alike." The "difficulty" is that thought and memory, dealing always with *idea*, cannot mediate to us knowledge of the time-conditioned subjective. They cannot find the ego. So far, the author is with Santayana when he, so to speak, out-Descartes Descartes. What needs to be reconsidered, however, is whether, in dealing with my past self, I am dealing always with something that is out of my present subjectivity and therefore only to be presented as a recollection—an *idea*, remembered or thought. Do my present and my past really stand outside each other like this? Is it possible that a subject-self confined to a durationless present, contemplating an object-self back in the past (or forward in the future), should be what this "self-consciousness", which I have, literally is? Such self-consciousness is a fact, and so it must be possible.—Ed.]

text and perspective, as well as for more deeply seated reasons, we may be thoroughly confused as to what has taken place in the recent past or even a moment ago. Indeed there are states of the self of which we may become fully conscious only after they are past; and (paradoxical as the statement may seem) the act of realizing them fully for the first time may be the act of recovering them in memory.[18] In other words, we may vividly remember experiences of which we were hardly conscious at the time.[19] But the really basic (the philosophical) problem has nothing to do with the supposed variability of our memories under different conditions. It is not a question whether in any particular instance we have reason to trust or to distrust our power of recollection, but whether anything whatever that comes to us in this form can establish its claim to our belief upon indisputable grounds. In brief, the problem is one which has to do with the *validity* of our memories in general. Here subjective certitude is obviously no criterion. There are incidents in what we assume to be our private past which stand out in our present consciousness with the utmost clarity of detail and with a strangely moving familiarity of atmosphere. We say we have a vivid recollection of them, or that it all comes back to us as if it were yesterday. What we usually fail to realize is the need of asking how it is possible to know that in a past, to which we have no access but our recollection of it, the experiences which it portrays were ever really ours. What we remember is present to us only in *idea*. How then can our memories guarantee the authenticity of their supposed originals?

The difficulty has been strikingly exhibited by Professor Santayana in his discussion of the philosophical scepticism of Des-

---

[18] Referring to his first visit to Oxford Sir Walter Scott writes: "My memory only at present furnishes a grand but indistinct picture of towers, and chapels, and oriels, and vaulted halls, and libraries, and paintings. I hope, in a little time, my ideas will develope themselves a little more distinctly, otherwise I shall have profited little by my tour." Letter to Miss Seward, quoted Lockhart, Vol. I, pp. 328-9, Macmillan, 1900.

[19] This looks like saying that secondary self-consciousness may in certain circumstances take precedence over primary. Such an admission would prove fatal to the distinction as I have represented it. As a matter of fact all that is implied is that primary self-consciousness may fall short of secondary both in vividness and in clarity; and this is quite in keeping with what I have said as to the variable character of the relation between the two. It is of the utmost importance that this possibility should be recognized. The ethical and religious experience of self-realization or "coming to oneself" depends upon the power of appreciating intensely in the secondary phase what was imperfectly appreciated in the primary phase of self-consciousness.

cartes.[20] The point is this. In doubting everything but his own existence Descartes does not go far enough. ". . . I have sought to carry [the Cartesian method] further," says Professor Santayana, "suspending all conventional categories as well as all conventional beliefs; so that not only the material world but all facts and all existences have lost their status, and become simply the themes or topics which intrinsically they are."[21] The fact is that existence, with its implications of past and future, is the "theme" which least of all permits of being treated as an immediately given. "Existence, then, not being included in any immediate datum, is a fact always open to doubt."[22] Not only therefore can we question our own existence, but, if we understand the method which has led us step by step to this final issue, we are bound to do so. To state the matter briefly, the ego whose existence we venture to question with such apparently conclusive results is necessarily an ego that reveals itself to us, as our memories and expectations reveal themselves, in the form of *something thought*. That is implied in the very fact that we find ourselves asking questions about it; for to ask questions is *ipso facto* to invest the object of them with the character of ideality. In so far then as the ego is permitted, even for one brief moment, to enter the region of Cartesian doubt, from the very nature of the case it is predestined to remain for ever an object of irresolvable uncertainty.[23]

17. The argument is not likely to pass unchallenged. It may be said, for example, that in this one instance—that of the ego—as Descartes assumed, the general principle connecting questionability and ideality does not apply. I may quite intelligibly ask whether I exist; but in the very act I immediately recover my foothold in the actual. Indeed the actuality of the questioner can never really be in doubt, since it furnishes the presupposition of the question.

[20] *Scepticism and Animal Faith.* Chaps. II to VI, and Chap. XXVII.

[21] *op. cit.*, p. 292.

[22] *op. cit.*, pp. 39-40.

[23] That Santayana finds a way out in the compulsions of animal faith is a fact that has no bearing upon our problem. His retreat from scepticism is a reaffirmation of the latter. "When it comes to assertion (which is belief) I follow Descartes in choosing discourse and (as an implication of discourse) my substantial existence as the objects of faith least open to reasonable doubt; not because they are the first objects asserted, nor because intrinsically they lend themselves to existence better than anything else, but simply because in taking note of anything whatever I find that I am assuming the validity of primary memory. . . ." *op. cit.*, pp. 292-3.

Such an attempt to rehabilitate the Cartesian contention (so in turn it may be argued) carries weight only in so far as the ego is conceived without regard to the temporal conditions of existence. As soon as these are taken into account Santayana's difficulty reasserts itself. The questionable ego must obviously be at the very least an ego of the past, and the statement that it is accessible to interrogation only in idea follows from this fact. Hence the impossibility of setting a limit to systematic scepticism by invoking the self-authenticating affirmations of self-consciousness. The "cogito" to which I appeal against the destructive suggestions of the intellect is a "cogito" that has been displaced into the debatable territory of past experience by the very affirmation which we seek to rest upon it.

This Scepticism Rooted in an Error of Diagnosis

18. The contention of the sceptic, then, is that a time-conditioned ego, although we may easily find grounds to justify a belief in it, is really unknowable. In view of the seriousness of this conclusion it would be well to take careful note of the concepts upon which it is based. An analysis of the latter reveals the following assumptions. By a "knowledge" of the self we are to understand no more than an act of mind whereby memories or ideas of a subjective past are evoked in consciousness. The factors involved are two in number.[24] There is a present activity of consciousness which is altogether subjective, and might be defined as "remembering past experience"; and there is the experience thus remembered, which is no longer subjectively present to the mind, but offers itself to the latter as an object of contemplation. It will be observed that subjectivity and present time go together (a point in which I heartily concur), while past time is assumed (it seems to me without adequate consideration) to imply objectivity pure and simple. Again the temporal divisions recognized are past and present, and the assumption is that no event can occupy both. Present time and its content must be conceived as altogether present. An event of which this cannot be said without qualification must therefore be conceived not as *partly* present, but as

[24] For the sake of simplicity I leave the future meanwhile out of account.

altogether past, and therefore accessible to consciousness only in the objective form of a recollection.

Now when past and present are made to stand out against one another in such unqualified antithesis, the resulting concept is that of an instantaneous present for ever repelling an indeterminate past—in other words, a durationless actuality reducing all durations to the ideality of a "has been, but no longer is."

That under these conditions we have no right to consider our ego-consciousness as amounting to indubitable knowledge of the self is a very modest conclusion. It is altogether too modest for the premises. The truth is that the assumptions under which the sceptical position is maintained are fatal not only to the claim which the self makes to necessary existence, but also to the supposed consciousness of self upon which the claim depends. In the first place a durationless activity of the subject cannot be a *consciousness* of anything. In the second place, if the supposed consciousness is that of an object-self in a time that is altogether past, it is difficult to see how it is possible for us to assume the identity of the latter with the subject-self that knows it in an altogether different time. To these objections there is no answer, and for the compelling reason that the underlying assumptions are mutually destructive. As I have pointed out, a self that is entirely past can exist for us only in idea; but there can be no *idea* of a self in a time that is completely present at a durationless moment, and is for that reason completely durationless. Thus the very conception to which Santayana has recourse in his attempt to discredit the Cartesian principle is itself discredited by his attempt to apply it.

19. The error is one of diagnosis. Our self-consciousness, which, whether legitimate or delusive, must be recognized as a fact, and is so recognized by Santayana, cannot be reduced without remainder to the activity of a subject-self in a durationless present, contemplating an object-self in an indefinitely extended past. Of the former, there can of course be no awareness until it has ceased to be our present subjective activity and has taken its place among the experiences which have become objects of consciousness, and thereby can no longer be known as *our experiences*. What we must realize is that we can have no consciousness of self as object until we have had consciousness of self as subject, that we can have no memories of ourselves which did not begin as conscious

experiences.[25] Santayana overlooks the necessity of primary self-consciousness as a precondition of secondary, and hence he is unable to accord to the latter the authenticity and importance that pertain to it by nature. It is only upon the assumption of such a precondition that secondary self-consciousness can be established as a vital element in the process of self-realization. As a first step in the correction of the sceptical fallacy we must proceed to modify the sharp antithesis of subjective and objective selfhood, with the correlative antithesis of a momentary present and a past of indeterminate duration. The demands of logic will be sufficiently met if it can be shown that in certain instances, or indeed in any single instance, the process of objectification or ideation is so closely integrated with the actual experience of which it is the transcript that the two between them constitute an indivisible unity of experience.

The Self-Conscious Being Is Actually in the Past State Which He Is in Process of Objectifying

20. Now I think it can be shown that such instances do occur in the sphere we are investigating—that of secondary self-consciousness. Let me try to make this plain by means of an illustration.

The tea-taster or the connoisseur in wine is a person qualified to pronounce judgments of value upon what in one of its aspects we should ordinarily account a physical substance. In the expressions he uses we find him referring to the wine or the tea. As a matter of fact the elements of experience involved are partly subjective and are so far subjectively discoverable. Leaving aside the difficult question whether the "taste" or flavour which we commonly attribute to objects of gustatory experience is itself to be classed as an object, like colour or sound, or as an "effect" upon us—that is, a modification of consciousness—we note the following analytically distinguishable moments in the process of investigation. The connoisseur must *taste*. That is to say, a subjective event of a well defined character must take place within the system of subjective

---

[25] This may appear to conflict with the admission I have already made that our memories may be fuller and richer than the original experiences to which they refer. The apparent contradiction, however, will be found to disappear when viewed in the light of my completed theory as to the relation of primary and secondary self-consciousness. From the standpoint of that theory as a whole the assertion of the text is in no way out of harmony with the view that our memories may be not merely a reproduction, but an amplification of their originals.

events which constitutes his experience and his mind. Whatever else is implied, we are bound at least to recognize at the outset an activity of primary self-consciousness. This is the first moment. The second takes the form of an appreciable pause. The expert is obviously preoccupied with something. He is waiting for the gustatory sensation to complete itself and to declare its quality unmistakably. The implication is that it takes time for such experiences to become subjectively articulate and to disclose their significance. I am not thinking of the processes whereby we elaborate our sensations intellectually—recognition, interpretation, classification—but of the fact that even at the level of our elementary sensory impressions there is such a thing as being relatively *unformed* and being completely *formed*, and that the passage from the first to the second requires time. The connoisseur then, having waited for the full revelation of a subjectivity that unfolds its secret by degrees, repeats the operation by tasting once more and pausing while the sensation acquires the requisite degree of definiteness. Perhaps the process is repeated again and again until the point is reached at which a verdict may be confidently pronounced.

It will be noted that what I have been describing is an experience or a sequence of experiences in time. Primary self-consciousness, therefore, which we detected at the beginning, will be present to the end. Throughout the successive phases of the action the subject has been *enjoying himself* in his sensations. But that is not all: he has been regarding the same sensations with studious attention. He has been cultivating their acquaintance by a deliberate preoccupation with them, and in so doing he has been turning his subjective states into *objects of interest*. In this way primary self-consciousness is reinforced and complicated by the intrusion of secondary. Our problem has to do with the relation between these two.

In the first place I would point out that the act of tasting and the attentive pause constitute an unbroken, though not an undifferentiated, continuum. Subjectively regarded, the experience is one and indivisible. It is not reducible to two distinct experiences, tasting and (shall we say?) savouring? Without the "savouring" the tasting is incomplete, and the savouring may consequently be interpreted as a fulfilment of the tasting. On the other hand the two phases of the experience are emphatically distinguishable, and the difference between them is in one of its aspects a temporal difference. The relation involved is difficult to put into words without the appearance of contradiction, and indeed it cannot be exactly expressed except in terms of the doctrine of time which has still to be set forth. The following points, however, may be made in advance of a complete statement.

(a) The total experience (which in its integrity might be described as "tasting with appreciation") includes both primary and secondary self-consciousness. (b) Since the latter presupposes the former, the secondary condition will naturally prevail in the closing rather than in the opening phases of the total movement. (c) At no point in the duration of the experience can the activity of secondary in relation to primary self-consciousness be described as *merely* remembering (or *restoring* in idea) a state of awareness which once was, but is no longer, subjectively present to us: at no point in the experience does the sensation completely lose its subjective actuality and connect itself with our consciousness of it exclusively through the relationship of objectivity. (d) Such being the case, we must conclude that the phase of primary awareness does not pass away when the phase of secondary sets in, but that the two are concurrently and inseparably present within the unity of an experience which is altogether one.

21. In "tasting with appreciation," therefore, we recognize a single subjective movement whereby the mind, in the active enjoyment of a gustatory experience of *itself*, endeavours by a heightened application of attentive interest to its own subjectivity, to invest the latter with a greater precision and wealth of significance. In the process a certain differentiation of consciousness occurs. A subjective state, by partially detaching itself from all others as a centre of studious concentration, becomes thereby to some extent objectified, but (in this case) without losing anything of its subjective intensity. Indeed the enhancement of the whole experience through attention is definitely subjective in its significance. The presumption is that there is something wanting to the primary experience until the secondary has provided it with a new context of relationship. Hence the secondary must be construed as a positive enlargement of the primary. But if so, it is impossible to treat the secondary as nothing but a questionable reproduction in idea of a presumptive (but necessarily uncertain) original.

22. From what has been said it should be clear that the primary and secondary modes of self-consciousness are here functionally related, and that between them they constitute the single system of experience described in the words "tasting with appreciation." Thus each phase is determined by the other, and but for the relation between them the integral experience would not be what it is. It should be once more obvious that in speaking of functional determination I am not thinking of the relation between an original experience and the revival of it in memory. The subjectivity of the original could hardly be considered as *determined* by the objectivity of the remembered, and between them the two could certainly not be conceived to constitute a single experiential system. Of course the illustration is drawn from a highly specialized type of experience, characterized by the brevity of its duration and by the exceptional concentration of self-consciousness in both the primary and the secondary mode. Above all the illustration owes its point to the fact that the two phases synchronize, and that the subjectivity of the primary so obviously enfolds and assimilates the element of objectivity due to the action of secondary self-consciousness.

A Longer Interval Makes No Difference of Principle

23. But while the peculiarities of the instance serve to bring out the fundamental features with exceptional force, it must not be thought that these features are restricted to experiences so limited. There are cases in which it is possible to establish a functional relation, of the type we have encountered in "tasting with appreciation," between acts of primary and secondary self-consciousness which are separated by a wide interval of time. At first sight this will doubtless appear an extravagant claim. Indeed it might seem as if the admission of a time interval would render it impossible to realize the condition already stated as necessary for the correction of the sceptical fallacy—namely, the modification of the antithesis between a subject-self of primary experience and an object-self of past.

24. The issue as a whole turns upon a single question, which may be variously expressed. When a long interval separates a state of secondary self-consciousness from the primary to which it refers, is it possible that the later state can do more than reproduce the earlier objectively in idea or memory? Is it possible that the *sub-*

jective identity of the earlier state can be in any way affected by the fact that it is succeeded by the later? If the answer is in the negative, it follows that between the two phases of self-consciousness there is not that intimacy of mutual determination which is required to constitute a single system of experience. In the second phase the subject will be found to contemplate the first as past, but without exercising any modifying influence upon it or bringing it, *subjectively speaking*, into a new perspective or context of interpretation. On this assumption it makes absolutely no difference to the past experience that at this interval of time it should have been followed by an act of recollection: we do not change our pasts by remembering them. If, on the contrary, there is something in the later state of mind which makes it impossible for us to think of it as the mere contemplation of its peculiar object (in this case an earlier subjective process, the act of primary self-consciousness), or as the mechanical reproduction of a mental past in a mental present—if, to adopt an alternative mode of expression, the earlier state, by entering into a new context of relations through the advent of the later, is actually amenable to retrospective modification, then the situation is radically altered. What are the facts of the case?

25. When we recollect a past phase of our selfhood (that is, when we are conscious of what we take to be such), we frequently experience a more or less profound emotional disturbance, and perhaps the conative strains of our nature are stimulated to exceptional activity. Obviously there is more here than is implied in the concepts *ideation, objectivation, mechanical reproduction.* The earlier phase of our subjectivity, which has become an object of contemplation, has power to move us deeply and to provoke us to action. This is the fact which we have to interpret.

It is not enough to say, as some will be sure to do, that the object, taken by itself, has in it, like other objects, something which moves us to aversion or the opposite. That objects of consciousness in general are found to be agreeable or the reverse is of course a matter of fact, but this is not the point. The anguish which I experience upon the recollection of what was once an incident or a prevalent tendency of my inner life is not to be explained as I explain the properties that offend me in an ugly picture, a musical discord, an economic heresy, a disastrous political policy, the conduct of a Nero, or generally speaking in

anything that makes its appeal to my susceptibilities in the medium of its objectivity as such. No object, *qua* object, ever pro
duces in my mind the painful feelings which I call shame, remorse
exasperation, or, contrariwise, the peculiar glow of satisfaction
the positive self-feeling and exaltation which the thought of som
achievement—some activity of self-expression or self-repression
sustained in the face of difficulty and of adverse inclination—oc-
casionally evokes. All that is most characteristic of these emotiona
experiences is attributable, not to the affective influence of object
upon subject, but to my consciousness that the object in this case
is *myself*. Beneath the subject-object relationship implied in
secondary self-consciousness there is a movement of the spirit in
which past phases of our inner being assimilate themselves to the
present of our subjectivity. In other words, our present experience
of past episodes in our spiritual history is an experience of what it
means to be the *subject* involved—that is to say, the spiritual
system within which, as functionally related elements of being, pas
and present come together.

When, for example, we suffer the pangs of remorse, the ex
perience is not to be described as a consciousness of something un-
pleasant in a no-longer-existent phase of our selfhood, a phase that
has become objectified for us by the interval which separates i
from the subjective present. On the contrary, what we feel is that
neither the interval of time, nor the process of objectification, nor
the multitude of our intermediate preoccupations has power to
separate our past from us. There is nothing in the temporal con
ditions of existence as such that can rupture or impair the subjective continuity of our being—a continuity that brings together
into a single system of experience the past which we deplore and
our present anguish of remorse. Thus the distinction of primary
and secondary self-consciousness, even when this is accompanied
and conditioned by a very considerable time interval, breaks out
within a subjective experience of the self which is continuous
throughout. It follows that the primary experience, though earlier
in time, cannot be unaffected by the subsequent consciousness of
it. The determinative relation is reciprocal, and that irrespective
of the temporal factor. As in the previous instance, primary and
secondary self-consciousness are functionally related within the
unity of a system which, ontologically speaking, is utterly and
absolutely subjective.

26. It remains to point out that what is true of the primary and secondary phases, when the latter operates as a consciousness of the past, is likewise true of them when it operates as a consciousness of the future. There are of course special difficulties here, with which, so far, we have not learned how to deal. But this much is obvious. Self-consciousness is not merely retrospective: it is also anticipatory in form. And since the future, like the past, exists for us *in idea*, a certain objectification (in this case highly tentative and provisional) will necessarily precede the realization of our actual future selfhood in the mode of subjectivity. "Objectification," however (whether in thought or in imagination), is a very inadequate expression of our total attitude to our personal future. We do not merely *contemplate* ourselves in imagined situations. We actively prepare ourselves for the coming event by a forward adjustment of our spiritual being, which is conative, and, it may be, definitely volitional in character. The future of experience, therefore, means much more to us than is implied in its ideality. It is sternly real, and the proof of this is the agitation it produces among the subjective powers that constitute our active nature. In the measures which we adopt to place ourselves in fitting relation to it there is profound subjective seriousness. We do not thus prepare to meet the non-existent. It will be further noted that in this instance, as in the previous, the ideal factor, though objectively presented, is understood to represent a state of the self, and therefore an entity belonging to that order which exists subjectively. It is really to a *self* of the future that the self of the present makes its adjustment, and the *idea* merely furnishes the light by which we seek to take the necessary measures. Once more an experienced continuity of subject-selfhood is the presupposition behind the constantly renewed activity of the spirit, whereby self-consciousness becomes successively differentiated as primary and secondary. What the subject-self at every point anticipates is *subject-selfhood*, articulated (it is true) in accordance with the latest phase in an ever-changing situation, but nonetheless quite definitely integrated with its own subjective antecedents.

Secondary Self-Consciousness thus a Function of Primary

27. From a consideration of the subject in these various aspects we return to the conclusion that secondary self-consciousness is a function of primary. It is so in the sense that both from the stand-

point of its existence as a mode of experience and from that of its significance as a revelation of what it means to be a conscious subject, it is determined by the initial and defining subjectivity of the system to which it belongs. On the other hand the specific character of that initial subjectivity is no less unmistakably determined by the inclusion of secondary self-consciousness among its modes. In this connection the extent of the time-span covered by the latter is of the utmost significance. One subjective system will differ from another in ways that are definitely determined by what I might call retrospective and proleptic capacity. The momentary glance of introspection, directed, in accordance with the psychologist's purpose, to the subjective content of the instant before, is significant only in the measure to which such experiences, when taken in functional relation to others, may be considered as contributing to the understanding of such a being as the subject-self. How great or how small that significance is I do not undertake to say. But it obviously represents a different order of magnitude from that of an experience in which the time component is measurable by years. There are instances in which secondary self-consciousness is correlated with the subjectivity of half a lifetime. For example, our attention may be powerfully directed to some inveterate disposition, whether to action or to feeling, as when we are obsessed by the consciousness of some bad habit or some vice which embitters all our memories and constitutes a standing challenge to all our efforts for a better future.

The opposing extremes are found on the one hand in the moment-to-moment type of experience which we assume to be characteristic of the lower animals, and, on the other, in that profound preoccupation with life as a whole which is peculiar to the developed moral and religious consciousness of man. It is only too obvious that the subjectivity of the brute creation,[26] when com-

---

[26] The attribution of a subjective nature to the non-human members of the animal kingdom rests upon the assumption that we are entitled to think of them as conscious beings. It will be remembered that subjectivity was defined in terms of experience, and that the definitory mark of experience was found in consciousness. The case of the lowest organisms, in which the evidence of consciousness is wanting, presents a difficulty. In view of the conception upon which our whole argument is based it would seem necessary to assume that a system from which consciousness is permanently absent cannot be a system of experience, and therefore cannot be characterized as subjective. As a matter of fact the solution is not so simple as this. There are aspects of the question which have not yet made their appearance, and cannot do so until we have considered the relation of subjectivity to life.

pared with our own, is deficient in many of the possibilities which we have learned to recognize as characteristic of the spiritual mode of being. This is due to the fact, however it is to be explained, that the power of secondary self-consciousness, except in the case of *homo sapiens*, is almost entirely undeveloped. The result is a certain inchoateness of spiritual modality, in which the inability to objectify the self of past and future experience brings out in striking form the nature of a life where the consciousness of self is altogether primary.

The Animal Mind

28. Animal existence, so far as can be judged from an observation of the behaviour in which it externalizes itself, is characterized by two opposite properties. On the one hand we note the intensity with which the stream of consciousness concentrates successively at certain points determined by the constitution and the vital needs of the psycho-physical organism. Whatever be the business of the moment, the animals are apt to be immersed in it; and in the sequence of their preoccupations there is a consistency and a stubbornness that savour of predetermination and fatality. On the other hand there is an almost total absence of those activities which in man imply the power to capitalize occasions long gone by in the interest of a future still remote. In even the higher mammals there is little evidence of an inner history of conscious consecutiveness; and the general impression which this type of being makes upon the mind of the observer is that of something aimless and unplanned—a series of occasions which, even when they bear the mark of a rigid biological periodicity, have no suggestion in them of a future projected in advance or a past transformed through contexts furnished by a retrospective consciousness of its significance.

29. From this account of the matter it should be obvious that we have no right in any absolute sense to deny self-consciousness to the lower animals. In so far as the evidence permits us to attribute any kind of consciousness to them, we must, in accordance with the principle involved, construe such consciousness as in some sense an inner revelation of their subjectivity.[27] Indeed when we view their nature from the first of the two standpoints which I have

---

[27] The same thing is true of the human infant.

suggested, the thought occurs that the absorption of the animal psyche in its own vital occasions is an instance of self-consciousness in one of its most extreme forms, and that for an analogue in our human experience we must look to the cultivated self-absorption of the mystic.[28] The parallelism is further borne out by the fact that the self-absorption which mysticism tries to render complete is conditioned by a drastic repudiation of the objectivist standpoint and by a refusal to admit the reality of time distinctions. What, however, for the human agent is an ideal to be achieved and a principle to be realized in practice, in the case of the lower species is the natural product of constitutional necessity.

30. These admissions must not of course be looked upon as giving the brute creation any superiority over mankind. Doubtless there are advantages (or at least compensations) in a mode of being so severely limited. Here there are no irksome responsibilities, no difficult adjustments to a remote future, no wrestlings with an ultimate destiny,[29] no lingering regrets, bitter memories, agonies of remorse. There is no tragedy (although to the eye of the sentimentalist—I use the term without reproach—there may be wistfulness and pathos) in the destiny of any living thing beneath the level of mankind. All of this, however, is to be construed not as a state of privilege, but as a badge of inferiority. The incapacity for secondary self-consciousness is a deprivation, as the capacity for it is an enlargement, of being in the spiritual sense. The human self is characterized by numberless possibilities not realizable by any of the lower orders, among others those embodied in religion and morality and in a plastic political and social system. What we call progress—the artificial adaptation and acceleration of nature's evolutionary movement—depends upon the same condition; and

[28] Of course this is not an adequate characterization of mysticism. For its complete expression the latter requires two statements. In the first of these the self (the Âtman) is everything; and mysticism may be defined as the attempt to obtain an experience which shall be an experience of the self and of nothing more. From the second point of view conscious selfhood is the type of unreality, and, in the form of self-will, the principle of evil. The latter proposition is the thesis of the exquisite quasi-mystical *Theologia Germanica.*

[For a full development of his thoughts on mysticism see the author's *Studies in the Philosophy of Religion*, Vol. I, Chaps. XII-XIV.—Ed.]

[29] C. E. Montague (*Disenchantment*, Chap. I, "The Vision") has commented on what must have been to many a first impression of army life in the late war—the sense that "life had undergone an immense simplification" through reversion to a more primitive ordering of existence. The author significantly adds: "Of course, an immense simplification of life is not certain to be a wholly good thing."

with the advent of progress history makes its appearance as a new and unprecedented phenomenon. It is only when man has been evolved that this great change occurs, and the order of events for the first time takes on the character of historicity. In man alone we note those unique powers of initiative and self-determination whereby the individual raises himself from the slough of his anonymity and reveals an identity no longer sunk in that of his kind. By the same powers the social group emerges, as something quite distinct in *genre* from the biological background of the species, and exemplifies the possibility of organizing a communal life on untried principles, where instinct gives place to conscious contrivance and to definite experiment.[30]

Now all these possibilities come to fruition in human experience. They are accessory to the way in which men and women *enjoy* themselves as spiritual beings. And since experience is the stuff of which spiritual beings are made, every accession of experience in any of these forms accrues to the latter as an increment of *being*. Indeed we may go further than this and assert that while the presence of consciousness warrants us in attributing to the lower animals a rudimentary selfhood of their own, it is only when we come to beings capable of secondary self-consciousness, developed in closest integration with primary, that we perceive the fundamental condition required for the realization of an ideally complete selfhood.

That condition is the conjunction of the object- and the subject-self and their integration into one. The points involved may be expressed in three propositions. (a) Wherever being takes the form of consciousness, a self is presupposed. This is the principle implied in primary self-consciousness, with which the experience of selfhood begins. (b) When consciousness is directed to an object which, considered in itself and apart from the relation of objectivity into which it has entered, belongs to the same subjective system to which the act of consciousness belongs, that object is no other than the self in one or other of its phases. This is the principle of secondary self-consciousness, in which the experience of selfhood terminates. Finally, the essential nature of selfhood comes out most

---

[30] Significant of the transition from an order of nature to a social order is the change of meaning which the Greek word κόσμος undergoes as it passes from the classical usage (the "world" around us) to that of the New Testament (a "world" of men).

explicitly as an identity of inner constitution when we realize (c) that the self which appears as a *presupposition*, is one with that which appears as an *object*, of consciousness. Thus the underlying principle of selfhood as such, the selfhood that goes behind all its own distinctions and embraces all its own differences, is the identity of the "self" implied in secondary self-consciousness with that implied in primary.

PRIMARY SELF-CONSCIOUSNESS AS REFLECTED IN FRENCH LINGUISTIC
EXPRESSION

The French language abounds in evidences of primary self-consciousness—e.g., reflexive forms with *intransitive verbs*, "je me tais," etc.
Generally speaking, French idiom is well suited to bring out the fact
that subject-consciousness is implied in subjective activity. Cf. the usage
in which the ordinary nominative of the first personal pronoun is so
completely absorbed into the texture of the verb that in order to draw
attention to its analytic identity, it must be separately expressed. "Moi,
j'aime." The significance of such linguistic devices is that the subject is
defining its selfhood in terms of the conscious experience expressed by
the verb. Thus the self is first posited with something approaching ex-
pletive force—"Moi!" Thereupon follows the statement of the spiritual
content—"j'aime," the activity of consciousness called loving. In this
case "self-consciousness" is not the subject's consciousness of the self as
object, but the self's conscious realization of its subjectivity. The "je"
has lost its force as an independent symbol carrying a distinct representation (sémantème), and has become an inseparable phonetic
element in a complex linguistic structure (morphème). *vid.* J. Vendryes,
La Langage, pp. 86-104. At an earlier stage in the history of the language the fusion was not so close, and the first personal pronoun could
appear apart from its verb. F. Brunot quotes from the *Roland*: "Fier de
ta lance e *jo* de Durandal," and recalls the ancient juridical formula:
"*Je*, soussigné, reconnais. . . ." *La Pensée*, Book VIII, Chap. VIII, p.
243.

CHAPTER VIII

THE PHYSICAL WORLD

The Physical as Spatial Is Objective, but Is Independent of Its Objectivity

1. In the preceding chapters I have set forth what seem to me the main considerations which serve to elucidate the nature of being in the subjective or spiritual form. The assumption throughout has been that this is one of the two modes in which reality finds independent expression. The other is the physical.

Now when we come to the physical mode, we are at once confronted with a disconcerting paradox, upon which I have already commented, namely, that in the more advanced stages of scientific investigation—the stages to which Eddington refers when he speaks of wave mechanics as corresponding to a "profounder level of conception"[1] —there seems to be nothing left to which the epithet "physical" can with any degree of significance be applied. Thus just as the most recent philosophical thinking, logical positivism, ignores or discredits the conditions upon which the *existence* of any conceivable world depends, so the most recent physics ignores or discredits the conditions required to invest the existing world with the character of *physical* reality.

This is of course no reflection upon science as such. What I have said does not affect the force of my observations in the opening chapter with regard to the progressiveness, the continuity and the communicability of scientific knowledge. The truth is that of all the facts which constitute the corpus of the scientifically knowable only a relatively small proportion are calculated to throw a direct light upon the nature of the physically real. Exact astronomical, geological and biological information, though scientific in the ordinarily accepted sense of the term, may leave us very much in the dark as to the essential nature of the forces at work in producing the celestial and terrestrial phenomena or the living bodies which furnish the object of research. Our difficulty is not that there is so little scientific knowledge of the world available, but rather (a) that so little of that knowledge is of service in the attempt to

[1] *New Pathways in Science*, p. 46.

define the physical mode of being, and (b) that where the sciences reach the limit of analysis, as in the electronic theory of the atom and in wave mechanics, we find ourselves engaged in the manipulation of concepts and of symbols for which it is difficult to discover an actually existing correlate among the objects which furnish a content to our experience of the outer world. It is for this reason that the laws of physics seem to have taken the place of the independently existing reality which they were originally designed to explain.

2. In view of the plight to which we have been reduced, it may not be considered too presumptuous if the philosopher, in the tentative and hypothetical way which befits the obscurity of the subject, should venture upon a few suggestions of his own. These will naturally have to do with the most general aspects of the case, such aspects as are of definitory significance and must be taken into account if we are to have a theoretical concept of the physical as such. For the detail we are entirely dependent upon the investigations of the physicist and the chemist, and anything advanced upon purely philosophical grounds must be taken as out of order if it runs counter to the facts for which science can adduce conclusive evidence. In what follows I shall be drawing largely upon the slowly accumulating stock of conclusions to which my argument so far has been found to point, and for the greater part my object will be merely to restate and to develop these conclusions in a context appropriate to our latest problem.

3. I begin by evoking once more the postulate of being. At the very least we must assume that a physical world *exists*, or that reality *exists* in the physical form. This assertion is not invalidated by the difficulties in which the science of physics is involved: on the contrary it gives expression to what is no less than a fundamental presupposition of all scientific inquiry. From the strictly philosophical point of view, however, the application of the postulate in a physical sense may require a word of justification. As a matter of fact the existence of the physical is implied in all that has been said as to the methodological advantages of treating the subjective or spiritual as an independent mode of being. This may be shown as follows.

4. If we recognize that systems of experience exist, and that they are closed to all that is not a function of their native subjectivity, then since our experience is not exclusively "of" itself (whether in

the form of primary or in that of secondary self-consciousness) we are forced to recognize the existence of something else—something that is neither a subjective event nor a system of such events, namely, the non-subjective *of which we have experience.* This necessarily reveals itself in the form of objectivity. Now we have seen that objectivity is not a mode of being, but a relation or the characteristic which anything acquires through standing in this relation. To say, therefore, that the non-subjective reveals itself in the form of objectivity is not to say anything about the mode of its being, although, of course, we know something of that mode when we know that it is non-subjective. Clearly the latter is the category to which the physical, if it exists at all, is to be assigned; but this does not take us very far. As I have pointed out, there are numberless objects of experience which, although they do not exist subjectively, are subjectively conditioned. These must be excluded from the concept of which we are in search. What remains is a non-subjective mode of being which is entirely unaffected by the relation of objectivity in which it stands to the subjective mode. That being in this sense exists can hardly be doubted, if there is anything to which the truths of physical science apply. The fact with which we are here dealing has definitory significance. I shall call it *the independence of the physical.*

Spaces Which Are Objective but not Independent. The Space of Perception and Its Derivatives

5. The next point is one which calls for careful statement and consideration. When we ask wherein precisely the independence of the physical consists, the answer, I think, must be: "Above all in its spatiality."[2] In this the physical presents itself in the light of a double contrast—on the one hand to the spiritual mode which, as I have tried to show, is altogether non-spatial, and on the other, to every spatial order which is not thus independent. In the latter category I include all forms of space (the n-dimensional, for example) which are intellectual constructions,[3] as well as others which depend upon the visual, the tactual, and, generally speak-

[2] The emphasis here lies where Hobbes placed it in his definition of body as "that, which having no dependence upon our thought, is coincident or coextended with some part of space." *De Corp.*, VIII, 1.

[3] Of course this does not mean that these are subjective or in any way capricious. If they are thought at all, they must be thought in accordance with the rules which hold for objects of this kind.

ing, the spatial imagination. I must add the space of objects seen in a mirror, the space of pictures (which is quite distinct from that of the canvas or the colours spread upon the latter) the space of dreams, mental images, imagined bodily sensations, and hallucinations. All of these are *mind-conditioned* spatial orders; and this fact, although it does not negative their objectivity, differentiates them sharply from the space of physical existence.

6. But what of the visible and tactual space of our ordinary working experience, which we are accustomed to consider "real"? The question that has to be settled is whether this kind of space exhibits that independence of mind which is the definitory characteristic of the physical. Whatever be the ultimate answer to the question, it is obvious that the space of ordinary experience is not dependent upon mind in the same way and to the same degree as in the case of the various other subjectively conditioned orders of spatiality to which I have just drawn attention. A comparison with the latter, therefore, by bringing out the precise points at issue, may reasonably be expected to lead us at least some distance in the direction of an absolutely independent space.

7. In any such comparison it is important to observe in the first place that our experience of three-dimensional space in the world of perceptual objects is presupposed in all other forms of spatial experience (whether perceptual or conceptual) with the sole exception of body-feeling. Thus (leaving the latter out of account as irrelevant to our present inquiry) we may construct the notion of an n-dimensional objective manifold by processes of pure thought; but the ability to interpret the construct as *spatial* depends upon the fact that we already possess a notion of space based upon our actual experience of it. An experience of "real" space is also a precondition of our ability to form spatial images; and the space of pictures, though quite distinct from that of the canvas and the pigments, is mediated to our consciousness by the spatiality of the latter. That is to say, if the canvas and the colours were not extended objects of vision, we should be unable to see the picture in a space of its own.

8. For the rest, the relation between an ostensibly "real" space and the more obviously mind-conditioned forms of extension varies with the modes of the latter. For example, the space of a picture differs in respect of this relation from the space of reflected objects. To see that this is so it is only necessary to consider the

way in which the third dimension is supplied in the two instances. In the case of the picture the element of depth is purely ideal, and the reason for this is to be found in the nature of the picture as a two-dimensional representation of a three-dimensional manifold— a representation which, so far as our consciousness of outward distance is concerned, owes nothing to the laws of binocular vision. The third dimension must therefore be supplied exclusively by the mind.[4] It is otherwise with mirror-reflected images. Here binocular vision plays the same part in determining our sense of outwardness as it does in the case of "real" objects. I do not mean to suggest that reflected space is *not* ideal in any of its aspects, including the third dimension; but in its ideality it is subject to conditions which are altogether absent from the space of pictorial representation. As one of these conditions, the determination of the third dimension in accordance with the laws of binocular vision calls for further comment.

9. The precise point is this. Since mirror depth is determined in the same way in which "real" depth is determined, it might seem that, so far at least as theory and definition are concerned, there is no reason for distinguishing between the two, and that the spatiality of a mirror is identical in nature with the spatiality of the "actual" world—that is to say, that it is itself "actual" or "real." Practical questions aside, the difficulty, as I have already explained, is that whereas points of "actual" space can be co-ordinated in a single system, and whereas the same is true of points in mirror space, no point in the latter can be coordinated with any point of the former *in the space of either*. The same mutual exclusiveness is illustrated in the case of motion. No object moving in "real" space ever passes out of this into the space of its own reflection; and no object moving in the space of a mirror ever passes into the space of its original. In this sense the two spatial orders do not unite in a single spatial system. It follows that we may have two (and perhaps more than two) systems of space which are identical in the principle of their organization, and in the optical

---

[4] An interesting analogy to the picture is the tessarac, which is a three-dimensional representation of a "four-dimensional cube." The fourth dimension of the latter is ideally constructed upon cues supplied by the structure of the tessarac itself. I used to possess a tessarac, which was made for me in wire by Professor Ramsay Traquair of McGill University.

laws that govern them, and yet, as systems of space, are indefeasibly distinct.

10. There is, however, another side to the truth. The mutual
exclusiveness of the two systems is not more obvious than the fact
that the one is a function of the other. Every point, every magnitude, every dimension, every motion in mirror space is determined by a prototype in the "actual" world. If y may be taken to
epitomize and symbolize the mirror space, and x to epitomize and
symbolize the "actual," we obtain the formula $y = F(x)$, which, in
accordance with the principle of reduplication, rests upon the prior
formula $y = F(xy)$. Thus x and y, although, as I have said, indefeasibly distinct, nonetheless constitute a single ontologically
heterogeneous system.[5]

11. The questions, relevant to our problem,* which arise at this
point have to do with the modality or ontological status of the
three systems involved—(a) that of mirror space, (b) that of
"real" space, and (c) that which unites the two.

(a) That mirror space is distinct from "real" space and is a
function of the latter does not seem to me to be decisive as to its
modality. That is to say, we are not entitled to assume, upon the
grounds stated, that what we are here dealing with must be something ideal rather than physical. So far as we know to the contrary,
there is no reason why there should not be two or more mutually
distinct systems of physical space. The question therefore as to the
modality of the extension which we perceive in a mirror must be
decided upon other grounds. These are supplied by a consideration
of the ontological character of mirror *objects* or reflections in general. The latter, it will be agreed, are not susceptible to physical or
chemical explanation. They are unanalyzable, imponderable, and,
while as spatial they have of course a magnitude of their own, they
are not measurable as the objects of physics and chemistry are
measurable. This is obvious enough as regards the third dimension;
but it is no less the case as regards the other two. The lateral extent
of a reflected object, for example, is not that of the distance which

---

[5] That there should be no difficulty in combining the idea that x and y are *distinct
systems* with the idea that between them they constitute a *single system* is sufficiently
obvious if we assume that the mirror is concave or convex. In this case the functional
relation remains, but the two systems of "real" and mirror space are differently
organized.

[*"Our problem"—of discriminating purely *physical* space from all the varieties of
mind-dependent space.—Ed.]

the image covers on the surface of the mirror. The latter may vary, while the former remains uniform. It will be said that the size of the reflection in mirror space is that of its original in "real" space, and that the dimensions of the reflection may be ascertained by measuring the original. The statement is in a sense true; but when its meaning is made clear, it is seen to imply that in the very act whereby we establish a quantitative identity between the original object and its mirrored duplicate, we relegate the two to separate and modally exclusive systems of being. Let me explain what I mean.

Suppose that the "real" object is three feet in length. That is a fact which we ascertain by methods to which the physicist has constant recourse. It is a fact which expresses a physical character of the object in question, and which therefore we may describe as itself "physical." The same cannot be said of the statement that the length of the object as seen in the mirror is three feet. This is a statement which from the standpoint of the physicist is entirely meaningless. The magnitude of such appearances lies beyond his province altogether. In so far as he deals with reflections he does so from a totally different standpoint, that, namely, of the sciences of optics and the physics of light. And from this point of view the size of the reflected object is emphatically not that of its original, but that of a space which is reckoned upon the surface of the reflecting medium in accordance with optical principles. To take the present instance, the image will be found to measure, not three feet, but possibly three inches or half an inch. In brief, the physicist has nothing to tell us about the world of objects which we see "in the mirror," although he has much to say about the play of light upon the mirror's surface, and generally speaking about the physical conditions which contribute to, although of themselves they do not explain, what we actually see under these conditions. By all the criteria which he applies the mirrored manifold has no existence in the physical world at all. The statement, therefore, that the reflection is identical in its dimensions with its physical prototype is tenable only upon a set of assumptions which go beyond the scope of those that serve to define the standpoint of physical science, and the implication is that we are here dealing not with one order of reality, but with two. Even upon this understanding the assertion is of very dubious propriety. To be exact, what we ought to say is not that the reflected object is three feet long, but that it is the reflection of an object of that length. From these considerations it is clear that the physical mode of being cannot be attributed to mirror space, any more than it can to the objects which occupy the latter. And, as there can be no question of mirror space existing in the subjective mode, we are driven to the conclusion that this type of spatiality is among the entities which are a joint product of conditions subjective and physical—in a word, that mirror space is a function of the physical in conjunction with the subjective conditions of perceptibility.

What Is Physical *in the Space of Perception*

12. (b) When we come to what I have called "actual" or "real" space, that is, the space of visible, tangible, three-dimensional "things" in the "outer" world, the same criterion must be taken as decisive. We have seen that, ontologically speaking, "things" are among the objects of our experience which are to some extent determined by the conditions that render them perceptible, or, more generally, by their correlativity to the subjective and psychophysical processes which are our integral reactions to them. This applies to these objects in their spatial and quantitative, as well as in their qualitative character. Many of their spatial properties and relations—those, for example, which we call "up" and "down," "before" and "behind," "to the right," "to the left," and, in some contexts, "great" and "small"—are such as involve a reference, direct or indirect, to our bodies and our body-feelings. The relations in question of course belong to the interpunctal system of observed space, and not to the felt space which I have defined as the system of all the loci to which our body-feelings refer. At the same time the interpunctal system, in those aspects of it to which I am here drawing attention, is so dependent upon the sensory and conative experience of the individual that science is compelled to ignore whatever characters of the objective manifold are so determined.

My general conclusion is that in so far as "real" space is to be identified with actually perceived space—the space, for example, in which the magnitude and clarity of visible objects varies with their distance from the observer, and in which distance is established by the muscular adjustments emphasized by Berkeley as the grounds of spatial inference—the element of extension is modally one with the element of objectivity itself. Both are subjectively conditioned. To the extent to which objects and "things" are mind-dependent, the same holds good of their spatial properties and relations. The expression "real" in this connection, therefore, cannot be interpreted in the sense of "physically real." To the modality of space in the aspect of its subjective determination I shall give the name "Berkeleian."

13. The Berkeleian properties are not, however, the only properties of "real" space.* Behind the magnitudes and relations of the perceived manifold there are magnitudes and relations with which the physicist deals by methods that indeed involve perception in their application, but, for their completion, require a certain strategy of thought. To this category belongs the technique of exact measurement, in which an attempt is made to eliminate the vagueness and uncertainty of perceived magnitude. The latter is the product of an inference from the psycho-physical system's reaction to its object, and it is correlated with our subjective impressions. For a method based thus upon the correlativity of the subjective with the objective, scientific measurement substitutes another procedure, one whereby the objective is itself made to furnish a standard for the measurement of all quantities. For example, the application of a graded scale to a measurable object neutralizes the relativity of the objective to our consciousness of it, and brings to light an aspect of the real which is independent of the fluctuating conditions of sensibility. The magnitude ascertained by measurement, although of course as an *object of consciousness* it is necessarily *related* to consciousness, is in no wise *subjectively conditioned*. Hence, as independent of the relation in which it stands to mind, it belongs to the *physical* character of the entity which sustains the relation.[6]

What is true of scientifically established magnitudes is true of everything in the spatial manifold that reveals itself, in the same way, as independent of the subjective processes by which it is known. This would apply to all spatial characters which are determined in strict accordance with the laws of optics, in contradistinction to the characters which depend upon the conditions

[*"Real" space, i.e., the space of perception.—Ed.]

[6] The point here is not that relativity as such is eliminated, but that the relativity eliminated is relativity to mind. If the Fitzgerald contraction and the phenomena upon which the Einstein theory is based may be taken as well authenticated, physical magnitudes vary independently of the subjective conditions of perception, and therefore in accordance with the definitory character of physical existence.

of visibility.[7] It would apply to the spatial factor in all the events which are symbolized by the equations of the physicist.

From this it will be seen that "real" space is only in part physical; in part it is mind-dependent. The distinction is one which must be taken into account in considering the third of our problems, which, it will be remembered, has to do with the modality of the system that unites "real" and mirror space.

14. (c) Ontologically speaking, mirror space, as we have seen, is insulated from "real." The two do not constitute a single system of space; and yet, since the one is a function of the other, in accordance with the principle of reduplication they must, as I have pointed out, be conceived to constitute a single system of some sort. The question is: What kind of a system?

Though each is incapable of assimilation to the spatial system of the other, when taken in conjunction they compose the identity of a system of points between which there exists a one-to-one relation. These points are all alike in space, but corresponding points are in different spatial systems. The only possible conclusion then would seem to be that the system which between them they constitute is a logical system. It should be further remembered that what is outside of the mirror is *visible* (that is, mind-dependent and not *physical*) space. Mirror space and "real" space (in its visible aspect) are therefore both subjectively conditioned. The subjective factor, however, is not the only one involved. The nature of the mirror as a reflecting surface, and the laws of light and of optics are no less contributory to the total effect. The situation as a whole is obviously complex, and it is necessary at once to disentangle and to correlate the various factors, subjective and physical, upon which the completed phenomenon depends.

First of all there exists a genuinely physical system, of which the spatial character is sufficiently attested by the appearance of a spatial coefficient in the laws of optics and of light, or—generally speaking—in the equations that make up the content of the science of physics. In so far as there are grounds for supposing that these laws are universally operative and that the phenomena which exemplify them are related in a spatial sense to all contemporaneous physical phenomena, we seem warranted in assuming a single com-

---

[7] The difference is that, for example, between the position, configuration and magnitude of a retinal image as contrasted with those of the corresponding object in visible space.

prehensive spatial universe as among the conditions implied in the physical mode of being. That is to say, whatever exists in the sense connoted by the term "physical" must conform to the laws that constitute the physical universe a single spatial system. At this point it is hardly necessary to add that this system, considered in and by itself, includes no vestige of the spiritual mode of being, and that, under the same qualification, it cannot be conceived as a function of the latter.[8]

In this it differs from the world of our perceptual experience—the ever-changing manifold of objects which spread themselves out before our senses, and to which we are constantly adjusting ourselves in ways that can only be described as spatial. Perceived space, as I have remarked, is a function of physical space taken in conjunction with the conditions (physiological and psychical) of perceptibility. The various relations involved may be symbolized as follows: If Ps = physical space, pr = perceived space, and C = the conditions referred to, then $pr = F(Ps + C)$. In other words, all the characteristic spatial properties of the world which we observe by means of the senses are what they are because it is so that they exist for percipient organisms in a world of physical space. The basic formula is of course expressible in the equation, $pr = F\{pr(Ps + C)\}$. By this we are to understand that the conjunction of percipient organisms with the space of physics is a fact that must be first read in the light of our spatial perceptions, if the latter are to be expressed as a joint product of that conjunction.

We have seen that mirror space is a function of perceived space, and that between them they constitute an interpunctal system based upon a one-to-one relation. From this it is clear that the space of reflected objects is non-physical in its modality. It is, however, physically as well as subjectively conditioned, the physical element being in this case represented by the body of fact embraced within the laws of optics. The remaining types of spatial system—those which are entirely the product of imaginative or intellectual construction—may be described as functions of our spatial experience. As such they are altogether non-physical; but in so far as our spatial experience is in part dependent upon physical conditions, the latter are among the factors upon which in the

[8] *vid.* Appendix to this chapter, p. 330.

end, and however indirectly, we are dependent for the power of investing the creations of thought and of imagination with a spatial character.

The Physical as Temporal

15. I pass to a second set of considerations—those having to do with temporal existence—which are of no less fundamental significance for the definition of the physical mode of being. And here we encounter a difficulty at the outset. Time is of the essence of all existence, and that irrespective of modality. For this reason it is impossible to apply the concept of time in general as a criterion of the physically real. The general concept must be modified in accordance with the nature of the datum before we can hope to utilize it in the definition of which we are in search. Our question, therefore, comes to this: In what way do the temporal conditions of physical existence differ from those of any other mode, and more particularly of the spiritual? The difficulty comes out at once if we consider that, whereas the physical and the spiritual *differentiate* themselves modally as the spatial and the non-spatial, they come *together* in virtue of their common temporal character. One thing is, however, clear. In so far as the distinction between physical and spiritual being defines itself as the difference between spatial existence and conscious existence, the time of the former must be conceived as a correlate of space, while the time of the latter is a correlate of consciousness and of such subjective processes as are functionally connected with the latter. Our first problem, therefore, is the correlation of space and time in the definition of the physical mode of being.

16. Once more we shall have to take our cue from the sciences which deal with the matter in hand, and more particularly from the science of physics. The question, however, at once arises how far scientific truth can be here assumed, and how far it can be utilized in the interest of a problem which is more definitely philosophical than scientific. My view is that it would not be enough merely to accept the conclusions of the physicist, which, in the present state of scientific thinking, are both tentative and controversial. What we have to do is rather to follow up the processes of thought by which the science which deals with the nature of the physical world comes to a gradual appreciation of the factors with which it is dealing. In this way the hidden character of the phys-

ically real will be found to emerge into view and to define itself progressively by a series of changes in the standpoint from which the attempt to understand it is conceived. Even in the absence of technical proficiency, a knowledge of these changes and of the considerations by which they were actuated may reasonably be expected to provide a certain insight into the nature of the reality with which we are trying to grapple. Such knowledge will necessarily be historical in form.

Light from the History of Science. The Greek Effort to Bring Process (the Temporal) into Structure (the Spatial) Intelligibly. The Milesians

17. In the history of physical science there is a phenomenon which arrests us by its persistence and by its constant reappearance in successive phases of thought. We encounter it alike in the naïve systems of the pre-Socratic schools and in recent advances of twentieth century physics. This phenomenon is the tendency to find the secret of *structure* in *process*, and so to interpret the spatial from the standpoint of the temporal. This is abundantly clear in the case of evolutionary biology. It has lately become hardly less clear in the sciences which deal with the inanimate. The time factor is now recognized to be of the essence of physical reality. Yet it has taken centuries to master this truth, and to unfold the implications of a principle that was vaguely divined almost from the first.

18. The opening phase in the history of Greek science* comprises a succession of systems which might be appropriately summarized as answers to the two questions: "What is it?" and: "How does it come to be?" These questions in a sense represent opposing tendencies in the history of scientific and philosophical inquiry. They give expression to what might be designated the Eleatic and the Heraclitean bias. In the course of development they become inextricably interwoven, sometimes with disastrous consequences. Of this we have sufficient evidence both in the ancient and in the modern era. Their mutual entanglement is responsible for the strange predicament of recent thinking, whereby nature is reduced

[*It seems permissible to observe here that the author's interest in Greek science and philosophy was of similar long standing and comprehensive scope to his interest in linguistic studies.—Ed.]

to a stream of events in time, all of whose distinguishable properties are timeless essences or eternal objects.

The doctrine of Thales that all things are water obviously presupposes the question: "What is it? What is the stuff of which the world is made?"[9] The answer given has only to be stated in order to suggest a second question: "How does water come to assume the various non-aqueous forms which so effectively disguise its identity"? Thus the first of our two questions leads directly to the second. That Thales himself ever definitely propounded this question can hardly be gathered from the scanty records of his teaching; but, as Professor Burnet points out, there are numerous phenomena of the natural world—evaporation, rainfall, nightmists, dew, subterranean springs and alluvial deposits—which, in an age of inexact and uncritical observation, might well have appeared to furnish ocular demonstration of the passage of matter from and to the liquid form.[10] In special cases of motion, such as the action of the magnet and perhaps the magnetic attraction of amber, the need of an explanation was met by a reversion to animistic conceptions.[11]

19. With his successor in the school of Miletus the identity of the substratum is determined by a line of thought in which motion plays a decisive rôle. It can hardly be doubted that Anaximander was led to his conclusion that the basic stuff is best defined as "boundless," by his consciousness of certain difficulties inherent in nature's ceaseless periodicity. Since the characteristic form of change is from one extreme to another—from warm to cold, from dry to moist, and back again—and since each of these extremes is by nature destructive of its opposite, it would seem inevitable that any departure from a state of perfect equilibrium, by placing one of the opposites in a position of incurable and progressive inferiority, would terminate in its eventual extinction. The result would be a static universe. This, however, is not in accordance with the facts. For every disturbance of the balance there is a compensatory change in the contrary direction—a circumstance which has no intelligible ground in the character of the opposites as such, and can be rendered thinkable only by the introduction of some

[9] Aristotle, *Met.*, A, 983 b.
[10] *Early Greek Philosophy*, 3rd ed., p. 49.
[11] *op. cit.*, p. 48.

factor specially designed to meet the needs of the case.[12] It is Anaximander's assumption that in the interplay of these mutually
destructive forces there is a principle at work whereby the loss on
one side or the other is invariably made good from an inexhaustible
reserve of being. Hence the boundlessness of the primeval stuff.

It will thus be seen that in dealing with the question what the
world *is*, or how its *being* must be characterized, Anaximander is
guided by his interest in certain temporal processes, and more particularly by his desire to explain how these processes continue to
propagate themselves under conditions which at every moment
threaten to bring them to an end. In brief, being has to take the
form of an ἄπειρον in order that becoming, as Aristotle puts it,
may not fail.[13] Behind the argument we detect what must have
been a necessary presupposition—the everlasting alternation of
the seasonal fluxes. In the logic of Anaximander's thought the infinitude of being is an inference from the assumed eternity of
change.

20. When we pass from general considerations dictated, as was
invariably the case among the early Greek philosophers, by a strict
regard for thinkability, to detailed cosmology, we find a similar
motive at work. The forms which nature assumes in our experience
are due to the specific character of the operations by which these
forms are evolved. We have just seen that the boundlessness of the
world-stuff is deduced from the eternity of the world-process. But
though thus deduced, it is necessarily posited as coequal with the
latter in the order of originality. The next step is obviously to
locate the primeval impulse, from which the whole world-move-
ment proceeds, in the boundless itself. It is only so that the latter
can be represented, with any degree of definiteness, as an operative
cosmic principle. The vague notion of an indeterminate expanse of
matter[14] must be fertilized by the conception of a process at work

---

[12] For a cogent statement of the view, so characteristic of the Greek mind in this phase
of its development, that the stability of the natural order is expressible not as "a determined sequence of events or mechanical causation," but as "an *ex post facto* readjustment," *vid. Greek Philosophy before Plato*, by Professor Robert Scoon, pp. 19 *sq.*

[13] *Phys.* Γ, VIII, 208, a, 8.

[14] The controversy as to whether the word ἄπειρον means "spatially infinite" or
"qualitatively indeterminate" is chiefly of philological interest. Burnet has advanced
good reasons against the view of Teichmüller and Tannery, who interpret the term in
the latter sense (*op. cit.*, 1st ed., text pp. 60 *sq.*, 2nd and 3rd ed., footnote pp. 60 and 58
respectively). But while admitting that *infinitude* is what is meant, we must acknowl-

within its undefined immensity. To the primitiveness of infinite stuff there must therefore be added the primitiveness of a world-informing activity, whereby the opposites are "separated off."

There has been some controversy as to the meaning of this phrase. Without drawing upon the pictorial imagination for sensory representations of the process, I venture to suggest that the essential point, upon which everything turns, is the question: "Separated off *from what*—from the Boundless, or from one another?" The evidence seems to be that what Anaximander had in mind was the formation of a world-order *from the Boundless* by some process of extraction or segregation.[15] But it is clear that since the opposites cannot be thought of as *removed* from the all-enveloping Boundless—*riddled out of it*,[16] so to speak, and set apart by themselves—segregation in this case can mean nothing but local differentiation *within the Infinite*. That the differentiation takes a spatial form is the result of translating into terms of physical necessity what must have been for Anaximander primarily a necessity of thought. Modes of being which are qualitatively incompatible must occupy different places in the real world. The theoretical implications of oppositeness are here seen unfolding themselves under the conditions of actual existence. But the time factor is also recognized upon empirical grounds. The opposites must *find their way* to the places which they occupy. They do so by a process of mutual segregation. That is to say, they *become* opposites in the act of differentiating themselves in space, and they take up their several positions in space because their synthetic incompatibility sunders

edge that Anaximander's conception must necessarily imply indeterminateness as well. Otherwise the ἄπειρον would be rendered useless for the very purpose for which the concept was devised—namely, as a co-solution to the problem of the opposites.

[15] Such at least is the more obvious meaning of the words which Simplicius quotes from Theophrastus: ἐνούσας γὰρ τὰς ἐναντιότητας ἐν τῷ ὑποκειμένῳ ἀπείρῳ, ὄντι δὲ σώματι, ἐκκρίνεσθαί φησιν Ἀναξίμανδρος. Burnet does less than justice to the importance of this passage. If it is true that the words ἐνούσας and ὑποκείμενον are "unhistorical," and that they represent an "accommodation" to Peripatetic ideas, the notion of a "separating out" is nonetheless quite obviously one of the keys to Anaximander's cosmology.

[16] For this very reason I cannot accept Burnet's striking conjecture (expressed more guardedly in his third edition) that "the term 'separating-out' suggests some process of shaking and sifting as in a sieve." The relation of the opposites to the Boundless after they have been "separated out" is not like that of the riddled to the unriddled mass, or of the grain to the chaff. The Boundless is still represented as "encompassing" all the worlds. This objection to Burnet's notion would of course disappear if the word ἐκκρίνεσθαι could be taken as referring explicitly, rather than (as I hold) by implication, to the separation of the opposites from one another.

them from one another. "Separation" is therefore the equivalent of oppositeness in a time-conditioned manifold of events. When read in the light of this truth, the question I have just proposed will be found to answer itself by destroying the alternatives on which it rests. The differentiation of the opposites from the Boundless and their differentiation from one another are not two events but one. In other words, the hot and the cold, with all the variations in the changing manifold of which these are the type, are separated from the infinite reservoir of being by the same process of differentiation by which they acquire the character of opposites.

When, therefore, Anaximander speaks of them as separated off *from the Boundless*, he is really asserting that the principle of change, whereby things come to differ from one another, must be interpreted as a principle of determinateness in the primordial being itself. Being must be viewed in the light of an aboriginal bipolarity. But the Boundless, which is Anaximander's answer to the question: "What is it?" is rendered available for the purposes of world-formation only through his answer to the question: "How does it come to be?"

The ensuing picture of the world is determined in every feature by the differentiating principle. The qualitative oppositeness of hot and cold is reflected in a further process of local segregation, whereby the cold, in the form of earth and water, accumulates in the centre of the forming world, while the hot spreads round this compressed nucleus as a sphere of flame, and is eventually broken up by the air which it attracts to itself. By a natural train of thought the initial differentiation gives rise to a system of roughly stratified elements. The distribution of those is pregnant with the suggestions of a more explicit theory of change.

21. From Anaximander the line of advance goes out in two directions to Anaximenes and Heraclitus respectively. In the hands of the former the conception of a stratified universe, the product of a first differentiation, passes into that of a graded system of differences evolved from a simple world-substance by the opposite processes of rarefaction and condensation. The effect of this change of viewpoint is to render the concept of a definitely identifiable primary substance unnecessary. If the only difference between things is one of relative density, there is no reason why the aboriginal stuff should be defined at all, much less that it should

be defined as air.[17] Water or earth would have done just as well. Process has displaced substance in significance as the key to world-building. The logic of Anaximenes' position points the way to the surprising turn which the argument takes at the instance of Heraclitus.

Science at an Impasse. Heraclitus' Exaltation of Process and Parmenides' Denial of Its Possibility

22. The clue to Heraclitus' system is to be found in a reversal of the basic assumption of Anaximander's cosmology. When Thales' successor described the opposites as "separated off," he had doubtless in mind, as I have said, their synthetic incompatibility. The same consideration forbade him to think of them as *coming from* or *passing into* one another. Hence the necessity of a neutral substratum, from which without contradiction they could be represented as originating by mutual differentiation. No such necessity exists for Heraclitus, and that because he refuses to admit the truth of the proposition behind the postulate of infinite substance. That the opposites cannot pass directly into or out of one another is an assumption to which our everyday experience effectually gives the lie. "Cold things become warm, and what is warm cools; what is wet dries, and the parched is moistened."[18] The conception of *transition into* is thus made to displace that of *segregation from* in the attempt to render nature's manifoldness and diversity intelligible; and with this change there goes a complete readjustment of the questions: "What is it?" and "How does it come to be?" The opposites are no longer the *products* of differentiation: they are actual *phases* in the process itself—a process which is one and continuous throughout.

In Heraclitus the tendency, which we have noticed as characteristic of scientific advance, to answer the first of our two questions in terms appropriate to the second reaches its extreme limit; and for that very reason (strange as the assertion may seem) the conception of process ceases for the time being to be scientifically fruitful. The reason is that the advance to the new point of view was too rapid for the slowly accumulating body of man's exact

---

[17] Of course, as Burnet remarks, there is no reason *why it should not*. My point is that the new conceptions which render the identification possible, at the same time deprive it of its force.

[18] Frag. 39, Burnet's translation.

knowledge of the world. Heraclitus' system is a metaphysical anticipation of truths which could not as yet be made available for purposes of physical investigation. At this point the scientific movement overreaches itself—or, to vary the metaphor, Greek science finds itself compelled to mark time until the speculative issues raised by Heraclitus and Parmenides have revealed the impossibility of further progress along the lines suggested by either of these thinkers. The exact nature of the difficulty can best be brought out by a further consideration of Heraclitus' system.

23. In order to see the bearings of this upon scientific knowledge it is necessary to realize the motive that led to its inception. Contrary to what we should expect, it was not a powerfully intuitive feeling, or a delicate sensitiveness, to the significance of change as such that induced Heraclitus to transpose the concepts of being and becoming. His motive was really that of eliminating the element of irrationality from becoming. Now the phenomenon of change (so it seemed to him) cannot be rationalized so long as we consider it as a predicament of being as such—that is to say, of what, by definition, is fundamentally unchanging. The only alternative is to eliminate being itself. Thus change becomes not only empirically apprehensible, but thinkable as well. Heraclitus was therefore led to formulate his doctrine of flux by the self same rationalistic bias which compelled his great opponent Parmenides to deny it.

To bring Parmenides and Heraclitus together on any other basis than that of their mutual antagonism may savour of paradox. But I cannot agree that any fundamental likeness subsists between Heraclitus and the contemporary thinker with whom it is most natural to connect him, M. Bergson. For Bergson it is the power of intuition that reveals the unbroken flow of real duration, the intellect that imposes the illusion of fixity. With Heraclitus the exact opposite is the case. The apparent fixity, in so far as it is not reducible to a product of strife or opposite tension,[19] is an illusion which must be dispelled by a reasoned argument, a λόγος, true for all time, and therefore timelessly true.[20] From this it follows that change as conceived by Heraclitus is not to be identified with creative evolution as conceived by M. Bergson. There is no place

[19] Burnet, Frags. 43, 44, 45, 46, 47, 62, 69 and 83. ("It rests by changing.")
[20] *op. cit.*, Frags. 1 and 2.

in the ever-moving system of things for the genuinely new and un-precedented.[21] All things come to pass in accordance with the "word."

24. Now (and this is another paradox) it is precisely his sense of rigid law, of rationality in nature's incessant fluxes that marks Heraclitus' system as belonging to the non-scientific phase of Greek thought. Of course science has to do with rigid law; it has to do with nature's fluxes. But the age was not yet near when the concept of law could be profitably applied to the variable content of time rather than to the changing content of space. In a word, the line of progress for natural knowledge was as yet, and was for centuries to come, in the direction of a purely mechanistic interpretation of nature. From this point of view all changes in the outer world are best represented as the successive configurations of a spatially ordered manifold, rather than as the spatially distributed manifestations of a temporally ordered continuum. It is therefore better to consider being as the fundamental reality behind becoming than to consider becoming as the fundamental reality behind being. With this in mind a mechanistic science proceeds to organize the complex content of experience in spatial constellations of contemporaneous elements; and the coordination of sequent constellations is essentially an extension of the same process. That is to say, it is an attempt to view the successive distributions of the contents of space in such a way that the later will appear as a variation upon (and indeed a reproduction of) the earlier. Each successive constellation is attributed not to the general nature of succession in time, but to the specific character of its spatial antecedent in the series. The transition from the one to the other is merely the interval that separates them—an interval to which it may be necessary to assign a quantity and a number, but never a character of its own.

25. The reason for Heraclitus' failure to provide a point of view from which, in accordance with the tendency we have been following, the concepts of process could be scientifically developed, is perhaps to be found in the fact that nature's sequences, though subject to a law which we have reason to believe universal, are by

[21] *op. cit.*, Frags. 20, 29. cf. the observations on what is "common"—i.e. like a law, comprehensive and universal, Frags. 91a, 91b, 92, 62. The point of my statement is in no way altered by the remark (Frag. 32) that "the sun is new every day." It is new in a strictly predetermined sense.

no means reducible to the formula of a transition between opposites, with the corollary of a periodic recurrence of every phase in the total movement. This formula rather suggests the mystical simplification of cosmic process in such doctrines as the Hindu and Pythagorean cycle of births, the Stoic ἐκπύρωσις (periodic conflagration),[22] the dialectic of nature and of history in German Idealism, and the Nietzschean Wiedergeburt. Such products of speculative thought and fancy have their origin in the attempt to show how time articulates itself in the form of events rather than how events in time effect a rearrangement in the otherwise unchanging contents of space. The difficulty is that the events in question, though preordained and clearly distinguishable, are correlated on a basis that is either purely qualitative (like the transition between opposites),[23] or purely speculative (like the dialectical movement and the world-cycle).What science demands is a quantitative correlation between the time factor and the space factor. But this was as yet too much to expect. What was within the compass of the scientific consciousness was the correlation of successive configurations of the content of space; and the business of science was expressible in the formula: "Given one of these (the *Hypothesis*), to find the other (the *quaesitum sive eventum*)"—or else: "Given each in turn, to establish an intelligible relation between them." That the transition from the first to the second was a process of some sort, and that every process is effected in a time that is continuous, was doubtless understood; but the attention was necessarily focused at two distinct points, the *terminus a quo* (definable as the moment of the first configuration) and the *terminus ad quem* (definable as the moment of the second). The reference of the latter to the former is the essence of a scientific explanation at the mechanistic stage of development. While, therefore, it is true that almost from the beginning of scientific inquiry the question as to what it *is* turns at once into the question *how it*

[22] Not that Heraclitus himself anticipated this doctrine. What he says about fire judging and convicting all things (Frag. 26) is to be understood as meaning that other things (water and earth, for example) will pass *in turn*, not all at once, through the phase of fire. On this point Burnet's argument seems to me conclusive. *op. cit.*, pp. 158 *sq.*

[23] It is true that Heraclitus represents the cosmic process as regulated in a quantitative sense. "This world . . . is now, and ever shall be, an ever-living Fire, with measures of it kindling, and measures going out." (Burnet, Frag. 20.) But this is only theory. As the measures referred to cannot be empirically or mathematically ascertained, the statement cannot be considered scientific except in an ideal sense.

comes to be, the latter question resolves itself back at once into the question what it *was*. Being is no less necessary for becoming than becoming for being. Transition is from a having *been*, and is a coming to *be*, or else it is from a *being* to an about to *be*. The anomaly in Heraclitus' system is that the terminal points in the process are to be viewed in the light of the transition between them, and not the transition in the light of its limiting moments. Hence it is necessary to answer the question: "What is it?" with a direct negative: "It is *not*."[24]

26. It would be beyond the scope of this inquiry to consider the system of Parmenides, which presents a point-to-point antithesis to that of Heraclitus, and is equally unfruitful in scientific results. The philosopher of Ephesus proves that being is incompatible with becoming: the philosopher of Elea replies by proving that becoming is incompatible with being.[25] From the standpoint of natural knowledge the rehabilitation of being is no less imperative than the recognition of change. The logic of Parmenides, like that of Heraclitus, ends in the negation of all science. And yet these two dialecticians, working at cross purposes, though from an identical motive, produced between them the movement of thought which was to carry the Greek mind to the culminating point of its scientific achievement.

Atomism as a Pis Aller *Solution. Science Launched Upon Its Long Spatio-Mechanical Development*

27. The atomic theory owes its inception to a single profoundly significant modification of Parmenides' conception of being and non-being in their mutual relation. Parmenides had agreed that non-being, since it is self-contradictory, is unthinkable. Hence it cannot *be*. We cannot attribute existence to that which *ex hypothesi* is non-existent. Now this is obviously true in an abstract logical sense. But there is another sense in which it apparently no longer holds. If being and non-being are given a physical rather than a logical significance, and interpreted as filled and empty

---

[24] The contradictoriness of this procedure is the gist of Parmenides' criticism, apparently directed (though not perhaps exclusively) against Heraclitus. "The other [way of search], namely, that *It is not* . . . that, I tell thee, is a path that none can learn of at all." Frags. 4, 5. cf. 6. Burnet, pp. 173-4.

[25] It should be understood that throughout the word "being" must be taken in the concrete sense (τὸ ὄν, das Seiende, *that which is*) and not in the abstract (τὸ εἶναι, das Sein, what it means *to be*). *vid.* Burnet, p. 178.

space respectively, it seems possible to think of both as existing.[26] The discovery (or perhaps I should say, the postulation) of a void, which had been denied by Parmenides[27] and Empedocles,[28] and had been identified by Alcmaeon with air,[29] and with breath or physical darkness by the Pythagoreans,[30] is an epoch-making event in the history of science—even if science of late has been unable to sustain the idea.

Filled space, as conceived by Democritus, conforms in a general way to the character of Eleatic being. Only, it is no longer one, but many. This is rendered possible by the fact that being itself is now conceived primarily in a spatial sense: it is that whose nature it is, first and foremost, to fill the spatial void. Now the idea of space carries with it the idea of externality, and therefore of multiplicity. Where being takes a spatial form, it must have parts, and the parts must fall outside one another. For this reason Zeno, perhaps with greater consistency than Parmenides, denied space and multiplicity together. Democritus assumes space, and with it he recovers the right to treat the world as a manifold. This consists of a vast plurality of atomically distinct units of physical being.

Zeno had denied infinite divisibility. The atomists agree with him in this. But they do so by assuming what Zeno in the course of his argument against space really denies, namely, the difference between space as such and the body that fills it. It is true that everything extended may be thought of as infinitely divided; but such division may not be physically possible. Thus we reach the conception of physical bodies, the atoms, which, while possessing a certain magnitude, do not admit of actual division.

28. What is really significant in the atomic theory is the fact that it represents a point of view required to render the conception of change once more available for the purposes of scientific progress. When being takes the form of indivisible units of filled space, becoming takes the form of motion in a void; and all the problems

---

[26] Whether such a thing as empty space *actually* exists in the physical world is another question, and one with which science was hardly in a position to deal competently until the conception of the atom as a bit of matter had given place to the theory of electrons and to wave mechanics.

[27] *The Way of Truth*, Frag. 2, Burnet, p. 173. cf. Frags. 6 and 8.

[28] Frags. 13 and 14, Burnet, p. 207. cf. Frag. 17, p. 208.

[29] *Aet.* IV, 16, 2. Arist., *Hist. An.*, A, 11. 492a 13. *vid.* Diels Vorsokratiker, p. 104. Burnet, p. 194.

[30] Burnet, pp. 108-9.

that arise in physics, cosmology and astronomy become problems in motion. Upon the basis of this conception of change, as change of place, it at length becomes possible in a scientifically profitable sense to answer the question: "How does it come to be?"

There is no evidence that Democritus ever tried to account for motion. This of itself may be taken as evidence that he never did. If so, he showed scientific insight. It is not the business of science to deal with the problem expressed in the Aristotelian phrase, ὅθεν ἡ ἀρχὴ τῆς κινήσεως—the problem how motion first got into the world.[32] The Heraclitean view of change as underived and fundamental now contributes to the scientific point of view. What science has to explain is not the origin of motion, but its characteristics, its conditions, and the forms which it assumes as these conditions vary. Science does so by observing these characteristics and conditions empirically and generalizing them as the laws of physics. In this its success is largely dependent on the standpoint from which it starts. The supreme contribution of Democritus to Greek science, and to science in general, was that by eliminating the confusions and irrelevancies inherent in the conception of change as a predicament of the opposites, and by placing research upon a quantitative and mathematical basis, he established that mechanistic theory which from his day almost to our own has been the world's refuge against the uneliminated vestiges of animism and antique superstition, and its chief guarantee of scientific progress.

Changes in the Spatio-Mechanical Picture. The Modern Effort to Accommodate the Temporal in the Spatial. Leibniz. Joule

29. In the modern era we find the same tendencies at work in forms appropriate to a later stage of thought. The union of the time factor with the space factor in a mechanistic theory of motion has paved the way for investigations which have exposed the inadequacy of that theory as an interpretation of certain types of fact—the types, moreover, which come nearest to expressing the ultimate nature of the physically real. Body in motion, which

---

[32] This remains true even when the point is reached at which motion is no longer, what it presumably was for Democritus, something ultimate and unaccountable, but is seen to be a phenomenon or phase of something more fundamental than itself.

seemed to Thomas Hobbes a sufficient explanation of all that is,[33] was indeed for long the best authenticated guide to scientific truth, and for that reason could be assumed, as it was by Democritus, without further question. But questions were bound to arise sooner or later, partly because the two fundamental concepts were not free from theoretical difficulties, partly because the facts could not in all cases be made to square with them. I have pointed out that the *origin* of motion as such is not a scientific problem. On the other hand the *differentiations* of motion—velocity, acceleration, direction—are among the most typical of the phenomena for which science undertakes to account.[34] These differentiations, however, are not fully explicable by reference to the fact of motion itself. The key to them must be sought in some principle behind the phenomenon.

30. A special difficulty is the interpretation of rest, which we have already considered in connection with the views of Descartes and Leibniz.* So long as motion was treated as an ultimate principle, there was no explanation of rest except as an opposite or a negation. This in itself was a defect in a doctrine based upon the matter-in-motion hypothesis. We have seen how Leibniz resolves the difficulty by interpreting rest as a limiting instance of motion. The effect of this (or, perhaps I should say, the precondition upon which alone the change of viewpoint became possible) was the reduction of motion from the status of an ultimate principle to that of a phenomenal manifestation, an externalization, of something more fundamental than itself—the "force" of which both rest and motion are the variable appearances. A similar conclusion, as I have also pointed out, results from the attempt to view the phenomenon of motion in the light of the principle of continuity.

31. Thus the dualism of motion and rest is overcome, but not the dualism of body and motion, or, to be more exact, of matter and energy. The latter was destined to propagate itself through still one other phase of thought, the nineteenth century physics, in which the recognition of matter and energy as basic forms of

---

[33] Motion is the sole cause of all phenomena. It is the only form of change, and it produces nothing but motion. *De Corp.*, VIII, IX, 7 and 9; XXV, 2; *Leviathan*, Part I, Chap. I.

[34] For Democritus the main problem was the explanation of the rotatory movement—the δῖνος, δίνη—of the world-system.

[*See I, 24, above.—Ed.]

existence was sealed by the formulation, upon empirical evidence, of the twin principles of the indestructibility of the one and the conservation of the other. The latter, announced as a law of nature by Joule in England, and by Mayer and Helmholtz in Germany, is the answer, brought up to date, to the immemorial question: "How does it come to be?" The world, as it reveals itself to us through the observation of its overt phenomena, is the product of an energizing principle which, in all its transformations, remains constant, and manifests its presence in the orderly changes to which the material substance of the world is subject. Physics and chemistry divide between them the work of extending and consolidating man's knowledge of the corporeal system upon a basis supplied by the apparently irrefragable concepts of energy and matter.

32. Behind these concepts, with whatever is new in them, we detect the features of an old world-picture, in which a variety of bodies are moved about by the application of force. But the picture was already obsolescent. In particular it was proving its inappropriateness as a representation of the events which chemistry was bringing to light in the minute systems of the physically real. The behaviour of the elements in relation to one another, when reduced to the scale of their atomic interaction, is quite unlike anything in the macroscopic world where bodies push and jostle, collide and gyrate in accordance with the mechanical laws of movement. Here we naturally think of the body first, as the constant subject of its own displacements, while its motions have about them the air of something relatively adventitious and (in spite of the uniformity of the laws which they exemplify) indefinitely variable. It is otherwise with the reactions of the atoms. These reactions present the appearance, not so much of externally induced predicaments, as of events which express the intrinsic nature of the atoms themselves in relation to other atoms.[35] So closely integrated are these events with the identity of the substances which sustain them that they may be looked upon as among the definitory properties of the latter.

[35] The expression "Wahlverwandtschaften" (elective affinities) which Goethe appropriates for the title of his novel, is of course metaphorical, but it draws attention to the fact that chemical action must be conceived as issuing from the inner constitution of the atoms, rather than as imposed upon the latter. The reactions of the elements to one another are selective responses of each to each.

The Position Today, and How It Has Been Reached.
(a) Matter as Motion. Kelvin, etc.

33. This transfer of emphasis from the concept of matter to that of process is the most characteristic feature in the science of today. In the light of what is now known of the minute structure of the physically real, the concept of the world as a material system pervaded by mechanical motion has been largely superseded by that of a system of events interpretable in scientific knowledge as a universal energy diversifying itself in forms which, under conditions of ordinary human experience, take on the aspect of body. In the attempt to understand the physical mode of being energy now comes first, and body is interpreted as a concentration of energy. To a much greater extent than at any other time the question: "What is it?" has been found to demand an answer in terms of the question: "How does it come to be?"

34. The advance from the first to the second point of view is illustrated by successive episodes in the history of physics and chemistry within the last sixty or seventy years. The detail of these, which is all-important for a strictly scientific assessment of modern developments, is beyond my competence. But it is not my purpose to assess the theories in question as a contribution to science. My object is to obtain a general perspective in which the new insight will be seen transposing old relations and transforming ancient prepossessions.

In the 'sixties of last century the traditional conception of the material world was challenged by Sir William Thomson (afterwards Lord Kelvin) in his theory (to which I have already alluded) of vortex atoms.[36] Helmholtz had announced the laws of rotatory motion in a perfect fluid—that is, "a homogeneous incompressible fluid devoid of all viscosity" or "fluid friction."[37] Thomson hastens to make use of Helmholtz' discovery in an attempt to reformulate the atomic theory. He maintains that every advantage which can be claimed for the "infinitely strong and infinitely rigid Lucretian atom"—in brief, its eminent suitability as an explanation of the permanent qualities of the various kinds of matter—can with

---

[36] *Proceedings* of the Royal Society of Edinburgh, Vol. VI, February 18, 1867, and of the Philosophical Society of Glasgow, Vol. VI, March of the same year.

[37] *Proc.* (Edinburgh), p. 94. Clerk Maxwell, *Scientific Papers*, Vol. II, pp. 466 *sq.*, art. "Atom," reprinted from *Ency. Brit.* In this article the writer gives an elaborate account and discussion of the vortex theory.

equal force be claimed for the "vortex ring" of Helmholtz,[38] and that certain additional advantages can be claimed for the latter. In particular the vortex ring succeeds, where the Lucretian atom fails, in explaining the vibrations of a molecule as shown by spectroscopic examination.[39] "But," to quote the words of Clerk Maxwell, "the greatest recommendation of this theory, from a philosophical point of view, is that its success in explaining phenomena does not depend on the ingenuity with which its contrivers 'save appearances,' by introducing first one hypothetical force and then another. When the vortex atom is once set in motion, all its properties are absolutely fixed and determined by the laws of motion of the primitive fluid, which are fully expressed in the fundamental equations."[40]

35. Now whatever the value of Thomson's hypothesis as a correction and enlargement of the atomic theory, the philosophical implications of the doctrine are of permanent interest, both as an early indication of the new direction which scientific thought was about to take, and as an anticipation of the final fate which awaited the concept of matter as a compact, inert, space-filling substance out of all *intrinsic* relation to time. This appears somewhat casually in the concluding phrase of a statement by Thomson himself on the special advantages of the vortex theory. ". . . The vortex atom," so the statement runs, "has perfectly definite fundamental modes of vibration, depending solely on that motion, *the existence of which constitutes it*."[41] How far the writer would have accepted the conclusions implicit in his own assertion is perhaps matter of doubt, but the logic of his position is brought out clearly by Clerk Maxwell.

The exact point might be stated as follows. The atomic theory (as Democritus himself already realized) is not an attempt to account for all the perceptually recognizable properties of macroscopic bodies. Its "only pretext" (to repeat Thomson's words, applied to the traditional doctrine) "is that it seems necessary to account for *the unalterable distinguishing qualities* of different kinds of matter."[42] That is to say, the scientist confines his attention ex-

[38] *Proc.* (Edinburgh), p. 94. The "vortex ring" is described in detail by Clerk Maxwell, *op. cit.*, p. 470.

[39] Clerk Maxwell, *op. cit.*, p. 471. *Proc.*, p. 96.

[40] *op. cit.*, p. 471.

[41] *Proc.*, p. 96. Italics mine.

[42] *Proc.*, p. 94. Italics mine.

clusively to the qualities of bodies (and to the bodies as definable in terms of the qualities) which he has learned to distinguish as permanent. It is his assumption (and the assumption is basic) that these properties will become scientifically intelligible if he can show that they have their definitory characteristics in what he takes to be the ultimate constituents of the material world. Now the properties which commend the vortex ring as a substitute for the Lucretian atom are not the definitory characteristics of the perfect fluid in which they are located. They are the properties of a *rotary motion* (a Wirbelbewegung), to which indeed that fluid is supposed to be amenable, although there seems to be nothing in the nature of the fluid, considered as a material substance, to suggest that it must needs be in such a state of motion. The concept of matter with which we have here to do is one which defines itself not in terms of, but in contradistinction to, the motion which is its occasional predicament. Thus we are driven to a quite untenable conclusion, very well stated by Clerk Maxwell. ". . . According to Thomson, though the primitive fluid is the only true matter, yet that which we call matter is not the primitive fluid itself, but a mode of motion of that primitive fluid. It is the mode of motion which constitutes the vortex rings, and which furnishes us with examples of that permanence and continuity of existence which we are accustomed to attribute to matter itself. The primitive fluid, the only true matter, entirely eludes our perceptions when it is not endued with the mode of motion which converts certain portions of it into vortex rings, and thus renders it molecular."[43]

36. As I have remarked, Thomson's position is untenable. Matter cannot be reduced to a "mode of motion," since the concept of motion presupposes the independent existence of matter. Timerding[44] has pointed out that the vortex theory is identical in principle with Descartes' explanation of the physical world. This is true only in the sense that Thomson employs the same concepts —matter, or extended substance, and motion—which form the basis of all Descartes' thinking about nature. Otherwise the vortex theory is a direct inversion of the Cartesian. The difference is that between representing motion as a mode of extension and representing extended substance as reducible to a mode of motion. What is really significant, however, is the fact that in so far as Kelvin's

[43] *op. cit.*, p. 472.
[44] Quoted Sedgwick and Tyler, *A Short History of Science*, p. 278.

doctrine reproduces the old categories, the objections brought by Leibniz against those will apply equally to the Kelvin doctrine. What is more, the Leibnizian solution will fit both cases alike. Thus while the characteristic properties of motion cannot be made to explain the permanent qualities of matter, without at once negating and presupposing material substance as such, there is no objection to reducing matter altogether to a concentration of energy, and explaining motion as a manifestation of the latter. And this in effect is the next step in the forward movement.

(b) Relativity

37. The various phases in the process whereby the concept of the physically real as matter in motion has been transformed may be brought together under two heads. One of these has to do with relativity, the other with the structure of the atom.

Of the former it will be enough to say that it has destroyed the commonly accepted notion of the relation between bodies and their movements in space, and has thereby broken down the dualism of matter and motion which was the mainstay of the mechanistic theory. That the magnitude of bodies is relative to their motion and varies with the latter is a truth which is not compatible with the view that motion is nothing but change of place—that is to say with a mere predicament of what must otherwise be conceived as an invariant term in a series of varying relations. Motion must now be reckoned among the factors upon which the quantitative identity of the physically real depends, and the physically real must in this aspect of measurability be conceived as a function of its own vicissitudes. These vicissitudes thereby acquire a certain definitory force. So far then as measurability (an eminently *physical* property) is concerned, we must not think of bodies as independent and self-determined,[45] nor of their movements as irrelevant to their identity. The substitution of a functional for a purely conjunctive relation in the theory of moving bodies has rendered the expression "matter *in* motion," if understood in one sense, scientifically obsolete; if understood in another, it has transformed the meaning of the phrase in accordance with a new insight into the facts. It should be noted, moreover, that if the inclusion of motion among the determinants of body compels us to revise

---

[45] Of course this statement in no way affects their independence of subjective conditions.

our ideas of the body, it has a similar effect upon our ideas of motion. The theory of relativity provides a new context of interpretation for the concepts of both. The total effect is to convert a constant into a variable, and to invest a variable with the significance of an ontological principle.

(c) Modern Atomic Theory

38. Motion, however, as we have seen, is at the best a superficial manifestation of something much more fundamental than itself—the energy of which the displacement of macroscopic bodies in space is only one among many phenomena. It is to this concept that we must now direct our attention. The successive steps in the process of thought which has completely revolutionized our view of the physical world have to do mainly with energy.

The starting-point is the notion of matter itself, which, as we have seen, is definable as a compact, inert, space-filling substance. What is scientifically significant in this is the fact that it admits of treatment in terms of quantity. Now the quantity of matter is its *mass*. Mass, therefore, may be taken as the definitory property of matter, as conceived by science. This brings us to the first step in the transformation of the concept. For scientific research has proved that mass and energy are identical. Thus the entity which first revealed itself as a principle of motion has come to be recognized as the reality behind the apparent inertness and passivity of the material form of being.

39. The next step involves a highly important change of viewpoint—no less than the provision of a new context for the conception of energy. For certain purposes it is customary to think of energy as it was conceived when the science of physics was still in the mechanistic phase of its development. The characteristic phenomenon is the movement of bodies; and the factors involved are space, time, mass, force, velocity and acceleration. It is the business of physics to show how these factors are coordinated in the explanation of movement. We know, for example, from experimental evidence, that acceleration may serve as a measure of the force involved, that velocity may be defined (in the formula $v = at$) as the product of acceleration and time, and that the distance traversed is proportional to the square of the time which the movement occupies. But the fact behind all the equations by which

these truths are expressed is merely the fact that a measurable content of space, a fixed mass, is found to occupy successive spatial positions at successive moments, under conditions which are constant for all events of this description. The significance of the time factor is that of a *condition* and no more. That is to say, when this factor occurs in an equation, what is meant is that it takes so and so many units of time for a certain spatial movement to complete itself—or (since movement and energy are measurable in terms of one another) for a certain amount of energy to be expended in the "work" represented by the movement. The time-measure is one thing, the quantity of movement or of energy measured by it is another; and the former contributes nothing to the *existence* of the latter, any more than a footrule contributes to the *existence* of the table which it tells us is five feet in length. The change of viewpoint to which I have referred as so important involves a new interpretation both of time and of energy through the discovery of a new relation between the two.

40. As originally introduced into physics, the concept of energy is really a generalization of all the changes to which bodies are liable as they pass from a state of rest to a state of motion and back again. The point of the concept is that the phenomenon of motion cannot be treated, as it was by Descartes (and in a sense by Newton[46]), as a thing by itself, but must, as Leibniz showed, be integrated with the phenomenon of rest. Energy is a quantity which requires for its expression an initial synthesis of the two opposing predicaments of body. Its identity is maintained and revealed alike in the kinetic and in the potential form, and the unit in terms of which it is measured (the erg or the foot-pound) is an ideal quantity which we posit *as there* whether or not it is manifesting itself in any observable change in the phenomenal manifold.[47] So conceived, it cannot be considered to *exist* as its manifestations exist. It is not, like them, an event in time, but merely a measure. What obviously exists is either body in motion or body at rest. And yet it is impossible to conceive of energy even in this phase of the conception, as definitely non-existent. In so far as it is identical with

---

[46] In his doctrine of the conservation of motion.

[47] Thus the erg is definable by reference to the dyne, as "the work done when a body acted upon by a force of one dyne moves through a centimetre in the direction of the force" (Watson, *A Text-Book of Physics*, 8th ed., 1929, p. 80); but the dyne is a mere *capacity* to produce a velocity of one centimeter per second in a mass of one gram.

mass, and mass is, physically speaking, the essence of body, the existence which we attribute to body must accrue to energy as well.

41. The situation is confused, and what is needed to put it right is clearly nothing more nor less than a synthesis of energy and duration. That is, the temporal factor must not be treated as extraneous to the spatial, but must be read into the concept of energy as a guarantee of existence. In brief, energy must be multiplied by time. This latest step has actually been rendered necessary as a result, not of such theoretical considerations as I have advanced, but of the new light thrown upon the nature of the physically real by the discovery of the ultra-atomic constituents of the latter. The phases in the process are once more two in number.

Bohr's Atom and Subsequent Advances Upon It

42. The first of these is represented by Bohr's theory of the atom, worked out in relation to the atom of hydrogen.[48] Of this theory the general features are well known. The hydrogen atom consists of one positive charge of electricity, the proton, which in this instance constitutes the nucleus, and one negative charge, the electron. The latter moves round the former in accordance with Coulomb's law of electric force. In the case of the other elements the structure of the atom is more complex, the nucleus consisting of several positive charges along with uncharged particles (neutrons) and a number of circulating electrons equal to the number of positive charges. So far the atom resembles a microscopic planetary system composed of a sun and its attendant satellites. It differs from such a system in certain peculiarities which mark the behaviour of the electrons in their orbits.

What happens is as follows. The energy of the atom may be augmented or diminished by the absorption or emission of wave-energy in the form of light. This means that radiation from or to the atom has the effect of disorganizing and reorganizing the latter. When radiation thus is absorbed or emitted, the electron "jumps" from one orbit to another. At this point Bohr's theory incorporates the results of Planck's discovery that radiant energy changes by discrete amounts. The different orbits in which, under the condition stated, the electrons may revolve represent a higher and a lower degree of energy, but in every case a degree that is fixed and

[48] In what follows I am indebted for such detail as I have thought fit to introduce chiefly to Eddington's *Nature of the Physical World*, Chaps. IX and X.

uniform, the "h-quantity" $= 6.55.10^{-27}$ erg-seconds. It is only when the increase or decrease has reached the h-quantity that the change of orbit takes place, and it does so instantaneously and without any intermediate process of transition. The electron, therefore, must not be thought of as passing continuously by spiral motion from one orbit to another, while the energy of the atom increases or decreases by continuous gradations. On the contrary the electron suddenly disappears from one orbit and reappears in another without passing through the intervening space at all. Clearly Bohr's conception of the atom as a tiny but picturable planetary system was quite inadequate to the expression of such behaviour. In Eddington's words: "The older quantum theory which treated the electron as a particle succeeded up to a certain point. But it never got so far as to formulate a system of laws of motion which would cover the jumps of the electron from one orbit to another. It was a collection of strange empirical rules rather than a systematic theory."[49]

43. In consequence of this, Bohr's model, which was the product of an incompletely successful attempt to unite quantum facts with the supposed atomic structure of the physically real, had to give place to a more highly coordinated system of notions, and one from which the last vestiges of the atom, as originally conceived, were destined to disappear. Schrödinger's hypothesis is one of several which, since the year 1925, have been devised as a solution to the difficulties in which Bohr's theory had become involved. The difference between the two points of view might be expressed by saying that Bohr attempted to square the quantum principle with the concept of the atom, whereas Schrödinger tried to construct a concept of the physically real which would square with the quantum principle. The result is wave mechanics.

The significance of the quantum theory in this application, and from the point of view of our problem, is to be found in the concretion of time and energy. As a result of this, the factor which so far has appeared as an extraneous condition of existence, a mere circumstance and a measure, now assumes the character of a component.[50] Being reveals itself in definitely identifiable parcels,

[49] *New Pathways in Science*, p. 43.

[50] To repeat a former analogy, the time factor is no longer applied to a quantity of energy as a footrule is applied to a spatial object. The relation is rather like that be-

definable by reference to a unit of duration. The erg yields its place to the erg-second, and the concept of energy to the concept of "action."[51] Action is the equivalent, in a four-dimensional space-time manifold, of what we call "energy" in the three-dimensional world of space. It is the amount of energy which occupies a volume of time, when the relation between the two is conceived as con-stitutive of each.[52] The h-quantity gained or lost when the electron jumps an orbit is a fixed amount of *action* measurable in terms of this unit. According to Schrödinger the physical world consists of action distributing and redistributing itself, in accordance with its four-dimensional character, in this medium. The atoms are sys-tems of the constituent events. They occur in the so-called sub-aether, which, I presume, is a hypothetical medium assumed for the events of which the atoms are themselves composed.[53] The sub-aether is a vibratory system of which the ripples or oscillations take place at a rate a million times faster than that of light. When a large number of these waves converge to constitute a disturbed area, the result is what the older physics called a particle.

44. The reinterpretation of the latter in terms of action makes it possible to understand how the electron can jump an orbit without passing through the intervening space. The difference between moving in one orbit and moving in another is merely that between two distributions of the action which fills the four-dimensional manifold and constitutes the sub-aether. In this way the idea of material particles moving from one place to another in a stated time is superseded by that of variations in a vibratory medium. That is to say, what was a centre of disturbance becomes relatively quiescent, and a quiescent centre becomes disturbed. From these conceptions we gather that the identity of the atom is that of an

---

tween a man's life and its duration. The duration is not one thing, the life another. Apart from time life is nothing at all. Hence the *units* of existence, for example, years, are to be construed as actual blocks of *existence*.

[51] The term is most unhappily chosen. In the purely physical world there is nothing to which the name of "action" can be appropriately annexed. Action implies an agent, and the only agents known to us are subjective systems.

[52] *vid.* Eddington, *The Nature of the Physical World*, pp. 179-80.

[53] The necessity of the concept is matter of controversy. So far as I can make out, the use of the term "aether" is of some value as calling attention to those aspects of space which come into view when space and time are integrated in the ways I have noticed. *vid.* Eddington, *New Pathways*, p. 39. Aether has been defined as "space endowed with certain properties," and as "the subject of the verb to undulate." *vid.* C. S. Darwin, *The New Conceptions of Matter*, p. 23.

electrically active area of space-time defining itself against other areas which are also electrically active, but in different degrees. In other words, the atom is a system of events, including the behaviour of the electron in each of its possible orbits and its behaviour in passing from orbit to orbit in accordance with "the *h*-rule." Within this system we distinguish the electrical charges, positive and negative, from one another, as well as from the space between them. This space, however, must be understood in a peculiar sense. It cannot rightly be described as empty. Of course if we abstract the electrons and protons in thought from their mutual relations and from the sphere of their activity, what remains is merely space and time. But in this case space and time have no existence, and space-time itself becomes a mere abstraction. What really exists is a system of forces whose variable interplay is interpretable in terms of spatio-temporal relations. These relations are an integral part of the system itself. They enter constitutively into the terms, that is, the protons and electrons; and the latter, which are relative to one another, thus spread themselves over the whole of the area affected.

45. The four-dimensional manifold and the events which are its content are of course not picturable in three-dimensional imagery. Yet it is permissible to draw upon the latter for analogies. For example, the relation of the atom, as originally conceived, to the four-dimensional events into which it has been resolved is like the relation of a sea-wave as seen by the eye to the actual event as known to the physicist. When you stand upon a breakwater and watch the incoming billows, as they define themselves against the sea-wall opposite, the phenomenon which presents itself for inspection is that of a volume of water moving onwards in a horizontal direction. But the particles of which these billows consist do not participate in the translatory movement, literally speaking, as we know, but vibrate at right angles to the direction in which the waves are travelling.[54] Thus a *movement* is propagated, say, from a point *a* to a point *b*, although no particle actually passes from the one point to the other. In the same way, but with variations due to the four-dimensional character of the event, when the quantum has been reached by radiation to or from the atom, and a consequent rearrangement of four-dimensional energy occurs, the event may be

[54] Watson, *Text-Book*, p. 346.

described as the displacement of an electron from one orbit to another, although nothing has actually been transported out of the first and deposited in the second.

The Resulting Predicament of Physics—That Nothing Physical Remains. This View Unwarranted

46. Before proceeding to sum up on the nature of the physically real as defined in terms of wave mechanics, I must revert to a point on which I have already dwelt.[55] Eddington insists that in passing from Bohr's model of the atom to wave mechanics, we have passed from a view which represents the extreme limit of physical analysis to a view from which all traces of what we can with any degree of significance describe as physical have disappeared. "The nearest we have got to objective reality is the world of protons and electrons; that is to say, such a world corresponds to the level of conception which physics had reached before it was forced to deviate towards a different aim. Between the universe of our experience and the universe of objective reality probability interposes like a smoke screen."[56] This is the predicament of physics to which I have repeatedly referred.

47. The grounds for Eddington's conclusion are two in number. (a) Wave mechanics knows nothing of individual electrons, or indeed of individual waves of radiation, but only of statistical averages; and (b) the most the physicist can assert is that under certain conditions there is a probability that an electron will be present.[57]

Now granted that this is a true account of the matter, the inference to be drawn from it is not that in the last analysis the physical has disappeared from the sphere of truth that is open to the physicist, but only that in the present state of scientific knowledge there are certain truths which do not reveal themselves except in the form of statistical averages and probabilities. In either case the reference in the end is necessarily to individual events, even if these events do not declare themselves individually. That "in the most

[55] Chap. III, Appendix A, and beginning of the present chapter.

[56] *New Pathways*, p. 46.

[57] A further complication arises over Heisenberg's principle of indeterminacy. But this does not really affect the main issue. If it is the case that at any particular moment only half the factors involved in a physical process are accurately determinable, this is a circumstance that seriously affects the *interpretation*, but does not prejudice the *existence* of a physical mode of being.

modern theories of physics probability seems to have replaced aether as the nominative of the verb to undulate" is surely a meaningless pronouncement.[58] If statements of probability have anything to do with an actually existing world, the probability in question must appear as a predicate and not as a subject of assertion. This is implied in Eddington's own language. ". . . Numerical probability is not an uncertainty; it is an ordinary physical datum —the frequency of a certain characteristic in a class."[59] The frequency of a characteristic is surely an adjectival conception which presupposes the class as a sustaining substantive. Furthermore it is not even to the class as such, but to the individual instance that the concept of *probability*, strictly speaking, applies. What applies to the class is the statistical average. Probability is a notion that arises when we express our knowledge of a group in terms appropriate to the constituent members. Thus, to take one of Eddington's happy illustrations, if "the class of all human births" is characterized by the property of being "equally frequent on all days of the week," "the probability that Mussolini was born on a Friday is 1/7."[60] That is clearly a truth about the birth of Mussolini, an individual event, and not about the class to which the event belongs; and if it is the case that the truth in question rests upon the prior assumption of a class, it is no less so that the recognition of the class presupposes the existence of its individual constituents. These are not all known to us, but if no single instance were known, we should have no grounds for assuming that such a class exists, and no statistical knowledge of the latter. Behind this knowledge stands the postulate of being; and being implies the existence of individual instances. It is to these (whether, individually speaking, they are known or not) that the notion of probability, as distinct from that of statistical averages, has reference.

48. It may be said that the probabilities of wave mechanics differ from other instances of probability in that here no individual undulation in space-time is independently knowable, and that for

[58] Eddington, *op. cit.*, p. 110. A good example of the liberties which a scientific writer permits himself to take with language is to be found in the passage from Professor Darwin's book to which I have already referred (note 53), where the author, having described the aether as "the *subject* of the verb to undulate," goes on to remark that this same aether "merely is a convenient noun to *describe* the properties of space," and that "it is often a convenient *grammatical construction* to have." (Italics mine.)

[59] *op. cit.*, pp. 115-16.

[60] *op. cit.*, p. 117.

this reason we have no means of identifying the entities with which the theory deals. This is of course a difficulty; but there is nothing new and unprecedented about it. From the day when Dalton in his *New System of Chemistry* revived the atomic theory with the announcement that "the ultimate particles of all homogeneous bodies are perfectly alike in weight,"[61] the chemist has been working not with individual atoms, but with vast aggregations of these in all sorts of complex combinations. In relation to these the atom may be said to define itself (upon circumstantial evidence) as the hypothetical unit—the chemically homogeneous and self-identical entity—which furnishes a substantival basis, a "nominative," to the statistical assertions which constitute the science of chemistry. In like manner, and with equal cogency, the physicist, reasoning back from the truths (if indeed they are such) of wave mechanics, may define the physically real as the system of actual events which we must assume if his equations are to have anything more than a purely logical significance. That these events are not severally identifiable is of no more significance than the fact that the chemist, even when he is said to "isolate" the atom of helium, is dealing not with a particular atom, but with a volume of this element. What is of real importance is that the postulate of being should not be lost sight of. If there is no evidence, circumstantial or otherwise, that anything exists corresponding to the equations of wave mechanics, that can only be construed as a reflection upon the theory itself. As a matter of fact the presumption is all in the opposite direction. For the first step in the newer physics has been to secure existence in incorporating the time factor (the universal condition of *being*), along with the spatial, in the concept of the physically real. The recognition of the quantum as an empirically verifiable and exactly measurable concretion of "action" must be placed in the balance, as a well authenticated revelation of the physical, against the theoretical and speculative character of wave mechanics.

Since All That Exists Is Temporal, the Spatial Can Only Exist if It Is Systematic

49. My general conclusion is as follows. In the absence of time, it is impossible to assign existence to space; in the absence of space,

---

[61] T. M. Lowry, *Historical Introduction to Chemistry*, p. 293.

it is impossible to assign a physical character to events in time. The significance of the spatial factor is that of a differentia. The temporal represents the generic aspect of existence. Where these two come together, as they do when energy is multiplied by time, the resulting concept is that of a physical mode of being. We may therefore with confidence assume the physical mode whenever the time factor, which is the guarantee of existence, is found co-ordinated with a spatial factor in the unity of an event. Such events occur independently of our consciousness, but not of one another. Between them, and between their constituents, there exists a functional relation. Hence they constitute systems, and perhaps in the end a single comprehensive system. It is from this point of view that their identity, and with it their existence, comes out most unmistakably.

The concept of system, in this connection, must not be regarded as a mere addendum or afterthought, inserted upon empirical grounds. On the contrary, it supplies the condition upon which alone the postulate of being authenticates itself in the realm of the physical, as now defined. To state the position briefly, system (or the unity which system implies) is the one thing needed to give the actuality of existence to events in space-time.

50. The point is this. Whatever *exists* must have *duration*. That is to say, it must retain its identity throughout a sequence of moments; and we must be able to say of it that it is one and the same in each of its successive phases. This implies that *successiveness* must be subordinated to *persistence* in a time-conditioned existence. The ontological status of selfhood, which we have considered at length, rests upon an exceptionally sustained application of this principle. We have seen reason to reject the notion of physical *selves*; but the recognition of physical *systems* is inseparably bound up with the recognition of duration as a condition of being. In the absence of system, duration disappears in mere succession, and time becomes nothing but change or transition. Now transition, as Heraclitus realized, is not interpretable in terms of being, but only of becoming; and a world of pure becoming is a world in which nothing *is*. To escape the implications of such a view recourse has been had to various devices of thought, all of them designed to restore the element of permanence.

51. These fall into two classes. The first includes the λόγος of Heraclitus himself, the Platonic Forms, and, in recent times, the

"essences" of Santayana and the "eternal objects" of Whitehead. In each case the permanent is the timeless, and the result is an impossible dichotomy of being and existence—on the one hand a ceaseless torrent of events, on the other a world of frozen essences. The second class is represented by the various types of mechanism, and particularly by the atomic theory in its earlier form. Here the attempt is made to provide for the element of permanence by separating the time factor from the content of space. Matter is the intrinsically unchanging: the atoms are its eternally self-identical units. Events in time make no real difference to the latter. But the conception of events that make no difference has proved quite inadequate as an expression of the nature of chemical combination. The identity of the atom does not define itself *against* its own predicaments. What *happens* to the unit of matter is something that must be taken into account in the attempt to identify the nature of that which gives its content to the spatial world.

The Possibility of Time-Conditioned Systems

52. From every point of view we are driven to the conclusion that the permanent cannot be identified with the non-temporal, whether in the form of space or of timelessness.* We must consequently seek it in the time-conditioned. The theoretical requirements of the case will obviously be met if the contents of any manifold, into which time enters as a component, can be shown not only to differentiate themselves, but also *to be thereby integrated*, in respect of their temporal character. This condition is fulfilled in so far as events and the constituents of events are functionally related and so organized together into systems. A detailed exposition of the subject calls for a special inquiry into the nature of time. Without such an inquiry, our treatment of the physical cannot be considered complete.

53. This latest phase of the argument is fraught with the possibility of serious consequences. Our attempt to understand the nature of the physical world has been based upon the assumption that the subject-matter can best be viewed in a context supplied by man's scientific knowledge of it. Now we are about to view the same subject-matter in a context supplied by the problem of time —that is to say, of the universal condition of existence. The pos-

[*I may again be permitted the remark that in the author's view, once we see the real nature of time we shall be under no temptation to discard it.—Ed.]

sibility for which we must be prepared is that the new procedure may bring to light aspects of the physical which are beyond the purview of the exact sciences. From the standpoint of the latter, the independence of this mode of being is axiomatic, and I have been content to accept the assumption without question. No attempt has been made to define the concept of independence except in so far as the latter has been taken to mean that the presence of a human consciousness in no way affects the existence of the unmistakably physical. Of course it is unlikely that we shall have occasion to abandon or to modify a view so abundantly confirmed by experience. The question is whether the unqualified admission of independence in this sense may be interpreted as implying that, absolutely speaking, and in every possible context, the physical can be conceived as something which requires no reference to any other mode of being.*

[*Though independence is stressed as the fundamental characteristic of the physical, the author does not seem to think the possibility is thereby ruled out, that that very independence is mind-conferred. The position seems to require some doctrine of creation; and this he in fact admitted and defended.

N.B. At this point in the MS., there followed a long discussion on time, unfortunately too incomplete for publication.]—Ed.

APPENDIX (*See note* 8, *page* 298)

The Existence of Space

The nihilistic tendency to which I have repeatedly drawn attention as implicit in the positivistic thinking of recent times has its repercussions in the doctrine of space. Thus, to quote from a very acute work written from this point of view: ". . . The truth surely is (to put it paradoxically) that there is no such thing as Space, but only *spatial objects*—that is, objects extended, standing in various relations of distance, direction and size to one another, and able to move in various ways. In other words, 'Space' is what Cambridge philosophers call an incomplete symbol: it is not the name of anything, but stands only for a set of facts about things." H. H. Price, *Perception*, 1932, p. 109. To this I should reply that if the "facts about things" are to be taken, in the strict sense, as timeless truths, then assuredly they have no existence; but if the "things" referred to are time-conditioned entities, as is implied in what is said about their being able to move, then the "facts" about them have reference to properties and relations of actual existents; and if the properties and relations have no existence, it cannot be true that they are "facts about things." It seems necessary, therefore, to assume that spatial characters exist. But they cannot do so without at the same time presupposing a comprehensive (and in the end an all-comprehensive) system of functionally-related spatial characters. This system is what is meant by Space.

PART II

THE NOTES FOR THE VANUXEM LECTURES

Part II

THE NOTES FOR THE VANUXEM LECTURES

CHAPTER IX

On Professor Santayana and Professor Whitehead*

1. Recapitulated.

(a) By "function" we are to understand a type of connection between entities which stand related as determinant and determined.†

(b) By "system" I mean a whole of functionally related elements.‡

(c) Applying these abstract concepts to the actual world of our experience, I hope to show that there exist only two types of system—the physical and the spiritual.

Each of these is ultimate, aboriginal, irreducible. Nothing ever passes from the spiritual mode of being to the physical or vice versa. Nothing that begins as a movement in space ever ends as a

[*The five chapters comprising Part II (numbered IX to XIII inclusive) contain the lectures as Dr. Bowman spoke them, so far as they survive in writing. Six were given. Five out of the six—i.e. all except lecture number one—do so survive, in varying degrees of fulness. And after much careful consideration of alternative ways of treating the material, the view was arrived at that the only method perfectly fair to both reader and writer would be to print the notes, in all possible faithfulness, exactly as they stood. This has accordingly been done, excepting only that in Chapter XIII I have felt compelled to leave out one allusion appropriate only to the time and the occasion; and that in one or two other places I have ventured to "graduate" abruptnesses of expression as I am sure the author would have wished.

In all but the last chapter of this Part, the numbering of the sections is the author's. It will be observed that some of these sections consist of mere headings. My excuse for printing them so is, again, necessity. To amplify them seemed presumptuous, while to omit them was to spoil what followed. Their omission would have completely dispersed that peculiar aroma of the lecture-room, which their retention seems somehow to preserve. And to preserve this was essential, it seemed to me, to this particular Part. For, as will be seen, the first portion of it (Chapters IX, X and XI) is a condensation for lecture purposes of the preceding Chapters I to VIII; while the remaining portion is a similar "platform" condensation of a further development of the author's thought which he did not have the opportunity to elaborate as he would have done, no doubt, in the same way.

No notes of the first spoken lecture exist. But the "recapitulated" first section above, indicates clearly that it covered almost the ground of our Introduction and Chapter I. —Ed.]

[†See pp. 17ff.—Ed.]
[‡ibid.—Ed.]

state of consciousness. And nothing that begins as *experience* of a conscious subject ever ends as a physical process.*

(d) And yet these two alternative modes of being, distinct and metaphysically irresolvable as they are, are not unrelated. Between them they generate a whole universe of possibilities and meanings. In particular, the world of values has its origin in the mutual interplay of the physical and the spiritual. This world has many provinces. To each of these I give the title of domain. Thus there will be a domain of goodness in each of the many senses of that term, a domain of beauty, of utility, of charm and sanctity.†

Pseudo-Monism in Contemporary Speculation

2. Now this whole structure of thought stands or falls with the conception of the spiritual as an order of reality, indisputable, autonomous and independent.

But the whole trend of modern thought is away from any such conception. Take, e.g.,

(a) Dewey's conception of experience—as a mere predicament of bodily existence: the soul is nothing but the bodily behaviour viewed in a special context. "The distinction between physical, psycho-physical and mental is one of levels of increasing complexity and intimacy of interaction among natural events. In the hyphenated phrase body-mind, 'body' designates the continued and conserved, the registered and cumulative operation of factors continuous with the rest of nature, inanimate as well as animate; while 'mind' designates the characters and consequences which are differential, indicative of features which emerge when 'body' is engaged in a wider, more complex and interdependent situation."

(b) Mind as emergent—Lloyd Morgan and Alexander. Mentality as a quality. Distinction between "the Deity"—substantival—and "Deity."

(c) Hatred of mind—D. H. Lawrence.

(d) Fear of mind. Whitehead's *Process and Reality*. Here he is never tired of warning us against the assumption that consciousness is a necessary ingredient in situations where we can hardly fail to take it for granted. He repudiates "the assumption that the basic elements of experience are to be described in terms of one or

[*See Chap. I, 14-19, pp. 31*ff*.—Ed.]
[†cf. pp. 349*ff*.—Ed.]

all of the three ingredients, consciousness, thought, sense-perception. . . . According to the philosophy of organism these three components are unessential elements in experience, either physical or mental."

(e) Consciousness as an iridescent film on the surface of bodily life. For me, consciousness is *not* a surface phenomenon but a substantial reality, with height and depth as well as length and breadth.

3. Modern philosophy and its leaning toward naturalism. Monism the motive.*

4. The modern position. It makes no struggle to reconcile the dual opposites. The opposition is simply obscured. The modern philosopher dismisses mind by ignoring it.

5. Santayana and Whitehead.
(a) Difference in their starting points—Santayana begins as a sceptic while Whitehead is constructive throughout.
(b) Identity in their conclusions.

Substances and Essences in Santayana's Thought

6. Santayana.
(a) Cartesian doubt. Santayana goes beyond the "cogito." The only "thinking" we can catch is a remembered thinking; and memory is deceptive.† He ends in a scepticism which is absolute and unrelieved.
(b) He falls back on faith. The drive of nature in us is towards ends that are predetermined by our heredity and by the physical conditions of existence. Thus, we believe in substance, not because the concept approves itself to our reason, but because, being the kind of animals we are, we cannot help it. Substance *strikes us irresistibly*, in the very process whereby we adjust ourselves, blindly but inevitably, to the world around us. The guarantee of substance is a certain "animal watchfulness," promoted by nature to guard the vital interests of the organism. From the standpoint of knowledge and the critic of knowledge "belief in substance is the most irrational, animal and primitive of beliefs; it is the voice of

[*cf., e.g. Chap. II, 1-4, pp. 51*ff*. and Chap. V, 1, p. 177.—Ed.]
[†cf. Chap. VII, 15-16, pp. 269*ff*.—Ed.]

hunger";[1] and the first revelation of it is in the appetitions and aversions of the animal ego. What that ego discovers of *self* or of *other*, assumes in the first instance the form of materiality; and the belief in the substance so generated is confirmed by the findings of a more developed experience—"The substance in which I am proposing to believe is not metaphysical but physical substance. It is the varied stuff of the world which I meet in action—the wood of this tree I am felling, the wind that is stirring its branches, the flesh and bones of the man who is jumping out of the way. Belief in substance is not imported into animal perception by language or by philosophy, but is the soul of animal perception from the beginning, and the perpetual deliverance of animal experience."[2] Of course, our first crude apprehension of it must be rectified and refined by a more adequate descriptive identification of its forms. But this process leads merely to an exacter knowledge of its constituents, and these, as they disclose themselves, appear with all the characteristic properties of substance.

To sum up, substances are "objects of belief posited in action," and as such they are to be distinguished from everything that does not prompt to action or challenge to belief. This brings me to the second fundamental conception in Santayana's philosophy—the conception of essences.

It will be remembered that animal faith is a reaction against *intellectual scepticism*. But it is not the only possible reaction. There is another, which Santayana describes as "retreating to the immediate"—that is to say, accepting the given at its face value and as it appeals to our rudimentary sensibilities, but without adding anything in the way of mental comment, whether affirmation or negation. In this, scepticism transcends itself and comes to rest in a vacancy of spiritual acquiescence. The indispensable condition is that the retreat to the immediate shall not stop until it has removed all interpretative accretions from the bare deliverances of experience. When this point is reached what remains over is a pure intuitable content, an essence.*

(c) Dualism. (i) Nature as flux. (ii) The realm of essences as eternal. Essences cannot be the source of anything. Nothing comes

[1] *S.A.*, pp. 190-1.
[2] *S.A.*, p. 201. [cf. Chap. II, 7*ff*., pp. 57*ff*.—Ed.]
[*cf. Chap. II, 9*ff*., pp. 60*ff*.—Ed.]

to be because the essences are brought to bear upon the plastic stuff of nature as a force is brought to bear upon a yielding mass.*

(d) Turning now from the objective realms of nature and of essence to the inner life of spirit, we find in Santayana a superb illustration of the tendency to which I have referred—the tendency to deny all substantial reality to spiritual being. This tendency assumes two forms. On the one hand spirit is immersed in the flux of nature; on the other, it is made to play like a phosphorescent sheen upon the surface of events.†

[*cf. *ibid.*, 10 (e), p. 63—Ed.]
[†cf. *ibid.*, 16*ff.*, pp. 70*ff.*—Ed.]

CHAPTER X

ON THE SPIRITUAL AND THE PHYSICAL

The Meaning of Spirit

1. Naturalism, which is an attempt to escape from the duality of nature and spirit, only results in rendering dualism incurable. Reducing nature and spirit to nature alone, the latter breaks out into a torrent of events on the one hand and a universe of frozen essences or eternal objects on the other. Thus arises a new duality.

2. Proposal to try duality of spiritual and physical.* Note that this does not imply dualism. No reason why reality should not include two irreducible modes of being without sacrifice of coherence.

3. Spirit.† The spiritual is the subjective, the mental, the personal. Spirit is a subjective system—subjectivity being the definitory concept.

4. What is subjectivity? The definitory concept is experience:‡ a person is a *system of experience.*

5. What is experience? It defines itself by reference to consciousness. It is the kind of system to which conscious states or processes belong.

6. What is consciousness? It is indefinable.

7. Consciousness and experience. These are not synonymous. Experience includes the unconscious. A problem is to distinguish unconscious states of a subjective system from those of a physical entity. They are not alike. Dewey is wrong when he remarks that a stick or a stone, because it exists and undergoes changes, has experiences. Whitehead is wrong also, who maintains that consciousness, thought, sense-perception are unessential elements in experience, and speaks of a *physical* as well as a *mental* form of experience. No experience is physical. All unconscious states of experience are mental. The point is that the unconscious states of

[*cf. e.g. Chap. II, 14*ff*., pp. 67*ff*.—Ed.]
[†cf. Chap. v, 8*ff*., pp. 181*ff*., and 14*ff*., pp. 189*ff*.—Ed.]
[‡cf. *ibid*., 26*ff*., pp. 199*ff*.—Ed.]

a spiritual being belong to the same system to which conscious states belong.*

The Objective, Selfhood, Personality†

8. Subjective and objective. The subjective is a mode of being. The objective is a relation. This is a reversal of ordinary usage of the terms.‡

9. Varieties of the objective§

(1) Such entities as exist subjectively.

(2) Such as are non-subjective, yet are subjectively conditioned; for example, the timeless truths of mathematics, contents of noun clauses, sum of a series such as $0 + 1 + 2 + 3 + 4 \ldots$

(3) The non-mental which exists independently—the physical.

(4) Things.

10. Summing up, there are three types of entity, (a) the subjective, (b) the objective that exists independently of its subjective conditions, and (c) the objective which is subjectively conditioned.

11. Certain distinctions remain. Self and selfhood.

(a) Definition. A self is a system defined by reference to its own internal structure.°

(b) There are only *subjective* selves. Contrast things, crystals.¶

(c) Reason for this: all consciousness is self-consciousness. In the very act whereby we realize what it is to have an object of experience, we experience what it is to be a subject.ᐃ The self-consciousness which precedes the possibility of introspection.

(d) Introspective self-consciousness, (1) primary, and (2) secondary.⊙

12. (e) The concept "person" and the concept "man."⁺

[*See the diagram in Appendix D to Chap. VI, above.—Ed.]
[†cf. Chap. VI, 9*ff*., pp. 224*ff*., and Chap. VI, 20*ff*., pp. 232*ff*.—Ed.]
[‡cf. Chap. VI, 7*ff*., pp. 223*ff*.—Ed.]
[§cf. *ibid.*, 11*ff*., pp. 226*ff*. Note that (1) and (3) are, ontologically, entirely independent of their objectivity, (2) and (4) not so. For the varieties of (2), and on (4) see *ibid.*, 16*ff*., pp. 229*ff*.—Ed.]
[°cf. *ibid.*, 20*f*., pp. 232*ff*., and 22*ff*., pp. 236*ff*.—Ed.]
[¶cf. *ibid.*, 28*ff*., pp. 241*ff*.—Ed.]
[ᐃcf. Chap. VII, 1*ff*., pp. 225*ff*.—Ed.]
[⊙cf. *ibid.*, 5*ff*., pp. 259*ff*., and 11*ff*., pp. 265*ff*.—Ed.]
[⁺cf., e.g. Chap. V, 8*f*., pp. 181*ff*.—Ed.]

CHAPTER XI

On the Physical, the Natural and the Spiritual

The Purely Physical*

1. The physical viewed in the light of what we know as to the structure of the atom.
Two phases of the theory.
(a) Bohr's model—not to be taken literally—and the conception of the atom as a planetary system, illustrated by reference to the hydrogen atom.
(b) Schrödinger's development.

2. Bohr's model. The electron moves in a circle or ellipse round the proton in accordance with Coulomb's law of electric force. The atom resembles a planetary system consisting of one sun and its satellite, but it differs from such a system in certain properties in the behaviour of the electron. The latter may assume more than one orbit, and the laws which determine the interorbital movement have no counterpart in stellar physics.

3. Jumping an orbit, as redistribution of the four-dimensional energy called "action" in a field of such energy. The paradoxical character of this may be mitigated by thinking of the way in which the horizontal movement of a wave may be propagated by a vertical movement of its constituent particles. The particles are displaced vertically.

The World of Perception and the World of Physics†

4. The physical and the perceptual. Whitehead and the problem of bifurcation. Eddington and the same problem, *vid.* his introduction to *The Nature of the Physical World*.

5. Conclusions reached so far.
(a) There are two mutually independent modes of reality, the spiritual and the physical. Each of these occurs in the form of a closed system.
(b) This conclusion is not accepted by Naturalism. It appears to end in dualism. In endeavouring to avoid the latter conclusion,

[*cf. Chap. viii.—Ed.]
[†cf., e.g. Chap. vi, App. A., p. 250.—Ed.]

Naturalism absorbs the spiritual into the physical. The result is a new dualism which breaks out within the physical itself. My contention, that the only way to avoid this is a frank acceptance of the fundamental duality with which I begin.

(c) The spiritual and the physical are not unrelated. My purpose is to explore the relations between the two; and it is my hope that by so doing we shall reach a position from which reality, in spite of the initial oppositeness of the natural and the spiritual, will reveal itself as a coherent whole.

6. Compare the titles of the last lecture and the present. (1) The spiritual and the physical. (2) The physical, the natural and the spiritual. Observe, a difference is implied between the natural and the physical.

(a) The physical is the real in that aspect which remains when every vestige of the spiritual has been withdrawn—a vibratory system of space-time. In a sense this is an abstraction, but it is not on that account a mere fiction. It is not non-existent. It exists as a smile exists on a face.

(b) The natural is the physical viewed in a perspective supplied by the spiritual mode of being.

My purpose today is to supply the perspective in question, to advance from the physical to the natural, from what is relatively abstract to what is relatively concrete.

7. The starting-point is the duality of the physical and the natural worlds. The two worlds are the subject of the amusing contrast which Eddington draws in the Introduction to his Gifford Lectures on *The Nature of the Physical World*.

The Identity of the Perceptual Object (A) as Perceptual

8. I shall now endeavour to show that the two worlds of Eddington dissolve into one world as soon as the light of spirit, which is conscious experience, is brought to bear upon them. My method will be to begin with the ordinary world of perceptual experience, and enquire whether, by a series of steps, under conditions which admit of exact statement, the perceptual world does not dissolve into the world of mathematical physics—in other words, whether the purely physical world be not a function of the perceptual, and the perceptual world a function of the physical.

(a) The first point is to discover how the identity of an object of perception is determined. The relevant considerations may be summarized as follows:

(i) Such an object is not to be identified with its perceptual manifestations, whether taken individually or in conjunction. For example, gold is not definable as "yellow," nor yet as "yellow + hard + heavy + soluble in aqua regia. . . ," etc.

(ii) On the other hand these perceptual manifestations are essential qualities of gold, in the sense that if under certain conditions, they failed to make their appearance, gold would not be what it is. They must, therefore, be included in any concept of gold that aims at completeness.

(iii) The object that possesses the qualities is not to be defined as an unknown substratum (Locke) nor as a logical construction (Russell). If the qualities are *its* qualities, they are its *manifestations*, and it is so far knowable through them. If they are qualities *of the object*, the object *is presupposed* in its qualities, and cannot be conceived as a mere abstractum of thought. The question therefore is: what is the alternative to defining the perceived object *either* as a logical construction *or* as an unknown substance?

(iv) The answer may be obtained by considering the nature of the object perceived in relation to the act of perceiving it. These two are the objective and subjective correlates in a single complex of experience. (α) The object perceived, even if it is partly conditioned by the percipient activity, has an existence of its own, which is quite distinct from that of the subjective factor. This is what is meant by calling it an object. (β) As an *experience* the act of perception is *immanent*. That is, it begins and ends in the consciousness of the subject. But the relation implied in the experience is *transitive*. This means that when a conscious subject is perceptually aware of objects, his experience is not merely (like conscious experience in general) an experience of self, it is an experience of self *in relation to* an Other, and therefore an experience of that other *in relation* to the self. The total experience therefore is that of transitive relationship (including the relata) within the necessary immanence of consciousness. (γ) But the act of perception is more than a cognitive state. It is a highly complicated but well defined and closely integrated attitude or adjustment of the whole self to external provocation—a definite concrescence of sub-jective activity in response to a concrescence in the world without. Thus, in the average perception, judgment and obscure bodily feeling, centred upon one or more organs of sense, combine in a single act of the spirit. That act is characterized by "intent" or *bearing*; and the object of perceptual experience is defined as the correlate of the percipient act determined by the intent of the latter. In so far as the act has a unity and identity of its own, the perceived object is a self-identical though complex structure. Its identity is that of the counter-thrust to which the action of the self is subject. (δ) A final point has to do with quantities. Objects of perception must belong to a certain order of magnitudes, and must bear a certain appreciable quantitative ratio to the organs of sense. Objective entities which conform to the quantitative con-ditions of perceptibility are our so-called "gross" or "macroscopic" structures: those that fall below this order of magnitudes are called our "microscopic" or "minute" structures. The relation between gross and minute structure is an all-important link in the chain of considerations binding together the world of perceptual ex-perience and the world of physics.

(B) *in Its Relations (of Interaction) with Other Objects*

(b) The identity of perceived objects has thus been established by reference to the percipient acts of which they are correlates. It is now necessary to consider these objects from a different point of view. Perceptual experience not only reveals their existence: it reveals the fact that they come and go, and displace one another in accordance with fixed and uniform rules. It is therefore possible to consider them from the standpoint not only of their relation to the percipient, but of their relation to one another. They have an identity which is determined by the latter kind of relation, as well as an identity which is determined by the former. The one may be called their *perceptual*, the other their *chemical* identity. The per-ceptual identity is the distinctiveness of an objective structure as defined by its perceptual qualities: the chemical identity is its distinctiveness as defined by the chemical reactions of its con-stituents. The two identities differ as one definition differs from another. But they do not differ in their incidence: they apply to one and the same entity, X, which, under certain conditions, manifests itself as an object of perception, and under others as the subject of very specific chemical reactions.

(c) The next step in this reduction, then, is to analyze the concept of chemical identity. Chemically considered, the whole world of objects divides into two types of structure, elements and compounds. The unit of being in the case of the former is the atom, in the case of the latter the molecule. The reactions which serve to define the chemical identity (of any structure) are characteristic events having to do with the relations of molecules and atoms, and in the end with the relations of the atoms to one another. Thus, from the chemical point of view, the identity of perceptual objects, which are gross structures, is determined by the identity of their atomic constituents. Things of sense are functions of their own atomic content. Hence it is necessary to discover what it is that determines the identity of the atoms.

(d) Underlying the question there is a fundamental assumption or principle of chemical science. Chemically considered, the atoms differ from one another as the elements differ, and in no other way. Each element is absolutely self-identical in all its chemical properties, and at the same time different from every other element. Similarly every atom of a single element is identical in character with every other, and different from every atom of a different element. It is thus the nature of the atom that determines the nature of each element when taken in bulk. The same thing is true of the molecule in relation to a compound: the properties of the molecule are the properties of the whole mass.[2] In the case of compounds, therefore, as in the case of elements, the chemical properties of the gross structures (i.e. the perceptual objects) are identical with those of the minute structures which compose them. The macroscopic and the microscopic systems are functionally related.

(e) The chemical identity of the atom is determined by two factors—weight, and the capacity or incapacity for entering into chemical combination, in fixed, measurable proportions, with other atoms. Thus the hydrogen atom may be defined as the lightest of all, and that which when combined with oxygen in a certain ratio

[2] vid., e.g., Foster, The Romance of Chemistry, pp. 33-4.

produces water. This is as far as the analysis of chemical identity will take us. The result of such analysis is to show that the gross structure of perceptible bodies is a function of their chemical constitution, and this, in turn, a function of their atomic composition. The next step leads to the analysis of atoms of different elements, and carries us beyond the science of chemistry as such into the realm of physics. When the process is complete a further set of functional relations will be found to have emerged, connecting physics with chemistry.

Our point of departure is the periodic law of elements discovered by Mendeléev about 1870.[3] If the elements are compared in respect of their atomic weights, they are seen to fall into a series. Now when the elements are arranged in order according to weight (from hydrogen, 1.008, at one extreme to uranium, 238.5, at the other) it is found that in their chemical properties they resemble, not those that stand nearest to them in the series, but certain others, which occur at regular intervals. A significant fact is that when elements resemble one another in their chemical properties—i.e. their reactions—they also resemble one another in their spectra, which are a *physical* phenomenon. In accordance with these types of resemblance the elements fall into nine distinct groups.[4] A special class is that of the inert gases which do not readily combine with other elements. Now what is called a "period" is the series of elements reckoned from an alkali to the next inert gas. The number of periods is seven and they are of unequal length.*

(f) The symmetrical character of these facts calls for an explanation. It is here that the transition to physics occurs. For the phenomena of the periodic law are correlated with certain characteristics in the structure of the atom, and the examination of these characteristics is the work of physics.

(g) The structure of the atom and the periodic law.

(i) The amount of electricity, positive and negative, in the atom, measurable by the number of electrons in the atom, corresponds to the atomic number of the element in question. For example in the first period (the first period consists of two elements, hydrogen

---

[3] *vid.* Bertrand Russell, *The ABC of Atoms*, Chap. II; F. Soddy, *Matter and Energy*; A. E. Garrett, *The Periodic Law* (The International Scientific Series, Vol. XCVI).

[4] Thus the 3rd, 11th, 19th, 29th, 37th, etc., in the total series constitute the group of alkalis, the 4th, 12th, 20th, 30th, 38th, etc., the alkaline earths; the 5th, 13th, 21st, 31st, 39th, etc., the earths. See Periodic Table on the following page.

[*The vertical columns in the Table.—Ed.]

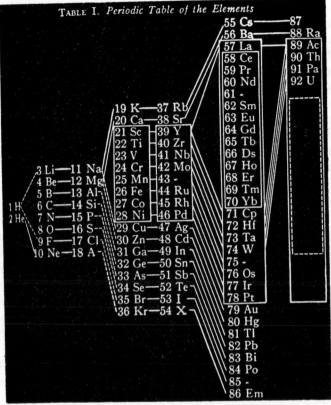

TABLE I. *Periodic Table of the Elements*

Reproduced by permission, from the *Encyclopedia Britannica*, Fourteenth Edition, Vol. II, page 643, Article "Atom" by Niels Bohr.

and helium: these are numbered 1 and 2) we find in hydrogen one positive and one negative charge of electricity, one proton and one electron. In helium there is twice the amount of positive

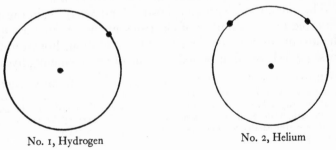

No. 1, Hydrogen   No. 2, Helium

electricity that there is in hydrogen. Hence, in order to balance this, there must be twice the number of electrons. This proportion persists throughout the whole series. Thus lithium, the third element, has three electrons, oxygen the eighth has eight, uranium the ninety-second has ninety-two.

(ii) The number of orbits or rings* corresponds to the number of the period to which the atom belongs. Thus the atoms belonging to the first period have only one ring.[5] Those belonging to the second period, *viz.* lithium, beryllium, boron, carbon, nitrogen, oxygen, fluorine and neon, have two, those belonging to the third period have three, and so on.

(iii) The distribution of the electrons among the different rings is in accordance with the following plan. The first atom in each period (always an alkali) has only one element in its outermost ring.[6] The last (an inert gas) has a number corresponding to the number of elements in the period. Thus the second period contains eight elements which are numbered three to ten. The first is lithium, the last neon. Hence lithium has one electron in the outermost ring and neon has eight. These symmetrical relations are subject to certain irregularities in the later periods; but the

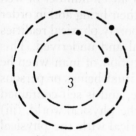
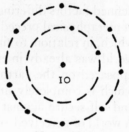

No. 3, Lithium   No. 10, Neon

variations are of a kind which suggests that they can be adjusted to the general form of the relational scheme. The conclusion, therefore, seems warranted that the chemical properties of the elements, which are determined by their atomic numbers and the periodic law, are functions of their physical properties, which are determined by the structure of the atom.

[*"Orbits or rings." *Read* "shells."—Ed.]
[5] Russell, *op. cit.*, Chap. III, pp. 39-40. [Again, "shell" *rather than* "ring."—Ed.]
[6] *op. cit.*, p. 32.

The Resulting Metaphysical Picture

(h) The chain of evidence is now complete, and may be abbreviated as follows:

X is a perceptual object or gross structure of sensory experience.

(i) The perceptual identity of X is a function of its chemical identity. That is, what the conscious subject shall perceive is determined by the chemical constitution of the object in relation to the subjective conditions of perceptibility. (ii) The chemical constitution of the gross structure is a function of the minute structures which compose it—in the case of compounds, the molecules, in the case of elements, the atoms. (iii) The identity of the minute structure (that is to say, in the last analysis, the atom) is a function of the atomic number and the periodic law, or, generally speaking, of the position of the individual atom in the series. (iv) This position in turn is a function of the atomic structure—and therefore of electronic events in the world of physics. The world of physics is thus identical with the world of perceptual experience, and between them they constitute nature in two of its fundamental aspects. Hence nature is not two things but one thing.

(i) The total situation now resolves itself into a number of well defined factors differing in the modality of their being and in order of metaphysical precedence. (i) A world of purely physical realities which, in relation to finite spirits, is original and underived. This world was already in existence for the reception of man when he appeared on the earth. (ii) A world of spiritual beings or persons which is completely underived from nature, and is self-contained and self-secure against all the processes of the physical world. (iii) A world of perceived objects which is identical with the physical world except for a certain unique relationship into which it has entered with percipient organisms, and for certain characteristics that have their origin in this relationship. So far as these characteristics are concerned, the world of perceived objects is neither original nor underived. It is a creaturely world, and implies the existence of both the world of physics and that of spiritual beings.

Genesis of the Values

(j) One word in conclusion with regard to the sensory qualities which are the definitory properties of perceptual objects. These have no existence in and by themselves. Their locus is in the world of physics, but the originative principle that calls them into being is resident in spirit. In relation to the sensory properties spirit is creative (but it requires the medium of the physical). When physical and spiritual come together the former bursts into life and displays itself in a rich variety of manifestations unknown before. Vibrations become colours and sounds. Space begins to glow and throb with meanings which the physical world cannot bring forth of its own accord, but which it contracts in the presence of the conscious subject. The elements of nature are bathed in the ethos of spirit. Such meanings, evoked by spirit in the medium of nature, belong to the realm of values. Sensory properties are values of the first or most elementary order: they are the condition upon which all the other values of the physical world depend. For example, an object which is round and red may be characterized by the property of beauty, if there is an appreciative consciousness to judge it beautiful. In this case the beauty is the beauty of the *object* and not of the appreciative consciousness; but in the absence of the latter the object would not have the property of beauty. Thus, just as sense qualities are functions of physical reality in relation to consciousness, so beauty, or, generally speaking, aesthetic value may be described as a function of the sensory qualities in a similar relationship. The same thing is true in respect of those qualities which we epitomize in the term "utility." Utility is a meaningless concept in the absence of conscious purpose; but granted the purpose, the utility of which it is a condition is a characteristic, not of the purpose as such, nor of the consciousness which sustains the latter, but of the *object*.

Classification of the Values

9. Objective values:
(a) Values of the first order—the sensory qualities.
(b) Values of the second order—the properties in sensory objects which we describe as pleasant, agreeable, etc. (e.g., in colour and sound). These may be further designated the primary or material aesthetic values. It is characteristic of them that they go directly with the sensory qualities as such, and do not imply a high degree of organization in the objects to which they are attached.

(c) Values of the third order—utilities. Utility is a value that accrues to objects in respect of their relation to one another and of a prior relation to the conscious subject.

(d) Values of the fourth order—the higher or formal aesthetic values. These differ from the primary aesthetic values in that they depend upon the *organization* of the objects to which they belong —e.g., a work of art. They further differentiate themselves from the primary in that they do not depend upon a mere *feeling of pleasure* evoked by the object *in the individual*, but upon a judgment of taste claiming validity for all mankind.[7] Beauty is an attribute of form and may be quite compatible with much that is ugly and revolting in the matter. (Compare almost any tragedy, the "Agamemnon"; Shakespeare's "Othello"; the novels of Dostoievsky; Rembrandt's picture of a butcher's shop; the case of discords in music.)

(e) Values of the fifth order—those we have in mind when we think of *truth* as a value. These might appear to be completely independent of the relation to a subjective being; but, as Professor Taylor has shown, while the truth itself may, theoretically speaking, be identified with that which merely is, and which, therefore, does not need to be known in order to be, it is only in relation to the mind of a knower, and to its character as knowable, that the truth acquires the property of being valuable.[8]

(f) Values of the sixth order. These accrue by association (or perhaps some deeper principle of unity) to the objects, places, institutions, which man has to regard as sacred. Sanctity is a quality which has its origin in the emotions and judgments which centre upon what is, in effect, the source of all value—spirit itself.

[7] *vid.* Kant, *Kritik of Judgment*, Part I, Div. I, par. 6, pp. 55-6. English tr., Second Moment.

[8] *The Faith of a Moralist*, First Series, pp. 39, 45-6, 47.

CHAPTER XII

On Spirit, Life and Time

Morality and the Body

1. The realm of nature. The world of pure physics is clothed in qualities which it acquires in a perspective supplied by spirit.

(a) The sensory properties—the product of a first impregnation of the physical, whereby the natural is born.

(b) The values—the product of a second impregnation (of the natural) whereby the values are born: (i) the primary or material aesthetic values, (ii) utilities, (iii) the secondary or formal aesthetic values, (iv) the value of truth, (v) sanctity.

2. The subjective equivalent of the values, or what it means to the subject of experience to create and to realize the values of the objective world.

Among the subjective values a first place to be given to morality. Morality immanent. It begins as an attitude of the spirit and it ends as an enhancement of the spirit's life. But it does so, through the medium of an activity rendered possible by the possession of an animal body.

3. The relation of body and mind. Spirit and nature. The realization of all values, whether objective or subjective, depends upon the fact that the human spirit does not make its approach to the physical world directly, but through the medium of a specialized structure, the body, which in its most obvious properties, belongs to nature rather than to spirit. It is as an embodied soul that man confronts the universe, and all the characteristic modes of his perceptual experience, with all the values that develop out of such experience, are due to this fact. Man's moral experience too is in no small measure dependent for *its* modes upon the same organic connexion. The consequences that accrue to man from the possession of an animal body are incalculable; and it is of vital importance that we should make no mistake about the mutual relation of the two constituents of his composite nature.

The Sense in Which Mind Is a Function of the Brain

4. The body-mind relation. This is a problem which has perplexed the mind of humanity through all the ages, yet the principle involved is very simple. In order to bring the issue to a head, let us recollect that all the questions involved are reducible to one: is consciousness, the characteristic mode of spiritual activity, reducible to a function of the brain? In view of the evidence I must answer in the affirmative. But having done so, I perceive that the problem is not disposed of. For this fact has still to be interpreted. Now there are two possibilities of interpretation. For the naturalist, to say that the mind is a function of cerebral activity is to include mind, along with bodily behaviour, in the system to which the brain belongs. In terms of the theory of functions and systems, the formula of naturalism would be:

$$y \text{ (mind)} = Fx \text{ (brain)}$$

the implication being that x and y between them constitute the purely physiological system $X\,Y$. Now this I dispute. My contention is that mind is a function of the brain only within the unity of a system which includes both. The formula, $y = Fx$, must always be read in the light of the further formula $y = F\,(x\,y)$. This is an application of the principle of Reduplication.* In other words, the statement that body and mind are functionally related is valid only upon the assumption that the two systems in question, which are closed to one another and mutually inviolable, nonetheless between them constitute a *comprehensive* system which is neither exclusively spiritual nor exclusively physical, but implies an order of reality in which spirit operates *through* nature, and nature reveals herself as plastic and responsive to the informing energies of mind. In the concluding lecture (XIII) I shall try to develop the logical and metaphysical implications of this conception. But before doing so it will be necessary to complete my account both of spirit as such, and of those modes of being which stand out in antithetical relation to the latter—the physical and the natural. The argument will centre upon two problems of fundamental import—the nature of life and the nature of time. It is in the latter above all that reality reveals its innermost secrets and fundamental divisions.

[* cf. Chap. 1, 4, p. 22.—Ed.]

Physical Time versus *the Time of Perceived Events or Kantian Time*

5. The doctrine of time.* The four forms of time, physical, perceptual, vital and spiritual. Consider the first two.

(a) Physical time, or the time of the purely physical. Three properties of time, (i) successiveness, which is absolute in the sense that if it is not there we cannot speak of time, (ii) irreversibility, and (iii) transitiveness, which are conditional properties. These are the three properties, and physical time-series are defined by them. The characteristic distinction here, is *before* and *after*. Can we speak of Past, Present and Future here? No point of reference. Present. This can only be supplied subjectively.

(b) Perceptual or Kantian time, the time of perceived events, i.e. events which, while objectively presented, are subjectively conditioned.† This is characterized by the same properties which belong to physical time, and by certain other properties derived from the condition under which perceived events occur. That condition is the relation under which all objects of perception, whether in the form of events or in any other form, stand to the consciousness of the percipient.

This is shown by Kant as follows: We experience the different phases of an event *successively*. That is to say, in the experience of an event, we have *a succession of experiences*. But in addition to this, we must have *an experience of their succession*. If so, the sequent moments must present themselves to consciousness concurrently. They must be experienced together as constituting the sequent phases of one and the same event. But in order to experience them in this way, the mind must perform the operation which Kant calls synthesis. Synthesis is the binding activity of consciousness whereby each phase of the event, as it gives place in perceptual experience to the subsequent phase, is retained by the imagination and added in thought to the experience of the moment. At every stage in the experience of an event, therefore, the mind must add something from an experience that has gone before to an experience that comes after. This means that the relation of before and after has acquired a new property. The after is not merely *subsequent to* the before: in a sense it must be thought of as ap-

[*With all that follows should be compared the author's paper on Spirit-time, given to the Aristotelian Society, June 1933, *Proceedings*, 1932-3.—Ed.]

[†The mind-conditioned non-mental, of Chap. VI, 15, p. 228.—Ed.]

propriating and including the before; and the before is not merely *prior to* the after: it incorporates itself in what is subsequent to it. Consciousness, so to speak, throws organic filaments across the ever-widening gulf of time and gathers to itself its own receding content of experience. This does not imply that the distinction of before and after, earlier and later, is done away with or obscured: it implies that the distinction is possible only upon the basis of an underlying unity. Within this unity before and after differentiate themselves from one another as "no longer" and "now" differentiate themselves in the unity of the composite whole "no longer now." That is to say, the "no longer" acquires the status of an ideal qualification in the actuality of the present moment; and the present owes its actuality to the fact that it sets a limit to the "no longer." "Now" is where "no longer" stops. It is a limit—πέρας as Aristotle called it. But as a *limit* it has no existence *of its own*, and none whatever except what it borrows from that self-same "before" which it turns into an ideality. When such is the case, *before* and *after* redefine themselves. They are no longer the articulations of mere successiveness. In the time of perceived events the characteristic relationship of physical time is transformed. *Before* becomes past and *after* present. *Thus the relation of past to present becomes the characteristic relation of Kantian time*—the time of perceived events.

Past and present. Perceived events, like perceived objects, are subjectively conditioned. This applies to their time relations. The distinction of past and present has no relevance to physical events except in so far as these report themselves in the experience of conscious subjects. Thus the present is determined subjectively. An event is present if it is being perceptually experienced. It is past if its relation to a present event is that of before to after.

The Time of the Spiritual, i.e. of Subjective Events

6. From the analysis of "Kantian" time it appears that the time of perceived events is determined by that of the act whereby they are perceived. If so, that act must itself be amenable to time relations. It must have a time of its own—a time which accrues from it to the events it renders perceptible. There must, therefore, be a time of subjective, as well as of objective, events. Subjective events or mental processes follow one another in time, and so con-

stitute a succession of experiences. Along with this, as in the previous case, there goes an experience of succession. Thus experience
comes in in two ways. In the one instance many experiences are
involved, and in the other only one. The one experience, however,
the experience of succession, is not unrelated to the many—the
successive experiences. Its relation to the latter is altogether *sui
generis* and is quite distinct from the relations of any one experience in the series to any other. It is not merely another experience added to them, but must be conceived as a comprehensive
subjective system within which they differentiate and organize
themselves, and of which they are the mutually related contents.
Every transition from one experience to another presupposes a
covering experience of transition. The former rests upon the latter
and is conditioned by it. In the order of reality the comprehensive
system is prior to its constituents. Thus both "Kantian" time and
the time of subjective events are determined by the Experience of
Time—which is a fact of the subjective or spiritual order. The
priority of the comprehensive system to that which it comprehends is a principle which plays a fundamental rôle in the development of experience, and it is well to have a name for it. A suitable
designation would be Comprehension or Convolution.

Retroactivity. So far, the only case that has been considered is
that in which x and y, *before* and *after*, have the value of past and
present.* In this instance, not only is the present affected by its
past, but the past is affected, and in some cases at least, actually
transformed by its present. Upon this assumption alone can certain of the most momentous possibilities of the moral life be explained and justified.† For example, x is a past action, y our present
consciousness or experience of x. Let y be a state of repentance—
i.e. a painful emotion having x as its object and including a judgment of wrong-doing. We repent what is past. But in order to
explain why we do so, and how it is that we are justified in so
doing, we have to think of $x + y$ as related in a more complicated
way than that of mere temporal succession. At the moment when
we committed the act x, we were not in a state of repentance. That
means that we did not view the act as we now view it; the act did
not have the significance and therefore the identity for us which it
has subsequently acquired. Morally considered, therefore, it ap-

[*i.e. not present and future.—Ed.]
[†cf. Chap. VII, 24f., pp. 279ff.—Ed.]

pears in the character of a quite different act from that for which we now repent. And yet there would be no point in repentance unless the act *repented* were *the same act which we committed in the past.* Their identity, however, can only be established upon the hypothesis that what is past can without loss of the old identity acquire a new identity from an experience that succeeds it in time. We are thus forced to the conclusion that something from the present spreads back over the past, transforming the latter with new and dynamically active meaning. A further inference is that moral agents must be responsible, not only, as is generally and rightly assumed, for their future conduct, but also for their past. If it were not so there would be no point in the command: "Repent." The call to repentance is an injunction to accept responsibility for our own past (and even, be it added, for a past for which we were not in the same measure responsible at the moment); and there is profound insight in the characteristically Christian notion that when we repent our past misdeeds, so far as *we* are concerned, they are wiped away and undone. In other words they are *transformed* as elements in the continuum of an experience which includes them along with the act of repentance. These possibilities may be summed up in the term Retroaction, which may consequently be defined as the power of the present to modify the past.

The Future

7. The full range of possibilities implied in the principle of convolution is, however, only revealed when we consider time not merely in its aspects of past and present, but also in its aspect of futurity. The concept of the future can be deduced from that of the past in its relation to the present. In order to show this we must begin with the *Experience of Time.* The principle involved is that every past began by being a present and every present by being a future.

Deduction of futurity. (a) When we speak of an experience of time, we think of time itself as related to experience. But the question must be asked: What time? Clearly the time of the events whose transition is the content of the experience. Of these events some are past and one is present. But the present and the past are experienced together, and the experience which unites them is a present experience. In this we see the difference that experience makes to time. If we think of the latter apart from experience, the outstanding fact is that one time differs from another. The physical world is a system characterized by such divisions. Experience, on the contrary, is a system in which past and present meet. But in order to understand how this is possible, it is necessary to think of experience not only as a system but as an activity. As such it possesses characteristic modes in which it expresses itself. Among these is that of reproducing the past ideally; and this is one of the things we mean by present time. The present therefore is a function of the activity of experience in relation to the past. (b) But this is only one-half of the truth. The relation to the past is only one of the temporal relations in which the system of experience stands. The act whereby that system of experience reproduces its own past is an act of self-adjustment. That is to say it is a relation which is also an activity—a relation sustained by an activity—or (perhaps more accurately) an activity sustaining a relation. But the activity is never complete, for the simple reason that before it can be completed, the present has become the past, and must itself be ideally reproduced. Such reproduction calls for another act of synthesis, that is, another experience in another present, and this, in turn, for still another, and so on ad infinitum. All of these fall within the system of the comprehensive experience, which remains one while the constituent experiences come and go within it. Inside this system each act of adjustment acquires a new character as it transpires. It is not merely the activity of relating an actual present to a past ideally revived, but also the activity of relating an actual present to an ideal present, which is yet *to be* realized, and by which the former is about to be displaced. In this way experience takes on the aspect of a continuous preparation for the displacement of the present into the past. This has the effect of bringing the present into a new perspective. Not only do we view it in relation to the past which it enables us to reinstate ideally; but we view it in relation to another present, so far also existing ideally, which we think of as ready to replace it when it itself becomes a past. This ideal present is what we call the future; and *since the recognition of it is implied in the adjustment to the past*, we may say that the adjustment to the past is also an adjustment to the future, and that past and future alike are functions of an ever-active, ever-moving present of experience. The time of experience, the time of personal existence, is always present time;

but it is a present to which past and future alike stand in functional relation.

8. The idea of the present as exercising a determining influence over the future is commonly recognized. A less familiar idea is that of the future as exercising a determining influence over the present. Yet such an influence follows as a corollary from the deduction of futurity, taken in conjunction with the principle of retroaction. The adjustment to the past only completes itself *when it has become* an adjustment to the future. This means that in the very act whereby the present sets a limit to the past, and establishes itself in relation to the latter as an *after* to a *before*, it is itself displaced into the past and becomes a *before* to a new *after*. It thus acquires a new meaning within the convoluted system which encloses it. In other words, every present is vitally affected not only by the fact that it follows its past, but by the fact that it anticipates its future. In order to be a present it must embrace elements of its own sequelae by a certain anticipatory power peculiar to experience or the spiritual mode of being. This characteristic of the time of spirit may be called Prolepsis. Prolepsis then is an exact analogue to Retroaction, when the relation involved is that of the future to the present. It is the retroactivity of the future. But as this retroactivity implies a forward adjustment of the spiritual system to meet the coming event, the term Prolepsis is the more suitable of the two.

9. The doctrine of time adds a further and quite conclusive argument to the refutation of naturalism. Every attempt to represent human life, in its subjective aspect, as a product of natural causes, or a function of natural forces within the purely physical, is negatived by a consideration of the time relations involved. Man's spiritual nature is definable as a system of experience, and such a system implies the recognition of past, present and future time, and of an organic connection between the three. The natural world of perceptual events permits the recognition only of past and present; whereas the time relations of the purely physical are limited to the distinction of before and after. It is therefore necessary to distinguish personality or spirit from nature in both of its aspects, the purely physical and the perceptual. In the former case all phenomena are the products or functions of the physical conditions, spatial and temporal, under which they come

into existence. In the latter, they are functions of similar conditions reinforced by a non-physical relation to some percipient organism. Strictly speaking, experience or spirituality is not a product of anything that is not already identical with it in character. *From the standpoint of matter and of physics*, the genesis of spirit is an insoluble mystery, and we can only say of it that like the wind it bloweth where it listeth and that we cannot know whence it cometh or whither it goeth. The truth is that in the spiritual world the characteristic fact is not sequence but synthesis; and synthesis cannot be explained in terms of sequence. There is nothing in physical nature, so far as we have considered the latter, corresponding to the mind's power of gathering together into an ideal whole the various experiences which occur at different times in the history of the conscious subject. The difference between nature and spirit, therefore, from the temporal point of view, is this, that whereas in the case of the former we explain every event by referring it to a previous event, in the case of the latter the relation of one event in time to another is quite unable to explain how *any* event comes to be an *experience*.

Time and Life

10. It will be seen that the theory of time has brought an unforeseen confirmation to our initial analysis of Reality as embracing two original modes of being and a third mode which is derived by functional relation from the compresence of the two former in the total scheme of things. But the analysis is incomplete. So far I have said nothing about a phenomenon of nature which stands out by itself in unmistakeable articulateness—the phenomenon of life, or of the bodily structures in which it incorporates itself. The reason for this is that the nature of living things, as I understand it, can be rendered intelligible only by a consideration of their time relations. It was therefore necessary to postpone the discussion of life until the doctrine of time had reached a certain stage in its development. As a matter of fact the doctrine of life is so integrally bound up with the time of the living body that, from the philosophical point of view, the two must be included within the ambit of a single problem.

Let me explain what I mean by the philosophical point of view, in contradistinction to the strictly biological. The science of biology, in common with all the sciences, is bound to isolate its data in one or other of the various contexts, or systems of relationship, in which they are found to occur. It is only so that truth, in its scientific aspect, can be discovered and made known. With philosophy it is quite different. Here the duty of the thinker is to view his data in every possible context of experience.

No conflict arises here provided (1) the biologist does not presume to treat the truth which he discusses within the relevant context, as equivalent to the truth when viewed within every possible context, and (2) the philosopher does not commit the error of ignoring or despising the patient labours of the biologist and the vast stores of knowledge which he has placed at the disposal of mankind.

In the present case the biologist must ignore and the philosopher must recognize the special context provided for life by the fact that living bodies and spiritual systems go together.

11. The nature of life in general. The English word "life" is ambiguous. It applies to two very different, though not unrelated modes of existence: (1) the existence of living bodies, and (2) the existence of subjective systems or persons. The idea of existence is common to the two cases; and upon the basis of this idea the two forms of life may be defined as, respectively, what is characteristic of the way in which living bodies exist, and what is characteristic of the way in which conscious subjects exist. In the first case life reveals itself objectively as a phenomenon of the natural world: in the second it reveals itself subjectively as what it means to be alive, when living and the consciousness of living are one. Thus life in the sense of biological subsistence is one thing, and life in the sense of personal existence is another. To live, as persons live, is to be the subject, not the object, of conscious states. Life, as they experience it, is identical with the experience of living. Nevertheless the living body is designed to sustain the meanings implied in the subjective mode of life.

12. The nature of living bodies. Among the attempts made to distinguish these bodies from all others the following are worthy of note.

(a) There are those which lay all the emphasis upon organization. Now organization cannot of itself be made the criterion. For, since all physical structures are organized, this conception (of itself) does not furnish the differentia which enables us to distinguish those that are alive from those that are not. It is sought to supply the missing differentia by qualifying the concept of organization in one way or another. Thus, e.g., (i) it is said that living bodies *are exceptionally complex organizations*. On this view the difference between the animate and the inanimate is merely one of degree. This, however, is not to render the distinction clear, but to obscure it. There are difficult border-line cases; and there are cases (e.g., crystals) in which the criterion breaks down altogether. In order to make the concept of organization adequate to the definition of life, those who adopt this view commonly add the concept of life to that of organization, which obviously assumes the very thing for which they are trying to account. Clearly complexity of structure, even if it is implied, is not a sufficient explanation of life. (ii) Again it is said that the organization of living bodies is marked by a peculiar closeness of integration. Although all bodies are organized, some organizations are more perfect than others. The bodies that possess this superior integration are distinguished as organic and as organisms. In this way the difference between the inanimate and the animate is defined as the difference between the inorganic and the organic. The characteristic fact about an organism is that, however differentiated the parts and diversified the function, it must be regarded as a structural and functional whole. In relation to this whole the parts assume the character of organs. That is to say, they are subordinate structures, each with its own specific function, and so connected with the others and with the main structure that the function of the organ is an activity of the organism. The conception of organism is not really adequate to the definition of life. Living bodies are certainly highly integrated organisms; but organism, however integrated, is merely the concrete equivalent of the abstract notion of organization: it is organization in actually existing individual structures; and as such it does not stand out against the general background of nature in such a way as to bring out clearly the differences which distinguish living bodies from others. Neither *integration*, therefore, nor *complexity* (and the two go naturally together) can be taken as a sufficiently clear differentia of life.

(b) Organization and integration, when taken by themselves, having proved inadequate, one may perhaps seek to locate the secret of bodily life in certain physiological properties and functions. That these are highly characteristic of living bodies cannot be denied. Examples are growth, proliferation, metabolism, respiration, the circulation of the blood, reproduction by kinds, regeneration of injured parts, the self-adjustment of the organism whereby, e.g., the proportion of certain chemical constituents in the blood is maintained at a uniform level in spite of variations in the external supply.[1] These various characteristics of living things differ greatly in significance as criteria of life. For example, in the history of crystals there is something closely resembling proliferation and reproduction; and the last-mentioned property, whereby the body regulates the assimilation of chemical substances does not (as Professor Haldane thinks) serve to differentiate living things in the most emphatic way from mechanisms. On the contrary, it is a property which the living body shares with self-regulating machines. If any use, therefore, is to be made of physiological characteristics, it is necessary to exercise a certain discrimination in the choice of those that are significant from the standpoint of this problem.

13. The processes to which I refer fall into two main groups. (a) There are certain of them, e.g., metabolism, respiration, circulation, systole and diastole of the heart, the action of sensori-motor arcs, whose movement is from one point to another and back again. These processes, which thus fall into a movement and a counter-movement, might be called the *pendular* or *circular* functions of the body. (b) In contradistinction to the pendular and circular functions there are certain processes to which these functions minister, but which affect the organism directly and as a whole. These processes are neither circular nor pendular, but represent the steady process of the body in one direction through the successive phases of its development from birth to death. They are the unique episodes in the body's history. Each of these, then, occurs only once in the life of the organism.[2] A typical example is growth: another is the series of processes that leads from adolescence to maturity and from maturity to senescence and death. We commonly distinguish the phases from one another; and it is true that they are theoretically distinguishable. They are not on that

[1] On this last point vid. J. S. Haldane, *The Sciences and Philosophy*, Lect. III, pp. 40-1 and 44-5.
[2] For an application of this idea to the question of reincarnation and repetition, vid. Taylor, *The Faith of a Moralist*, First Series, p. 320.

account actually separable. Each of them is what it is by reason of its position in a single, unbroken movement of life. The life-process as a whole, therefore, is presupposed in each of its successive phases. Each moment in the process is at once an epitome of what has been and an anticipation of what is to be. The time of the living body is so far like the time of experience—spirit-time— rather than the time of physics.* The movement of life is not like the movement of a projectile in space, but like that of a snowball gathering substance as it goes. Its *afters* are not merely subsequent to, but inclusive of, its *befores*; and its befores are all adjustments to its afters. Life, therefore, transforms the time of physics into another kind of time; and the time of life, like the time of experience, is characterized by the distinctions of past, present and future.³ It is this fact above all, which distinguishes the living body from other corporeal structures, and fits the former to enter into a single ontological system† with the spiritual mode of being, and to be the vehicle for the moral purposes of mankind. Life, as I understand it, from the standpoint of philosophy, is a reverberation of spirit into the world of nature; the living body a physical structure permeated by subjectivity and vibrating in spirit-time.‡

[*The moral significance of this parallel is developed further in Part III. See, e.g., below, Chap. xvi, 19*ff.*, pp. 406*ff.*—Ed.]

³ *vid.* Bergson, *Creative Evolution*, Chap. i.

[†A heterogeneous system, of course, cf. I, 6, and II, 8-19.—Ed.]

[‡The obvious sense here again would seem to be that spirit is able to become present *to* the physical (and so to occasion the emergence of the world of sensory properties and of values) only by first having entered into functional relation *with* it, via the body. Life is the adaptedness of the body to sustain this relation. And the body itself—or the life that is in it—is here being described as a "reverberation" of the spirit.—Ed.]

CHAPTER XIII

On Creativity and Incarnation

Time and Morality

1. The specious present. There are two possible views of the present.

(a) On the one hand it may be conceived negatively as a dividing line or a point separating the past from the future. So regarded, it is a limit of each against each, and is one and the same in relation to both. That is, the "now" which limits the past against the future, also limits the future against the past. This may be called the *parietal* conception of the present. If taken as adequate or complete, it ends in contradiction. Thus, upon this view, the present would be a durationless moment. But as time is made up of infinite presents, it would have to be thought of as itself durationless. Again, this view would lead to a difficulty pointed out by Aristotle. If "now" is a durationless division, "it is not time but only an attribute of it."[1] There remain the past and the future. But the past, as Aristotle puts it, is the part of time that "has been and is not."[2] Clearly this view is destructive of the existence of time.

(b) The present may be conceived not as a pure limit but as a meeting-place, or synthesis, of the past and the future. It cannot, however, be so conceived if it is a durationless point. Hence it is necessary to think of the present as having a certain extensity. It is a present that endures. Such a present is known as "specious," and the conditions of its realization are found in what has been said about convolution, with the implied concepts of retroaction and prolepsis. The specious present is sustained by an act of synthesis which combines elements of a "just past" and a "just about to be" in a single structure of experience—an experience which actually is and is therefore in the full sense of the term "present." The time so characterized may be designated spirit-time in contradistinction to the space-time of the physical world.

If the present has duration, the question will arise: how much time does it take to make a present? We speak of the present geological era, the present century, the present year, day, hour,

[1] *Physica*, Δ, xi, 220 a, 21-2.
[2] *op. cit.*, 217 b, 33-4.

instant. So regarded the present is obviously a shifting quantity and a convention, of which the significance is purely pragmatic. Any stretch of time may be considered a present, according to the point of view and the purpose implied. And yet it is obvious that such a conception would involve the whole problem of time in hopeless confusion. If time is real and if its divisions are significant, it follows that there must be some method of converting a conventional into a real present. How can such a method be discovered?

The answer is, by going back to the principle which underlies the division of time into past, present and future—the principle which enables the time of physics to acquire the properties characteristic of spirit-time. That principle is experience. It is experience which furnishes the point of reference from which certain times take on the aspect of the past, and others the aspect of the future.

The next question that arises is this: how is the criterion of experience to be applied in the definition of an extensive present? The answer is easy. Experience is not an otiose condition of passive contemplation—a mere receptivity of successive states of consciousness. It is an active adjustment of the spirit, and indeed of the total psycho-physical organism, beginning with what I shall call an incitement and terminating in a satisfaction or perfected achievement. The answer to my question is implicit in these statements. The measure of a true extensive present is the temporal span of a completed adjustment. Within the total curvature of such a movement there will be, at each successive moment, elements which are before and elements which are after; but there will be no element which is not altogether present: so:

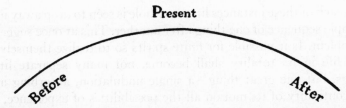

Present

Before   After

This theory has the advantage of rendering the conception of present time exact and real, while allowing for the indefinite variability of the definitory span. Thus, like the waves which occur in water, in air, in the sub-ether of the physicist, the undulatory movements of the life-force differ in length, in amplitude, and in their periods. There are vast adjustments which carry on their bosom numberless minor contributory adjustments, as a long Atlantic roller carries on its surface a thousand smaller waves and ten thousand tiny ripples. Each of these minor movements represents an authentic present within the amplitude of a greater but no less authentic present. To take a homely illustration, we may think of the golfer addressing the ball. He has for his "present" purpose to make a satisfactory shot; but this purpose of his falls within a wider scheme, which is equally his present purpose, that of—let us say—having an enjoyable game of golf. And if all his golfing be an enterprise which he undertook with an object in view, perhaps his health, then that object too is his authentic present purpose; as, once again, a whole life policy might be, in which health itself is only one, and not the first, consideration.

2. The question must be asked: Is there any limit to this process whereby the present of experience expands with our growing purposes, and contracts to the measure of the small contributory movements? The answer is that it all depends on the kind of life we lead. Let me give three typical instances.

(a) The life of the libertine: a continuous passage from one moment of delirious but short-lived pleasure to another—a case of *short* waves.

(b) The life of projects, the realm of economic and technical endeavour, building a bridge or a skyscraper, carrying out a reform of the administrative services. If the span of the specious present is measurable by the length of time from the inception to the completion of the project, we have here plainly a life of longer movements.

In each of these instances life as a whole is seen to drop away into a simple sequence of one thing after another. This at once suggests a problem. Is it possible for finite spirits so to realize themselves, that life in its totality shall become, not many separate little things, but one great thing—a single undulation, absorbing into the continuity of its motion all the possibilities of experience, all projects, purposes, endeavours, all disappointments and successes, all joys and sorrows, and so neutralizing the divisions of time, and coming to itself in the completeness of a life that is altogether one? The achievement of such life is the ideal possibility which we call *morality*. The *moral life* is the life that is lived as a perfect whole—

the life in which all impulses, emotions, aspirations, energies are organized together and enlisted in the service of one supreme ideal, definable as life itself.

3. (c) But that is not yet the full problem. A final possibility remains to be explored. Have we reasonable grounds for supposing that even man's terrestrial existence, which terminates with the death of the body, is but a passing phase of his spiritual experience —an experience which continues in successive waves of vital energy, perhaps in embodied form, perhaps in incarnation after incarnation? Is death the *end* of life, or an *episode* in life? The question is one which depends entirely on the ultimate relation of the two original and mutually independent modes of being upon which we have dwelt throughout, the physical and the spiritual.

In the course of these lectures the way has been prepared for the problem by which we are now confronted. Above all it has been established that there are numberless possibilities of being for which the purely physical is not accountable. The rich and varied manifold of the sensible, which we see around us, is the composite product of the physical and the spiritual. Take spirit out of the world, and "nature" disappears, leaving only a barren waste of undulating ether waves, for ever in motion, breaking out here and dying down there, reinforcing one another and obliterating one another by the process known to the physicist as interference. Exciting as they are, and abundantly worthy of the best efforts of the man of science to understand them, I think it will still be acknowledged that they represent existence at the very lowest level. They are not non-existent, but the being which we feel ourselves entitled to attribute to them is being reduced to a minimum —being almost at the point of extinction.* Above all they are wanting in that inwardness of being which we call selfhood, and therefore the mode of their existence is that of uttermost dependence. At every point they are conditioned and sustained by the external relations in which they stand to one another. Taken in their totality, however, they constitute a single independent

[*It has not been said that they *are* extinct. The author is here apparently taking a certain attitude towards the conception of a limit. He is assuming the possibility, without being over a given limit, of being absolutely at it. The idea of an independence of mind, which is mind-conferred—the idea of an absolutely-other-than-mind, which yet is (by mind itself) required to be, and to be just such—seems to involve this assumption.—Ed.]

order of reality—the physical—a reality that fills all space and all time, and stands out in eternal and irresolvable antithesis to the spiritual mode of being.

When we come to spirit the contrast is almost overwhelming. Existence is here raised to the highest power in a mode of being that internalizes everything it touches, incorporates every experience to the unity of a system that is inviolably immanent, and absorbs into the unbroken continuity of subject-selfhood, the successive barriers opposed to its triumphal progress by the arch-divider time.

The Physical as a Creation

4. How are these two modes of being to be brought together in thought? One thing at least is certain. Their relation is that of a higher to a lower, of that which *is* in the fullest sense, to that which all but *is not*. But we must go further than this.

I have insisted on the originality and mutual independence of the spiritual and the physical. But this independence has to do with their respective modes of being. The physical is emphatically *not* the spiritual nor the spiritual the physical; and nothing but confusion can result from the failure to maintain the distinction in all its force. But the mutual *independence* of the two *modes* does not prejudice the question of the conditions by which *existence* in these modes is determined and maintained; and the questions still remain: How does spirit come to be, how does it continue to be? How does the physical world come about, how does it maintain its existence?*

But the first of these two sets of questions savours at once of the paradoxical. For in raising it we are asking: How does *being at the highest* come to be? The only possible answer is that it comes to be because it is being at the highest. Spirit *is*, because it cannot quench the exuberance of the energies of self-realization. It is otherwise with the physical. The secret of being at the lowest can

[*A distinction is apparently intended here between the physical *mode of existence* and *its existence in* that mode. The thought is undoubtedly difficult, but not, I think, entirely obscure. The meaning would seem to be that though the physical is to be taken as not dependent on spirit for its *mode* of existence, i.e. for *what* it is—and it is indeed very little—it must be construed as dependent on spirit for the fact *that* it is. If so, the position seems to imply a lower limit of *whatness*, with the attitude to the notion of a limit suggested in the last footnote.—Ed.]

only be resolved by looking towards being in its fulness. In other words, the physical is a creation of the spiritual.

5. It is not, of course, an easy viewpoint to take. The thought that anything "can come into being or pass away" has been discredited ever since Parmenides, for the dilemma it contains. That which comes to be is either made from something, and then it is not created; or it is made of nothing, in which case it can be nothing. The dilemma has its sphere of validity. It holds for the physical world. Physical processes are all non-creative. We only confuse the issue when we speak of the "creative advance" of a nature which is "closed to mind." The physical cannot creatively advance. The *ex nihilo nihil* must hold good in any universe which consists solely of atoms changing their places, or even in one in which, in the language of Jeans, "everything is waves." Creation is possible when one factor is physical and the other spiritual.*

6. But deep in the history of science a tendency relevant to this issue has been at work, which has only come to full fruition in our own time. The original Democritean overemphasis on spatiality has had to be corrected, and time has had to be recognized as an integral factor in the physically real. With this there has entered into the nature of physical reality a character which, in the last resort, can only be spiritually understood. A relation to the spiritual which we can only call creaturely is thereby indicated in the nature of the physical itself. For the definition of creation is the functional dependence of the physical world in its entirety on the energies of spirit. Now it is clearly not from our individual spirits that these energies can be conceived to go forth. We must assume a spirit adequate to the task. We must assume God. God is the metaphysical correlate of the creative activity which we are compelled to assume in order to account for the existence of the physical world.

God

7. In the concept of God, the definitory notion must be that of eternity. He is the eternal spirit—this, not in the timeless sense, but in the sense of an everlasting endurance. The being of God defines itself in relation to its time conditions, as an absolutely

[*A brief discussion of the idea of Creation which may be compared with the above will be found in the author's *Studies in the Philosophy of Religion*, Vol. II, Chap. xxv. —Ed.]

perfect adjustment of every past to every future in a present that is infinite in each direction.

8. God and the created universe. The spiritual mode of being, like the physical, is to be conceived as a vibratory system; vibrating in the non-spatial time of the spirit, as the other does in space-time.

The vibrations or undulatory motions of the spirit are non-spatial. What is the meaning of this statement?

It means that for purposes of His own, the divine Being creates within the ambit of His nature, a region where the undulations of His spirit die out in infinitesimal vibrations and cease to function as a time-compelling power of consciousness. Space is the unconsciousness of Omniscience, the unconsciousness of God; and the creation of a spatial universe is one of the ways in which the Creator diversifies the infinite, unbroken curve of His existence. The vibrations of the physical world are the faint overtones of the divine orchestration. Or, to vary the metaphor, they are the last ripples that break the surface of the creeks and backwaters of existence, where being dies away into nothingness because it ceases to be spiritual.

9. A last question concerns the relation of physical and spiritual in its bearing on the idea of a divine incarnation. Has God a body, as finite spirits have bodies? And would it be correct to represent the physical world as the *body* of God? I venture to answer the question in the negative, and for this reason. It is not body in general but only *living* body that clothes the spirit as a garment and serves it as an organ; and the condition of this possibility is that the elements of nature, physical and chemical, be so re-organized and so vitalized that their rhythms conform to the characteristic periods of spirit-time. So understood, man's embodied life must be interpreted not as a product or function of nature's impersonal forces, but as an activity of incarnation. It is the spirit that organizes the body and not the body the spirit. Incarnation, therefore, is not an anomaly. It is the universal principle of human life.* But the incarnate life may vary infinitely in its *capacity to*

[*"It is the universal principle of human life." The author seems throughout to think of two distinct ways in which the two modes of being interlock. (a) The sacramental universe arises from their *conjunctive compresence*. But (b) they only become

express the inner life of spirit; and the supreme tragedy of human history is man's continuous, conscious failure to realize within him, in adequate motions and effective forms, what he feels to be the energies of a nature akin to the divine. In his anguish of self-defeat he looks around him for a spirit like himself, incarnate in human form, to which to stretch out hands of appeal. Is not this in fact the supremely characteristic phenomenon of our modern civilization? And is there not something pathetically familiar, even immemorial in the contemporary cult of the deified tyrant? But what are the marks by which we should *know* a saviour of mankind? Who is he? Surely the answer is, He, wherever he may be found, in whom the light of the spirit breaks most unmistakeably through the meshes of the flesh. And the supreme test is that the spirit should flame forth more and more radiantly as the body goes down before the embattled forces of nature, that the ideal forms of spirituality should emerge with ever-growing clarity and splendour as the powers of evil close in; that the unseen energies of a hidden life should transmute disaster into triumph. Where these symptoms appear we may with safety assume incarnation of the divine, the presence of God's delegate on earth. But here we are within the region of the historical, and the question that arises in every mind is beyond the field of the philosopher. Each must

so compresent, in virtue of an entirely different kind of union with the physical, a *functional* union, into which spirit has also entered, in the heterogeneous system called the psycho-physical organism—for which latter union the author seems to have regarded life in the biological sphere as the preparation.

If this interpretation is correct, if life is in this manner an adaptation of the physical and material, fitting it for that functional (as distinct from merely conjunctive) union with spirit, which enables spirit, in turn, by its compresence or conjunction with the physical (in a heterogeneous system) to give rise to "nature" and clothe matter with the significance which makes the universe sacramental; then surely it would seem to be the principle, not of *human* life only, but of *all* life, to prepare matter to house, embody or "incarnate" spirit. And such would seem to be the way in which we ought to take the "reverberation" metaphor, at the close of Chap. xii, p. 363, above. It may be that the author, like many others, tends to use theological terms in senses deviating somewhat from the traditional; but surely there is some legitimate sense in which the idea of incarnation is central to his whole philosophy.

A flavour of neo-Platonism is perhaps discernible in the author's ultimate conception, given in this chapter, of creation—as an incident in the self-overflowing of spirit. On the other hand, if, when we view the spirit as rising through the physical to confront the physical (the function of life) we can also take the view that that through which spirit thus rises is its own creation, we get something reminiscent of the "rocket" metaphor of M. Bergson.—Ed.]

answer it for himself. I am restricted to general principles. But I think it fair to say nonetheless that in my own view, if there be anything in this long drawn out argument, the doctrine of the incarnation of God in the man Jesus, is the one possible solution for the tragedy of a world that has lost itself.

PART III

SUPPLEMENTARY DISCUSSIONS

CHAPTER XIV

THE THEORY OF VALUES

Nature and the Values

1. Being assumes three characteristic forms: (a) the purely physical, (b) the spiritual and (c) a world of perceived objects which is identical with the physical except for a certain relationship—itself non-physical—into which it has entered with percipient organisms, and for certain characteristics which have their origin in this relationship. So far as these characteristics are concerned, the world of perceived objects presupposes the existence both of the physical and of the spiritual mode of being.

So far, the emphasis has been placed on the ontological independence of the physical and the spiritual. But this is only one side of the truth. The recognition of (c) as a dependent mode brings both of the two independents into a new perspective. Since the sensory properties of the natural world are functions of the relation between the spiritual and the physical, that relationship is seen to be a necessary presupposition of all our perceptual experience of the world. In view of the numerous new possibilities that thereby come to light, the compresence of spirit with its other in the total scheme of things is a fact of no less importance than their ontological independence. It has been shown that there are certain possibilities of being—e.g., sound and colour—which arise in the outer world by the instrumentality of mind. These reveal themselves as *objects* and not as *states* of consciousness. Hence they do not exist subjectively. Yet they are subjectively conditioned. What exists subjectively is our consciousness of them. This consciousness belongs to the subjective system of our experience. The latter is in consequence profoundly affected by the fact that through the creative energies of spirit the physical world has given rise to the acquired character—natural. Thus it is no less true that the physical is affected by its relation to the spiritual than that the spiritual is influenced by its relation to the physical. There are numberless possibilities of spiritual self-realization which arise only through this relationship. When all these possibilities, objective and subjective, which presuppose the compresence of the two independent modes of being are considered together, the generic term which best expresses their nature is the term "value." It is the presence of value which gives to the universe its aspect as sacramental.

(a) The Objective Values

2. The natural classification of values is into objective and subjective; of which the former falls into a number of orders or classes, the first of those being the sensory qualities. Objects which are characterized by these qualities, through the presence of the physical to consciousness, may be characterized by still further qualities under the same condition. For example a colour or a sound, besides having the definitory property of redness or of pitch, may have a character which we describe in the epithets "pleasant," "agreeable" or the like. This character may be designated *charm*. Charm in an object is the correlate of pleasure in the conscious subject, and it is generated by a second application of the same principle which gives rise to the object of sensory experience itself. Just as the sensory object is a function of its own *physical conditions* in relation to a percipient, so the charm which accompanies it is a function of the *sensory object* in relation to an appreciative consciousness. For this reason the values which we summarize in the term "charm" may be designated values of the second order. From another point of view they may be described as the primary or material aesthetic values. By this is meant that their power to provoke pleasurable feeling in us is due entirely to their intrinsic character as sensory objects in relation to consciousness, and that apart altogether from the objective *context* in which they make their appearance. Questions of composition, proportion, harmony, design, or generally speaking organization, do not arise at this point. The sensory content excites us in and by itself, and we can neither be praised nor blamed for being susceptible to such excitement. We are not yet in the region of genuine artistic values, where taste becomes amenable to standards. The taste involved in primary aesthetic experience is nobody's business but that of the individual himself; and the only rule that is at all relevant is that expressed in the maxim *De gustibus non est disputandum*.

3. Values of the third order may be designated Utilities. Utility is a value that accrues to objects in respect of their relation to one another and of a prior relation to the conscious subject. For example, an instrument or machine is characteristically related to the product which it brings into existence. Its relation to the latter is that of a cause to an effect. But before this relation can be established, each of the terms must have entered into another relation with the mind of a conscious subject—the inventor of the process or the actual producer who handles the instrument. This conscious subject adjusts the terms to one another, but first of all he adjusts them severally to himself in idea. That is to say, he forms a concept of the effect as something desirable, and of the instrument as an efficient mechanism for the production of the latter. In the context of his thought and his desires the relation of cause and effect becomes the relation of means and end. Thus the intervention of mind converts a mechanical relation of cause and effect between two objects (see figure below) into an ideal relation of means and end between the same two objects, through a still further relation between each of the objects and the subjective processes of the agent. When this elaborate system of connections has been established, the result is the value called utility. As in the previous instances, utility is generated as a new meaning by the cooperation of the physical and the spiritual. This value, however, differs from the last in that the implied correlation is not between a single object and the consciousness of it, but between a system of mental processes and a complex set of relations in the physical world.

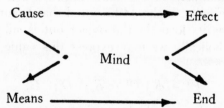

The relations between the first three orders of objective value may be conveniently symbolized as follows:

$$V^1 = \phi \, (Ph + C)$$
$$V^2 = \phi \, (V^1 + C)$$
$$V^3 = \phi \, \{(O^1 - R - O^2) + C\}$$

where V = value, ϕ = function, Ph = the physical, C = consciousness, O = object, and R (in the last equation) = a relation of cause and effect.

4. Relations also play a fundamental part in values of the fourth order—those which we summarize in the term beauty. In contradistinction to the second class, these may be described as the higher or formal aesthetic values. They differ from the primary or material in that they do not depend upon the pleasurably exciting character of individual sensory presentations, but upon the power of an ordered composition to provoke the mind to admiration. The secret of beauty is the way in which the sensory contents are organized together into a structure which satisfies because of its harmonious relations, its proportions and its completeness. Beauty is thus an attribute of form rather than of matter, and is quite compatible with a total absence of charm or attractiveness in the sensory constituents of the composition. It is not to these but to the structure as a whole that the designation "beautiful" is strictly speaking applicable (cf. any tragedy, the Agamemnon, Othello, Dostoievsky's novels, Rembrandt's picture of a butcher's shop, use of discords). A further vital difference between the primary and the higher aesthetic values is that the former rest upon the private susceptibilities of the individual, whereas the latter imply a standard of judgment which is assumed to be universal. The proof of this is that a specific judgment of beauty is challengeable, whereas a judgment of hedonic sensitiveness is not. You can impugn the taste of the individual in the one case, but not in the other. To be unimpressed by beauty argues a defective power of appreciation. Finally, it should be noted that beauty, like charm and utility, has its locus in the object but is subjectively conditioned. Symbolically we may express this value of the fourth order so:

$$V^4 = \phi \left\{ (O^1 - R - O^2) \cdot C \right\}$$

where R = the relations which constitute form.

Sanctity, Truth

5. In addition to the foregoing there still are two types of value which differ from those already enumerated in that the objects to which they are attached do not belong exclusively either to the physical or to the natural world. These are *truth* and *sanctity*.

Sanctity finds its object primarily in the spiritual mode; while the locus of truth is the ideal.*

Sanctity may be described as a value of the fifth order. It belongs to everything which man has learnt to regard as sacred and that irrespective of the modality of its being.

6. The condition under which this value arises is as follows. All values without exception have their origin in a relation to spirit. Hence the *being* of spirit itself, i.e. its life, must be the *supreme* value. Now spirit or personality exists subjectively. In each individual person being takes the subjective form. But all the modes of existence may enter into the relation of objectivity. In the present instance this means that the personality of one individual, though in itself subjective, may take on the character of an object in the experience of another. One person may be known by another. Now among all the possible objects of experience, personality is the transcendently valuable. It is so for the reason stated—namely, that it is itself the source of all values. Hence there is something in it calculated to fill the mind with awe. In its presence we feel a certain constraint, varying all the way from the bashfulness of the child in the presence of his elders to the profound reverence of the disciple for the master and the worshiper for his God. In all our contacts with it, it invites us to *look up*, as to a superior form of being. The meaning which it contracts, in relation to our consciousness of it, is not like any other meaning. We do not enjoy it as we enjoy a pleasurably exciting object of sense or a beautiful composition. There is no context of experience in which it may appropriately be treated as a mere utility—i.e. as a means to some end which is not its own but that of another. To exploit a person is to degrade the spiritual to the level of the natural. It is to violate its subjectivity, and this is an offence against the very principle of values itself. Hence the Kantian maxim: "So act as to treat humanity, whether in thine own person or in that of any other, in every case as an end withal, never as a means only."[1]

At the same same, personality is not merely a restraining, far less a repelling object. It is uniquely attractive. No other mode of

[*The author sometimes treated "truth" before "sanctity." Here he treats "sanctity" first. The point is unimportant.—Ed.]

[1] To this may be added a further maxim: "Never forget that a person, even if his being in the first instance reveals itself to you objectively, is not a mere *object* of *your* experience, but is far more fundamentally the *subject* of his *own*, and must therefore be treated with the respectful consideration due to his character as a conscious self."

being can rightly be described as "endearing," and to no other can the predicate "dear" be directly applied. If it is true that the presence of one spiritual being has a profoundly disturbing influence on another, the reason is that it evokes an enhanced self-consciousness in the latter. And self-consciousness is the active principle of self-realization. Ontologically speaking, we are dependent on the stimulus of other subject-selves for the development of our own subjectivity, that is to say for our very being as subjects of experience. Intersubjective communion is the element in which spirit lives. It is so for the following reason. Personal relations are not mere relations between terms. They are experiences, and therefore they enter into the constitution of the beings between whom they hold as relations. If such a relation exists between two persons A and B, the relation is A's experience of B and B's experience of A. And since every person is the system of his own experiences or subjective states, it follows that his inner being is vitally modified by the personal relations which enter into it. Hence the value of spirit to spirit is incalculable. It belongs to an order of magnitudes which is incommensurate with that of any other value. And this is what is meant by sanctity. In terms of the fundamental principle involved, therefore, sanctity may be defined as the infinite value of spirit to spirit.

7. But the principle has been extended by association to everything that stands in a peculiarly intimate relation to the spiritual mode of being, everything that ministers to it as an organ, or symbolizes it as an emblem, that commemorates phases of its time-conditioned existence, or brings home its import with exceptional power, or is in any way connected with the fundamental hopes and fears that centre on the life and death of human individuals. The sanctity of objects, places and institutions is a value which these entities contract exclusively through their association with the fundamental sanctity of personal existence.[2] Sacred objects may be devoid of other forms of value—charm, utility, beauty. Yet their association with the source of all values renders them of priceless worth in the eyes of those for whom this association outweighs all other considerations.

[2] Examples: Amulets, charms, fetishes; the totem; the human body; "that dear face"; the memorials of childhood; the appurtenances of death; a lock of hair; the precincts of a church; the sacramental elements.

8. Values of the sixth order have their locus in the ideal realm of *Truth*. Like all others this type of value is subjectively conditioned. It owes its existence to a relation between the facts known and the mind that knows them. From certain points of view it might appear as if the facts could not possibly owe anything to the purely extraneous circumstance that someone has become acquainted with them. But this is not so. When it becomes an object of consciousness—i.e. the content of a judgment—fact contracts a new significance through the new context or system of relations into which it has entered. It has ceased to be a time-conditioned particular, and has acquired the character of timeless value. As truth it conforms to the conditions by which values are determined.

(b) the Subjective Values

9. The second class of values is the subjective. To each of the objective values there corresponds a subjective equivalent; to the sensory properties the consciousness of them, i.e. sensation; to charm and beauty, aesthetic satisfaction of the primary and the higher types respectively; to utility, the appreciation and realization of the uses of things; to sanctity, the emotions of awe and reverence or regard for spirit as such; and to truth, the comprehension of reality as distinct from mere appearance, illusion and falsehood.

The Conception of Moral Value as that which Characterizes Human Approximations to a Finished Spirituality, *Filling Spirit-Time*

10. So far, no place has been found in the realm of values for morality. It is obvious that it belongs to this realm. The language in which we refer to it implies that it is conceived as a value. In the attempt to identify it, the foregoing analysis may be taken as a clue. For example, it may safely be assumed that the principle which is operative throughout will be operative here also. That is to say, morality will be found to have its explanation in a relation to spirit. The question is, what kind of relation?

The answer presupposes a further question, and one having to do with the locus of ethical value. Where is moral goodness to be found? What is the sphere of its relevancy? To what does it attach itself as an adjectival qualification? Clearly to human actions and to the persons of whom the actions are a revelation. We speak of actions and of agents as good or as wanting in goodness. When viewed in the light of a moral assessment, personality appears as character; and it is primarily to character that the epithets "good" and "bad" apply. Human actions acquire their moral significance as expressions of character. Morality is thus a value which accrues to character and to conduct through a relation of these to the fundamental principle of all values—personality itself, or the subjective mode of being.

This statement, however, is fraught with two serious difficulties. (i) If moral value has its locus *in personality*, and its origin and principle in a *relation to* personality, it would seem that personality must be conceived as related to itself. (ii) Morality is a value which may or may not be realized, or which may be realized in indefinitely varying degrees, in the lives of different persons or in that of one and the same person. All human beings are morally imperfect: some characters are so deficient in moral value that we apply such epithets as "worthless," "good-for-nothing," etc., to them. But these admissions appear to conflict with the proposition that since personality is the source of all values, it itself must be the supreme value. In other words, the value of the subjective is first postulated unconditionally, and then it is suggested that it is subject to conditions which may or may not be realized.

11. The solution to the paradox involves the conception of spirit-time. Subjective systems are amenable to time relations. In so far, however, as the time in question is spirit-time, synthesis prevails over mere sequence. This is one of the differentiating marks of the spiritual mode of being. But the differentia is realizable in infinitely varying degrees. No finite subject can ever absorb the whole manifold of its temporally ordered experiences into the unity of a complete synthesis; and persons differ indefinitely in their approximation to this ideal. Their failure must be construed as a defect in spirituality. Where integration is loose and the power of synthesis restricted, personality in the conscious subject has about it something of the character of an ideal still to be realized. Morality, then, is a value which accrues to human behaviour and to human character in so far as, under the limitations of a time-conditioned existence, these are conducive to and expressive of a finished spirituality. The precise significance of this assertion can be made clear only by a detailed analysis of human nature and of the processes by which it develops through the successive stages of life.

CHAPTER XV

THE DEVELOPMENT OF MAN'S SPIRITUAL BEING, COGNITIVE AND CONATIVE

1. Personality is a subjective system of experience, but in the case of man, it makes its appearance in conjunction with a special type of animal organism. From the beginning of life it is as a *psycho-physical* and not as a purely psychical or as a purely physiological system, that every human being exists. This fact has an important bearing upon man's development as a moral agent. The spiritual in him evolves within a matrix that is not exclusively spiritual. That matrix is the instinctive life, and the psycho-physical units of human nature are the individual instincts.

The Instincts

2. Of the instincts in general, the following characteristics may be noted:

(1) They are common to man and the lower animals.

(2) They must not be identified with reflex action. Reflex action is a component, but there is a mental component as well. Instinct is the *psycho-physical* unit, at once of human nature and of human behaviour.

(3) The mental component has three aspects, distinguishable but not separable—the cognitive, the affective and the conative.

(4) Instincts frequently occur in interconnected series, the conclusion of one furnishing the stimulus to the next. The order is irreversible.

(5) Sometimes the total action requires the cooperation of an internal and an external stimulus.

(6) The significance of the total action appears in the end to which it leads, the special satisfaction in which it terminates. Every instinct subserves some purpose in the economy of life; and it is this purpose which reveals the meaning of the process as a whole.

(7) How the instincts originate. In the case of the individual they are not the product of experience, education, training, learning. Unlike habits, they are not acquired but are the spontaneous responses of the psycho-physical organism to an environment to

which it has become adjusted by centuries of evolution. Instinctive processes occur where the organism and the environment most completely interpenetrate. So far as the individual is concerned, the instincts are part of his racial inheritance. In Professor Hocking's phrase, they must be regarded as "hereditary paths of least resistance" or as "a foreshortened education."

3. Instinct, then, may be defined—modifying McDougall—as a racially inherited psycho-physical disposition, common to man and the lower animals, and expressing itself in a tendency (1) to exercise selective discrimination in favour of certain types of stimuli, (2) to experience a characteristic emotional excitement when the appropriate stimulus occurs, and (3) to react to the stimulus in a more or less stereotyped fashion.

The relation between the physiological and the mental component may be construed as follows. At the beginning of life in the case of man, and throughout life in the case of the lower animals, the physiological process is in advance of the mental. When the stimulus occurs the reaction follows of its own accord and without the special intervention of a directive intelligence. Consciousness normally makes its appearance at two points: in relation to the stimulus, and in relation to the reaction. (1) It is usually necessary that the stimulus should be felt, or that the object which propagates it should be perceived. On the other hand (2) in relation to the reaction—the bodily process is reflected in consciousness; i.e. it too is *felt*. In neither case does the presence of consciousness seriously interfere with the physiological operation. Clearly, if man is to develop in a moral sense, it can only be upon the condition that in the course of his life the initial relation between the two components of instinct be reversed. That such inversion is possible in the case of man is due to certain features in his original instinctive equipment as contrasted with that of other living things.

Development in the Instinctive Life. The Principle Involved

4. The instincts fall into two classes representing different levels of development. One of these is characteristic of certain lower forms of animal life. The other is characteristic of the higher mammals. In the former class (known as the epicritic) the instincts are noted for their fineness of discrimination and precision of execution, in the latter (protopathic) class, for the absence of these qualities.

The epicritic type of instinct is found in extreme form among insects; in man the instinctive life is protopathic. It is confused, that is to say, and inefficient. When the reaction occurs, it is not graduated to meet the vital needs of the organism, but occurs with full force whether the situation calls for a sustained or for a slight reaction. It is evident that the ungraded, protopathic, "all-or-none" type of instinct is the more rudimentary, the epicritic the more highly developed.[1]

5. It might seem strange at first sight, that as we ascend in the evolutionary scale, from relatively low types of animal life to the very highest, the characteristic instinctive reactions should become not less but more primitive. This fact, however, should be read in connection with the whole range of activity open to man and the lower animals respectively. Where the instincts are prevailingly epicritic, the behaviour of the species is restricted to certain narrow channels and is rigidly predetermined. Efficiency is purchased at the cost of flexibility, variety and freedom. Only a few stereotyped activities are possible, and when the conditions are given these activities occur with mechanical regularity. All individuals in the group act alike. There are no significant departures from the standard responses to stimulus. Where, on the contrary, as in the case of man, the instincts are of the protopathic type, i.e. where they are less highly evolved, their relative inchoateness renders them more easily modifiable. Being less rigidly defined, they enter into all sorts of dynamic associations. Sometimes they *inhibit*, sometimes they *reinforce* one another; and generally speaking the resulting mode of life is marked by a high degree of flexibility and a rich variety of activities. It is only under these conditions that freedom and morality are possible. Morality, therefore, presupposes the *protopathic* type of instinct. The same is true of progress. In the case of the insects, the epicritic instincts represent the limit of development. It is impossible to advance further in this direction, because at this point insect life attains a virtual perfection of adjustment. When the epicritic stage of evolution is reached, therefore, we come to the end of a process.

6. In the case of man instinct is not an end, but a beginning; and it is natural that the instincts should remain at a relatively primitive stage of development, because in the advance of human life the instinctive stage is eventually left behind. On the other hand,

[1] *vid.* Rivers, *Instinct and the Unconscious*, Cambridge Press, 1920.

where perfection of adjustment occurs at the level of instinct, there is no incentive for the organism to advance beyond. A perfected instinctive system makes for arrested development. Insect life represents a cul-de-sac in the path of the life force.

The principle of this advance is a readjustment of the mental to the physiological component in instinct. At the beginning of life the physiological factor is completely in the ascendency: the mental factor has no directive or controlling influence. In the course of time this relationship is reversed. The mental factor takes command of the total movement, and the physiological assumes the character of an organ or instrument for the achievement of ends that are conceived and prescribed in advance by consciousness. This rearrangement is rendered possible by the fact that in man the instincts do not normally occur as isolated units of behaviour but in associative groups. When such a group comes into action, the mental component of each of the associated instincts tends to sink to the level of unconsciousness, and, as in the case of learning to swim or to walk, there emerges a new and more complex state of consciousness. This is the (psychical) concomitant, M, not of the minute contributory units of behaviour, but of the activity in its complex totality. Furthermore, in the very process whereby the mental factor becomes complex, it becomes integrated and autonomous. Our subjective life is no longer a mere reflection into consciousness (m^1, m^2, etc.) of events (ph^1, ph^2, etc.) that are going on of their own accord in the body. It has become a system of thoughts, emotions and native impulses or volitions, organized together in ways that express the nature, not of the body but of the mind. Thus:

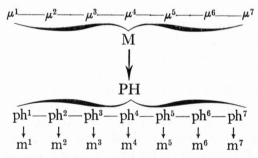

$$\mu^1\text{---}\mu^2\text{---}\mu^3\text{---}\mu^4\text{---}\mu^5\text{---}\mu^6\text{---}\mu^7$$

$$M$$

$$\downarrow$$

$$PH$$

$$ph^1\text{---}ph^2\text{---}ph^3\text{---}ph^4\text{---}ph^5\text{---}ph^6\text{---}ph^7$$

$$\downarrow\quad\downarrow\quad\downarrow\quad\downarrow\quad\downarrow\quad\downarrow\quad\downarrow$$

$$m^1\quad m^2\quad m^3\quad m^4\quad m^5\quad m^6\quad m^7$$

7. In the transition from a physiologically determined experience to a spiritually directed behaviour, there are two main stages. The first extends roughly from infancy to adolescence,

the second from adolescence onwards. In the earlier portion of the first stage we are chiefly preoccupied with learning the art of managing the body and using the organs which nature has provided for the furtherance of life (hands and feet, eyes and ears and tongue). Later, we are equally occupied with exercising the mind upon certain more or less stereotyped problems. Throughout this period as a whole, our ends are generally prescribed for us by others and imposed upon us by social sanctions. It is our business to become expert in the use of the requisite means whether physical or mental. Morality begins here, but only in a limited sense. The ethical life of a child is restricted by the fact that he is not yet fully responsible for the choice of ends. When the later stage is reached the restrictions of childhood are largely removed, and the choice of ends becomes the greatest of all our responsibilities. We are now moral agents in the full sense of the term. A man's character is to be estimated chiefly by reference to the kind of ends he habitually chooses, and especially by reference to the question whether he has succeeded in defining the end of life as a whole.[2]

8. As the simpler "units of behaviour" coalesce in complex patterns or systems, their mental ingredients begin to contract relations amongst themselves. In this way there is generated a spiritual order of life which is largely independent of the natural order with which it is correlated. The process may be viewed, not only from the standpoint of conscious experience as a whole, but from the several points of view implied in the cognitive, the affective and the conative aspects of conscious experience.

The Evolution of a Finished Spirituality
(a) on Its Cognitive Side

Let us consider first the cognitive life. The raw material and the primitive form of cognition are to be found in *sensation*. This may be defined as the mental correlate of stimulation. When a stimulus occurs in the body, consciousness takes the form of sensation. In the development of the cognitive life we may note the following.

9. (a) Sensation as such. Sensation may be regarded from two points of view. Subjectively considered, it is a mental state. But states of consciousness have their objects. For the object in this case we may adopt the term *sensum*—e.g., *blue*, in contradistinc-

---

[2] Compare the difference that results from defining man's chief end as pleasure, acquisition, sex, service of humanity, "to glorify God and enjoy him for ever."

tion from *seeing* blue, *sound* as distinct from *hearing*, and so on. Sensation is the rudimentary form of cognition, corresponding to the "unit of behaviour."

(b) A certain difficulty arises in connection with the conception of sensation as such. Our sensations, to begin with, are no better than vague feelings. Later, they become exact and well defined. But when this point is reached they are no longer mere sensations. They have become perceptions, and their objects *percepts*. A percept is a sensum interpreted, identified, distinguished and perhaps classified. The paradox of the situation* is that in order to have a well defined sensory experience it is necessary to advance beyond the merely sensory to the perceptual phase of consciousness. Sensa complete themselves only when they are more than sensa.

10. (c) A difficulty, again, arises in connection with perception. A percept or identified sensum is possible only by an *act of judgment*. In order to have a fully developed sensory experience of blue, it is necessary that the presented content should be *perceived* as blue; but this in turn implies that it is *judged* to be this specific colour and nothing else. The content of our perceptual experience is therefore not merely a sensory presentation. It is an object upon which a judgment of identification is centred. Thus, just as a completed sensum implies an act of perception, so every act of perception implies and anticipates a more advanced mental operation, the act of judging.

11. (d) The effect of judgment upon the percept. When the percept is identified by the act of judgment it contracts a new character, the character of universality. *This blue* is an individualized example of *blue in general*. But *blue in general* is not the object of sensory or perceptual experience, it is an object of thought —that is to say, a concept or idea in the mind. Thus just as the completed sensum implies a percept, the completed percept implies a concept. When this point is reached a new possibility arises. Concepts may exist in the mind without the support of perceptual experience. It is possible to *think* blue without perceiving a specific example. Thus we attain the power of free ideas. A free idea is an element in judgment and implies the latter. It is the product of thinking pure and simple. When a judgment occurs in the absence of sensory or perceptual experience, the objects rep-

[*"The paradox"—the appearance of contradiction that is in all dialectical movement.—Ed.]

resented are ideas, and the judgment is the system of their mutual interrelation.

12. (e) Judgments and systems of judgment. Not only do concepts stand related to one another in the system of the judgment, but judgments come together in more complex systems of thought. Such systems are the product of reflection brought to bear upon some province of experience. Every science is one such system— i.e. an organized body of interrelated judgments upon some aspect of the natural world. Other systems are those which embody a man's professional knowledge, his views on education, his political or economic creed. One body of organized judgments differs from another in comprehensiveness. The greatest comprehensiveness is aspired to by philosophy and religion. Here we have an attempt to think the fundamental aspects of experience together. The product is a total outlook on reality. Such a total outlook, when brought to bear on the practical conduct of life, may be called a policy. A policy of some sort is essential to a developed morality.

(b) on Its Conative Side

13. Turning to morality and policy, we note five points.

(a) Morality implies a system of judgments upon the meaning of life as a whole. The judgments constitute what are called a man's principles. His policy is the complete system of these. In the absence of such a policy a fully developed moral life is impossible. The possession of a policy, therefore, must be considered among the conditions of morality.

(b) This does not mean that it is the only condition. A man with a well defined and well sustained policy may not be a good man. His policy may be mistaken. Conversely the absence of a policy need not imply badness. A man's instincts may be sound and wholesome without a policy. But so long as his life is lived mainly on the plane of instinct, he cannot be considered an ethically mature or developed person. A completed moral life, then, demands two things, a policy of some sort, and the right sort of policy; what might be called, quite simply, the good man's policy; of which the following subsidiary points are to be noted.

14. (i) The good man will think of his life as characterized by a certain unity. His ideal will be that of a completely integrated system of experiences. The moral life, as he sees it, will be as far removed as possible from a mere sequence of occasions, oppor-

tunities, impulses in response to stimulation. Coherence will be of the essence of moral living.

(ii) He will realize that the psycho-physical life of instinct can never of itself furnish an adequate basis for the complete integration of the spiritual self. It is true that the instincts tend to coalesce in associative groups. They do so naturally, and without the conscious and deliberate intervention of the subject. But the spontaneous coalescence of instincts always falls very far short of a general unification of personality. For one thing, the number of instinctive activities which combine in response to any stimulus is always limited. Certain tendencies of our nature are thus developed at the expense of others. The ideal of a perfected humanity is not thus attainable. In the second place, when the instincts coalesce by natural affiliation, they do so under the attractive power of a single major instinct—maternity, gregariousness, pugnacity, curiosity, food-seeking, escape, self-assertion, submission, acquisitiveness, sex. No one of these, even if accompanied by a cluster of cognate impulses, is fitted to act as a principle for the organization of the spiritual life as a whole. It follows that:

(c) in moral policy the principle of integration must be sought beyond the level of the instinctive life as such, even at its points of highest development—that is to say, the ideal of a moralized existence can be realized only in the second of the two phases in the transition from a physiologically to a spiritually determined behaviour. Morality demands the elevation of the spiritual principle to a position of complete and permanent ascendency over the instinctive life—in other words, the effective displacement of a psycho-physical by a purely spiritual determinism.

15. (d) For the realization of this ideal there are certain necessary conditions. (i) We must have attained the capacity for secondary self-consciousness,* in the most extended sense. This means that we must be aware of ourselves as the subjects of an experience extending continuously into the past and potentially into the future. (ii) We must realize that our selfhood is incomplete. It is so in the sense that the activities which are its temporal contents have been largely the responses of the psycho-physical system to momentary stimulus or to incitements which affect us on one side of our nature only, and fall far short of expressing what is desirable as a whole. Even if we succeeded in attaining our ends,

[*Chap. VI, 6ff., pp. 260ff.—Ed.]

our life assumes the aspect of a series of gratified desires rather than of a permanently satisfied self. Thus the consciousness of personal continuity is accompanied by a distressing sense of discontinuity in our interests and achievements. Life appears to us to be a succession of many unimportant things, rather than one thing of fundamental value. (iii) Along with this sense of actual incompleteness there must go the ideal of a completed selfhood—that is, of a mode of being in which the infinitely variegated activities of life are all duly correlated and subordinated to one great end. The discovery of such an end is the supreme achievement of morality on its cognitive side.

A Finished Spirituality as Cognitive of an End. Defining the End

16. (e) Finally, the definition of the end may be arrived at by a process of elimination. Generally speaking the condition to be fulfilled is that of supplying some object in life capable of satisfying man's fundamental craving for the power to experience life as one, and so realize the ideal of completed selfhood. Clearly, the problem has to do with experience in its temporal aspect.

17. As we have insisted the fundamental characteristic of spirit is its unique power to bring a variety of times together into a single system of involuted time. Always, by its very nature, the time of experience in all its forms is necessarily involuted. Every present is a specious present. But it may be so in various degrees. In the life of pleasure, for example, the limits of involution are determined on the one hand by the stimulus or incitement, on the other by the gratification achieved. These limits are very restricted. Pleasure is a shortlived experience. Once the culminating point has been reached, a phase of life is at an end; and we must begin all over again. A life that is planned as a succession of gratified desires, therefore, resolves itself into a series of disconnected episodes. For, as has been often observed, the life of pleasure is subject to what might be called the moral law of diminishing returns. With each succeeding gratification the capacity for pleasurable excitement decreases and the stimulus must be intensified, until the point is reached at which the capacity for pleasure is reduced beyond the possibility of effective stimulation. The pursuits which once produced intense gratification now no longer have that effect, they have become distasteful and perhaps disgusting. But by this time they may have become habitual, so that the subject finds

himself saddled with habits he may have learnt to loathe but cannot break. Not only has life resolved itself into a series of discontinuous activities, but these activities themselves have lost all value, and become meaningless.

18. We have already said something concerning the life of practical projects, whether social, political or economic. Unlike the life of pleasure, the life of projects is actuated on each occasion, not by psycho-physical stimulus but by the definite consciousness of a remoter end to be achieved. This end exists, for the agent, at first, in idea. In this case the involution may be quite extensive. We may labour steadily and consistently for years to attain a certain position in society, to achieve a political programme or reform, to amass a fortune; and we may succeed. But the fact remains that no one of these ends is sufficiently comprehensive to satisfy the deepest cravings of the spirit. If success crowns our efforts the project comes to an end, and like Othello we feel our occupation gone. Life loses its significance and with its significance goes its interest. One cure for this is the discovery of fresh projects, but these lead to the same predicament and leave us in the end with a sense of frustration.

19. The life of pleasure and the life of successive projects must therefore both be rejected as failing to fulfil the conditions required to render a single system of experiences completely integrated under a supreme end. There remains one possibility. The object which is alone capable of concentrating upon itself the sum-total of the forces, cognitive, affective and conative, of man's spiritual being—the object to which man's nature may go out as an undivided whole of spirit in a sustained act of intellectual affirmation, emotional abandon, and volitional self-surrender, can be no other than the promotion of the spiritual mode of being itself, wherever it exists. Thus the moral end, which is at the same time the principle of spiritual integration, is definable as the service of spirit by spirit. This is an end sufficiently comprehensive in its scope to be capable both of engaging all the energies of our instinctive and psychical nature and of organizing these energies together into the unity of an experience which is altogether one. But what is meant by the promotion of the spiritual or the service of spirit by spirit, can be made fully clear only by considering the subject in its emotional aspect; to which we shall turn in the following chapter.

CHAPTER XVI

The Development of Man's Spiritual Being, Affective and Conative

The Affective Side of the Developed Spirit. Emotion and Sentiment. Part Played by the Proleptic Tendency of the Mind

1. Just as the cognitive side of experience develops in complexity and independence, so the emotional side develops under the same conditions into something having a relatively permanent identity and an inner constitution of its own. When the affective components of instinct are organized into permanent systems they become sentiments.[1]

Something of the principle of the organization may be suggested diagrammatically thus:

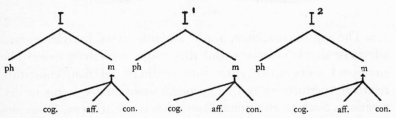

I = Instinct
ph = The physical component
m = The mental component, cognitive, affective and conative.

When the instincts coalesce, their emotional ingredients may unite to form a new complex emotion, which is different in quality from any of its constituents, and is not a mechanical product of them. Such complex emotional states are excited by objects and situations which provoke more than one instinct at the same time. McDougall has enumerated some of these compound emotions. Admiration, for example, combines wonder, which is the affective ingredient in the instinct of curiosity, with negative self-feeling which is the affective ingredient in the instinct of submission. Hence admiration is a binary emotion. Awe is tertiary. It unites

[1] *vid.* McDougall, *Social Psychology*, Chaps. v and vi; Shand, *The Foundations of Character*, Chaps. iv and v.

admiration, with its two constituents, and fear.[2] A further advance in complexity is implied in reverence. This emotion McDougall analyzes into awe and gratitude. The latter is described as "a binary compound of tender emotion and negative self-feeling." Hence reverence will include the four emotional constituents, wonder, fear, tender emotion and negative self-feeling, the last being derived from two sources, first as a constituent in awe, and secondly as a constituent in gratitude. Thus:

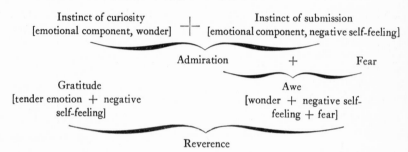

Instinct of curiosity   Instinct of submission
[emotional component, wonder] ─┼─ [emotional component, negative self-feeling]

Admiration   +   Fear

Gratitude   Awe
[tender emotion + negative   [wonder + negative self-
self-feeling]   feeling + fear]

Reverence

2. The sentiments, then, imply a synthesis of the elementary affects or simple emotions. But they imply something more. The emotional units which enter into synthetic relation, constitute relatively permanent and independent emotional systems or dispositions. Such an emotional disposition is a sentiment. Examples are love and hate. Our next task is to glance briefly at this relation of sentiment and emotion.

3. (a) An emotion or affect is a transient experience of the conscious subject which comes and goes with the stimulus or the object that promotes it. A sentiment is a permanent organization of the emotional self, which determines what particular emotional experience shall arise in consciousness in response to any stimulus or in any situation. Thus emotions exist only in the form of definitely conscious states. Sentiments exist whether or not for the time being we are conscious of them. When they emerge out of the unconscious they take the form of emotions specially designed to give expression to them under the circumstances of the case. The sentiment of hatred, for example, persists through a succession of conscious

[2] McDougall, *Social Psychology*, p. 135.

and unconscious phases. In the conscious phase it may become the emotion of anger or angry contempt. Thus:

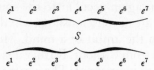

e = emotions about to be organized into sentiment S.

ε = emotions which give temporary expression in consciousness to sentiment S.

(b) The same emotional ingredients may enter into different sentiments. But they enter in different ways and under different conditions. For example, fear, anger, joy and sorrow may combine to give temporary emotional expression to the settled sentiment of love. "In the presence of anything we love we are disposed to feel joy, and in prolonged absence from it, sorrow, and at the suggestion of danger to feel the fear of losing it, and when it is attacked, to feel anger against the assailant."[3] The same four emotions, under different conditions, enter into the sentiment of hate. Thus if we hate a person we feel sorrow, anger and fear in his presence or at his success, and joy in his absence or at his discomfiture.

4. (c) The sentiments are not generated from the emotions by mere association or by any process of mechanical conjunction. Love, for example, is not the mere sum of joy + sorrow + fear + anger; and if it is so defined it will be impossible to distinguish love from hate. The appearance of any particular affect and the precise quality of the affect are determined by the sentiment of which it is the manifestation. The principle involved is that the sentiments are not organized by the emotions. On the contrary, the emotions are organized by the sentiments.

5. But if the sentiments are compounded of the emotions, the emotions must come first in the order of development. If the emotions are organized by the sentiments, the sentiments must be already there as a principle of organization. This is the difficulty to which we already saw the solution, in an application of the principle of prolepsis. In this there is an exact parallel between the development of the emotional and that of the cognitive life.* Just as sensations anticipate and imply the perceptions which succeed them in

---

[3] Shand, *op. cit.*, Chap. IV, p. 35.
[*cf. the "paradox" of p. 388.—Ed.]

time, and these in turn the still later judgments and concepts, so the elementary or crude emotions anticipate and imply the sentiments. But this possibility is again peculiar to the spiritual mode of being. Every elementary state of consciousness, whether cognitive or emotional, occurs within the ambit of a mind. Moreover it is not conveyed into the mind from without. Rather it is the inner response of a subjective system to incitement. The existence of such a system is therefore the precondition, both in an ontological and in a temporal sense, of all its individuated contents or experiences as those occur in time. Thus when a particular sensation or emotion arises in consciousness as a result of stimulation, it immediately finds itself within a subjective context having a certain extensity in time. This context includes elements not only from among the antecedents, but also from among the sequelae, of the momentary conscious state. The experience of the moment is what it is because of what comes after as well as because of what comes before. Its identity as a subjective event is determined in part by its relation to a future development of the system as a whole. From the very instant at which an emotion makes its appearance in consciousness, it is transformed by the fact that in accordance with the proleptic tendency of the mind, an emotional structure anticipates and determines the momentary excitements which are among its contents.

The Affective Side of the Developed Spirit in Relation to the Cognitive

6. There is a correlation of emotional and cognitive as aspects of experience. The objects of cognitive experience, sensa, percepts, judgments, concepts and policies are at the same time objects of emotional experience. There is thus a reciprocal correspondence between the emotional and cognitive phases of our awareness. The two develop together. As sensa and percepts give place to judgments and concepts, the emotions become organized into sentiments. Sentiments therefore arise in us by the same process that gives rise to the power of thinking. The affective states which accompany the objects of sense before the latter have been organized and interpreted by concepts are crude, elementary emotions. They are further characterized by momentariness and instability. The development of the emotional life to the level of sentiment implies the development of the cognitive life from the level of sensory and perceptual experience to that of free ideas. We can feel transient

pleasure and pain, fear and anger, in the presence of a perceived object; but in order to love or hate, to reverence or despise anything, we must learn to think it. All the higher emotional possibilities imply the emancipation of the mind from the bond of sense[4] by the power of free ideation.

7. The moral life has its emotional structure. (a) Just as on the cognitive side, moral development implies the transition from the crudeness of sensory experience to systems of judgment and thought, so on the emotional side the same development implies a transition from the crudeness of elementary affective experience to the organized systems of sentiment. The limiting case is that in which the sentiments are organized together into one comprehensive system centred upon a supreme object—an object capable of dominating and integrating the emotional life as a whole. This system is the affective correlate of a policy. What a policy is on the intellectual side, the comprehensive sentiment is on the emotional side—viz. a total system of feelings or a master feeling epitomizing such a system and brought to bear upon the practical conduct of life. When such a system exists, it represents the value of life in its entirety—what alone makes life worth living.[5]

(b) When the emotions are thus gathered together into a supreme sentiment, the result is emotional permanence or stability. This is essential to a morally developed character.

(c) Along with this stability, and as a necessary precondition of it, there goes the capacity to sustain an emotional attitude indefinitely in the absence of the object that evokes it. An emotionally mature character is one that has rendered itself independent of the moment-to-moment incitements of sensory experience. The highest possible achievement in this respect is the ability to conceive and to sustain a powerful sentiment towards an object of which we have had, and perhaps can have, no sensory experience at all.[6]

---

[4] cf. Helen Keller, *The Story of My Life*, pp. 22-4.

[5] cf. the Apostle's words: "For me to live *is* Christ." Phil. i. 21. Also "For I am persuaded that neither death nor life, nor angels, nor principalities, nor powers, nor things present, nor things to come, nor height, nor depth, nor any other creature, shall be able to separate us from the love of God, which is in Christ Jesus our Lord." Rom. viii. 38-9. It is noteworthy how the concentration of the emotional life upon one supreme object gives that life a complete unity in spite of vicissitude.

[6] This is the crowning possibility to which the Apostle refers in the words: "Jesus Christ; whom having not seen, ye love." 1 Peter i, 7-8. For a cognitive parallel *vid.* John xx. 29, "Blessed are they that have not seen, and yet have believed."

8. (d) Again, as on the cognitive side the possession of a policy does not of itself guarantee morality, so on the emotional side the displacement of the crude emotions by settled sentiments is not all that morality implies: and the question arises as to the kind of sentiment capable of furnishing the emotional condition and content of the good life—what might be called the moral sentiment.

The Governing Affect in the Spiritual Life: Reverence. The Nature of this Sentiment. McDougall's Analysis

All values have their origin in the existence of the spiritual. On its cognitive side morality is the intellectual recognition of this fact, and the organization of the cognitive life around it. This is the essence of the good man's policy. On the emotional side the question is: What is the sentiment that goes with the intellectual appreciation of the original and absolute value of spiritual existence? The answer is *reverence*. In its affective aspect the moral life is a life dominated by reverence for personality. Reverence is the subjective realization of the value called sanctity; and the good life is the life in which a consciousness of the sanctity of the spiritual prevails steadily through all the occasions and vicissitudes of human experience.

9. As to the nature of reverence, McDougall's analysis[7] may be taken as basis, but it requires supplementation and modification in certain essential respects.

(a) It is not enough to represent the sentiment as compounded of four independently existing elementary emotions. In accordance with the principle of prolepsis, the sentiment must be taken first, and its components represented as its differentiated contents. Their exact character, therefore, is determined by the nature of the system which they presuppose. Thus the fear involved is not just any kind of fear, but the kind that is peculiar to the sentiment of reverence. And so of wonder and negative self-feeling. A further interpretation of these constituent emotions is necessary.

10. (b) The reinterpretation we would submit is as follows:

(i Of fear there are two main types, the natural fear of danger and "numinous" fear.* The former (*a*) is centred on any object or eventuality that threatens our life or is fraught with pos-

---

[7] *vid.* p. 394, above.

[*With all that follows, here, compare *Studies in the Philosophy of Religion*, Chap. VII, on "The Numinous and the Holy."—Ed.]

sible pain or disaster. Its sphere is the natural life of man, and its object is *circumstance*. Characteristic examples of the objects of natural fear are fire and water, famine, disease, pain, poverty. Against such dangers we arm ourselves in advance. (β) Numinous fear, on the other hand, is not the dread of any natural eventuality but a peculiar apprehension which assails us when the natural enters a context of the supernatural—in other words, when we find ourselves in the presence of the spiritual or subjective mode of being. In so far as it is possible for one person to fear another person *as such*, the emotion is not natural but "numinous" fear. The latter may be defined as "the spirit's fear of spirit." It is specifically this kind of apprehension that enters as a constituent into the sentiment of reverence.

11. The question inevitably arises: What is there in the spiritual mode of being that it should be an object of fear? Why should one person fear another person *as such*? I venture to explain as follows. The presence of another person has a disturbing effect upon the natural flow of the instinctive life. It produces a sudden transition from primary to secondary[8] self-consciousness. When this occurs we become acutely aware of our ontological status as spiritual beings—the subjects of an experience. This new consciousness of self is a necessary condition of any well developed sense of moral good and evil. The reason is that the distinction of good and evil has its source in subject-selfhood, the principle of all values. Where the values are objective—i.e. where they have their locus in *objects* of experience—it is possible to become aware of them without being conscious of the relation to the spiritual being by which they are conditioned. But moral value has its locus not in the objects around us, but in ourselves. Hence a consciousness of self is implied in our consciousness of such value. Man first realizes his nature as a moral being when he realizes that he is a person; and the principal agency in evoking secondary self-consciousness is intersubjective contact with other subject-selves. Now the accession of self-consciousness is a disturbing, and may even be a profoundly distressing experience. It has about it something of the force of a rebuke. Our primitive instinctive nature is confronted by a higher nature that is spiritual through and through, and the conjunction is felt as an embarrassment. Hence the fear which attends

---

[8] *vid.* above, Chap. VII, 6*ff.*, pp. 260*ff.*

every advance in self-consciousness. We feel embarrassed in the presence of another subject because that presence places a constraint upon instinct.[9] Our consciousness of this restraint, on its emotional side, is numinous fear—an ingredient in the sentiment of reverence.

12. (ii) The *wonder* which McDougall includes as a further ingredient is also of a special kind. As there are two main types of fear, so of wonder. One is merely the emotional accompaniment of intellectual and scientific curiosity—i.e. of the desire to know.[10] Now knowledge proceeds by analysis and causal explanation. It accounts for a substance by breaking it up into its constituent elements or parts, and for an event by resolving it into a product of constituent events. When the limit of analysis is reached, the explanation is considered complete: the instinct of curiosity is satisfied and wonder ceases.[11] This type of wonder, then, aims at its own extinction through a completed exploration of the object. On the other hand there is a kind of wonder which does not seek satisfaction in dismembering its object, but in contemplating it in its unimpaired integrity. For example, when a great work of art evokes our admiration, we do not seek to dispel the feeling of wonder by analyzing it into its constituents or by asking how it was produced. We take it as a whole; and outside the whole the parts are meaningless. What really excites our wonder is the mystery of its *indefeasible concreteness*. It is not a subject for analysis but a θαῦμα marvel and mystery, an object to be contemplated (θάομαι) in silent and inextinguishable wonder.[12] Now this sense of the mysterious finds its most fitting object in the concreteness of living structures; and for this reason primitive peoples regard living things with a peculiar awe.[13] The highest point is reached when the life in question is spiritual life, and the structure in question is a subjective system or personality. We are now in the presence of the supreme mystery—what Otto has called the *mysterium tre-*

[9] Compare the embarrassment of the vying disciples in the presence of the child set in their midst. Mark ix. 33-7.

[10] cf. Aristotle, *Met.*, A, 982b.

[11] Aristotle, *op. cit.*, A, 983a.

[12] Note that the θαῦμα is a μυστήριον—a mystery; and in the presence of a mystery we become still. μύω, to close (the mouth?).

[13] e.g., Totemism. [cf. the author's *Studies in the Philosophy of Religion*, Chap. III. —Ed.]

mendum. Wonder and numinous fear have become inextricably blended.

13. (iii) The element of *negative self-feeling* also is insufficiently defined by McDougall. Such feeling may be no more than a sense of debasement, and, as such, it may be a debasing emotion. But when it is found in the sentiment of reverence, the negative feeling, while it debases, also exalts.[14] And the reason is that the being in whose presence we feel debased is of like nature with ourselves —a spirit or subjective system. Thus in paying homage to personality in another we are paying homage to personality in ourselves. When we prostrate our nature before the principle of selfhood in any being, we achieve the morally necessary attitude of self-respect. With these modifications McDougall's definition may stand. Reverence includes numinous fear, the negative self-feeling that exalts and the wonder that is still in the presence of the spiritual.

The Effect of Reverence

14. Now, reverence *works*. Reverence might be described as an emotional purge of life. Its function is to purify and exalt the instincts. This can be shown by a consideration of typical cases. Human behaviour may be taken to fall into three main divisions according to the nature of the relationship involved:

(1) Relation of persons to the natural world around them.

(2) Relation of persons to persons.

(3) Relation of the individual subject to itself—i.e. to its own states and activities.

(1) The ethical principle involved in *the relation of persons to the natural world* is that the supernatural, which is the spiritual, should always prevail over the natural. Morality demands that in all relations between persons and things the ontological superiority of the subject over the object should be asserted and maintained. This means that the material necessities and resources of life must

---

[14] cf. Dante's phrase, applied to the Virgin:

> Vergine, madre, figlia del tuo figlio,
> *Umile ed alta* piu che creatura.

Paradiso, xxxiii, 1-2; and *vid.* Taylor, *Faith of a Moralist*, Vol. I, p. 310. Also, "For thus saith the high and lofty One that inhabiteth eternity, whose name is holy; I dwell in the high and holy *place* with him also *that is* of a humble and contrite spirit, to revive the spirit of the humble, and to revive the heart of the contrite ones." Isa. lvii. 15; and *vid.* Paul Elmer More, *The Sceptical Approach to Religion*, p. 128.

be relegated to an inferior position as means to an end, and that, unlike persons, they must never be treated as ends in themselves. The case is different when the point of the object is not utility but charm or beauty. Aesthetic significance is not a means to anything else, but a self-substantiating value, the realization of which has therefore the force of an end. But the end in question is still subordinate to the principle by which it is determined. In the last resort the value of a beautiful object resides in its capacity to give pleasure to a conscious subject. The fundamental and therefore the supreme value is always an attribute of the spiritual as such. Morality requires (among other things) the emotional recognition of this. Where such recognition is not forthcoming the result is an inversion of values. We become the slaves of an interest in *things*, of a desire for them, or of the emotions which depend for their maintenance upon the existence of things. From this disaster we are normally saved by the power of habitual reverence—for ourselves and for other persons. Thus *self*-respect prevents a man becoming a glutton or a miser. Reverence for *others* should prevent him indulging the instinct of acquisition in ways that involve social injustice.

15. The effect of reverence (2) upon instinctive behaviour *towards persons* can be briefly indicated by considering a series of instincts:

(a) The sex impulse[15] unregulated by a reverent regard for its object and the vital (which are the spiritual) interests of the latter, implies a violation of the sanctity of personality—a breach of Kant's rule that persons should never be treated merely as a means to our satisfaction, but always as ends in themselves. The life of sex becomes moral to the extent to which it is placed in an emotional context of which reverence is the principle. It thereby becomes an outlet for the expression of personality. In human experience sex is a function not of our animal nature but of the spirit. Its purpose in the economy of the conscious life is to minister to the legitimate craving for a personal relationship which shall be complete—i.e. a relationship of perfect intimacy, and one in which the element of tenderness shall have the fullest scope. Hence the

---

[15] *vid.* Hocking, *Human Nature and Its Remaking*, Chap. XLII, "Christianity and Sex Love"; J. G. Fichte, *Science of Rights*, First Appendix, "Fundamental Principles of the Rights of Family," English tr., pp. 391 *ff.*

degrading and enervating form of self-indulgence which the cultivation of sex becomes where personal regard is lacking.

(b) The parental instinct under the same conditions, i.e. if uncontrolled by a reverent regard for the vital interests of its object, likewise degenerates into a subtle and cruel form of self-indulgence.

(c) Gregariousness without reverence is an instinct which leads to every form of social oppression and injustice. The *rights* of the individual are inevitably ignored when there is no *regard* for the personality of the individual.[16]

(d) Combativeness has an entirely different quality according as it is accompanied or unaccompanied by respect for the enemy and by self-respect. Contrast modern warfare and the ideals of chivalry.

(e) Curiosity tempering itself by respect for the privacy of the individual may be contrasted with curiosity giving itself rein. One might instance the use and abuse of the confessional.

(f) Self-assertion. The principle here is to repress the instinctive, in order that the spiritualized self may be asserted. Respect for the spiritualized self is the condition involved.

(g) Submission—if of spirit to spirit—is not degrading.

16. When reverence is (3) the basis of the relation of *the self to itself* this relation takes the form of self-respect. This sentiment is a fundamental condition of morality. It is always directed to the total system of personality—personality as such or as an ideally integrated whole—and never to the momentary states or subordinate systems within the whole. Self-respect forbids us to degrade our spiritual being in its entirety to the service of an individual instinct or group of instincts. When such degradation occurs what is wrong is that we are deficient in self-respect. Without self-respect the life of the individual is either emotionally unintegrated or else it is integrated around one of the major instincts or a group of these. In the first case the result is an undeveloped, in the second a misdeveloped and defective character. Self-respect, it will be noted, implies a consciousness of the self as a whole or as the unified system of its own subjective contents or experiences. This in turn implies that ability to experience life as one, which figures in the good man's policy. Finally, the ability in

---

[16] Compare youth in the place of power, with its overriding intolerance; or again the cynicism of government by propaganda and advertisement.

question presupposes retroactive and proleptic activity in the involuted time of the spirit.

Is Such an Emotional Attitude within Our Command?

17. There is a problem of the emotions and the ethical imperative. For the moral life demands a certain emotional attitude and the question arises: can we meet the demand? Can we, by any effort within our power, achieve the sentiment upon which the moralization of our conduct and our character depends? In brief, is it possible to *command the emotions*?[17]

At first sight the answer to this question appears to be in the negative. The volitional control of the emotions and sentiments would seem to be beyond our power. We cannot produce a state of fear or anger by a simple fiat of the will. We cannot love or hate at the word of command. The very fact that we distinguish conation as the *active* aspect of experience, from feeling, would appear to imply the passivity of the latter; and some writers, e.g., Fichte, have definitely represented feeling or emotion as the passive factor in the life of the self.[18]

This point of view, however, rests on a limited and partial reading of the facts of experience. If it is a fact that we cannot, by a direct act of the will, remove one emotional disposition and create another, it is no less a fact that emotional changes occur, and that in the course of their lives men and women acquire dispositions which, to begin with, were beyond their capacity. Such changes must be determined by conditions of some sort. They do not just happen; and, if so, the question arises whether, among the conditions which lead to emotional transformation, there may not be some which lie definitely within man's power as an active being. Again, while it is true that the affective side of experience is distinguishable from the conative or active, the distinction is purely theoretical. There is no actual experience that is exclusively affective or exclusively conative. Every experience is both. Action and emotion in every instance go together, and each has a determining influence on each. This truth has an important bearing upon the question of the conditions under which the emotional life of the individual may be transformed. Even if it is impossible to alter our sentiments by direct volition, radical changes in the emotional self may nevertheless be induced by *what we will*, and by the active and consistent pursuit of a certain policy. Thus by willing a

---

[17] *vid.* Hocking, *Human Nature and Its Remaking*, Chap. xl, pp. 363-4.
[18] *vid. Das System der Sittenlehre*, Werke, IV, p. 44, English tr., p. 48; *ibid.*, p. 107, tr., p. 111.

course of conduct, we may be contributing to the sum-total of spiritual conditions upon which the emotional requirements of morality depend. A moral disposition may be *cultivated* by a sustained effort of the moral will.

18. What, then, should we will? One solution might be a direct pragmatic method.[19] We might feel that the way to induce the emotional disposition desired is to act as if we already possessed it. This is not without its uses. It rightly emphasizes the active and practical nature of the moral life; and it recognizes the solidarity, actual and ideal, of action and emotion. It is reasonable therefore to expect certain results from such a course. On the other hand, this method involves certain theoretical defects, and is fraught with practical danger. For example, while it is actuated by the praiseworthy motive of bringing our feelings into line with our conduct, its *first* effect is to divorce our conduct *from* our feelings. Now it is true that morality does frequently demand the dissociation of our actions and our emotions; but such dissociation, if sustained beyond a certain point, generates various forms of insincerity—culminating, it may even be, in hypocrisy. It is only in the case of the crude, momentary emotions that dissociation is permissible. Where the permanent emotional dispositions and the prevalent activities are concerned, any such dissociation is a form of untruth. The direct pragmatic method, therefore, must be strictly subordinated to the fundamental principle that in the moral life the organized systems of feeling and the typical modes of action must be kept in close correlation.[20] There remains an indirect method, which is also pragmatic. This consists in the cultivation of a policy and the steady pursuit of aims embodying the best that is known to us. Such a course of life, implying the consistent direction of the attention to the highest objects, brings its emotional correlate with it.[21] An intense preoccupation with the ideal, sustained by an effort of the will cannot fail to change the currents of the emotional life.

[19] *vid.* Hocking, *Human Nature and Its Remaking*, pp. 364-5.

[20] cf. Kant and Fichte on this question. Kant, *Grundlegung* (*Fundamental Principles of the Metaphysic of Morals*) tr. Abbot, First Section, p. 18; Fichte, *Das System der Sittenlehre*, Dritter Absch., §24, Werke, IV, pp. 310-11, English tr., pp. 325-6.

[21] cf. Paul: "Finally, brethren, whatsoever things are true, whatsoever things are honest," etc. Phil. iv. 8.

These conclusions imply the assumption of a will. Such an assumption demands a consideration of the remaining aspect of conscious experience—the conative.

The Evolution of a Will

19. The will must not be conceived as an original faculty given to man at birth as a power to do what he likes. At the beginning of life "what he likes" is a meaningless phrase. Man acquires "likes" and "dislikes" only as a result of growing experience; and the power to "do" is subject to a similar condition. The power to *do what we like*, therefore, is an acquired power. Obviously, then, the question of the will must be treated from the same standpoint from which the other aspects of the conscious life have been treated—viz. that of man's gradual development as a spiritual being. Here the starting-point is the conative feature in the mental constituent of the instinctive life.

Conation is psychical activity; and to say that every mental state has a conative aspect is to say that the life of the mind defines itself as a perpetual *doing something*. The precise degree and mode of its activity, however, varies with the varying levels of development. The conation which goes with the rudimentary instinctive life of the infant is little more than blind impulse—the psychical element in the response to stimulus. As such, it is not as yet directed by consciousness to any well defined goal. It is only after the conative life has been developed to a certain point by practice and experience that man is able to foresee the end of his actions from the beginning, and to direct his conduct accordingly. He is thus an active being long before he is capable of acting for conscious ends or willing these ends in advance. If the will may be defined as the power of deliberate, self-directed action to self-chosen ends, it is obvious that that power is not the *presupposition* but the *product* of man's spiritual evolution.

The problem of the will is therefore in the first instance the problem of man's development on the conative side of his nature. The principle of that development is identical with that which applies in the case of cognition and emotion. Just as there is a type of cognition and a type of affect, so there is a type of psychical *activity* or conation, that goes with the individual instincts, viz. impulse.[22] In the same way, when the cognitive and emotional

[22] cf. the German *Trieb*.

factors become organized into distinct spiritual systems of thought and sentiment respectively, the conative factors that accompany the former become organized into a corresponding system of conscious activities. Thus:

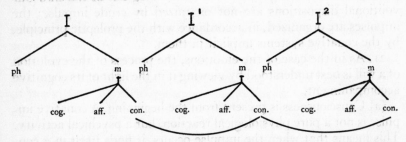

Furthermore, just as the instinctive life develops into (a) cognitive systems or policies and possibly a comprehensive or supreme policy, and (b) emotional systems or sentiments and possibly a supreme emotional disposition or ruling sentiment—so (c) it develops into conative systems and possibly into an all-comprehensive conative disposition. This last is the activity of the conscious subject as a whole realizing itself as a completely organized and unified system of spiritual energies. It is to this system alone that the name "will" is applicable. Its constituent acts are called volitions. Thus:

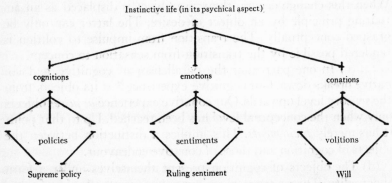

20. We must now consider how the conative impulses come to be organized into volitional systems. There is here a further parallelism with the cognitive and affective aspects of experience. If it is true that the will is a *product*, and that it is evolved out of the elementary conative energies, the evolutionary *process* is not a

mere mechanical redistribution and collocation of existing units, but is similar to the process whereby the policies and sentiments are evolved out of their respective rudiments. The organizing principle is to be sought not at the beginning but at the end. Our volitional dispositions are not organized by crude impulse: the impulses are organized, in accordance with the proleptic principle, by the conative systems implicit in them.

21. As in the case of the emotions, the process of the evolution of a will is best understood by viewing it in the light of its cognitive accompaniment.

(a) Consciousness is present from the beginning. A conative impulse is not a pure physiological reaction, but a psychical activity. This means that when the impulse occurs, it finds itself in a context which is spiritual in character—a context of conscious experience. In such a context it is more than a mere impulse or psychical reaction: it is an experience of subject-selfhood, a revelation of the self to itself.

(b) The conative life in its development follows the same general lines as the cognitive. Where the cognitive life is still in the phase of sensory experience, the conative takes a form in which crude impulse preponderates. The object of sense functions as the stimulus or incitement to impulsive activity. It is only when the thinking stage is reached, that the impulse gives way to definite volition. When this change occurs, the sense object is displaced as an actuating principle by an object of desire. The latter can only be grasped conceptually. The transition from impulse to volition is rendered possible by the transition from sensation to concept.

22. (c) In one particular the parallelism of cognitive and conative breaks down. Our cognitive experience *has* its objects from the sensory level upwards. Our conative experience *acquires* objects only when the conceptual level has been reached. Up to that point it has merely *incitements*. This implies a distinction between the objects of cognition and those of conative endeavour.

(d) The objects of cognition present themselves under a form of actuality. That is to say they impress us as actually *there* for our inspection.[23] Objects of conation on the other hand, appear under a form of non-actuality. What impresses us about them is that they

---

[23] This is so even when they are subjectively conditioned. It is not in the nature of knowledge to draw attention to the fact that its objects may depend for their existence upon the mind that knows them.

are *not* there, that they are not available for our use or enjoyment until by our action we have called them into being or realized them. At the first, then, they exist for us only ideally, or as concepts; and this applies to the objects of appetition or desire however rudimentary in character. Even if the object is merely the gratification of the senses, we experience it first of all as something absent, something *to be* achieved. What *is present* is merely the *idea* of the gratification desired, and the state of desire itself. The conative life, therefore, is characterized by the fact that as soon as it becomes conscious of its objects, it draws upon the power of ideation, and this irrespective of the question whether these objects are gross and sensual or spiritualized and refined.

In the scale of conations, sensual desires do not necessarily correspond to sensory objects in the cognitive scale. They may rather correspond to concepts. This is one of the principles on which the distinction of moral good and evil depends. Impulses are neither good nor bad until, by the power of ideation, their objects have become clear—i.e. until they have become desires. When this point is reached they are *either* good *or* evil according as they serve to promote the spiritual above the psycho-physical or the psycho-physical above the spiritual. But in either case moral credit and moral blame do not accrue to the individual until the desire has been received into a still more comprehensive system of conations, and has been thereby either rendered effective, suppressed, destroyed, or at the least modified in morally significant ways. This means that it is our volitions rather than our desires that determine the ethical value of our attitudes and our conduct. No guilt attaches to evil desires until they are willed. And credit attaches to good desires only under the same condition.

23. What do the volitions mean to the will in the evolution of the conative life? The will is compounded of individual volitions. It is therefore the final product of development and comes last in the order of time. On the other hand it is no less true that every volition is definable as *an exercise of the will*. Apparently, then, the existence of the will is already presupposed in the volitional activities which are the condition of its evolution. Once again, we are in the presence of proleptic activity.[24]

Volition is a psychical activity based upon a prior activity of desire. The latter furnishes the presupposition and starting-point

[24] For the emotional parallel, see section 5, p. 395 above.

of the former. But the relation between the two may vary from positive to negative. In the one case the desire is reinforced and rendered effective, in the other it is inhibited by the energy of the volition. (a) Where the relation is positive the desire anticipates its own gratification. It completes itself ideally in a context which includes eventualities still to be realized. Without this forward adjustment of the conative system, desire would not be what it is. It must therefore be conceived as an exercise of conative energy actualizing itself within a larger system of psychical activity—that, namely, which comprises the action requisite to the gratification of the desire. This larger system is the volition in question. Volition, therefore, is a psychical compound in which, to the original energy of the desire, there is added what might be called the further energy of fulfilment. This is the increment of action required in order to carry the desire to the point of achievement; and the question arises: where does this increment originate?

The only possible answer is that it must have its source in the native activity of the subjective system as such. It is not a product of already existing subjective forces, but a coming into existence of a new force, which, in relation to its own effects, must be interpreted as genuinely creative. The fact which comes to light when this new force makes its appearance is the fact that every exhibition of volitional energy presupposes the activity of a spiritual system which, in all its manifestations, remains indissolubly one with itself. The energy of this system is the will. The will is therefore presupposed in every volition. At the same time the volitions are necessary to render the will effective—i.e. to give it actuality in a world of accomplished deeds. The total relationship amounts to this. The volitions are only *possible* because of the will to which they give articulate expression: the will depends for its *actuality* upon the volitions which give expression to it.

(b) The second case is that in which our volitions run counter to, and inhibit, our desires. In this case it is not less, but even more, apparent that the energy of volition must be that of the subject-self as such, rising up in opposition to one of its own conative tendencies. The very possibility of such a volition clearly presupposes a will which actualizes itself in the volition.

Freedom

24. Here arises the problem of freedom, which in the abstract is not to be defined as indetermination but as self-determination, or as the property of a self as such. It appears therefore that selfhood is the precondition of free action. This condition is realizable only when being takes the form of subjectivity. Liberty is the exclusive prerogative of subject-selves; but it is realized by such selves in varying degrees. Where the integration of the subjective system is incomplete the self is not altogether free. This is the case wherever the spiritual is still to any extent dominated by the psycho-physical. Only a system in which the spiritual is absolutely supreme can claim the privilege of perfect liberty. But the absolute supremacy of the spiritual is at the same time the ideal of moral perfection. If follows that moral perfection and liberty are one. They are both definable in terms of completed personality. Finally, since will is the activity of subject-selfhood or personality as such, there can be no positive question whether the will is free. It is bound to be free if it is really a will. Freedom is part of the definitory concept of a will completely moralized. Where liberty is problematical is in the case of the subordinate conative systems or volitions. It has been vehemently asserted and denied that in the act of volition we are free. In support of the first contention it is pointed out that at the moment of decision we have an irresistible consciousness of our own liberty. The counter-assertion is that this consciousness is purely illusory and is due to our ignorance of the factors by which our decisions and our actions are alike determined. Both positions are vitiated by dogmatism and by failure to understand the nature of spirit in relation to time. In so far as our conative activities are determined by what is prior to them in the order of development, they cannot be rightly designated the activities of a perfect subject-self; and therefore they fail to comply with the formal condition of liberty. On the other hand, in so far as our volitions imply the proleptic adjustment of a partial selfhood to an ideal subject-self; in other words, in so far as they may be accurately described as "an exercise of the will," they do comply with the condition: we have every right to regard them as free.

APPENDIX

APPENDIX

Other Writings by the Author

BOOKS

Sonnets from a Prison Camp, xii, 152 pp., London, John Lane, The Bodley Head, 1919.

The Absurdity of Christianity, 64 pp. Student Christian Movement Press, 58 Bloomsbury Street, London, W.C.1., 1931.

Studies in the Philosophy of Religion, edited by Professor N. Kemp Smith, 2 Vols., xlviii, 423 and 438 pp., London, Macmillan Company, 1938.

ARTICLES

"Difference as Ultimate and Dimensional," *Mind*,[1] Vol. XIX, N.S., No. 76, October 1910.

"The Sistine Madonna," *Hibbert Journal*,[2] Vol. X, No. 4, July 1912.

"The Elements and Character of Tolstoi's *Weltanschauung*," *International Journal of Ethics*,[3] Vol. XXIII, No. 1, October 1912.

"The Problem of Knowledge from the Standpoint of Validity," *Philosophical Review*,[4] Vol. XXXIII; No. 1, January 1914, No. 2, March 1914, No. 3, May 1914.

"Kant's View of Metaphysics," *Mind*,[1] Vol. XXV, N.S., No. 97, January 1916.

"Aristotle, *Metaphysics* X (I) b. 1056B, 27-32," *The Classical Review*,[5] Vol. XXX, No. 2, March 1916.

"Kant's Phenomenalism in its Relation to Subsequent Metaphysics," *Mind*,[1] Vol. XXV, N.S., No. 100, October 1916.

"Is Christianity a Bridge between East and West?" *Asia*,[7] Vol. XXIV, No. 7, July 1924.

"Is a Conflict with the Far East Inevitable?", *Princeton Alumni Weekly*,[6] Vol. XXV, No. 15, January 21, 1925.

"The Nature of Objective Mind," *Proceedings of the Aristotelian Society*,[8] Supplementary Vol. VII, 1927.

[1] Published by the Macmillan Company, Ltd., St. Martin's Street, London, W.C.2.
[2] Published by Constable & Co., Ltd., London.
[3] Published by Sherman, French & Company, Boston, Mass.
[4] Published by Longmans, Green & Co., Lancaster, Pa.
[5] Published by John Murray, Albemarle Street, London, W.
[6] Published by Princeton University Press, Princeton, N.J.
[7] Published by Asia Magazine Incorporated, 40 East 49th Street, New York.
[8] Published by Williams and Norgate, 14 Henrietta Street, London, W.C.2.

"Adult Education and Vocation," *The Journal of Adult Education*,[9] September 1927.

"The Princeton System: a Great University Experiment," *Glasgow Herald*,[10] March 20, 1928.

"Human Nature and Education," *The Scottish Educational Journal*,[11] Vol. XI, No. 3, January 20, 1928.

"The Mind of Primitive Man," *Proceedings* of the Royal Philosophical Society of Glasgow,[12] Vol. LVI, 1928.

"Ten Years After: Our National Position," *Glasgow Herald*,[10] November 10, 1928.

"Ten Years Ago—and Now," *The Welsh Outlook*,[13] Vol. XV, No. 11, November 1928.

"The Idea of Immortality," *The Scots Observer*,[14] December 1, 8, 15, 1928.

"Religion and the Tragic Sense of Life,"[15] *The Evening Citizen*, March 23, 1929.

"A Highland Preacher," *Scots Observer*,[14] September 4, 1930.

"Address on Robert Burns," *The Falkirk Herald*,[16] January 31, 1931.

"Christian Morality and Self-Expression," *The Student World*,[17] Third Quarter, 1931.

"The Kingdom—East and West," *Church of Scotland Congress Message*, Edinburgh, 1931.

"Is War Christian?" *The Scots Observer*,[14] February 4, 1932.

"When a Nation is not a State," *Daily Record and Mail*,[18] May 3, 1932.

"The Twentieth Century is not Interested in Religion," *The Scots Observer*,[14] May 26, 1932.

"Temperance in Scotland," reprinted by the Glasgow Presbytery Committee on Temperance from a letter in the *Glasgow Herald*,[10] October 8, 1932.

[9] Published by The British Institute of Adult Education, 39 Bedford Square, London, W.C.1.
[10] Published by George Outram & Co., Ltd., Buchanan Street, Glasgow, Scotland.
[11] Published at 47 Moray Place, Edinburgh, Scotland.
[12] Published by the Society, 207 Bath Street, Glasgow, Scotland.
[13] Published at 8 Broad Street, Newtown, Mont., Wales.
[14] Published by Scottish Publications, Ltd., 7 Royal Bank Place, Buchanan Street, Glasgow, Scotland.
[15] Published in Glasgow, Scotland.
[16] Published at Falkirk, Scotland.
[17] Published by the World Students' Christian Federation, 13 Rue Calvin, Geneva, Switzerland.
[18] Published by The Associated Newspapers, Ltd., 67 Hope Street, Glasgow, Scotland.

"The Religious Aspects of Temperance," *Life and Work*,[19] October, 1932.

"The Peace Ballot: Questions of Life and Death," *Forward*,[20] April 6, 1933.

"Triumph over Idleness," The Clydebank Press,[21] April 28, 1933.

"Man and the Eternal Order," *The Scots Observer*,[14] April 29, 1933.

"Spirit-time," *Proceedings* of the Aristotelian Society,[8] 1932-3.

"Jesus Christ in His Own Time," *The Baptist Times*,[22] June 8, 1933.

"Human Life and the Medical Profession," *McGill Medical Journal*,[23] 1934.

"Edward Caird, 1835-1908," *Glasgow Herald*,[10] March 22, 1935.

"The National Declaration on The League and Armaments," *Weekly Herald*,[10] March 30, 1935.

"Is it possible to be good without being a Christian? If so what difference does being a Christian make to a man?" in *Asking Them Questions, Problems in Religious Faith and Life*, Oxford University Press, 1936.

REVIEWS

(a) In *The Review of Theology and Philosophy*.[24]

Vol. II, No. 10, April 1907, *An Introduction to Philosophy*, by George Stuart Fullerton.

Vol. III, No. 4, October 1907, *Les Bases de la Philosophie Naturaliste*, by André Cresson.

Vol. III, No. 9, March 1908, *Sensations Païennes*, by Dr. Paul Hartenberg.

Pessimisme, Féminisme, Moralisme, by Camille Bos.

Vol. IV, No. 4, October 1908, *The Philosophy of Loyalty*, by Josiah Royce.

(b) In *Mind*,[1] N.S.

Vol. XVII, No. 68, October 1908. *Die dritte Dimension: Eine philosophische Erorterung*, by A. Levy.

ibid. The Will to Doubt. An Essay in Philosophy for the General Thinker, by Alfred H. Lloyd.

Vol. XIX, No. 73, January 1910, *Das Verhältnis der Verstandeserkenntnis zur Sinnlichen in der Vorsokratischen Philosophie*, by Dr. Ernst Arndt.

---

[19] Published at 22 Queen Street, Edinburgh, Scotland.
[20] Published by Forward Printing & Publishing Co., 26 Civic Street, Glasgow, Scotland.
[21] Published at Clydebank, Scotland.
[22] Published at 4 Southampton Row, London, W.C.1.
[23] Published at Montreal, Canada.
[24] Published by Otto Schultz & Co., 20 South Frederick Street, Edinburgh, Scotland.

ibid. Über die Erkennbarkeit der Gegenstände, by Hans Pichler.

Vol. XIX, No. 76, October 1910, *Science et Religion*, by E. Boutroux.

Vol. XX, No. 79, July 1911. *Proceedings of the Aristotelian Society.*
N.S. Vol. X.

Vol. XXI, No. 81, January 1912. *Prolegomena zur Naturphilosophie*, by Hermann Graf Keyserling.

ibid. XXI, No. 82, April 1912. *Individualism*, by Warner Fite.

Vol. XXIII, No. 89, January 1914. *Philosophische Kultur, Gesammelte Essais*, by Georg Simmel.

ibid. Introduction to Empiricism and Intuitionism in Reid's Common Sense Philosophy, by Oliver M. Jones.

(c) In other Periodicals

Oxford Magazine,[25] December 6, 1934, *Nature, Man and God*, by William Temple, Archbishop of York.

CONTRIBUTED PREFACES

To *Empiricism and Intuitionism in Reid's Commonsense Philosophy*, by Olive M. Jones, Princeton University Press, 1927.

To *Scots Theology in the Eighteenth Century*, by the Rev. Alexander McNair, London, James Clark and Co., 1928.

To *Memorial Exhibition of Pictures by the Late Norah Neilson Gray*, Glasgow, 1932.

VERSE

"The Chestnuts," *Princeton Alumni Weekly*, Vol. XXII, No. 10, December 7, 1921.

"Thanksgiving," written in captivity. *Glasgow University Magazine*, Vol. XLIV, No. 5, 1932.

"Propitiation," *ibid.*, Vol. XLIV, No. 6, 1933.

"Glengarnock," *ibid.*, Vol. XLIV, No. 7, 1933.

"Abel's Morning Song," *ibid.*, Vol. XLIV, No. 8, 1933.

"Virgo Mortua," *ibid.*, Vol. XLIV, No. 9, 1933.

"The Voice of She-oishne." A Sonnet, *ibid.*, Vol. XLIV, No. 10, 1933.

[25] Published by The Oxonian Press, Ltd., Queen Street, Oxford, England.

INDEX

INDEX

Where chapter number is given, the subject forms the general subject of the chapter.